LIFE
IN THE MIDDLE AGES

I & II

RELIGION, FOLK-LORE
AND SUPERSTITION

CHRONICLES, SCIENCE
AND ART

LIFE
IN THE MIDDLE AGES

PART II

RELIGION, FOLK-LORE
AND SUPERSTITION

CHRONICLES, SCIENCE
AND ART

LIFE
IN THE MIDDLE AGES

SELECTED
TRANSLATED AND ANNOTATED
BY
G. G. COULTON

I & II

RELIGION, FOLK-LORE
AND SUPERSTITION

CHRONICLES, SCIENCE
AND ART

CAMBRIDGE
AT THE UNIVERSITY PRESS
1967

PUBLISHED BY
THE SYNDICS OF THE CAMBRIDGE UNIVERSITY PRESS

Bentley House, 200 Euston Road, London, N.W.1
American Branch: 32 East 57th Street, New York, N.Y. 10022

First edition in one volume   1910
  (Constable & Co. Ltd)

Second edition in four volumes   1928
  (Cambridge University Press)

Reissued in two volumes   1967
First paperback edition   1967

First printed in Great Britain at the University Press, Cambridge

Reprinted by photolithography in Great Britain by
Butler & Tanner Ltd, Frome and London

To
MY WIFE

PREFACE

TO THE SECOND EDITION

(January 1928)

THE original volume was felt by some readers to be rather bulky; here, therefore, it is divided into separately purchasable parts, arranged roughly according to subject. The first and largest deals with *Religion, Folk-Lore and Superstition*; the second, with *Chronicles, Science and Art*; the third, with *Men and Manners*; the fourth, with *Monks, Friars and Nuns*. The first is enlarged by the addition of three extracts which were not in the first edition, two of which refer to subjects of considerable recent interest, St Joan and the Inquisition. The fourth volume is considerably enlarged, especially by the inclusion of My Lord Abbot from *Petit Jean de Saintré*. I have been able to correct a few mistakes and add a few notes; otherwise, there has been little opportunity of bringing the book up to date. For the rearrangement of the extracts and the revision of the proofs, and much other help, I am indebted to my wife.

G. G. C.

ST JOHN'S COLLEGE
CAMBRIDGE

PREFACE

TO THE FIRST EDITION
(May 1910)

THIS book appeals to the increasing body of readers who wish to get at the real Middle Ages; who, however impatient of mere dissertations and discussions, are glad to study genuine human documents, and to check the generalizations of historians by reference to first-hand facts. The Author has, therefore, attempted to compile a catena of such documents, each more or less complete in itself, but mostly too long for full quotation by historians. Moreover, he claims to cover a wider ground than most of the formal histories. The records here printed represent thirty years' study among all kinds of medieval writings, and could scarcely be outdone in this respect but by scholars who have better work to do. They have been chosen as specially characteristic of the period, and as appealing also to that deeper humanity which is common to all minds in all periods. They treat of clergy and laity, saints and sinners; spiritual experiences, love, battles, pageants, and occasionally the small things of everyday life. Drawn from six different languages, the large majority of these extracts are here translated for the first and perhaps the last time, since they are only the cream from bulky and often inaccessible volumes. A few are from manuscripts. If, on the whole, religious life is more fully represented here, and that life itself in its least conventional aspects, this want of strict proportion is more or less inherent in the plan of the work. We do not go abroad to meet Englishmen, or into the Middle Ages for the commonplace; though an occasional touch of this kind may help to show us the essential uniformity of little things in all ages. We most want to hear of those who, for good or evil, stand apart from the rest; and in the Middle Ages, as now, the evil generally lent itself best to picturesque description. The Author has, however, done all he can, consistently with any measure of historical truth, to avoid those darkest sides of all upon which the scope of his *From St Francis to Dante* compelled him to dwell at some length.

Several of the best books, being easily accessible elsewhere, are omitted here. From one or two more, only just enough is given to indicate the value of the rest, already sufficiently translated. It was impossible, within any reasonable compass, to exploit the rich mine of Franciscan and Dominican records also; a small fraction of these have already been printed in *From St Francis to Dante*, and the rest are reserved for a later volume. With these necessary exceptions, it is hoped that the present selection may be in some real sense representative. How far it is from being exhaustive, those will know best who have read most widely. From such critics the Author can only claim indulgence for this first attempt in English to cover Medieval Life as a whole.

G. G. C.

40 MILL ROAD
EASTBOURNE

CONTENTS

PART I: RELIGION, FOLK-LORE AND
SUPERSTITION

			PAGE
1	The First Millennium	*Ralph Glaber*	1
2	A Miracle of St Scothinus	*Acta Sanct. Hib.*	8
3	Another	,,	8
4	Another	*Acta Sanct. Bolland*	10
5	An English Saint Rescued	*Eadmer*	12
6	A Confirmation Scene		14
7	Popular Canonization	*Guibert de Nogent*	15
8	The Jackdaw of Rheims	*Exord. Cicterc.*	22
9	Monastic Poverty	,,	24
10	Hugh of St Victor's Purgatory	*Etienne de Bourbon*	25
11	The Changeling Monk	*John of Worcester*	26
12	Heretical Puritanism	*Ralph of Coggeshall*	29
13	A Precious Windfall	*Life of St William*	32
14	A Batch of Superstitions	*Bart. Iscanus*	33
15	The Priest of Evil Omen	*Jacques de Vitry*	35
16	Superstition Punished	*Wright's Latin Stories*	35
17	Masses and Money	*Petrus Cantor*	36
18	Ancestry of Henry II	*Trevisa's Higden*	39
19	The Jew Converted	,,	40
20	Medicine and Magic	*Harleian MS.*	41
21	A Saint in Need	*Adam of Eynsham*	43
22	The Broken Vow	,,	46
23	Priests in Purgatory	,,	47
24	The Vision of Paradise	,,	47
25	The Child and the Christ	*Vincent of Beauvais*	52
26	A Vision of King Arthur	*Lanercost Chron.*	52
27	Travellers' Tales	,,	54
28	A Noble Pluralist	,,	54
29	The Boy-Archdeacon	*Jacques de Vitry*	56
30	The Exacting Bishop	,,	56
31	The Simple Knight	,,	57
32	A Knotty Question	,,	57
33	The Usurer's Fate	*Caesarius of Heisterbach*	58

CONTENTS

PAGE

34	Mary and Christ	*Caesarius of Heisterbach*	62
35	The Same	„	65
36	Cuckoo, Cuckoo!	„	66
37	The Impenitent Heretic	„	66
38	The Storm of Béziers	„	67
39	The Sin of Tournaments	„	68
40	Apostles by Lot	„	69
41	The Sacrament as a Charm	„	70
42	Ordeal and Miracle	„	73
43	The Knight and the Crucifix	*Matthew Paris*	75
44	Norman Parish Priests	*Odo Rigaldi*	79
45	Pauper Funerals	*Etienne de Bourbon*	84
46	Unsuccessful Magic	„	85
47	Iconoclastic Usurers	„	86
48	The Wise Confessor	„	87
49	The Anatomy of Heresy	„	87
50	The Irishman and the Devil	„	88
51	Pilgrims' Disorders	„	89
52	The Sin of Dancing	„	90
53	A Bishop and his Flock	„	91
54	Saint Greyhound	„	92
55	Boy Archdeacons	„	94
56	Cathedral Visitations—Rouen	*Odo Rigaldi*	95
57	Cathedral Visitations—Exeter	*J. de Grandisson*	96
58	Cathedral Visitations—Exeter	„	98
59	Cathedral Visitations—Exeter	„	99
60	Cathedral Visitations—York	*Chapter Acts*	101
61	A Saint's Apology	*St Bonaventura*	104
62	The Sheep and the Goats	*Thomas of Chantimpré*	109
63	A Christmas Pageant	*Joannes de Caulibus*	109
64	The Cardinal's Gospel	*Carmina Burana*	112
65	Pardoners and Heretics	*Berthold of Ratisbon*	113
66	A Mother's Tears	*Thomas of Chantimpré*	118
67	A Strange Election	„	119
68	The Accursed Talmud	„	121
69	The Pluralist's Fate	„	122
70	The Maiden's Psalter	„	123
71	Hugh of St Victor's Purgatory	„	124
72	Priest and Penitent	„	125
73	Discipline and Humility	„	126
74	A Psychological Problem	„	127

PAGE

75	The Sin of Dancing	*Thomas of Chantimpré*	128
76	A Narrow Escape	,,	129
77	Who Sups with the Devil ——	,,	131
78	The First Sight of a Saint	*Peter of Sweden*	132
79	The Saint's Friends	,,	136
80	Sacred Love	*Christina von Stommeln*	137
81	The Answer	*Peter of Sweden*	139
82	An Undergraduate's Letter	*Brother Maurice*	140
83	Troubles and Trials	*Christina von Stommeln*	142
84	Balm in Gilead	*Peter of Sweden*	144
85	Last Days	*Anon.*	148
86	Grin and bear it	*Wright's Latin Stories*	149
87	Psalm-skippers	,,	149
88	The Blasphemer's Reward	,,	150
89	The Host Maltreated	,,	151
90	Tit for Tat	*Liber Exemplorum*	152
91	Vengeance Deferred	,,	152
92	A Short Way with all Devils	,,	155
93	The Resourceful Jongleur	*Jean de Beaume*	156
94	The Lay-brother and the Devil	*Chron. de St-Denis*	157
95	Witchcraft Extraordinary	,,	160
96	A Precocious Miracle-Worker	,,	163
97	The Beatific Vision	,,	164
98	The Same	*G. Villani*	167
99	Relics at St-Omer	*Anon.*	168
100	Hermits and an Hermitess	*T. Walsingham*	170
101	A Miraculous Statue	,,	174
102	Another	*Meaux Chronicle*	175
103	The Little Red Man	*T. Walsingham*	176
104	A Popular Miracle	*J. de Grandisson*	177
105	Another	,,	180
106	A Bishop *In Partibus*	,,	184
107	Graven Images	*Eustache Deschamps*	188
108	Gossip in Church	*La Tour-Landry*	189
109	Chaucer's Archdeacon	*Anon.*	191
110	A Sermon against Miracle-Plays	*Reliquiae Antiquae*	191
111	Ah, Constantine!	*John Gower*	196
112	A Programme of Reform	*Humbert de Romans*	199
113	A Second	*Guillaume ie Maire*	200
114	A Third	*Guillaume Durand*	201
115	Pulpit Cursing	*John Myrc*	205

			PAGE
116	The House of Prayer	*John Myrc*	207
116 A	Joan of Arc	*Johann Nider*	210
116 B	Torture and Evidence	,,	213
117	Wives and Widows	*St Bernardino*	217
118	Medieval Freethinkers	,,	229
119	A Determined Preacher	*Johann Busch*	230
120	Exorcism by Common Sense	,,	231
121	A Saint in Purgatory	*Dormi Secure*	232
122	Popes and Heresy	*Jacobus de Marchia*	235
123	The Odour of Heresy	,,	236
124	English Tails	*Golden Legend*	238
125	Prophets without Honour	*Johann Geiler*	239
126	Knotty Problems	*Peter Schott*	241
127	Paul's Walk	*Guillaume Pepin*	243
128	Abuse destroyeth not Use	*Sir Thomas More*	245

PART II: CHRONICLES, SCIENCE AND ART

			PAGE
1	Difficulties of the Medieval Encyclopaedist	*Vincent of Beauvais*	1
2	The Same	*Trevisa's Higden*	2
3	The Earliest Recorded Alpine Climb	*Chronicle of Novalese*	3
4	Another	*Vincent of Beauvais*	5
5	Another	*Chronicle of Brother Salimbene*	5
6	Vivisection	*Guibert de Nogent*	7
7	"Who builds good Churches must himself be good"	*Life of St Stephen*	8
8	Architectural Miracles	,,	10
9	The Religion of Learning	*Abelard*	11
10	History by Revelation	*Henry of Tournai*	14
11	The Religion of Church-building	*Haimon of Dives*	18
12	Father, Forgive them!	*Prior Geoffrey*	23
13	The Same	*Life of St Théodard*	24
14	The Same	*Adhémar de Chabannes*	24
15	The Eighth Lamp of Architecture	*Petrus Cantor*	25
16	The Earthly Paradise	*Trevisa's Higden*	28
17	Richard I and the Jews	,,	31
18	Bishop and Pope	,,	34
19	Fortifying a Town	*Lambert of Ardres*	35

CONTENTS

20	Natural History	*Jacques de Vitry*	38
21	Clerical Examinations	*Sarum Registers*	39
22	Another Batch	*Rouen Registers*	42
22 A	Clerical Ignorance	*Erasmus*	48
23	The Wandering Jew	*Matthew Paris*	50
24	Lion Taming	*Villard de Honnecourt*	53
25	Roger Bacon's Despair	*Roger Bacon*	55
26	A Lesson in Anatomy	*Berthold of Ratisbon*	63
27	The Proud Professor	*Thomas of Chantimpré*	65
28	An Author's Foreword	*Ramon Muntaner*	66
29	The Siege of Perelada	*"*	67
30	A Brief Romance	*"*	69
31	Oxford Manners	*Coroners' Rolls*	73
32	The Perfect Leech	*Anon.*	77
33	A Small-Beer Chronicle	*T. von Wolfhagen*	78
34	The Romance of Noah	*Queen Mary's Psalter*	84
35	A Bishop's Latin	*R. de Graystanes*	86
36	Manners at the University of Rome	*Anon.*	87
37	A Knight-Errant	*Sir Thomas Gray*	89
38	Chaucer's March	*"*	91
39	Clerical Innkeepers	*Council of Cologne*	91
40	Tourney and Masquerade	*H. Knighton*	93
41	The French Pope	*"*	94
42	The Spaniards on the Sea	*Froissart*	95
43	A Picturesque Bandit	*"*	103
44	The Conquered English	*T. Walsingham*	106
45	A Good Pope	*Meaux Chronicle*	107
46	A Nation in Arms	*Anon.*	108
47	A Clerical Reference Library	*Hamo of Hythe*	111
48	Educational Reform	*J. de Grandisson*	113
49	A Romance of Ruth	*La Tour-Landry*	114
50	The Master of Oxford's Catechism	*Rel. Antiquae*	115
51	Various Heights of Men	*"*	117
52	Inscriptions in Books	*Anon.*	118
53	Student Bandits in 1422	*Pleas to Parliament*	119
54	Talbot's Death	*Mathieu de Coussy*	121
55	Book-keeping by Double Entry	*Johann Busch*	128
56	A Page's Quarrel	*Götz von Berlichingen*	131
57	An Ancient Feud	*"*	133
58	The Iron Hand	*"*	135
59	Behind the Scenes at a Miracle Play	*Anon.*	138

CONTENTS

			PAGE
60	The Same	*Anon.*	141
61	The Half-Closed Bible	*Sir Thomas More*	142
62	Shylock in Provence	*Jean de Bourdigné*	147
63	The End of a World	"	151

INDEX TO PART I 155

INDEX TO PART II 175

LIST OF ILLUSTRATIONS
IN PART I

A Saint's Bones Unearthed . . . . . *page* 5

Clothes on a Perch 11

The Shrine of St Alban carried Abroad 19

The Cellarer at Work 27

A Medieval Mill 59

Death of Matthew Paris 77

Gambling and Beggary 81

Bagnorea 105

A Cripple 182

St Martin's Mass 190

Conjugal Amenities 223

IN PART II

An Auto-da-Fé of Jews . . . . . *page* 32

The Earthworks of Ardres 36

The Lion and his Tamer 54

Limburg from the South-West 79

Albert III, Duke of Austria, and Founder of the Order 81
        of Tailed Knights

Noah and his Ark 85

Réthel in the Ardennes 92

A Ship of War . . . . *page* 96

A Sea-Fight 101

A Mêlée 109

The Dying Warrior 125

Götz's Iron Hand 136

A Miracle of Our Lady 139

PART I

RELIGION, FOLK-LORE
AND SUPERSTITION

Ralph Glaber was put by his uncle to a monastic school, and took the vows in due course. His wandering and somewhat irregular life was partly spent in the Monastery of St Bénigne at Dijon (see Vol. IV), and seems to have ended at Cluny somewhere about 1044, at which date his Chronicle finishes. In spite of his crabbed style, he is one of the very few French chroniclers of the tenth and eleventh centuries who are worth reading: "it is, with the *Miracles de Saint-Benoit*, the most precious source we possess for manners and ideas in France at the end of the 10th and beginning of the 11th century" (G. Monod, in *Revue Historique*, t. XXVIII, p. 272). Certain exaggerated deductions drawn from him by modern writers, as to the overwhelming significance of the year A.D. 1000, have been corrected by Jules Roy in his admirable little monograph *L'An Mille* (Hachette 1885). It was not only at and about this date that our forefathers expected strange events: the medieval mind was perpetually haunted by the expectation of Antichrist, and even Sir Thomas More seems to have believed that the end of all things was at hand in his own days. The following extract is from Migne's edition (*P.L.* vol. 142, coll. 635 ff.).

1. THE FIRST MILLENNIUM

WARNED by the prophecy of Holy Writ, we see clearer than daylight that in process of the Last Days, as love waxed cold and iniquity abounded among mankind, perilous times were at hand for men's souls. For by many assertions of the ancient fathers we are warned that, as covetousness stalks abroad, the religious Rules or Orders of the past have caught decay and corruption from that which should have raised them to growth and progress.... From this [covetousness] also proceed the constant tumult of quarrels at law, and frequent scandals arise, and the even tenour of the different Orders is rent by their transgressions. Thus also it cometh to pass that, while irreligiousness stalks abroad among the clergy, froward and incontinent appetites grow among the people, until lies and deceit and fraud and manslaughters, creeping abroad among them, draw almost all to perdition! And, since the mist of utter blindness hath darkened the eye of the Catholic Faith (that is, the prelates of the Church), therefore their flocks, ignorant of the way to salvation, fall into the ruin of their own perdition.... For whensoever religion hath failed among the pontiffs, and strictness of the Rule hath decayed among the abbots, and therewith the vigour of monastic discipline hath grown cold, and by their example the rest of the people are become prevaricators of God's commandments, what then can we think but that the whole human race, root and branch, is sliding willingly down again into the gulf of primaeval chaos? ... And because, in fulfilment (as we see) of the Apostle's prophecy, love waxeth cold and iniquity aboundeth among men that are lovers of their own selves, therefore these things aforesaid befel more frequently than usual in all parts of the world about the thousandth year after the birth of our Lord and Saviour.

For, in the seventh year before that date, Mount Vesuvius (which is also called Vulcan's Caldron) gaped far more often than his wont and belched forth a multitude of vast stones mingled with sulphurous flames which fell even to a distance of three miles around; and thus by the stench of his breath he began to make all the surrounding province uninhabitable.... It befel meanwhile that almost all the cities of Italy and Gaul were ravaged by flames of fire, and that the greater part even of the city of Rome was devoured by a conflagration. During which fire, the flames caught the beams of St Peter's church, beginning to creep under the bronze tiles and lick the carpenters' work. When this became known to the whole multitude that stood by, then, finding no possible device for averting this disaster, they turned with one accord and, crying with a terrible voice, hastened to the Confession[1] even of the Chief of the Apostles, crying upon him with curses that, if he watched not over his own, nor showed himself a very present defender of his church, many throughout the world would fall away from their profession of faith. Whereupon the devouring flames straightway left those beams of pine and died away.... At this same time a horrible plague raged among

[1] The part of the choir in which the celebrant makes his confession before saying mass. This was usually just in front of the altar steps. See Dom Martene, *De Antiquis Ecclesiae Ritibus*, lib. I, c. iv, art. 2, *ad fin.*

men, namely a hidden fire which, upon whatsoever limb it fastened, consumed it and severed it from the body.[1] Many were consumed even in the space of a single night by these devouring flames.... Moreover, about the same time, a most mighty famine raged for five years throughout the Roman world, so that no region could be heard of which was not hungerstricken for lack of bread, and many of the people were starved to death. In those days also, in many regions, the horrible famine compelled men to make their food not only of unclean beasts and creeping things, but even of men's, women's, and children's flesh, without regard even of kindred; for so fierce waxed this hunger that grown-up sons devoured their mothers, and mothers, forgetting their maternal love, ate their babes. [The chronicler then goes on to speak of two heresies which arose in France and Italy, of the piety of King Robert of France, etc., etc.]

So on the threshold of the aforesaid thousandth year, some two or three years after it, it befel almost throughout the world, but especially in Italy and Gaul, that the fabrics of churches were rebuilt, although many of these were still seemly and needed no such care; but every nation of Christendom rivalled with the other, which should worship in the seemliest buildings. So it was as though the very world had shaken herself and cast off her old age, and were clothing herself everywhere in a white garment of churches. Then indeed the faithful rebuilt and bettered almost all the cathedral churches, and other monasteries dedicated to divers saints, and smaller parish churches.... When therefore, as we have said, the whole world had been clad in new church buildings, then in the days following—that is, in the eighth year following the aforesaid thousandth after the Incarnation of our Saviour—the relics of very many saints, which had long lain hid, were revealed by divers proofs and testimonies; for these, as if to decorate this revival, revealed themselves by God's will to the eyes of the faithful, to whose minds also they brought much consolation. This revelation is known to have begun first in the city of Sens in Gaul, at the church of the blessed Stephen,

---

[1] St Anthony's fire, one of the curses of the Middle Ages, which modern medicine has traced to poisons generated in corrupt rye-bread.

ruled in those days by the archbishop Leoteric, who there discovered certain marvellous relics of ancient holy things; for, among very many other things which lay hidden, he is said to have found a part of Moses' rod, at the report whereof all the faithful flocked together not only from the provinces of Gaul but even from well-nigh all Italy and from countries beyond the sea; and at the same time not a few sick folk returned thence whole and sound, by the intervention of the saints. But, as most frequently befalleth, from that source whence profit springeth to men, there they are wont to rush to their ruin by the vicious impulse of covetousness; for the aforesaid city having, as we have related, waxed most wealthy by reason of the people who resorted thither through the grace of piety, its inhabitants conceived an excessive insolence in return for so great benefits. . . . At that time, moreover, that is in the ninth year after the aforesaid thousandth anniversary, the church at Jerusalem which contained the sepulchre of our Lord and Saviour was utterly overthrown at the command of the prince of Babylon. . . . After that it had been overthrown, as we have said, then within a brief space it became fully evident that this great iniquity had been done by the wickedness of the Jews. When therefore this was spread abroad through the whole world, it was decreed by the common consent of Christian folk that all Jews should be utterly driven forth from their lands or cities. Thus they were held up to universal hatred and driven forth from the cities; some were slain with the sword or cut off by manifold kinds of death, and some even slew themselves in divers fashions; so that, after this well-deserved vengeance had been wreaked, scarce any were found in the Roman world. Then also the bishops published decrees forbidding all Christians to associate themselves with Jews in any matter whatsoever; and ordaining that, whosoever would be converted to baptismal grace and utterly eschew the customs or manners of the Jews, he alone should be received. Which indeed was done by very many of them for love of this present life, and impelled rather by fear of death than by the joys of the life everlasting; for all such of them as simulated this conversion returned impudently within a brief while to their former way of life. . . .

A SAINT'S BONES UNEARTHED

From MS. Cotton. Nero, D i, fol. 21b, representing the discovery of St Alban's bones in accordance with a divine revelation to King Offa II. The text illustrated is Matthew Paris, *Vita Offae Secundi*; the drawings in this MS. have often been attributed to the author's own hand, but are probably by another contemporary monk of St Alban.

After the manifold signs and prodigies which came to pass in the world, some earlier and some later, about the thousandth year from our Lord's birth, it is certain that there were many careful and sagacious men who foretold other prodigies as great when the thousandth year from His Passion should draw nigh. [Glaber here goes on to relate the rival claims of the Greek Church, the growth of heresy in Italy, the success of false miracles wrought by evil spirits, and another three years of famine and cannibalism; after which a series of church councils were held for peace and reform.] Then were innumerable sick folk healed in those conclaves of Holy men; and, lest men should think lightly of mere bursten skin or rent flesh in the straightening of arms and legs, much blood flowed forth also when the crooked limbs were restored; which gave faith to the rest who might have doubted. At this all were inflamed with such ardour that through the hands of their bishops they raised the pastoral staff to heaven, while themselves with outspread palms and with one voice cried to God: Peace, peace, peace! that this might be a sign of perpetual covenant for that which they had promised between themselves and God; on condition that, after the lapse of five years, the same covenant should marvellously be repeated by all men in the world in confirmation of that peace. That same year, moreover, so great was the plenty and abundance of corn and wine and other fruits of the earth, that men dared not hope to have so much during all the five years next to come; for no human food was aught accounted of save flesh or choice victuals, and this year was like unto the great Jubilee of ancient Mosaic times. Next year again, and again in the third and fourth years, the fruits were no less abundant. But, alas for shame! the human race, forgetful of God's lovingkindness and prone from its very beginning to evil, like the dog returning to his own vomit again or the sow that was washed to her wallowing in the mire, made the covenant of their own promise of none effect in many ways; and, as it is written, they waxed fat, and grew thick, and kicked. For even the princes of both orders, spiritual and secular, turned to covetousness and began to sin in theft and greed as grievously as before, or even worse. Then those of middle rank and the poorer people, following the example of the greater, declined into horrible crime. For who ere now had heard of such incests, adulteries, and illicit alliances between close kindred, such mockery of concubines and such emulation of evil men? Moreover, to fill up the measure of so great wickedness, since there were few or none among the people to correct the rest, and to rebuke such crimes, therefore the prophecy was fulfilled which saith, "And it shall be as with the people, so with the priest"; seeing especially that all the rulers in those days, both secular and spiritual, were mere boys. For in those days, through the sins of the people, that saying of Solomon's was fulfilled: "Woe to thee, O land, when thy king is a child." For even the universal Pope of Rome himself, the nephew of the two popes Benedict and John who had preceded him, was a boy scarce ten years old, whose money and treasures had procured his election by the Romans; by whom in process of time he was dishonourably treated and oftentimes cast forth, so that he had no power.[1] Moreover, as we have already said, the rest of the prelates in those days owed their promotion rather to their gold and silver than to their merit. Alas for shame! It is of such that the Scripture saith—nay, rather God's own mouth—"They have been princes, and I knew not." At this same time so innumerable a multitude began to flock from all parts of the world to the sepulchre of our Saviour at Jerusalem, as no man could before have expected; for the lower orders of people led the way, after whom came those of middle rank, and then all the greatest kings and counts and bishops; lastly (a thing which had never come to pass before), many noble ladies and poorer women journeyed thither. For many purposed and desired to die before they should see their homes again. . . . Moreover, some of those who were then most concerned in these matters, being consulted by many concerning the signification of this concourse to Jerusalem, greater than the past age had ever heard of, answered with some caution that it portended no other than the advent of that reprobate Antichrist, whose coming at the end of this world is prophesied in Holy Scripture.

---

[1] "The foulness of his conversation and life is horrible to relate," notes Glaber of the same Pope on a later page (698). This was the lowest ebb reached by the Papacy until the fifteenth and sixteenth centuries.

Nos. 2 and 3 are from the *Acta Sanctorum Hiberniae* of John Colgan, an Ulsterman who became Professor of Theology at Louvain. "Colgan" (writes Henry Bradley in the *Dict. Nat. Biog.*) "was an accomplished Irish scholar, and his large use of early documents in that language gives great importance to his work, which displays much critical sagacity." The lives are seldom exactly dated, but are mostly of great antiquity.

2. A MIRACLE OF ST SCOTHINUS
(*AA.SS. Hib.* vol. 1, p. 10.)

WHEN therefore St Scothinus, by these and other severe chastisements, had purged himself from all molestations and imperfections of lustful desires, as though he followed after the purity of an angel here on earth, then began other corporeal creatures also to obey him and recognize him as an angel of God; wherefore he oftentimes walked dryshod over the sea, without help of boat. Once, while he thus walked on the sea to pass into Britain, he met with the ship that carried St Barry the Bishop; who, beholding and recognizing this man of God, enquired of him wherefore he thus walked on the sea. To whom Scothin answered that this was a flowery field whereon he walked; and presently, stretching his hand down to the water, he took from the midst of the ocean a handful of vermilion flowers which, in proof of his assertion, he cast into the Bishop's lap. The Bishop for his part, to maintain his own truth, drew a fish from the waters and cast it towards St Scothin; whereupon, magnifying God in His marvellous works, they departed with blessings one from the other.[1]

3. ANOTHER OF ST GERALD, ABBOT OF LISMORE
(*Ib.* p. 600.)

BEHOLD, a messenger came from the king with the news that his only daughter was even now dead: at which tidings the king, who had no son, was sore afraid. But presently, recovering, he said to his peers, "O counsellors of my bosom

[1] This same or a similar miracle, as Colgan notes, is told in the Life of St David concerning St Barry and St Brandan. The reader may find it in full on p. 428, § xviii.

and faithful friends of my secret thoughts, let none of us reveal my daughter's death to these stranger saints; but let us say that mine only son is dead." And he added: "Unless they raise up to me a son instead of that daughter, I will cast them all into prison." When therefore the holy Abbot and his elder companions were brought into the royal presence, then said the king: "If ye would found in our domain an abbey rich in lands and goods, then beseech your God to raise up from the jaws of hell my son who is even now dead, the only hope of my kingdom; but if ye may not obtain this, then shall ye depart dishonoured from our realm, or remain as slaves among us." The holy men, hearing this, hastened to the chamber where the royal maiden lay dead; then the Abbot St Gerald turned to the corpse[1] and prayed: "O Eternal God, Who art the protector of all that trust in Thee, Who takest away the anguish of Thy faithful people, Who didst dry up the Red Sea for the captive Israelites and miraculously loose Peter from his bonds, have mercy and loose us also, who are prisoners to these barbarians, from this perilous pass into which we are come by the death of the King's daughter, insomuch as Thou mayest make of this dead maiden, by Thy marvellous power, a living youth, granting to him quick motion and sense through our ministry." After which prayer the king turned to him and said, "O man of God, saving thy reverence, it is my only son who is dead, and whom I beseech thee to vouchsafe to raise up." Then said St Gerald, "Be it son or daughter, may God Who giveth life to all, and to Whom all things are possible, vouchsafe to raise thee up a male child." Whereupon, making a sign of the cross, he poured water into the maiden's mouth from that stone which he ever carried with him from his mother's womb; and, to the amazement of all beholders, a royal youth arose forthwith from the bier; by which unwonted miracle their infidelity was scattered, and the faith of them that believed was made more strong. . . . Then the king and his dukes endowed this new son with thirty townships of land, together with all the appurtenances thereof.[2]

---

[1] The text, by an obvious error, has "he turned to the King."

[2] Upon this the learned Father Colgan notes: "This tale of one sex changed into another may be thought of doubtful authenticity, since no such story is

Acta Sanctorum Bolland. Julii II (July 6th); Life of St Goar, possibly by a younger contemporary. The Saint, who died about A.D. 650, built himself a little hermitage, at which two legates of the Bishop of Trèves once chanced to attend a very early mass: after which, out of hospitality to them, their host ate and drank. They, at the Devil's instigation, and in the hope of extorting money from him, accused him of "eating or drinking intemperately in the early morning." St Goar, compelled to go with them to the Bishop, miraculously milked three wild does on the way to refresh his two persecutors.

4. ANOTHER OF ST GOAR

BEHOLD, the man of God entered into the palace where the Bishop sat; and looked about forthwith for a place where his disciple might stand, and where he might hang or hide his own cape. Seeing therefore, in a corner of the chamber, how a sunbeam slid through a little window, he or his servant took this for an oaken pole;[1] so that he hanged up his cape thereon and bade his attendant stand there. Which when Bishop Rusticus and his clergy saw, he said: "See ye now what he will do! This case is not of God; if it had been, he would not have eaten or drunken so early, for the saints of old entered through almsgiving and fasting into the kingdom of Heaven, and became friends of God. Now therefore I know not what this case may be. He eateth and drinketh at dawn, he milketh wild beasts, he hangeth his cape on a sunbeam. Let him come near and render account, whether he do this for God's sake or for the Devil's."

Then they enquired of the man of God, who answered and said: "God of all justice and might, Thou knowest that I nowise consent to the Devil's part, nor desire to consent; nor

recorded in the histories of Ireland concerning any son of a king or chief, and events so rare are rarely omitted by accurate historians. But, seeing that it is no easier for the Creator to change one shape into another (which, as we read, He hath oftentimes done) than to transmute one sex into another, I see no reason why this so clearly possible event should be thought altogether incredible. See Jocelin in the *Acts of St Patrick*, c. 84 and 85 and 150; St Eninu in the *Tripartite Life*, par. 2, c. 16, and our notes on those passages, where we have made many remarks concerning wondrous transformations. Moreover, in the Life of St Abban, which we shall print below under the 16th March, we read of a female child turned into a male."

[1] Clothes were mostly hung on such *perches*, even in Kings' chambers: see the accompanying illustration.

know I that my cape hangeth on a sunbeam, for methought it was an oaken perch. Moreover, it was by no witchcraft that

CLOTHES ON A PERCH
From a fifteenth-century French MS. in T. Wright's *Homes of other Days*, p. 158.

I milked those beasts; but God ordained them for me at that very hour, that He might show His marvels to these unbelieving folk whom thou hast sent to me. In that I ate or drank at dawn, the Lord Who seeth all hearts knoweth that I did this not for gluttony but for charity's sake. [St Goar was triumphantly acquitted; and the same miracle is related of three later saints—St Aicaire, St Amable of Riom, and Pope Celestine V of the *Gran Rifiuto*.]

The two following extracts are from Eadmer, the Saxon monk who became St Anselm's confidant and biographer. I give them here only because they are necessarily much abbreviated in Dean Church's delightful *St Anselm*. The first is from a description of Anselm's first visit to England in 1079, on which he stayed long with his friend and fellow-monk Lanfranc, Archbishop of Canterbury. It was now that Eadmer first saw and heard the great man (*Vita S. Anselmi*, lib. 1, c. v, § xlii).

5. AN ENGLISH SAINT RESCUED

MOREOVER Lanfranc was but a half-fledged Englishman, as it were, nor had he yet formed his mind to certain institutions which he had found here; whereof he changed many for excellent reasons, but others of his own will and authority. Since, therefore, he purposed to change them, and had now the company of his like-minded friend and brother Anselm, he said to him one day in more familiar converse: "These English, among whom we live, have set up certain saints to worship them; concerning whose merits, as related by their countryfolk themselves, I have sometimes pondered, and cannot resolve the doubts of their sanctity that arise in my mind. And, lo! here is one of them, laid to rest in this same holy See whereunto God hath called me, a good man indeed, and in his lifetime an archbishop here. Him they number not only among the saints but also among the martyrs, though they confess that he was slain not for confessing Christ's name but for refusing to ransom himself. For when (to tell it in their own words) his adversaries and God's enemies, the heathen, had taken him, and yet for reverence of his person had granted him leave to redeem himself, they demanded from him an immense ransom; and he, seeing that he could by no means collect such a sum without stripping his vassals of their money, and, perchance, bringing some under the hateful yoke of beggary, chose rather to lose his life than to keep it on such conditions.

I would fain hear therefore, dear Brother, thy mind also on this matter." Thus did he, as a novice in English citizenship, briefly propose this question to Anselm.... But Anselm, as a prudent man, answered this prudent man simply according to the question proposed, saying: "It is manifest that he who feareth not to die rather than to commit even a light sin against God, would still less fear to meet death rather than to provoke God by a grievous sin. Now it would indeed seem a more grievous sin to deny Christ than that any earthly lord should somewhat oppress his subjects by taking away their money for his own ransom. But this Elphege refused to do the lesser evil; much more, then, would he have refused to deny Christ, if the furious band had constrained him thereunto by the threat of death. Wherefore we may understand that his soul was possessed with exceeding righteousness, when he chose rather to offer up his life than to violate charity and offend his neighbours. It is plain, then, that he was far from that woe which our Lord threateneth to him through whom the offence cometh; nor (as I think) is he undeservedly counted among the martyrs, since he is truly recorded to have borne death willingly for so high and righteous a cause. For even the blessed John Baptist, who is believed and worshipped by the whole church of God as one of the chief among the martyrs, was slain not for a matter of denying Christ, but for refusing to conceal the truth; and what matters it whether a man die for righteousness or for truth?"... To which Lanfranc answered, "I confess that I vehemently approve and revere the subtle perspicacity and the perspicacious subtlety of thy mind; and, taught by thy clear reasoning, I trust henceforward heartily to worship and venerate the Blessed Elphege as a truly great and glorious martyr of Christ, so help me God!" Which, indeed, he afterwards so devoutly performed, that he caused the life and passion of that saint to be diligently compiled... and authorised and bade it to be read or sung in God's Church, whereby he did no little to glorify the martyr's name in this country.[1]

---

[1] It must be borne in mind that the canonization of saints was not formally reserved to the Holy See until A.D. 1170; before that time it lay at the diocesan's discretion.

6. A CONFIRMATION SCENE

(Ib. lib. II, c. iv, § 38.)

ANSELM, therefore, set out from Wissant early on the morrow, and came after certain days to St Omer, where he was received with joy by clergy and monks, and detained for five days; during which time, at the prayer of the canons, he consecrated an altar. After which there came to him certain honourable men of those parts, kneeling at his feet and beseeching him to confirm their children by the laying on of hands and anointing with sacred oil. To whom he made answer forthwith: "Not only will I gladly receive those for whom ye pray in this matter, but others also who present themselves shall not be rejected." They, marvelling at the great man's benignity in so easy a condescension, were rejoiced above measure and gave him thanks; and, when their children had been confirmed, they forthwith filled the whole city with the words which they had received from his lips. Then might ye see men and women, great and small, pouring forth from their houses and outrunning each other in their haste to reach our lodging and share in so great a sacrament; for it was now many years since any bishop had suffered himself to be employed in any such office among them.[1] At last, on the sixth day, when he had already confirmed an innumerable multitude, and we were on the point of setting forth, and the long journey of this day compelled us to ḥasten, behold! a maiden came into the house as we were leaving it to mount our horses, and besought with lamentable affection of piety that she might be confirmed. Some of our companions, hearing this, were grievously troubled, and beat her down with contradictions, as folk who were already wearied with such matters. In short, though the holy man would have condescended to the maiden's prayers, yet these held him back and persuaded him to turn a deaf ear unto her, objecting the length of that day's journey,

---

[1] The medieval bishops had no settled times or places for confirming. It was usual for the people to try to catch them like this on their way through the district. It was frequently complained that many folk died thus unconfirmed. Archbishop Peckham complained in 1281 that there were "numberless people grown old in evil days who had not yet received the grace of confirmation." Compare also vol. II, no. 10.

and the perils which commonly threaten travellers by night, especially in a strange country; and showing that very many stood at the door intent upon this same matter, ready to burst in if he granted this one request. But when he had gone a little forward, then the father bethought himself what reasons he had followed and what he had done; whereupon, accusing himself of grievous impiety, he was so cut to the heart with grief that, for all the rest of his life on earth (as he often confessed) repentance for that deed never departed from his mind.

Guibert de Nogent, from the first publication of his works in the seventeenth century, has been known as one of the most interesting autobiographers of the Middle Ages: his *Treatise on Relics* and *God's Dealings through the Franks* [*in the Holy Land*] are no less interesting. His style, especially in his *Own Life*, is involved and obscure, quite apart from corruptions of the text; but he was one of the most honest and learned writers in an age of great intellectual activity; and, though he took St Bernard's side against Abelard, he shows a critical acumen which can seldom be paralleled in any period of the Middle Ages. Born near Beauvais in 1053, of noble blood, he lost his father in childhood and his mother at the age of twelve by her retirement to a convent. His old master having at the same time become a monk, Guibert ran wild for a few years. At last, through his mother's and master's influence, he took the vows at St Germer, that magnificent abbey-church which may still be seen between Gournay and Beauvais. The regularity of his life and his fame as a student earned him the honourable position of Abbot at Nogent-sous-Coucy. After playing a conspicuous part in the church politics of 1106 and succeeding years, he retired again to the peace of his abbey, wrote several books of great value, and died between 1121 and 1124. More specimens of Guibert's work would be given here, but that his life and writings have quite lately been admirably treated in a monograph by a scholar of great promise whose early death has aroused much sympathy (Bernard Monod, *Le Moine Guibert*, Hachette, 1905).

7. POPULAR CANONIZATION
(Guibert's *Treatise on Relics*, bk. i, chap. i, col. 614.)

WHAT shall I say of those [saints] whose fame is supported by no shred of testimony from without, and who are rather darkened than illustrated by the fact that they are believed to be celebrated in certain worthless records? What shall I do in their case whose beginnings and middle life are apparent to no man, and whose latter end (wherein all their praise is sung) is utterly unknown? And who can pray for their intercession when he knoweth not whether they possess any merits before God?... I have indeed known some men possessed of a certain saint, as they called him, brought from Brittany, whom they long revered as a confessor; until, suddenly changing their minds, they celebrated him as a martyr. When I enquired closely into their reasons, they had nothing better to plead for this man's martyrdom than for his aforesaid confessorship. I call God to witness, that I have read—and read again in utter loathing to them that were with me—in the Life of Samson, a saint of great reputation in France and Brittany, concerning a certain abbot whom that book names St Pyro. When, however, I sought into the latter end of this man whom I held for a saint, I found his special mark of sanctity to be this: to wit, that he fell into a well while drunken with wine, and thus died. Nor have I forgotten the question propounded by Lanfranc, Archbishop of Canterbury, to his successor Anselm, then Abbot of Bec, concerning one of his predecessors who had been cast into prison, and was slain because he would not ransom himself.... Let the pontiffs therefore see to it, let the guardians of God's people see to it, and provide that, if the people have a zeal of God, they may at least have it according to knowledge, lest they sin by offering aright and not dividing aright.[1] If the prophet say truly, "Woe unto them that call evil good and good evil," then what perversity can be greater than to thrust men upon the sacred altars who perchance, in their lifetime, deserved to be thrust forth from the Church itself!

I have indeed seen, and blush to relate, how a common boy, nearly related to a certain most renowned abbot, and squire (it was said) to some knight, died in a village hard by Beauvais on Good Friday, two days before Easter. Then, for the sake of that sacred day whereon he had died, men began to impute

---

[1] Referring to Levit. i, 17, and ii, 6, with a play upon *divide*, which might also mean *discern*. See also St Bernard, *Epp.* 4, § 3 and 87, § 3.

a gratuitous sanctity to the dead boy. When this had been rumoured among the country-folk, all agape for something new, then forthwith oblations and waxen tapers were brought to his tomb by the villagers of all that country round. What need of more words? A monument was built over him, the spot was hedged in with a stone building, and from the very confines of Brittany there came great companies of country-folk, though without admixture of the higher sort. That most wise abbot with his religious monks, seeing this, and being enticed by the multitude of gifts that were brought, suffered the fabrication of false miracles. Even though the covetous hearts of the vulgar herd may be impressed by feigned deafness, affected madness, fingers purposely cramped into the palm, and soles twisted up under men's thighs, what then doth the modest and wise man, who professeth to aim at holiness, when he maketh himself the abettor of such things? Oftentimes we see these things made trite by vulgar gossip, and by the ridiculous carrying round of sacred shrines for the sake of collecting alms; and daily we see the very depths of some man's purse emptied by the lies of those men whom St Jerome calleth *rabulas* in mockery of their rabid eloquence; who shake us so with their rogueries, and bear us along with such religious flattery that (to quote that saintly Doctor again) they gobble more busily than parasites, gluttons, or dogs, and surpass ravens or magpies with their importunate chatter.

But why do I accuse the multitude, without citing specific examples to rebuke this error? A most famous church[1] sent its servants thus wandering abroad [with its shrine], and engaged a preacher to seek alms for repairing its loss. This man, after a long and exaggerated discourse on his relics, brought forth a little reliquary and said, in my presence, "Know ye that there is within this little vessel some of that very bread which our Lord pressed with His own teeth; and, if ye believe not, here is this great man"—this he said of me—

---

[1] Probably the Cathedral of Laon, which our author knew very well. It was burned down in 1112 and sent round its shrine to beg for help; cf. Guibert's autobiography, col. 938, and Herman's Book of Miracles performed on this tour, *ib.* col. 963. It is noteworthy that the large majority of the miracles there described belong precisely to the three classes which Guibert describes as most easily feigned.

"here is this great man to whose renown in learning ye may bear witness, and who will rise from his place, if need be, to corroborate my words." I confess that I blushed for shame to hear this; and, but for my reverence of those persons who seemed to be his patrons, which compelled me to act after their wishes rather than his, I should have discovered the forger. What shall I say? Not even monks (not to speak of the secular clergy) refrain from such filthy gains, but they preach doctrines of heresy in matters of our faith, even in mine own hearing. For, as Boethius saith, "I should be rightly condemned for a madman if I should dispute with madmen." . . .

If, therefore, it be so doubtful a matter to judge of the claim to martyrdom, how shall we decide in the matter of confessors, whose end is often less certain? What though the common consent of the Church agree in the case of St Martin, St Remy, and such great saints, yet what shall I say of such as are daily sainted and set up in rivalry to them, by the common folk of our towns and villages?—Let them tell me how they can expect a man to be their patron saint concerning whom they know not even that which is to be known? For thou shalt find no record of him but his mere name. Yet, while the clergy hold their peace, old wives and herds of base wenches chant the lying legends of such patron saints at their looms and their broidering-frames; and, if a man refute their words, they will attack him in defence of these fables not only with words but even with their distaffs. Who but a sheer madman, therefore, would call on those to intercede for him concerning whom there is not the merest suspicion left in men's minds to tell what they once were? And what availeth that prayer wherein the petitioner himself speaketh in utter uncertainty of him whom he would make into his intercessor with God? How (I say) can that be profitable, which can never be without sin? For if thou prayest to a man whose sanctity thou knowest not, then thou sinnest in that very matter wherein thou shouldst have prayed for pardon; for though thou offerest aright thou dividest not aright. . . . But why should I labour this point at such length, when the whole Holy Church is so modest of mouth that she dareth not to affirm even the body

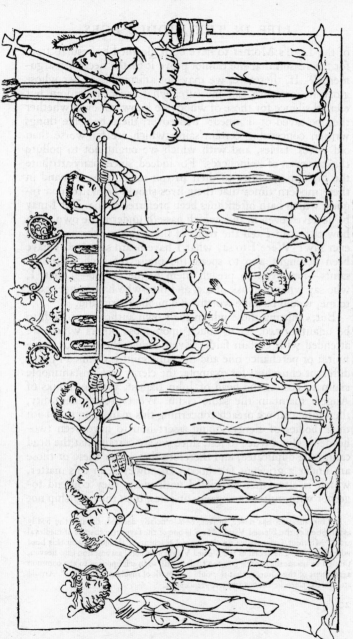

THE SHRINE OF ST ALBAN CARRIED ABROAD

From a MS. of Matthew Paris (1260), figured in J. Strutt's *Manners, Customs, etc.,* pl. LXIV. In the original the monk carrying the book is chanting, "This is in truth the martyr." (MS. Nero, D. 1, fol. 22a.)

of the Lord's Mother to have been glorified by resurrection, for the reason that she cannot prove it by the necessary arguments![1] If, therefore, we may not affirm this of her whose glory no creature can measure, what must we enjoin but eternal silence for those of whom we know not even whether they be saved or damned? Moreover, there be some things written concerning certain saints which are far worse than old wives' fables, and with which we ought not to pollute the ears even of swineherds. For indeed, since many attribute the highest antiquity to their patron saints, they demand in these modern times that their lives should be written: a request which hath oftentimes been preferred to me. Yet I may be deceived even in that which passeth under mine own eyes; how then can I tell the truth of those things which no man ever saw? Were I to say what I have heard said (and I have been besought also to speak the praises of such unknown saints—nay even to preach them to the people—) then I, who say what men ask of me, and they who have suggested it to me, would be alike worthy of a public reprimand.

But, omitting those whom their own authority proveth to be unauthorized, let us touch upon those others which are attended with certain faith. Even among these, error is infinite; or perchance one and the same saint is claimed by two different churches; for example, the clergy of Constantinople claim to possess the head of John Baptist, yet the monks of Angers maintain the same claim. What greater absurdity, therefore, can we preach concerning this man, than that both these bodies of clergy should assert him to have been two-headed? But a truce to jest, since we are certain that the head cannot be duplicated, and therefore that either these or those are under a grievous falsehood. If, however, in this matter, which is altogether associated with piety, they contend together with mutual arrogance and lies, then they worship not

---

[1] This question has never, in fact, been officially decided, though the bodily assumption of the Blessed Virgin Mary is one of the favourite themes of medieval art. "Melchior Canus sums up the general teaching of theologians on this head when he says: 'The denial of the Blessed Virgin's corporal assumption into heaven, though by no means contrary to the faith, is still so much opposed to the common agreement of the Church, that it would be a mark of insolent temerity.'" Arnold and Addis, *Catholic Dictionary*, s.v. *Assumption*.

God but the Devil. Therefore, both the deceived and the deceivers worship wrongfully that very relic wherein they make their boast. If, however, they worship an unworthy object, it is evident how great must be the peril to which all the worshippers are exposed. Even though, not being John Baptist's head, it be that of some other saint, even then there is no small guilt of lying.[1]

But wherefore speak I of the Baptist's head, when I hear the same tale daily concerning innumerable saints' bodies? In truth my predecessor, the Bishop of Amiens, when he would have translated the body of St Firmin (as he thought) from the old shrine to a new, found there no shred of parchment— nay not even the testimony of a single letter—to prove who lay there. This I have heard with mine own ears from the Bishops of Arras and Amiens. Wherefore the Bishop wrote forthwith on a plate of lead, that it might be laid in the shrine; FIRMIN THE MARTYR, BISHOP OF AMIENS. Soon afterwards, the same thing was repeated at the monastery of St Denis. The abbot had prepared a more splendid shrine; when lo! in the ceremony of translation, while his head and bones were loosed from their wrappings, a slip of parchment was found within his nostrils, affirming him to be FIRMIN, BISHOP OF AMIENS....

Hear now an illustration of our complaints, which may pass judgment on these instances aforesaid. Odo, Bishop of Bayeux, eagerly desired the body of St Exuperius, his predecessor, who was honoured with special worship in the town of Corbeil. He paid, therefore, the sum of one hundred pounds to the sacristan of the church which possessed these relics, that he might take them for himself. But the sacristan cunningly dug up the bones of a peasant named Exuperius and brought them to the Bishop. The Bishop, not content with his mere assertion, exacted from him an oath that these bones which he brought were those of Saint Exuperius. "I swear," replied the man, "that these are the bones of Exuperius: as to his sanctity I cannot swear, since many earn the title of saints who are far indeed from holiness." Thus the thief

[1] Amiens also claimed to possess the Baptist's head: but this tradition was apparently still without authority in Guibert's days.

assuaged the Bishop's suspicions and set his mind at rest. But the townsfolk heard of the bargain which the custodian had made with their patron saint, and called him before them; whereupon he replied: "Search again the seals on his shrine; and, if ye find them not unbroken, let me pay the penalty!" See now what disgrace this Bishop's bargain brought upon religion, when the bones of this profane peasant Exuperius were thrust upon God's holy altar, which perchance will never more be purged of them. I can recall so many like deeds in all parts that I lack time and strength to tell them here; for fraudulent bargains are made, not so much in whole bodies as in limbs or portions of limbs, common bones being sold as relics of the saints. The men who do this are plainly such of whom St Paul speaketh, that they suppose gain to be godliness; for they make into a mere excrement of their money-bags the things which (if they but knew it) would tend to the salvation of their souls.

8. THE JACKDAW OF RHEIMS

From Migne, *Pat. Lat.* vol. 185, col. 1144.
This is perhaps the earliest version of the now famous legend.

ALBEIT all who call themselves Christians are as it were naturally persuaded, by that Faith wherewith they have been imbued, that the sentence of excommunication is no less than a separation from God and an estrangement from eternal life; yet, for that hearts benumbed with negligence are sometimes more easily moved by examples than by preaching, I have thought it necessary to show how terrible is this peremptory sentence to a rational creature, when even a brute beast is thereby sometimes subjected either to death or to some most grievous calamity.... This monastery [of Corvey] in the time of the last Emperor Frederick [Barbarossa, d. 1190] was ruled by one Conrad, who, according to the pompous custom of prince-abbots, among other gauds of worldly glory, wore gold rings—in a spirit far different from that of the truly poor and humble-minded abbot-founder of Clairvaux, who (we find it written) delighted more in rake and hoe than in mitre and ring. Now it came to pass one day when he sat at meat and, in courtly fashion, had laid down a precious golden ring for the sake of washing his hands, that some trifle or some serious matter intervened, and the ring was left, somewhat too negligently, on the table. Meanwhile a tame raven, whom the abbot's courtiers kept as a pet, watching an unguarded moment, caught the ring in his beak and flew away swiftly to his nest without conscience of his own guilty theft. When, therefore, the feasters' hunger was satisfied, and the meats removed, and the guests arisen from the table, then the abbot learned his loss, blamed his servants' negligence, and bade them seek the ring forthwith in every corner: which, however, could nowhere be found, nor could the thief be discovered. Whereupon the abbot, suspecting both guests and servants, and stirred to fervent indignation, sent word to the parish priests of the great and wealthy town which was situated hard by the abbey and subjected to its rule, bidding them publicly launch the most grievous sentence of excommunication upon him who had not feared to defile himself with this crime. The sentence was proclaimed; and, as all rational beings in those parts found in their guiltless conscience a crown of innocence, so the irrational creature itself could not escape the temporal penalties of that curse, whereof the eternal pains could take no hold upon his fragile and shortlived condition. For this thief, guilty yet unaware of his own guilt, began to sicken little by little, to loathe his food, to cease more and more from his droll croakings and other irrational follies whereby he was wont to delight the minds of fools who neglect the fear of God; then he began even to droop his wings; and at last his very feathers fled from the corruption of his decaying flesh, exposing him as a miserable and marvellous spectacle to all beholders. It came to pass one day that, as the abbot's household disputed one with the other, in his presence, concerning this portentous change in the bird, and concluded that so great a marvel must have some cause, one of them said half in jest to the abbot: "Ye ought to consider, my lord, whether by chance this be the thief whom ye seek, and whether this loathsome plague which ye behold be not the token of that curse wherein he is involved." At which word all were astonished; and the abbot bade one of his servants straightway to climb the tree wherein this bird had his nest, and to turn over diligently his couch of straw and plaited twigs. The servant climbed, found the ring forthwith, cleansed it from the filth that disfigured it, and laid it within the abbot's hands, to the amazement of all that stood by. Wherefore, since the wretched thief, who suffered these horrible pains for his crime and yet had no guilty conscience thereof—when he, as we must believe, had been discovered by the finger of God, then the lord abbot, by the advice of prudent men, sent word to the priests who had pronounced this sentence of excommunication, to proclaim that the ring was now restored, and the curse of none effect. Whereupon, even as at first the aforesaid bird had sickened by slow degrees, and visibly languished from day to day under that insidious disease, even so he now began slowly to revive and to recover his former strength; until at last, by a plain miracle of God, he was wholly restored to his first health and beauty.

9. MONASTIC POVERTY
(*Ib.* col. 1345.)

ABRAHAM of blessed memory, formerly abbot of Prateae [near Bourges], of whom it is reported that he kept his virginity intact, by Christ's bountiful gift, until the day of his death, was a man of exceeding sanctity and unmatched meekness, and bare the Lord's yoke from his youth unto the end of his life. This man, being young both in age and in Religion, hid without permission in his pallet a small piece of new cloth wherewith to patch his frock. After a while he sought it and found it not, even though he turned his whole pallet over and over again; whereupon he withdrew abashed and, smitten with remorse of conscience, hastened to wipe out this stealthy theft in secret confession. But some time afterwards, as he stood alone in the kitchen washing the dishes, lo! this piece of cloth fell suddenly through the air and was placed in his hands as though some man had borne it to him. He recognized it forthwith and, looking around on all sides, seeing no man either up or down, he knew for a certainty that it had been stolen by some foul fiend who, after his confession, had been unable to keep it. Whereupon he became aware how perilous and terrible is even the least private possession to those who have professed a life of purity and perfect poverty: even as we read that a certain nun suffered the rebukes of the devil on her deathbed for the sake of a slender thread of silk which she had laid away without leave in her bed.

Now this good and pious man, for his exceeding purity of mind and body, was wont to receive many consolations from God and His saints, and especially from the blessed Mother of God, so that this same most holy Queen, coming sometimes in visions and telling him of things that should come to pass, after the most sweet words which she would speak unto him at such kindly visitations, would press upon his pure lips, with a scarce credible condescension, the most chaste kiss of her mouth. One night, however, he dreamed that he strove in disputation with certain faithless Jews concerning the Christian religion. When therefore they had long debated, suddenly so great a stench exhaled from those reprobates and infected his nostrils, that the bitterness of this most dismal odour awakened him. Yet, even when the sleep had left him, for many days afterwards he still smelt in his waking hours that same foul stench which had first assailed him in his dream. Nay, not only so, but even as often as any cause demanded that he should speak with Jews, or see them near him, or enter their houses, or pass by them, so often was he wont to smell that intolerable exhalation. Moreover, these things which we have even now related of the aforesaid man, we learned from his own mouth in private talk.

10. HUGH OF ST VICTOR'S PURGATORY

From the *Anecdotes Historiques* of Etienne de Bourbon, p. 223.

I HAVE read in a book of examples how Master Hugh of St Victor, after his death, appeared in grievous affliction to a certain holy man, beseeching his prayers and those of all good men. When therefore he enquired the reason of this affliction, Master Hugh answered that it was for his *zenedoxia*, and disappeared. And he, having enquired the sense of the word, found that it signified in the Greek tongue *Vainglory*.[1]

11. THE CHANGELING MONK

From the Chronicle of John of Worcester (Oxford, 1908), p. 46, under the year 1138.

MEANWHILE the report of this following miracle was noised abroad. There is in the archbishopric of Trèves a certain noble monastery named Prüm, dedicated to SS. Peter and Paul, and founded in ancient days by Pippin, King of the Franks, father to Charles the Great: from which monastery this strange and unheard-of event is reported by all that dwell therein. One morning, when the Cellarer of the monastery, followed by his servant, had entered his cellar to give out wine as usual for the sacrifice of the altar, he found one of the casks, which he had left full the day before, emptied even to the hole of that peg which men call *bung* or *spigot*, and the wine spilt over the whole pavement. Wherefore, groaning sore at this loss that had befallen, he rebuked the servant that stood by his side with many harsh words, saying that he had doubtless closed the spigot carelessly on the day before and thus caused this grievous damage: after which he commanded the man, under threat of punishment, to reveal this accident to no man; for he feared lest, if the Abbot should hear it, he would thrust him forth with contumely from his office. Again at nightfall, before the Brethren went to rest, he entered the cellar and closed with all diligence the spigots of the wine-casks; after which, locking the door, he sought his couch. Nevertheless on the morrow, when he entered his cellar according to custom, he found another cask emptied down to the bung-hole as on the day before, and the wine still flowing. Seeing which, and not knowing to whose negligence he might attribute this loss, he was cut to the heart and sore

[1] Like most Greek words in medieval Latin, this has suffered sad distortion; it ought to be Kenodoxia.

THE CELLARER AT WORK

From an illuminated initial of the early fourteenth century (MS. Sloane, 2435),
reproduced in H. Shaw's *Dresses and Decorations*.

amazed; and, again commanding his servant to breathe no word of what had happened, he fortified the spigots with all possible diligence, one by one, before seeking his couch that evening; after which he lay down sadly and anxiously to sleep. Having arisen at dawn and opened the cellar, he found the spigot drawn from a third cask, and the wine spilt even to the hole. Therefore, being stricken with terror, as well he might, at all these marvels, and no longer daring to conceal the common loss, he hastened to the Abbot and, falling at his feet, confessed all things in order, even as he had seen them. The Abbot therefore, having taken counsel with the Brethren, bade that all the spigots of the wine-casks should be anointed at nightfall with holy chrism; which was duly performed. The aforesaid Brother, therefore, having come to his cellar with the morrow's dawn, found a little black boy, wondrous small, clinging with his hands to one of the spigots: whom he seized forthwith and brought to the Abbot, saying, "Lo! lord, this little boy whom thou seest is he who hath brought upon us all that loss which we have suffered in our cellar"; and with this he told how he had found the urchin hanging to the spigot. Then the Abbot, marvelling beyond all belief at the figure of that child, took counsel and bade that a monk's frock should be made for him, and that he should be set to associate with the school-boys in the cloister. It was done as he bade; and this same child dwelt night and day with the school-boys. Yet he never took food nor drink, nor spake to any man, whether openly or in secret; and, while the rest slept at night-time or at mid-day, he would sit on his bed weeping and sobbing, without rest or intermission. Meanwhile another Abbot came to pray at this monastery, where he was detained for a few days; before whose face the school-boys often passed as he sat with the Abbot and the elder monks; at which times this little child, stretching out his hands to him, would look up with tearful eyes as though he besought some grace. After a while, seeing that he oftentimes did thus, the Abbot marvelled at his dwarfish stature and enquired of those that sat by, "Wherefore then will ye keep so small a child in your convent?" Whereat they smiled and answered, "Nay, my lord, this boy is not such as ye think"; and with that they told him of the damage which he had done unto them, and how he had been found hanging by the hands to the spigot of that cask, and how he had borne himself as he went in and out among them. At which that Abbot was sore afraid; and, groaning aloud: "As soon as may be," quoth he, "cast ye him forth from your monastery, lest ye incur greater loss or more grievous peril! This is manifestly some devil lurking in human form; nevertheless God's mercy hath protected you through the merits of the saints whose relics are here kept; so that he could not do you further hurt." So, at his command, the boy was forthwith brought into their presence; where, when stripped of his monkish frock, he vanished like smoke from between their hands.

12. HERETICAL PURITANISM

From the Chronicle of Ralph, Abbot of Coggeshall (R.S., pp. 121 ff.). Ralph's record is especially valuable during the years that came under his own experience (1187–1224).

IN the days of Louis [VII, 1137–1180], father to King Philip of France, while the errors of certain heretics, who are commonly called Publicans, spread secretly through many provinces of France, a marvellous thing befel in the city of Reims, in the matter of an old crone infested with this plague. The lord William, Archbishop of that city and uncle to King Philip, was riding one day for pastime without the city, attended by his clergy; when one of his clerks, Master Gervase of Tilbury,[1] seeing a maiden walking alone in a vineyard, and impelled by the wanton curiosity of youth, went aside to her, as we have heard from his own mouth in later years when he was a Canon. Having saluted her and asked whence she came, and who were her parents, and what she did there alone, having also observed her comeliness for a while, he began at last to address her in courtly fashion and prayed her of love *par amours*. "Nay," replied she, with a simple gesture

---

[1] "Gervase of Tilbury, an historian of the thirteenth century, whose career as a wandering scholar is very interesting, was for some time in the service of Otto IV, and was made Marshal of the Kingdom of Arles by him" (*Dict. of Eng. Hist.*).

and a certain gravity in her words, scarce deigning to look at the youth, "Nay, good youth, God forbid that I should ever be thy leman or any other man's; for if I were once thus defiled, and lost my virginity, I should doubtless suffer eternal damnation.beyond all help." Hearing which, Master Gervase forthwith knew her for one of this most impious sect of Publicans,[1] who in those days were sought out on every hand and destroyed; more especially by Philip Count of Flanders, who by an act of righteous cruelty punished them without mercy; yet some had already come over to England, who were caught at Oxford, and ignominiously branded on the forehead with a white-hot iron at Henry II's bidding, and banished the realm. While therefore the clerk aforesaid disputed with the maiden, confuting this answer of hers, then the Archbishop came up with his train; and, hearing the cause of this dispute, he bade them take the girl and bring her with him to the city. Then, when he had addressed her in presence of his clergy, and proposed many texts and reasonable arguments to confute her error, she answered that she herself was not so well-instructed as to refute such weighty objections, but confessed that she had a mistress in the city who would easily refute all by her reasonings. When therefore she had revealed this woman's name and abode, the crone was forthwith sought out by the servants, and set before the Archbishop. She, therefore—being assaulted on all sides with texts from Holy Scripture, both by the Archbishop himself and by his clergy, that they might convince her of so heinous an error—yet she, by a certain sinister subtlety of interpretation, so perverted all the texts they cited, that all understood clearly enough how the Spirit of All Error spake through her mouth. For she replied so easily, with so ready a memory, to all the texts and stories objected to her, whether from the Old or the New Testament, as though she had acquired a knowledge of the whole Scriptures[2] and had been always practised in answers of

[1] Many sects of medieval heretics were accused, and in some cases probably with truth, of adopting the extreme Manichaean doctrine which condemned even marriage.

[2] It was a constant complaint of medieval preachers that the heretics knew the text of the Bible so much better than the average orthodox; see my *Medieval Studies*, no. VII, p. 10.

this kind; mingling falsehood with truth, and baffling the true explanation of our faith with a certain pernicious understanding. Since therefore the obstinate minds of both women could be recalled neither by fair words nor foul, nor by any citations or texts of Scripture, from the error of their ways, therefore they were shut up in his prison until the morrow. On the next day they were summoned again to the Archbishop's hall, before him and all his clergy, and in the presence of noble men; where they were again publicly challenged to renounce their errors, and many reasons were again alleged. Yet they would by no means admit his salutary warnings, but rather persisted immovably in the errors they had conceived; wherefore they were unanimously adjudged to the stake. When therefore the fire was already kindled in the city, and they should have been dragged by the serjeants to the penalty to which they had been condemned, then that wicked mistress of error cried aloud: "O madmen and unjust judges! Think ye to burn me now with your fires? I fear not your doom, nor shudder at the flames ye have prepared." With these words, she suddenly drew from her bosom a spool of thread, which she cast through a great window of the hall, yet keeping the clue in her hand, and crying with a loud voice in all men's hearing: "Catch!" No sooner had she spoken this word, than she was caught up from the ground, and followed the ball like a bird through the window, under all men's eyes: for, as we believe, those same evil spirits bore her away who of old lifted Simon Magus into the air.[1] But what became of that witch, or whither she was spirited away, no man of that company could discover. Meanwhile the maiden, who had not yet come to such a pitch of madness in that sect, remained behind. No persuasion of reason, no promise of riches, could recall her from her foolish obstinacy; wherefore she was burned to death, to the admiration of many who marked how she uttered no sighs, no tears, no laments, but bore with

[1] For this legend see Vincent of Beauvais, *Spec. Hist.* lib. ix, c. 12, and the *Golden Legend* (Temple Classics, vol. iv, p. 15): "Then said Simon: it is not as thou sayest, but I shall show to thee the power of my dignity, that anon thou shalt adore me; I am first truth, and may flee by the air; I can make new trees and turn stones into bread; endure in the fire without hurting; and all that I will I may do. So Peter disputed against all these, and disclosed all his malefices."

constancy and cheerfulness all torments of the consuming flames, even as the martyrs of Christ (yet for how different a cause!) who were slain in old times by the heathen in defence of the Christian religion.[1]

13. A PRECIOUS WINDFALL

From the contemporary *Life*, written by a disciple of St William, canon of Ste-Geneviève at Paris, and afterwards abbot of Eskilsoe in Sweden and of St-Thomas-du-Paraclet. It will be found in *AA.SS. Boll.* April 6th (vol. I, p. 633, § 58).

WHILE Abbot William was yet in this corruptible body, weighed down with old age, two teeth were torn from his head, which he committed to Brother Saxo, saying: "Keep these two teeth in thy charge, and see that thou lose them not." He did as the Abbot had required him, pondering in his own mind wherefore this command had been laid upon him. When however the Lord had taken him away from before our face, then his surviving disciples, in memory of so holy a Father, besought that somewhat might be given to them of his possessions or of his garments; among whom one Brice, the Sacrist, complained that naught had fallen to his share saving a fur cap which the Saint had been wont to wear on his head. To which complaints this Brother made answer to whom these teeth had been entrusted: "I will give thee

---

[1] That incidents of this kind were not infrequent, we may gather from the learned and orthodox Petrus Cantor (*Verbum Abbreviatum*, Migne, *Pat. Lat.* vol. 205, p. 230). After complaining that the Church of his time dealt more harshly with heretics than the pagans had dealt with the early Christians, he goes on, "Moreover, certain honest matrons, refusing to consent to the lasciviousness of priests 'of the seed of Canaan' [Daniel xiii, 56 *Vulg.*] have been written by such priests in the book of death, and accused as heretics, and even condemned by a certain notoriously foolish zealot for the Christian faith, while rich heretics were simply blackmailed and suffered to depart. One man, because he was poor and pallid, though he faithfully confessed the faith of Christ on all points, and sheltered himself under the hope thereof, yet was burned because he said to the assembled bishops he would by no means submit to the ordeal of red-hot iron unless they could first show him that he could do so without mortal sin and without tempting God. Hearing this, they abandoned him with one accord [to the secular arm], telling the king that it was not lawful for them to be present at a judgment which involved the shedding of blood."

no small gift—nay, a mighty one, a pearl of price, no less than a tooth of our Father who in his lifetime loved thee not only with a special love, but thee above all others." With these words he delivered to him the tooth; and the Sacrist, rendering manifold thanks for this grace conferred upon him, took the tooth and held it in that dear veneration which it deserved. Oh what gifts did God afterwards confer upon mortal men through that tooth!—gifts which, if they were written down, man's weak intellect would never be content to believe!

14. A BATCH OF SUPERSTITIONS

Superstitions condemned in the *Poenitentiale* of Bartholomew Iscanus, Bishop of Exeter, 1161–1186. (MS. Cotton. Faust. A. viii, fol. 32, printed in *Rel. Ant.* I, 285.)

(i) WHOSOEVER shall strive to take away from another, and gain for himself, by any incantation or witchcraft, another's plenty of milk or honey or of other things; (ii) Whosoever, ensnared by the Devil's wiles, may believe and profess that they ride with countless multitudes of others in the train of her whom the foolish vulgar call Herodias or Diana, and that they obey her behests; (iii) Whosoever has prepared a table with three knives for the service of the fairies, that they may predestinate good to such as are born in the house; (iv) Whosoever shall have made a vow by a tree or water, or anything save a church; (v) Whosoever shall pollute New Year's Day by magic enquiries into the future, after the pagan fashion, or who begin their works on that day, that they may prosper better than in any other year; (vi) Whosoever make knots or sorceries and divers enchantments by charms of witchcraft, and hide them in the grass or in a tree or in a branching road, in order to free their beasts from murrain; (vii) Whosoever shall have set his child on the house-roof or in an oven [or *furnace*] to recover its health,[1] or for the same purpose shall

---

[1] "Ellen Cushion and Anastatia Rourkes were arrested at Clonmel on Saturday, charged with cruelly illtreating a child, three years old, named Philip Dillon. The prisoners were taken before the Mayor, when evidence was given showing an

have used charms or characters or anything fashioned for divination, or any artifice whatsoever save only godly prayers or the liberal art of medicine; (viii) Whosoever, while gathering medicinal simples, shall have said any charm save such as are godly, as the Lord's Prayer or the Creed or suchlike; (ix) Whosoever, labouring in wool or dyeing or other works, shall use charms or lay spells thereon that they may prosper; or who shall forbid the carrying away of fire or aught else from his house, lest the young of his beasts perish; (x) Whosoever shall work witchcraft from a dead man's funeral or corpse or garments, lest the dead folk take some vengeance, or lest some other die in that same house, or to obtain thereby some other profit or well-being; (xi) Whosoever on St John's Day shall have wrought any witchcraft to foretell the future; (xii) Whosoever shall believe that good or evil comes to him from the croak of a jackdaw or raven, or from meeting a priest or any animal whatsoever; (xiii) Whosoever shall cast into his barn or his cellar a bow, or any other plaything soever wherewith the devils called fairies should play, that they may bring the greater plenty; (xiv) Whosoever, in visiting the sick, shall conceive any omen of good or evil from the motion of any stone on his outward or homeward way, or by any other sign whatsoever; (xv) Whosoever shall believe that a man or woman may be changed into the shape of a wolf or other beast; (xvi) Whosoever shall spy out the footsteps of Christian folk, believing that they may be bewitched by cutting away the turf whereon they have trodden;[1] (xvii) (From the Council

extraordinary survival of superstitious belief. It appears that the neighbours fancied that the child, which had not the use of its limbs, was a changeling, left by the fairies in exchange for the original child, while the mother was absent. Prisoners entered her house and placed the child, naked, on the hot shovel, under the impression that this would 'break the charm.' The poor little thing was severely burnt, and is in a precarious condition. Prisoners, who were hooted by an indignant crowd, were remanded" (*Lynn News*, 24 May, 1884). Etienne de Bourbon, as will presently be seen (Extract 54 below), tells a similar tale from his own experience.

[1] A correspondent contributes an admirable analogy to *Notes and Queries* (17 September 1910). It is quoted from p. 245 of the *Report of the S.P.G.* for 1910. "A girl, because of a rival of her own sex, in the case of a man paying his affection to the latter, was told by her mother to gather up the 'track' of her feet— *i.e.* by taking up the sand on which she had walked—and putting this in a cloth to place it over the fire, when by burning the rival will in turn shrivel up, and so meet her death."

of Agde.) The priest must enquire whether there be any woman who professeth to be able to change men's minds by sorcery and enchantments, as from hate to love or from love to hate, or to bewitch or steal men's goods: also whether there be any professing to ride on certain nights and upon certain beasts with a host of demons in women's shape, and to be enrolled in the company of such. Let any woman of this sort be chastised with birchen twigs and cast forth from the parish.

15. THE PRIEST OF EVIL OMEN

From Cardinal Jacques de Vitry's *Exempla*, ed. Crane, p. 112: T. Wright, *Latin Stories*, p. 77.

In certain districts I have seen men when they meet priests [the first thing in the morning] forthwith crossing themselves, saying that it is an evil omen to meet a priest. Moreover, I have heard on sure authority that in a certain town of France wherein many of all conditions died, men said among themselves, "This deadly plague can never cease unless, before we lay a dead man in his grave, we shall first cast our own parson into the same pit!" Whence it came to pass that, when the priest came to the edge of the grave to bury a dead parishioner, then the countryfolk, men and women together, seized him, arrayed as he was in his priestly vestments, and cast him into the pit. These are inventions of the devil and demoniacal illusions.

16. SUPERSTITION PUNISHED

T. Wright, *Latin Stories*, p. 110.

Here is an example of a woman who used to make the sign of the Cross, as it is said, when she met her priest in the morning, and who answered that she did this lest some mishap should betide her that day. Whereunto he said: "Dost thou believe that it will be the worse to thee for having met me?" And she replied: "I fear it." Then said he: "It shall indeed be to thee as thou hast believed; for thou shalt have *one* mishap because thou hast met me." And, seizing her by the shoulders, he cast her into a muddy ditch, saying: "Be it unto thee even as thou hast believed!"

In Germany the same superstition was attacked in the thirteenth century by the Franciscan Berthold of Regensburg (ed. Pfeiffer, vol. I, p. 264): "Thus some folk believe in unlucky meetings, and that a wolf is lucky to fall in with—a wolf, that doth evil to all the world, and is so unclean a beast that he stinketh in men's nostrils and no man may thrive within scent of him!—and again they believe that an anointed priest is unlucky to meet; yet all our faith lieth on the priest, and God hath exalted him above all men!"

Petrus Cantor, "Peter the Precentor," was also Rector for many years of the Cathedral School at Paris—*i.e.*, of perhaps the busiest centre of learning in Europe. In 1191 he was chosen Bishop of Tournay; but the election was contested, and he willingly withdrew his claim; soon afterwards he entered a Cistercian monastery, and died in 1197. Cardinal Jacques de Vitry, who had known him personally, described him as "a lily among thorns, or a rose among thistles....A man mighty in word and in deed...whose uprightness of life added weight and gravity to his doctrine." The following extract is from his *Verbum Abbreviatum* (Migne, *Pat. Lat.* vol. 205).

17. MASSES AND MONEY
(Cap. xxvi, col. 97.)

LIKEWISE I say that temporal things should not be set among spiritual things in order that men may perform these latter, or at least perform them more promptly and swiftly.... To this purpose is that detestable example of the clergy who, playing at dice, fled in a disorderly and indecent fashion to vespers when they heard that there would be vesper-money for singing that service, and that it would be distributed beforehand in the church.[1] Another example is that of the prelate who besought the choir of his church to make St Stephen's day a feast of double solemnity in silken vestments

---

[1] To ensure regularity of attendance on the part of ministers at the great cathedral and collegiate churches, the authorities paid a considerable part of their salaries in ready money, handed over each time in the vestry to such only as had attended that particular service. See vol. IV for those who waited about the church for their "distributions" without properly celebrating the service.

and ecclesiastical chants, but who could only obtain it by promising to his clergy an annual feast, and by doubling the payment for mattins that night; so that they thus rather celebrated the Feast of the Double Money than the Feast of St Stephen.... When the bell rang for the hour of distribution at a certain church, and a bar was set across the entrance to the choir, the clergy ran as though to a solemn feast, even as old women run for the greased pig;[1] some stooping below to enter, others jumping over the bar, and others rushing in disorderly fashion through the great portal, whereby it is lawful for no man to enter save only for the dignitaries of the church. By reason of which baseness of filthy lucre, a certain layman besought one of the clergy not to attend at that service, for very shame's sake. But what could he do? If he entered into the choir, he would risk the suspicion of covetousness among the laity; if not, the clergy would suspect him of pride.... What can be more despicable than that the laity should call two of the services in a certain church, the *Lord's Hours*, for the singing of which there is no certain payment, and the rest the *Penny Hours*, nay, rather the Devil's hours? ...In short, even as it was honourable and laudable, before the ordinance of this miserable bargain, to enter the choir and perform divine service assiduously, so it is now dishonourable and of evil report, since this assiduity bringeth us rather the repute of covetousness than of devotion: so that now, in the words of the poet, "the Church (a name once noble and venerable) is prostituted, and sits like a harlot gaping for gain."

If this venality, the leprosy of Gehazi and the simony of the Magus, is so foul and damnable in the mere appendages to the Sacraments, as we have said above, then how much more so in the very substances of the Sacraments, and especially in the Eucharist?[2]... What, pray, is the cause why the other church services remain in the simplicity and purity of their first institution, and are never doubled, and this alone [of the Mass] is doubled, contrary to its first institution? Certainly

---

[1] *Tanquam vetulae ad unctum.* See Strutt, *Sports and Pastimes*, bk. IV, chap. iii, § xxxi, and Ed. Derembourg, *Vie d'Ousâma*, Paris 1889, p. 479.

[2] It was at this time still illegal to demand any fixed sum for saying mass: voluntary offerings might be accepted, but no fixed charge was allowed.

the cause is in the offerings: for at the Mass we offer and at no other service.... And, sad to relate, from such offerings altars are erected, sanctuaries are adorned, and monasteries built, by monks who thus abuse the Apostle's precept, "asking no questions for conscience' sake": though the Apostle speaketh only to such as sometimes ate with idolaters, that they might preach unto them. Moreover, we sell Christ more shamefully than Judas did; for we are worse than he. He, when his family was in need, sold one whom he believed to be a mere man; but we, Him Whom we know to be God and Man. He for thirty pieces of silver, and we for the vile price of a penny. He again, repenting (though with no true repentance), brought back the thirty pieces and cast them from him; but there is none among us in the Church who casteth away such ill-gotten gains. Moreover his thirty pieces, being the price of blood, were not put into the treasury: but nowadays from base oblations and ill-gotten gains altars are raised, churches and suchlike buildings are made.... Moreover (I say it even weeping), this sacrament alone is turned by some to magic arts, men celebrating masses over images of wax as a curse upon others; nay even, for such a curse, they sing the Mass of the faithful ten times or more, that their enemy may die by the third day or at least within a brief while afterwards, and may be laid with the dead in the grave. Some, again, have invented a Mass for the slaughter of those lately slain round about Jerusalem, as of newly-made martyrs: by which Mass they think to entice to themselves the greater oblations, by reason of the favour that men bear to such men slain [on the crusades]. To expel this many-headed disease from the Church I see but this one remedy; to wit, that there should be few churches, few altars therein, few and picked men to be ordained, and even those already ordained to be sifted before admission: above all, the strictest choice of such as are set over the lesser priests: and the extreme remedy, deliberated by Pope Gregory VIII, would be the abolishment of all oblations save thrice a year, namely at Christmas, Whitsuntide, and Easter, and on the Feast of the church's patron saint, and in presence of a dead body, and on any anniversary day. See how there was in all Israel only one temple, one tabernacle, one altar of offerings in the open court of the temple! for there was indeed in the Holy Place an altar of incense, yet naught was offered thereon save a little frankincense. Of this multitude of altars Hosea spake in detestation, saying, "because my people hath made many altars to sin, altars are become to him unto a sin: they shall offer victims, and the Lord will not receive them." Wherefore, after the example of this one temple, we should have a single church in each city—or, in a populous city, a few churches, yet all subject to one greater church. For the multitude of chapels hath begotten unlawful ministries, with many other portentous and strange things.

Ralph Higden, a monk of Chester, died in 1364. His *Polychronicon* is not only a digest of such chronicles as the author could get hold of, but also a popular encyclopaedia: it has no original merit, but is most valuable as showing a learned man's outlook on the world during Chaucer's boyhood. The book was translated in 1367 by John Trevisa, chaplain to Lord Berkeley, and is printed in the Rolls Series.

18. ANCESTRY OF HENRY II
(R.S. vol. VIII, p. 31.)

FOR that every man that readeth in book should have the less wonder of the ungracious issue and end of this king and of his sons, we shall take heed of this king's beginning, and whereof he came both on father's side and mother's side. Also of the condition of his wife, by whom he gat his sons. Geoffrey Plantagenet came of the children of a countess of Anjou, that was espoused only for fairness of body. She would seldom come to church, and then unnethe[1] she would abide the secrets of the mass. The earl her husband took her, and was ware of that doing, and ordained four knights to hold her in church; and she threw away her mantle that she was y-holden by, and left there her two sons under her right side of her mantle, and with her other two sons that she had under the left side of her mantle she flew out at the window of the church in sight of all men, and was never y-seen after that time. Afterward

[1] Scarcely.

Richard king of England told oft this tale, and said that it was no wonder though they that cometh of such a kindred grieved each other, as they that come of the devil and should go to the devil. Also in a time king Henry sent a clerk to his son Godfrey earl of Brittany, for to reform and make full peace, and the son answered the clerk in this manner: "Why art thou come to disinherit me of my right of my kind birth? knowest thou nought that it belongeth to us properly by kind,[1] and it is y-pight[2] upon us by kind of our forefathers, that none of us should love other? Then travail thou nought in vain to put away kind." Also this king Henry's mother was y-wedded to this Geoffrey, leaving her earlier husband, that was a pilgrim and lived as a hermit, and this king Henry came of them twain in his latter marriage. Also of this Henry, while he was a child y-nourished in the king's court of France, saint Bernard the abbot prophesied and said in presence of the king: "Of the devil he came, and to the devil he shall"; and meaned thereby both the tyranny of his father Geoffrey that gelded the bishop of Seez, and his own cruelness that slew St Thomas of Canterbury.[3]

19. THE JEW CONVERTED

(R.S. vol. VIII, p. 247.)

AT Toledo in Spain a Jew digged in his orchard to make him a vineyard; there he found a stone whole and sound in every side. In the middle of that stone he found a book, as great as a psalter with treen[4] leaves, written in Greek, Hebrew, and Latin, and spake of the three worlds from Adam to Antichrist, and declared the property of men, and set the beginning of the third world in Christ in this manner: "In the third world God's Son shall be born of a maid Mary, and He shall suffer the death for salvation of mankind." The Jew read this and was baptized anon....

---

[1] Nature.   [2] Fixed, fastened.
[3] Cf. Gibbon, *Decline and Fall*, chap. lxix, note 15.
[4] Wooden (tree-en.)

Burchard, Bishop of Worms, writing about A.D. 1020, condemned all who observe certain rites, or make certain incantations, "in the gathering of medicinal herbs; save only with the Creed and the Paternoster, in honour of God and our Lord" (*Decretum*, lib. X, c. 20; cf. c. 43). We remember, however, that Chaucer's Doctor of Physic worked by astrology, and that "his study was but little on the Bible." The fact is that some sort of ceremonial was generally considered a necessary part of all medieval medicine; and that, while one patient would sing Psalm xvi, drink his draught out of a church bell, and get a priest to say a prayer over him at the conclusion, others, again, had greater faith in the frankly pagan leechcrafts which still survived. A twelfth-century medical treatise in the British Museum (MS. Harl. 1585, fol. 12a ff.) gives the following two incantations. One of the two illuminations which accompany it in the MS. is reproduced in *Social England*, illustrated edition, vol. II, p. 118.

20. MEDICINE AND MAGIC

HOLY Goddess Earth, parent of Nature, who dost generate all things, and regenerate the planet which thou alone showest to the folk upon earth: Thou guardian of heaven and sea, and arbiter of all the gods, by whose influence Nature is wrapt in silence and slumber, thou art she who restorest day and puttest the darkness to flight, who governest the shades of night in all security, restraining at thy will the mighty chaos, winds and rain and storms, or again letting them loose. Thou churnest the deep to foam, and puttest the sun to flight, and arousest the tempests; or again at thy pleasure thou sendest forth the glad daylight. Thou givest us food in safety by a perpetual covenant; and, when our soul fleeth away, it is in thy bosom that we find our haven of rest. Thou too art called, by the loving-kindness of the gods, the Great Mother, who hast conquered the god of mighty name. Thou art the force of the nations and the mother of the gods, without whom nothing can be born or come to maturity. Mighty art thou, Queen of the Gods! thee, O Goddess, I adore in thy godhead, and on thy name do I call; vouchsafe now to fulfil my prayer, and I will give thee thanks, O Goddess, with the faith that thou hast deserved. Hear, I beseech thee, and favour my prayers; vouchsafe to me, O Goddess, that for which I now pray to thee; grant freely to all nations upon earth all herbs that thy majesty bringeth to life, and suffer me thus to gather this thy medicine. Come to me with thy healing powers;

grant a favourable issue to whatsoever I shall make from these herbs, and may those thrive to whom I shall administer the same. Prosper thou all thy gifts to us, for to thee all things return. Let men take these herbs rightly at my hand; I beseech thee now, O Goddess, may thy gifts make them whole; suppliant I beseech thee that thy majesty may vouchsafe me this boon.

The next incantation, fol. 13 b, is addressed to the herbs themselves.

Now, all herbs of might, I beseech you and supplicate your majesty; ye whom our Mother Earth hath brought forth and given as a gift to all nations, upon whom she hath conferred the gift of healing, and majesty in the sight of all men; be ye now a help and a profit to me. This I pray and beseech, with all supplication, be ye here present with all your virtues, (for she who hath created you hath given me leave to pluck you now, with his favour to whom the gift of healing hath been vouchsafed); and, so far as your virtues may extend, give ye healing and a good case and the grace of health. I beseech you grant me now by your virtue that whatsoever I distil from you may work with all power to a speedy effect and a happy issue. Grant that I may ever be permitted, by the favour of your majesty, to pluck you and to gather fruit in striving for you: grant this, and I will give you thanks in the name of the majesty which hath brought you to life.

Extracts 21–24 are from the so-called *Revelation to a Monk of Evesham*, first printed in English in 1483, and reprinted by Prof. Arber. *The Cambridge History of English Literature* (vol. II, p. 318) has an account of this beautiful book, which is not only very scanty but very incorrect: the true facts are to be found in Mr H. L. D. Ward's article on pp. 421 ff. of the *Journal of the Archaeological Association* for 1875. The monk was really of Eynsham near Oxford, and his vision was written in Latin by Adam, subprior of that monastery, who was then chaplain to St Hugh of Lincoln. This same Adam wrote in later years the beautiful Life of St Hugh, which has been published in the Rolls Series, and to which Froude devoted one of his *Short Studies*. A monk named Edmund, who had long been ailing, fell into a trance on the night before Good Friday, and awoke from it only with the sound of the Easter bells. He then told to those who stood by his bedside all that he had seen in Purgatory and Paradise; like Dante, he saw many great men known to him only by name, and many obscure folk whom he himself had known in life. The first passage here describes the death of a goldsmith with whom the monk had once been intimate. The spelling of the Old English version has here been modernized, and a few words altered.

21. A SAINT IN NEED
(p. 48.)

MY dear friend, (he said,) all ye together in the world hold me as lost and damned, not knowing the goodness and mercy here of my present lord saint Nicholas, the which had not suffered me an unhappy and an unprofitable servant of his to be damned and lost everlastingly....

Ye knew well how I disposed me in my living when I was in the world, as those things that were open to man's sight. Also I continued in the foul sin of drunkenness unto my last end, of an evil custom. Nevertheless it was not my will, for greatly it displeased me and mickle I sorrowed that I could not leave that vice. Soothly oftentimes I rose against myself, surely purposing to leave and cast away the foul vice of drunkenness that I was holden in. But, anon, what for the lust of drinking and the importunity of fellowship that I drank with, I was constrained to drink after the measure of mine old custom, whereby I was overcome and drawn again bound into lust and custom of the same sin, that was in mine own unmeasurable taking and appetite. Truly among this, by the mercy of God, the which will that no man perish, in my most blessed lord St Nicholas whom now ye follow graciously and presently, and whose parishioner also I was, such devotion I had that for any occasion I never left, but whatsoever I might do to his worship I did it full devoutly. And how mickle ever I gave me towards even to drunkenness, I used evermore to be at matins, for anon as they rang I would be there, and oftentimes before the parish priest. Also I found continually a lamp, of mine own cost, in St Nicholas' chapel. And those things that were necessary to the ornaments of all the church, as in lights or any other things, I would diligently ordain therefore, as [though] I had been his familiar servant and manciple. And where I had not sufficient of mine own goods to do it, I would move others of the parish to help as it seemed needful. Soothly the gifts that men or women gave, I took them, and to honourable uses full truly I spent them. Also twice in the year, that is at Christmas and at Easter, I would clean confess me of all my sins as well as I could to our parish priest, taking penances for them, and in part I did fulfil them diligently. Truly I did not observe and keep those things that I was commanded of my ghostly father, for oftentimes I left some things that I should have done, and [*word omitted*] those things that I should have been ware of. And of the commandment of my ghostly father I fasted the days of Advent as I did the Lent season; to the which days of Advent I added of mine own free will as many days before Advent as would make up the number of the days of Lent. And so on Christmas Day I would be houseled and receive the Holy Sacrament of our Lord's precious Body and Blood. But, alas, for sorrow! when that I should have been, that holy day of our Lord's birth, more holier and devouter in my living than other times, I turned me contrary unto other works and businesses of a worldly custom; wherefore it happened unto me also in mine last end that the wicked angel of the devil Sathanas, the which is causer and kindler of all evil, scorned me.... Soothly on Christmas Day, after that I had received the good Lord that I cannot remember without great horror and heaviness, I was drawn of an evil custom (as I said before) by overmuch drinking the same day into drunkenness again, to the great injury and wrong of such a Lord whom I had received a little before into my soul. And on the morrow I went to church as I used to do, sore wailing the foul vice the which I did the day before, purposing to beware of it and to do no more; but it was as void and vain. For by the occasion that I had of drinking, and the devil's stirring me thereto, I was destitute and lost the stableness of virtue and the mighty purpose of soberness that I had conceived; and so I fulfilled not my purpose in deed, but foul as I did yesterday so I did to-day, and by the delectation of over mickle drinking fell down again to drunkenness. Soothly the next day after following, the which is the third day after Christmas Day, I left not mine old custom of drinking, whereby I had lost the virtue of soberness and all my wits also. When it was dark night, I went out of the place where I drank, and came home and went to bed as I was clothed and shod, and a little I slept. And anon I woke, and would have risen, and said, as I had weened, that then it had rung to matins. But my wife told me Nay! and so I laid me down again. Truly then first I took a sleep, and anon after I took my death. And how I felt death suddenly come upon me I will tell you. A certain devil that tempted and stirred me to the vice of drunkenness thought to himself that an I died in such a peril without any contradiction he would me draw to hell, presuming also to have then power on me to do whatsoever he would, for mine obedience and consenting in that vice to him. But again full mickle he dreaded lest, by the merits of my patron St Nicholas, I should any time prevail against him by amendment of my living if I lived any longer; and so by his presumptuous power cruelly me strangled. Truly I felt him like an owl go into my mouth, the which oftentimes full evilly I opened to drink, and so through my throat slyly came down to my heart. And anon I knew that it was the devil. Notwithstanding I was yet mindful of the mercies of God and also of mine own wretchedness, and with stable purpose vowed in my mind to God that I would purely and wholly confess me of all my sins, and utterly for ever forsake the vice of drunkenness. And to this I called as inwardly as I could on St Nicholas to be my borrow.[1] Soothly to this avisement unnethe was granted me the space of a moment. Truly then the wicked spirit sat down anon upon my heart and clipped[2] it with his cursed arms on every side. Also he drew out of his mouth an horrible vomit of venom and cast it all abroad, and so in the space of a twinkling of an eye he expelled and cast me out of my body. And anon after that, I was had forth through dark places by the cruel and incredible madness of wicked spirits, the which all to-beat me, tore me, sticked me, drew me and all to-brent[3] me, and carried me with them I wot not whither, but as they would to everlasting torments. Then anon my most meek and dear advocate St Nicholas, to whom I called with all mine heart at my last end, and whom ever in my life I have worshipped though I were a sinner, came then and mightily took and delivered me out of their hands, and here hath set me in this place of purgatory for my purgation. And,

---

[1] Pledge, or guarantor.   [2] Embraced.   [3] Burnt.

howbeit that I suffer here sore and hard penance, I count it lightly while I have no dread of the wicked spirits, and also that their tyranny and importable[1] cruelness is ceased and gone from me. And soothly after this for certain I am and trust to have rest and everlasting joy by my lord St Nicholas. . . . O, he said, soothly an if I had known, when that I was in the world living, such things as I know now, I would have taught and defended all the world from that great hurt and damage how the people and folk might be sure and safe from the falling of sudden death. Truly and verily, an the Christian people would write daily on their foreheads and about the place of their heart, with their finger or in any other wise, these two words that containeth the mystery of the health and salvation of mankind, that is to wit and to say JHESUS NAZARENUS, without doubt the true people of our Saviour Jesu Christ should be harmless and preserved from such a great peril and hurt.

22. THE BROKEN VOW
(p. 74.)

AMONG them that brake their vows I saw a young knight brenning[2] in the midst of fire whom I knew sometime full well. And as I enquired of him why he was put in so great pain, this he told me. "My life," he said, "that I lived was but barren and vain and also vicious; for I was insolent and nice in pride and elation, and foul and unclean by the vice of lechery. Notwithstanding for this I am now specially punished, because I cast away from me the sign of the holy cross, the which I had taken upon me in a vow that I made to go to the Holy Land, howbeit that I took the cross not for devotion but for vain glory, the which I loved to have had of the lord that I served. Truly every night I labour in going as mickle as I may to make an end of that pilgrimage, but what for feebleness of strength and contrariness of the weather and also sharpness of the way, I am let [so] greatly that unnethe I may go at one time a full little day's journey. Soothly when the morning beginneth, flyen to me wicked spirits being mad in

---

[1] Insupportable.   [2] Burn.

all cruelness, and drawen me again to the place of my pains, where evermore, all the daytime, I am greatly pained in fire; nevertheless with a certain amendment of lesser disease, though it be little. And again when night cometh, I am restored to the place where I left last my journey, and so I go forth on my pilgrimage; and when the morning is come I am drawn again and cast to pains. And all that have vowed to go to the Holy Land, and after did cast from them their cross, and went not thither, in like wise as I go, they be compelled to do their pilgrimage: if so be they may have the grace of God in their last end to repent them, as I had to repent me for breaking of my vow, and then by the wholesome remedy of confession this sin that was deadly sin may be changed to a venial sin. Otherwise all that break that same vow be put to eternal damnation.

23. PRIESTS IN PURGATORY
(p. 81.)

ALSO many priests that by the grace of God left their vicious living of unchastity in very contrition of heart with confession of mouth when they lived, and because they had not done penance sufficiently, I saw them tormented in innumerable pains. Truly then I thought to myself that full few priests were there found, of the great number that is of them in all the world that had deserved pains after their death for breaking their chastity; and to this it was so answered: "Therefore full few be here tormented of the number of such persons, for unnethe it is seldom seen that any man of them were verily penitent and contrite while they lived for their sins; wherefore it is no doubt but that the great multitude of them be utterly damned."

24. THE VISION OF PARADISE
(p. 107.)

FURTHERMORE now when we were past all these places and sights aforesaid, and had gone a good space more inward, and ever grew to us more and more joy and fairness of places:

also at the last we saw afar a full glorious wall of crystal whose height no man might see and length no man might consider: and when we came thither I saw within-forth a full fair bright shining gate, and stood open, save it was signed and laid over with a cross. Truly thither came flockmeal the multitude of those blessed souls that were next to it, and would come in at that fair gate. The cross was set in the midst of that gate; and now she was lift up on high and so gave to them that came thither an open and a free entering; and afterward she was letten down again, and so sparred others out that would have comen in. But how joyful they were that went in, and how reverently they tarried that stood without abiding the lifting up of the cross again, I cannot tell by no words. Soothly here St Nicholas and I stood still together; and the liftings up of the cross and the lettings down again, whereby some went in and some tarried without, I beheld long time with great wonder. And at the last St Nicholas and I came thither to the same gate hand in hand. And when we came thither the cross was lifted up; and so they that were there went in. Soothly then my fellow St Nicholas freely went in and I followed; but suddenly and unadvised the cross of the gate came down upon our hands and departed me from my fellow, St Nicholas; and when I saw this, full sore afeard I was. Then said St Nicholas to me, "Be not afeard, but have only full certain faith in our Lord Jesus Christ, and doubtless thou shalt come in." And after this my hope and trust came again, and the cross was lift up, and so I came in: but what brightness and clearness of light was there-withinforth, all about, no man ask nor seek of me; for I can not only [not] tell it by word but also I cannot remember it in mind. That glorious shining light was bright and smooth, and so ravished a man that beheld it that it bare a man above himself by the great brightness of light; in so mickle that, whatsoever I saw before, it was as nothing methought in comparison of it. That brightness, though it were inestimable, nevertheless it dulled not a man's sight; it rather sharpened it. Soothly it shined full marvellously, but more inestimably it delighted a man that beheld it, and wonderfully compelled a man's sight to see it. And withinforth nothing I might see, but light and the wall of crystal through the which we came in. And also from the ground up to top of that wall were degrees ordained and disposed fair and marvellously, by the which the joyful company that was come in at the aforesaid gate gladly ascended up. There was no labour, there was no difficulty, there was no tarrying in their ascending; and the higher they went the gladder they were. Soothly I stood beneath on the ground, and long time I saw and beheld how they that came in at the gate ascended up by the same degrees. And at the last as I looked up higher I saw in a throne of joy sitting our blessed Lord and Saviour Jesus Christ in likeness of man, and about Him as it seemed to me were a five hundred souls which late had climbed up to that glorious throne, and so they came to our Lord and worshipped Him and thanked Him for His great mercy and grace showed and done to them. And some were seen on the upper parts of the wall as they had walked hither and thither. Truly I knew for certain that this place, where I saw our Lord sitting on a throne, was not the high heaven of heavens where the blessed spirits of angels and the holy souls of righteous men joy in the sight of God, seeing Him in His majesty as He is; where also innumerable thousands of holy spirits and angels serve Him and assist Him: but then from thence withouten any hardness or tarrying, they ascend up to the high heaven, the which is blessed of the sight of the everlasting Godhead, where only the holy angels and the souls of righteous men that be of angels' perfection see the invisible and immortal King of all worlds face to face, the which hath only immortality, and dwelleth in light that is inaccessible: for no man may come to it, the which no mortal man seeth neither may see. Soothly he is seen only of holy spirits that be pure and clean, the which be not grieved by no corruption of body neither of soul. And in this vision that I saw, so mickle I conceived in my soul of joy and gladness that whatsoever may be said of it by men's mouth full little it is, and unsufficient to express the joy of mine heart that I had there.

Therefore, when I had seen all these sights aforesaid and many other innumerable, my lord St Nicholas that held me by the hand said shortly this to me, "Lo son," he said, "now partly after thy petition and great desire thou hast seen and beholden the state of the world that is to come, as it might be to-possible. Also the perils of them that offenden and earn the pains of sinners; the rest also of them that have done their purgation; the desires of them that be going to heavenward; and the joys of them that now be come to the court of heaven; and also the joy of Christ's reigning. And now thou must go again to thyself and to thine, and to the world's fighting. Truly thou shalt have and perceive the joys that thou hast seen, and mickle more, if thou continue and persevere in the dread of God." And when he had said this to me, he brought me forth through the same gate that we came in; wherefore full heavy and sorry was I and more than a man may suppose; for well I knew that I must turn again from that heavenly bliss to this world's wretchedness. And greatly he exhorted me, how I should dispose me to abide the day of my calling out of my body in cleanness of heart and of body, and meekness of spirit with diligent keeping of my religion. "Diligently" (he said to me) "keep the commandments of God, and dispose thy living after the example of righteous men. And truly so it shall be, that after the term of thy bodily living thou shalt be admitted blessedly to their fellowship everlastingly."

And while the holy confessor St Nicholas this wise spake yet with me, suddenly I heard there a solemn peal and a ringing of a marvellous sweetness, and as all the bells in the world, or whatsoever is of sounding, had been rungen together at once. Truly in this peal and ringing brake out also a marvellous sweetness, and a variant mingling of melody sounded withal. And I wot not whether the greatness of melody or the sweetness of sounding of bells was more to be wondered. And to so great a noise I took good heed, and full greatly my mind was suspended to hear it. Soothly anon as that great and marvellous sounding and noise was ceased, suddenly I saw myself departed from the sweet fellowship of my duke[1] and guide St Nicholas. Then was I returned to myself again; and anon heard the voice of my brethren that stood about our bed; also my bodily strength came again to me a little and a little, and mine eyes opened to the use of seeing, as ye saw right well. Also my sickness and feebleness by the which I was

[1] Leader.

long time full sore diseased was utterly excluded and gone from me, and sat up before you so strong and mighty as I was before by it sorrowful and heavy. And I weened that I had been then in the church afore the altar, where I worshipped first the cross. . . .

[To which the writer of the work adds an epilogue.]

Many instructions and open examples be here at the beginning of this narration that evidently proven this vision not to be of man's conceit, but utterly of the will of God, the which would have it shewed to Christian people. Nevertheless, if there be so great infidelity or infirmity of any persons that cannot believe to these things aforesaid, let them consider the great sickness and feebleness of him that saw it, so suddenly and so soon healed into a very witness and truth of this vision that he saw. Also let them marvel the great noise that was about him, and also how that he was pricked in his feet [by the Brethren] with needles, by the which he could not in any wise be moved. Furthermore let them take heed to his eyes that were so far fallen down into his head, and [how he] was not seen unnethe to breathe the space of ij days, and also after a full long space of hours unnethe [at the] last might be perceived in him a full small moving as a thin thread in his vital veins. Also let them consider his continual weeping and tears the which he had afterward many days. . . . [But] full delectable it was to him, as he said, from that time forth, as oft as he heard any solemn peal of ringing of bells; because it would then come to his mind again, the full sweet peal and melody the which he heard when he was among the blessed souls in Paradise. Soothly, after that he was come to himself and his brethren had told him that now is the holy time of Easter, then first he believed, when he heard them ring solemnly to compline[1]; for then he knew certainly that the peal and melody that he heard in Paradise with so great joy and gladness betokened the same solemnity of Easter in the which our blessed Lord and Saviour Jesus Christ rose up visibly and bodily from death unto life; to Whom with the Father and the Holy Ghost be now and evermore everlasting joy and bliss. Amen.

[1] The last of the day-services.

The following anecdote from the Speculum Historiale of Vincent of Beauvais, lib. VI, c. 99, occurs also in a MS. of the Bibliothèque Nationale of the end of the twelfth century. See Toulmin Smith, *Contes de Nicole Bozon*, pp. 140, 279.

25. THE CHILD AND THE CHRIST

THERE is a famous city on the Rhine named Speyer, where men worship an image of St Mary, Mother of God, with her child. A little child, while his mother was praying afar, came to this statue with a slice of bread in his hand, and broke off a crumb which he held out to the image of the wailing Child, beseeching it in such words as German children are wont to babble, "Puppe, pappe! Puppe, pappe!"[1] At length, when the boy insisted, the image of the almighty Babe is said to have embraced him and addressed him thus, "*Puppe*, weep not; within three days thou shalt *pappen* with Me." His mother heard and trembled, and related this miracle to the senior canon, who even then came to the spot; and he, considering the matter carefully, replied, "Take heed! for after the day thus named thou shalt have thy child no more." The child was seized at once with a fever and died on the third day; wherefore he doth now most undoubtedly feast among the Innocents of Bethlehem.

The so-called *Lanercost Chronicle*, from which these extracts are taken, was not written at the monastery of that name, as earlier antiquaries supposed, but by a Grey Friar, probably of Carlisle. It extends in its original form to 1307, but is partly based on older materials. Like nearly all compilations by the early friars, it is full of picturesque anecdotes and human touches. It was edited for the Maitland Club by Father Stevenson in 1839. A translation of the greater part of it by Sir Herbert Maxwell has been printed in the *Scottish Historical Review*; though not always accurate, it is very readable and interesting.

26. A VISION OF KING ARTHUR
(p. 23, A.D. 1216.)

SEEING that we here mention Peter des Roches, Bishop of Winchester, I will set down that which I have heard from my elders. This man, vain-hearted and worldly, as is too

[1] "Little boy, eat!": cf. Dante, *Purg.* xi, 105. In the next line the sense seems to require the genitive *cunctipotentis*.

customary among our bishops, once assembled his huntsmen according to custom, and repaired to one of his church forests for the chase of wild beasts, when he should have taken his pleasure in the solace of men's souls. When therefore the beaters were scattered apart throughout the wood, it came to pass that the Bishop went by a certain glade wherein he found a fair new mansion that he had never seen before. He marvelled at its beauty, and hastened to see it, wondering sore who might be its builder. As he drew near, there came to meet him certain marvellously clad attendants, who forthwith invited him to come without delay to the banquet of their king, who even now awaited him. He hesitated and excused himself, saying that he had with him no garment fit for a bishop to sit down to meat in; but they, laying a proper mantle upon his shoulders, brought this guest to the king's presence, before whom he made obeisance. He was set at this great prince's right hand, where the more delicate dishes and drinks were ministered unto him. Yet he was not so stupefied but that he asked the king, among the rest who sat at meat, who he was and whence he had come thither; who confessed himself to be Arthur, once lord of the whole realm of Britain. Peter, clapping his hands for joy, asked whether he were among the saved; to whom the king made answer: "In truth, I await God's great mercy." Then said the Bishop: "Who, my lord, will believe me when I tell how I have to-day seen and spoken with King Arthur?" "Close thine hand!" quoth the king; and he closed it. Then said he: "Open!" and from the open hand there flew forth a butterfly. Then said Arthur: "All thy life long shalt thou have this memorial of me, that, at whatsoever season of the year thou wouldst fly one of these insects, thou mayest do thus and thou shalt have it [in thy hand]." Which blessing became in process of time so notorious that men often begged a butterfly of him for his benediction; and many called him the Bishop of the Butterfly. What Arthur's soul, yet mortal, intended hereby to teach, let him perpend who can guess better than I.

27. TRAVELLERS' TALES

(p. 97, A.D. 1275.)

I N these days there tarried at Hartlepool in England, William, Bishop of the Orkneys, an honourable man and a lover of letters, who related many marvels of the islands subject to Norway, whereof I record some here that they may be remembered. He told how, in one part of Iceland, the sea burneth for a whole mile round, leaving foul and black ashes behind. Elsewhere fire bursteth from the earth at certain times, after five or seven years' space, suddenly consuming villages and all on its path, nor can it be quenched or put to flight save by holy water consecrated by the hand of a priest. More marvellous still, he told us how men may plainly hear in that fire the lamentations of souls there tortured.[1]

(p. 131, A.D. 1289.)

The aforesaid Bishop [Hugh Biblinensis] told us again how, from that place on Mount Olivet where our Lord answered to the scoffs of the Jews, "If these should hold their peace, the stones would immediately cry out," even unto that gate of Jerusalem wherethrough He rode on the ass to His passion, thou canst not pick up a pebble and break it, but thou wilt find in the midst thereof the form as of an human tongue, as if in fulfilment of the Creator's will.

28. A NOBLE PLURALIST

(p. 158, A.D. 1294.)

THERE died in London Bogo de Clare, illustrious in name but not in life; whose end, as men report, was not very honourable [clarus] yet accordant to his deserts; for he had held innumerable churches, and had ill governed such as Christ had bought with His trading.[2] For he was a mere

---

[1] This was of course the common medieval belief: cf. the vision in Thomas of Eccleston (R.S. p. 67) of Frederick II borne off by devils to Etna.

[2] Or possibly, "had bought for him to deal with": the text seems corrupt here. There are elsewhere a good many words evidently misread by the editor: e.g. the *curalis exercens* of the next line should obviously be *curialis existens*. Similarly in

courtier, who cared not for Holy Orders but quenched the cure of souls and squandered the revenues of his churches; nor did he esteem Christ's spouse highly enough to provide the church out of her own revenues with necessary vestments untorn and undefiled; as might be proved by many profane instances, whereof I will tell one by way of example. In the honourable church of Simonburn, whereof he was rector, on the holy day of Easter, I saw, instead of a reredos over the high altar, a wattle of twigs daubed with fresh cow-dung; yet that living was valued at seven hundred marks yearly. Moreover he was so wanton and wasteful that he gave the old queen of France for a gift a lady's chariot of unheard-of workmanship; to wit, all of ivory, both body and wheels, and all that should have been of iron was of silver even to the smallest nail, and its awning was of silk and gold even to the least cord whereby it was drawn; the price whereof, as men say, was three pounds sterling; but the scandal was of a thousand thousand.[1]

the Maitland Club *Illustrations of Scottish History* (Battle of Neville's Cross, fol. 242a), the same editor prints *inniscata* and confesses himself puzzled: the word is plainly *inuiscata*, which makes just the sense required.

[1] We must multiply these moneys, of course, by 15 or 20 to get modern values. In the last line but one the word *thousand* has evidently dropped out between *three* and *pounds*, unless we are to suppose that this was only the price of a single cord. Bogo de Clare, though his clerical income would have compared poorly with that of William of Wykeham or Cardinal Wolsey, seems to have been the most notorious pluralist of the thirteenth century; the author of the Worcester Chronicle speaks of him with bated breath (*Annales Monastici*, R.S. vol. IV, p. 517). It is some satisfaction to know that he and another of the same feather did not collect their rents without friction; the tenants of Rotherfield rebelled against Bogo's bailiff in 1283 and destroyed his tallies, while in 1299 there was a more formal insurrection "with banners displayed" against an alien rector of Pagham (*Victoria Hist. of Sussex*, vol. II, p. 12). Another significant entry is among the pleas before the royal justices at Oxford in 1285 (*Oxford Hist. Soc.* vol. XVIII, p. 211). "The jurors present that Richard Everard and Walter de Chawsey, Bailiffs of Bogo de Clare, have lately raised a gallows within his domain of Holywell, some ten years past, they know not by what warrant. And a certain Thomas de Bensington was caught with a certain mare, and taken to the said Bogo's Court, by sentence whereof he was hanged at those gallows; and Alice le Welsh was hanged there also. Wherefore the sheriff was bidden to send for the said Bogo and bailiffs. And the said Bogo came and said that he held his church [of Holywell] by gift of the lord Henry, father of the present king, which church he found seised of the aforesaid liberties; and that all his predecessors, parsons of the aforesaid church, were seised of the same from time immemorial." The jury admitted his right, which was indeed unquestionable: but the entry is significant as showing how the growing ideas of the age were to some extent shocked by this anomaly of a rector who, as lord of the manor, had the right to hang men and women.

Jacques de Vitry studied at Paris, was ordained priest in 1210, and devoted himself to preaching by the advice of the Blessed Mary of Oignies, whose life he also wrote. After her death in 1213 he preached the crusade first against the Albigensians and then against the Saracens. In 1214 he was elected Bishop of Acre; here he worked many years with his accustomed zeal, until at last, disheartened by the vices and failures of the crusaders, he resigned in or about 1227. Next year he was made a cardinal, and in 1239 elected Patriarch of Jerusalem; but the Pope was unwilling to spare him. He died probably in 1240. A passage from one of his letters, recording his enthusiasm for the new-born Franciscan Order, may be found in Sabatier's *St François d'Assise*, c. xiii, p. 261. His *Historia Occidentalis* and *Historia Orientalis* describe the age in language even more unfavourable than that of Roger Bacon and others quoted in this book; but the main human interest of his works is contained in the *Exempla*, or stories for the use of preachers, published by Professor Crane for the Folk-Lore Society in 1890. A good many of these had already appeared anonymously among T. Wright's *Latin Stories*. Professor Crane's edition, though of very great value, contains a good many misreadings which I have been able to amend by collations procured from the Paris MS. References are to folios of the MS. Lat. 17509 of the Bibliothèque Nationale, and to pages in Crane's edition.

29. THE BOY-ARCHDEACON

(fol. 4, p. 1.)

How wretched and mad are those men who commit the cure of many thousand souls to their little nephews whom they would not trust with three pears, lest they should eat them![1] I have heard how one of these boys, after receiving an archdeaconry from a bishop his uncle, was set solemnly in his stall during the ceremony of installation, and was found not yet to have outgrown the needful ministrations of his nurse.

30. THE EXACTING BISHOP

(fol. 10, p. 2.)

I HAVE heard of a certain priest who could not satisfy the bishop's cook, who demanded innumerable dishes to be prepared for his master's use; until at last he cried in weariness and

---

[1] For this story see Extract no. 55.

grief, "I have no more now to give but ribs of the Crucifix!" which indeed he caused to be roasted and placed before the bishop on the table.[1]

31. THE SIMPLE KNIGHT
(fol. 105, p. 62.)

I HAVE heard how a certain knight, who never heard the truth in preaching nor had been well instructed in the faith, and who, being asked why he went not gladly to hear mass, (which is of such dignity and virtue that Christ and His angels ever attend upon it,) answered in simple words: "This I knew not; nay, I thought that the priests performed their mass for the offerings' sake." But, after hearing the truth, from henceforward he began gladly and devoutly to hear mass.

32. A KNOTTY QUESTION
(fol. 113, p. 68.)

I HAVE heard how a certain woman, in her extreme simplicity, would not receive the sacraments from unworthy priests, and that she did this not from settled malice but from ignorance.[2] God, wishing to recall her from her error, sent in her dreams a vehement and almost intolerable thirst; and it seemed to her that she was over a well whence a certain

---

[1] It was very frequently complained that the expense of entertaining Bishops or Archdeacons on their visitations pressed unduly upon monks and clergy. A theological dictionary of the early fourteenth century (see vol. III, no. 56) has on fol. 135a, "But thou wilt say: 'What can the wretched rector do? For the Rural Dean visiteth him with two horses... and the Archdeacon with five or seven... and the Bishop with twenty or thirty... and the Archbishop with forty or fifty.'" The author then does his best to reconcile the rectors to this burden by reasoned argument.

[2] This was still a vexed question in the thirteenth century. In 1074, Pope Hildebrand attempted to stop clerical concubinage by forbidding the laity to attend the ministrations of unworthy priests. The effect of this was so disastrous that the doctrine was finally abandoned. St Thomas Aquinas, while admitting it in theory, fears its dangers in practice (*Summa*, pars. iii, quaest. 83, art. 9). The fact was that it lent too strong a handle against the Church, and encouraged heretics who maintained that the virtue of the Sacrament was annulled by the unworthiness of the minister. The duty of abstention from the ministrations of sinful priests became a Wycliffite doctrine: see H. C. Lea, *Sacerdotal Celibacy*, 3rd ed. vol. I, p. 473.

leper drew water as clear as crystal, with a most comely vessel and a golden cord. Seeing therefore that many went up and drank, she also came forward; but the leper withdrew his hand, saying: "Thou who dost disdain to take the sacraments from evil priests, how wilt thou accept water from a leper's hand?" Most abominable, therefore, is that doctrine of the heretics who say that the virtue of the sacraments hangeth upon the lives of the ministers.

Caesarius of Heisterbach was possibly born, and certainly educated, at Cologne, then one of the richest and busiest cities of Europe. After some inward struggles, he was at last converted by the story of the harvester-monks and the Virgin Mary (vol. IV, no. 16); upon which he entered the Cistercian monastery of Heisterbach in the Siebengebirge. In this house, then at the height of its efficiency and influence, he finally became Prior and Teacher of the Novices, for whose special guidance he wrote his delightful *Dialogus Miraculorum*, one of the most intimate documents of the Middle Ages. He also wrote a few biographical and chronological treatises, and a book of Homilies. All these were apparently written between 1220 and 1235: the last dated event he mentions occurred in 1233. The Dialogue was printed five or six times between 1475 and 1605; the Homilies only once, in 1615. The author's faults are those of his time; his virtues of earnestness and vividness will perhaps be apparent even from these extracts. Father B. Tissier, reprinting him in 1662 in the *Bibliotheca Patrum Cisterciensium*, praises him as just the author to arouse the slumbering embers of strict Cistercian observance, and adds: "yet it is lamentable that this authority, who has deserved so excellently of the Church, should now at last, after so many centuries, be called not only fabulous but even erroneous; whereas, if he be attentively read even by a jealous critic, nothing can be found in him strange to Catholic doctrine" (t. II, *Preface*). The modern view is rather that of Father Karl Unkel: "The almost scrupulous love of truth which Caesarius shows in his anecdotes is well known, but equally so is his great credulousness" (*Annalen des Historischen Vereins f. d. Niederrhein*, Heft 34, 1879, p. 5). The interlocutors in the Dialogue are Caesarius himself, and a novice whom he is instructing. I quote by volume and page from Joseph Strange's critical edition (Cologne, 1851).

33. THE USURER'S FATE
(Caes. Heist. vol. 1, p. 70.)

IN the days when John the Master of Schools at Xanten, and Oliver, Master of Schools at Cologne, preached the crusade against the Saracens in the diocese of Utrecht (as I

A MEDIEVAL MILL

(From Viollet-le-Duc's *Dict. de l'Architecture*, vol. VI, p. 409.

was told by brother Bernard, who was then Oliver's colleague and fellow-preacher) there was a certain peasant named Gottschalk, if I remember rightly, who busied himself with usury. He took the cross with the rest; not from devotion, as events showed, but through the importunate urgency of the bystanders. When, by Pope Innocent's command, the dispensators collected ransom-money from the aged, the poor, and the sick, this same usurer feigned poverty and gave one of the dispensators about the sum of five marks, thus deceiving the priest. His neighbours afterwards testified that he might have given forty marks without thereby disinheriting his children, as he pretended. But God, who could not be deceived, presently put a terrible end to his trickery. The wretch sat about in the taverns, provoking God and mocking His pilgrims with such words as these: "Ye fools will cross the seas and waste your substance and expose your lives to manifold dangers; while I shall sit at home with my wife and children, and get a like reward to yours through the five marks with which I redeemed my cross." But the righteous Lord, willing to show openly how great pleasure He took in the travail and cost of the pilgrims, and how hateful in His eyes were the fraud and blasphemy of this scoffer, gave over the wretched man to Satan, that he might learn not to blaspheme. As he slept one night beside his wife, he heard as it were the sound of a mill-wheel turning in his own mill that adjoined his house: whereupon he cried for his servant, saying, "Who hath let the mill-wheel loose? Go and see who is there." The servant went and came back, for he was too sore afraid to go further. "Say, who is there?" cried the master. "Such horror fell upon me at the mill-door," answered the fellow, "that I must perforce turn back." "Well!" cried he, "even though it be the Devil, I will go and see." So, naked as he was, but for a cloak which he threw over his shoulders, he opened the mill-door, and looked in: when a sight of horror met his eyes. There stood two coal-black horses, and by their side an ill-favoured man as black as they, who cried to the boor, "Quick! mount this horse, for he is brought for thee." He grew pale and trembled, for the voice of command sounded ill in his ears. While therefore he hesitated to obey, the Devil cried again,

"Why tarriest thou? cast aside thy cloak and come.' (For the crusader's cross, which he had taken, was sewn on to his cloak.) In brief, feeling desperately in his heart the force of this devil's call, and no longer able to resist, he cast off his cloak, entered the mill, and mounted the horse—or rather the Devil. The Fiend himself mounted another; and, side by side, they swept in breathless haste from one place of torture to another, wherein the wretched man saw his father and mother in miserable torments, and a multitude of others whom he knew not to be dead. There also he saw a certain honest knight lately dead, Elias von Rheineck, castellan of Horst, seated on a mad cow with his face towards her tail and his back to her horns; the beast rushed to and fro, goring his back every moment so that the blood gushed forth. To whom the usurer said, "Lord, why suffer ye this pain?" "This cow," replied the knight, "I tore mercilessly from a certain widow; wherefore I must now endure this merciless punishment from the same beast." Moreover there was shown him a burning fiery chair, wherein could be no rest, but torment and interminable pain to him who sat there: and it was said, "Now shalt thou return to thine own house, and thou shalt have thy reward in this chair." Within a while the Fiend brought him back and laid him in the mill, leaving him half-dead. Here he was found by his wife and family, who brought him to bed and asked where he had been, or whence he came. "I have been taken to hell," he answered, "where I saw such and such tortures: where also my guide showed me a chair, which (as he said) was prepared for me, and wherein after three days I was to receive my reward." The priest was called forthwith, whom the wife besought to comfort his weakness, relieve his despair, and exhort him to those things which belonged to his salvation. But when the priest warned him to repent of his sins and make a clean breast in confession, saying that none should despair of God's mercy, he answered: "What avail such words as these? I cannot confess; I hold it useless to confess; that which is decreed must be fulfilled in me. My seat is made ready; after the third day I must come thither, and there must I receive the reward of my deeds." And thus, unrepentant, unconfessed, unanointed and unaneled, he died on the third day and found his grave in hell; and whereas the priest forbade him Christian burial, yet he took a bribe from the wife to lay him in the churchyard; for which he was afterwards accused in the Synod of Utrecht and punished I know not how. It is scarce three years since these things came to pass.

34. MARY AND CHRIST
(Caes. Heist. vol. i, p. 78.)

THERE lived not five years since near Floreffe, a Praemonstratensian monastery in the diocese of Liège, a noble youth whose father died and left wealth proportionate to his greatness and his state. The youth was knighted and, within a brief space, striving after earthly glory, he fell into extreme poverty. For he was altogether given up to tourneying for the sake of worldly glory, and he spent lavishly on minstrels and buffoons: until, his yearly revenues no longer sufficing for such prodigality, he was compelled to sell his paternal heritage. Now there lived hard by a knight rich and honourable though a courtier, to whom the aforesaid youth partly sold, partly pledged, his estates; and now, having no more to sell or mortgage, he purposed to go into exile, thinking it less intolerable to go begging among strangers than to bear the shame of poverty among his kinsfolk and acquaintance. But he had a steward, a man of iniquity, Christian by name but unchristian in deed, and utterly given up to the service of the fiends. He, seeing his master so sad, and knowing well the cause, said to him, "My lord, would ye fain become rich?" "Gladly," answered the youth, "so that it were with God's blessing." To whom the steward: "Fear not, only follow me, and all shall be well." Forthwith he followed after this wretch, (as Eve after the serpent's voice and a bird after the fowler's snare,) doomed to be quickly caught in the devil's toils. The steward led him that same night through a wood into a marshy place, and began to converse as with another person. "To whom speakest thou?" said the youth: but this Unjust Steward answered to his master, "Only keep silence, and care not with whom I may speak." When therefore he spake a second time, and the youth asked again the same question, the steward answered, "My speech is with the Devil." Then was the young man seized with a great horror: for who indeed would not have been dismayed at that spot and hour to hear such speech as this? For the steward said to the Devil, "Lord, behold I have brought hither this noble youth my master, beseeching your grace and your majesty that he may be thought worthy to be restored by your help to his former honours and riches." Then said the Fiend, "If he will be my devoted and faithful servant, I will give him great wealth, and add thereunto such glory and honour as his forefathers never had." Then answered the steward, "He will gladly and faithfully obey you for such a reward." "If then," said the Devil, "he would fain receive such gifts at my hand, he must forthwith renounce the Most High." While the young man, hearing this, refused to obey, the man of perdition said to him, "Why do ye fear to utter one little word? Speak it, and renounce God." At length the wretched youth was persuaded by the steward to deny his Creator with his mouth, to repudiate him with his hands,[1] and to do homage to the Devil. When this crime had been committed, the Devil added, "The work is yet imperfect. He must renounce also the Mother of the Most High; for she it is who doth us most harm. Those whom the Son in His justice casts away, the Mother, in her superfluity of mercy, brings back again to indulgence." Again the serpent whispered in the youth's ear, that he should obey his lord in this also, and deny the Mother even as he had denied the Son. But at this word the youth was utterly dismayed, and being moved beyond all measure, he said, "That will I never do!" "Why?" said the other, "Thou hast done the greater deed, do now the lesser; for the Creator is greater than the creature." But he replied, "I will never deny her, even though I must beg from door to door for all the days of my life": and he would not consent. Thus therefore both departed, leaving the matter yet unfinished, but burdened with a heavy load of sin, both the

---

[1] *Exfestucare*: see Du Cange, *Glossarium*, s.v. Festuca. This was a formal legal proceeding, quite different from Vanni Fucci's blasphemous gesture in Dante (*Inf.* xxv. 1–3).

steward who had persuaded and the youth who had consented. And as they went together they came to a certain church, the door whereof had been left half-shut by the bell-ringer as he went out. Whereupon the youth leapt from his horse and gave it to the steward, saying, "Wait here for me until I return to thee." And entering the church before dawn, he fell down before the altar and began from the depths of his heart to call upon the Mother of Mercy: (for upon that altar stood the image of the Virgin Mother herself, holding the Child Jesus in her lap.) And lo! by the merits of that most glorious Star of the Sea, the true dayspring began to arise in the heart of this our youth. Such contrition did the Lord vouchsafe to him for the honour of His Mother, whom he had not denied, that he roared for vexation of spirit, and filled the church with the wild vehemence of his lamentations. At the same hour the aforesaid knight, who had all the youth's lands, turned aside by God's providence, (as it is believed,) to that same church; and, seeing it empty and thinking that service was being held there, (especially for the clamour that he heard within,) he entered alone. Then, finding this youth so well-known to him weeping before the altar, and supposing that he wept only for his own calamity, he secretly crept behind a column and awaited the issue of the matter. So when the youth dared not to name nor call upon that terrible Majesty whom he had denied, but only importuned His most loving Mother with lamentable cries, then that blessed and singular Advocate of Christians spake thus through the lips of her statue, "Sweetest Son, pity this man." But the Child made no answer to His Mother, turning His face from her. When therefore she besought Him again, pleading that the youth had been misled, He turned His back upon His Mother, saying, "This man hath denied Me, what should I do to him?" Thereupon the statue rose, laid her Child upon the altar, and threw herself on the ground at His feet, saying, "I beseech thee, Son, forgive him this sin for my sake." Then the Child raised His Mother up and answered her, "Mother, I could never deny Thee aught: behold, I forgive it all for thy sake." He had first forgiven the guilt for his contrition's sake, and then at His Mother's intercession He forgave the penalty of the sin. ¶ *Novice.* Why was He so hard to His so beloved Mother? ¶ *Monk.* That He might show the youth how grievously he had sinned against Him, and the more to punish the very sin against Himself by grief of heart. So the youth arose and left the church, sad indeed for his fault, but glad to have found mercy. The knight left the church secretly after him, and, feigning ignorance, asked him why his eyes were so wet and swollen; to whom the youth answered, "It is from the wind." Then said the knight, "My lord, the cause of your sadness is not hidden from me. I have an only daughter: if ye will have her to wife, I will restore with her all your possessions, and make you heir in addition to all mine own riches." The youth answered joyfully, "If ye would vouchsafe to do thus, it would be most pleasant unto me!" The knight went back to his wife and told her the whole story in order; she consented, the wedding was celebrated, and the youth received all his lands again for his wife's dowry. He still lives, I think, and his wife's father and mother; after whose death their inheritance will fall to him.

35. THE SAME
(Caes. Heist. vol. ii, p. 382.)

A CERTAIN lay-brother of Hemmenrode was somewhat grievously tempted; wherefore as he stood and prayed he used these words, "In truth, Lord, if Thou deliver me not from this temptation, I will complain of Thee to Thy Mother!" The loving Lord, master of humility and lover of simplicity, prevented the lay-brother's complaint and presently relieved his temptation, as though He feared to be accused before His Mother's face. Another lay-brother standing behind the other's back smiled to hear this prayer, and repeated it for the edification of the rest. ¶ *Novice.* Who would not be edified by Christ's so great humility?

36. CUCKOO, CUCKOO!

From T. Wright's *Latin Stories*, p. 42. On p. 74 of the same book is a
very interesting pendant, from MS. Reg. 7, E. iv. A very similar story
is told of a Cistercian lay-brother (Caes. Heist. vol. 1, p. 295).

A CERTAIN woman was sick unto death, and her daughter
said unto her: "Mother, send for the priest to confess thy
sins." To whom the mother: "To what profit? If I am
sick to-day, I shall be whole to-morrow, or the day after."
But the daughter, noting how she grew worse, brought in
many neighbours to give her like warning; to whom she:
"What say ye or what do ye fear? I shall not die for twelve
years. I have heard a cuckoo who told me so." At length
in that peril of death she grew dumb. Then her daughter sent
for the priest, who came and brought all that was needed,
and coming to her asked whether she wished to confess anything. But she only said: "Cuckoo!" Then when the priest
offered her the Lord's Body and asked again if she believed
that He was her Saviour, again she answered: "Cuckoo!"
The priest therefore went home, and soon after she died.

37. THE IMPENITENT HERETIC
(Caes. Heist. vol. 1, p. 298.)

ABOUT that time, under Archbishop Reinhold, many heretics
were taken at Cologne, who, having been examined and convicted by learned men, were condemned by sentence of the
secular courts. When, therefore, the sentence had been pronounced and they were to be led to the stake, one of them
called Arnold, whom the others confessed as their master—
as those have related who were there present—begged that
bread and a bowl of water might be given him. Some were
willing to grant this; but prudent men dissuaded them, lest
aught should thus be done by the devil's work which might
turn to the scandal and ruin of the weaker brethren. ¶ *Novice:*
I wonder what he desired to do with the bread and water?
¶ *Monk:* As I conjecture from the words of another heretic,
who some three years since was taken and burned by the King

of Spain, he would fain have made a sacrilegious communion with them, that it might be a viaticum to his followers to their eternal damnation. For there passed by our monastery a certain Spanish abbot of our Order, who sat with the Bishop and Prelates of churches to condemn this same heretic's errors; and he reported the heretic to have said that any boor at his own table, and from his own daily bread, might consecrate the Body of Christ: for this cursed man was a common blacksmith. ¶ *Novice:* What, then, was done with the heretics at Cologne? ¶ *Monk:* They were brought out of the city and all committed to the flames together, hard by the burial-ground of the Jews. When, therefore, they began to burn sore, then in the sight and in the hearing of many this Arnold, already half burned, laid his hand on the heads of his disciples, saying: "Be ye constant in your faith, for this day ye shall be with Laurence."—Yet God knoweth how far they were from the faith of St Laurence! Now there was among them a comely maiden, but an heretic, who was withdrawn from the flames by the compassion of certain bystanders, promising that they would either give her in marriage or place her, if she preferred, in a convent of nuns. To this she did indeed consent in words; but when the heretics were dead she said to those who held her: "Tell me where lies that seducer!" When, therefore, they had shown her Master Arnold's corpse, she tore herself from their hands, covered her face in her garment, fell upon the body of the dead man, and went down with him to hell, there to burn for ever and ever.

38. THE STORM OF BÉZIERS
(Caes. Heist. vol. 1, p. 301.)

THE preacher and chief [of this Crusade against the Albigensians] was Arnold, Abbot of Cîteaux, afterwards Archbishop of Narbonne. The Crusaders, therefore, came and laid siege to a great city named Béziers, wherein were said to be more than 100,000 men. So these heretics, in the sight of the besiegers, defiled the volume of the Holy Gospels in such wise as may not be repeated, and threw it from the wall against the Christians, after which they shot their arrows and cried,

"Behold your law, ye wretches." But Christ, the Author of the Gospels, suffered not unavenged this injury inflicted upon Him, for certain camp-followers, kindled with the zeal of faith, like lions, even as they of whom it is written in the Book of Maccabees, laid their ladders to the wall and went up fearlessly, so that the heretics were struck with terror from God and fell away from the walls; and these first, opening the doors to them who followed, took possession of the city. Learning, therefore, from their own confession, that Catholics were mingled with heretics in the city, they said then to the Abbot, "What shall we do, lord? We cannot discern between the good and evil." The Abbot (fearing, as also did the rest, lest they should feign themselves Catholics from fear of death, and should return again to their faithlessness after his departure,) is said to have answered: "Slay them, for God knoweth His own." So there they were slain in countless multitudes in that city.[1]

39. THE SIN OF TOURNAMENTS
(Caes. Heist. vol. II, p. 327.)

ON the night after the day when the army of the Duke of Louvain was slaughtered by the men of Liège, a certain servant of the Count of Lose, passing by Montenaeken, (which was the place of slaughter,) about nightfall, saw there a vast tournament of devils; and methinks these unclean spirits would never have exulted so greatly but that they had taken some great prey there: for there is no question but that such as are slain in tournaments go down to hell, if they be not helped by the benefit of contrition.

[1] Caesarius is the only authority for this incident of the siege, which happened some 15 or 20 years before he wrote: but the story is perfectly consistent with what we know from many other orthodox sources. This same Arnold, for instance, wrote off at once to tell the Pope how "the city of Béziers was stormed, and our men, sparing neither rank, nor age, nor sex, smote some 20,000 inhabitants with the edge of the sword." To this Innocent III, good and great man though he was, replied in terms of triumphant congratulation, exulting that God had not consumed the heretics with the breath of His nostrils, but had allowed "as many as possible of the Faithful to earn by their extermination a well-merited reward," *i.e.* as he explains lower down, "the salvation of their souls." Both letters are printed n Innocent's Register, bk. XII, nos. 108 and 136.

40. APOSTLES BY LOT
(Caes. Heist. vol. II, pp. 129-133.)

IT is a very common custom among the matrons of our province to choose an Apostle for their very own by the following lottery: the names of the twelve Apostles are written each on twelve tapers, which are blessed by the priest and laid on the altar at the same moment. Then the woman comes and draws a taper; and whatsoever name that taper shall chance to bear, to that Apostle she renders special honour and service. A certain matron, having thus drawn St Andrew, and being displeased to have drawn him, laid the taper back on the altar and would have drawn another; but the same came to her hand again. Why should I make a long story? At length she drew one that pleased her, to whom she paid faithful devotion all the days of her life; nevertheless, when she came to her last end and was at the point of death, she saw not him but the Blessed Andrew standing at her bedside. "Lo!" he said, "I am that despised Andrew!" from which we can gather that sometimes saints thrust themselves even of their own accord into men's devotion.... Another matron, desiring to have a special Apostle, proceeded after the same fashion; but, having drawn the Blessed Jude (as I think), she cast that taper, apostolic name and all, behind the altar-chest; for she would fain have had one of the more famous Apostles, as St John the Evangelist or the Blessed James. The other, therefore, came to her in a dream by night and rebuked her sternly, complaining that she had displeased him and cast him shamefully behind the chest; nor was he appeased even so until he had added stripes to words, for she lay palsy-stricken on her bed for a whole year long. ¶ *Novice.* Is it lawful thus to choose Apostles by lot? ¶ *Monk.* It is written that St Matthew the Apostle was chosen by lot; yet not that he should be preferred to the rest, but that the number of twelve, diminished through Judas, should be filled up. Nevertheless I think that lots of this kind have come down by tradition from the election of St Matthew. I have heard at Cologne a learned priest publicly reproving such elections in church; "all the Apostles," said he, "are equally holy, wherefore all should be equally honoured by us; or, if we are to show special honour to any, it should be in my judgment to the blessed Peter, through whom our country was converted to the faith, and whom Christ appointed as a special Apostle to us.[1]

41. THE SACRAMENT AS A CHARM

(Caes. Heist. vol. ii, p. 170.)

I THINK it is less than two years now since a certain priest who doubted of the Sacrament of Christ's Body celebrated mass in the town of Wildenburg. As he was reciting the canon of the mass, with some hesitation concerning so marvellous a conversion of bread into Christ's Body, the Lord showed him raw flesh in the host. This was seen also by Widekind, a noble standing behind his back, who drew the priest aside after mass and enquired diligently what he had done or thought during the canon; he, therefore, terrified both by the vision and by the question, confessed and denied not how at that hour he had doubted of the sacrament. And each told the other how he had seen raw flesh in the host. This same Widekind had to wife the daughter of Siegfried of Runkel, a niece of the abbess of Rheindorf, who told me this vision last year. Wouldst thou also know what the Lord shows to priests of evil life, for that He is crucified by them?... A certain lecherous priest wooed a woman; and, unable to obtain her consent, he kept the most pure Body of the Lord in his mouth after mass, hoping that, if he thus kissed her, her will would be bent to his desire by the force of the Sacrament. But the Lord, (who complaineth through the mouth of the Prophet Zacharias, saying: "You crucify me daily, even the whole nation of you":)[2] thus hindered his evil doing. When he would fain have gone forth from the church door, he seemed to himself to grow so huge that he struck his head against the ceiling

---

[1] St Bernardino of Siena records with disapproval this lottery of Apostles for patron-saints (*Opera*, vol. i, p. 53): yet it was in this way that St Elizabeth of Hungary chose St John for her special Apostle (J. B. Mencken, *Scriptores*, ii, col. 2013).

[2] Caesarius here misquotes Malachi iii, 9, with a side reference to Zachariah xii, 10: cf. the 27th anecdote of his eighth book.

of the sacred building. The wretched man was so startled that he drew the host from his mouth, and buried it, not knowing what he did, in a corner of the church.[1] But, fearing the swift vengeance of God, he confessed the sacrilege to a priest his familiar friend. So they went together to the place and threw back the dust, where they found not the appearance of bread, but the shape, though small, of a man hanging on the cross, fleshy and blood-stained. What was afterwards done with it, or what the priest did, I forget, for it is long since this was told me by Hermann our Cantor, to whom the story was fairly well-known.... ❡ *Novice.* If all priests heard such stories, and believed in them, I think that they would honour the Divine Sacraments more than they do now. ❡ *Monk.* It is somewhat pitiful that we men, for whose salvation this Sacrament was instituted, should be so lukewarm about it; while brute beasts, worms, and reptiles recognize in it their Creator.... A certain woman kept many bees, which throve not, but died in great numbers; and, as she sought everywhere for a remedy, it was told her that if she placed the Lord's Body among them, this plague would soon cease. She therefore went to church and, making as though she would communicate, took the Lord's Body, which she took from her mouth as soon as the priest had departed, and laid it in one of her hives. Mark the marvellous power of God! These little worms, recognizing the might of their Creator, built for their sweetest Guest, out of their sweetest honeycombs, a tiny chapel of marvellous workmanship, wherein they set up an altar of the same material and laid thereon this most holy Body: and God blessed their labours. In process of time the woman opened this hive, and was aware of the aforesaid chapel; whereupon she hastened and confessed to the priest all that she had done and seen. Then he took with him his parishioners and came to the hive, where they drove away the bees that hovered round and buzzed in praise of their Creator; and, marvelling at the little chapel with its walls and windows, roof and tower, door and altar, they brought back the Lord's Body with praise and glory to the church. For though God be marvellous in the saints, yet these His smallest

[1] Churches were very commonly unpaved at this date.

creatures preached Him yet more marvellously. Yet, lest any presume to do this again, I will tell thee of a terrible thing which the mistress [of novices] at Sankt Nicolas Insel[1] told me last year. There was in that island a demoniac girl, a lay-woman, whom I also have seen there. A certain priest inquired of the devil that was in her,[2] why Hartdyfa of Cochem had been so cruelly tormented for so long a time; and the demon answered through the girl's mouth, "Why? she hath well and abundantly deserved it; for she sowed the Most High on her cabbage-beds." The priest understood not this saying, nor would the devil explain it further; he therefore sought out the woman Hartdyfa and told her of the devil's words, warning her not to deny if she understood them. She confessed her fault forthwith, saying, "I understand only too well; but I have never yet told it to any man. When I was young, and had got me a garden-plot to till, I took in a wandering woman one night as my guest: to whom when I complained of the ravage of my garden, telling how my cabbages were eaten up with caterpillars, she replied, 'I will teach thee a good remedy. Take thou the Lord's Body and crumble it up and sprinkle the crumbs over thy cabbages; so shall that plague cease forthwith.' I, wretched woman, caring more for my garden than for the Sacrament, having received the Lord's Body at Easter, took it from my mouth and used it as she had taught me, which did indeed turn to the comfort of my cabbages, but to mine own torment, as the devil hath said."
¶ *Novice.* That woman was more cruel than Pilate's minions, who spared the dead Jesus and would not break His bones.
¶ *Monk.* Wherefore even to this day she is punished for that enormous fault, and her tortures are unheard-of. Let those who turn God's sacraments to temporal profit—or, more abominable still, to witchcraft—mark well this chastisement, even though they fear not the guilt.[3]

[1] A convent of Augustinian nuns on an island in the Moselle.
[2] Many of Caesarius' anecdotes rest upon this medieval belief that mad folk had the spirit of prophecy, the devil speaking through their mouths.
[3] This eighth book of Caesarius contains many other tales of this abuse of sacraments for purposes of witchcraft; but the foregoing specimens will suffice for most readers.

42. ORDEAL AND MIRACLE

(Caes. Heist. vol. II, p. 243.)

DOM BERNARD of Lippe, who was once an abbot and is now a bishop in Livonia, is wont to tell a miracle contrary to this last. "I knew, (he said,) a fisher in the bishopric of Utrecht who had long lived incontinently with a certain woman; and, because his sin was too notorious, fearing one day to be accused at the synod then impending, he said within himself: 'What wilt thou now do, poor wretch? If thou art accused of incontinence in this synod and must confess, thou wilt forthwith be compelled to take her to wife; or if thou denyest it thou wilt be convicted by the ordeal of white-hot iron and be still more confounded.' So, coming forthwith to a priest (rather, as the event showed, from fear of punishment than from love of righteousness), he confessed his sin, asked counsel, and found it. 'If,' said the priest, 'thou hast a firm purpose never to sin again with her, then thou mayest carry the white-hot iron without further care and deny thy sin; for I hope that the virtue of confession will free thee.' And this he did, to the amazement of all who well knew his incontinence. Lo! here by God's power, as in former examples, the fire restrained its force against its own nature; and, as thou shalt hear later, it grew hot even more marvellously against its nature. To be brief, the man was absolved. Many days afterwards, as he rowed with another fisher at his work on the river, and the house of the aforesaid woman came in sight, then the other said unto him: 'I marvel greatly, and many marvel with me, wherefore the iron burned thee not at the synod, though thy sin was so notorious.' He, boasting unworthily of the grace that had been conferred on him (for he had already conceived the purpose of sinning again), smote the river-water with his hand and said: 'The fire hurt me no more than this water!' Mark the marvellous justice of God! He who had guarded the penitent in His mercy, punished now by a just and strange miracle the same man when he relapsed: for no sooner had he touched the water than it was to him as white-hot iron. He drew back his hand suddenly and cried aloud; but he left his skin in the water. Then, in tardy repentance, he told his comrade all that had befallen him."

Our fellow-monk Lambert was wont to tell a like miracle to this. A countryman who had a feud against another gave money to a certain wicked man of the Order of wandering Religious, (whereof there are many,) that he might burn the other's house; which this man, entering under the cloak of religion, set afire at a convenient time. Again this abandoned wretch, forgetful of the hospitality he had received, set fire to the same house for the same bribe, after that it had been rebuilt. The master, troubled at this double loss, accused all of whom he had any suspicion, but they purged themselves by the ordeal of white-hot iron. Again the burned house was rebuilt; and this iron which had been used for the ordeal was thrown into one corner of it. To be brief, that false religious vagrant came again, corrupted by his former covetousness, and was received with all kindness. He marked the aforesaid iron and asked what purpose it served: to which his host answered: "I know not who has twice set fire to my house; and, though I had suspicion of certain men, they have borne that iron at white-heat and yet were not burned." Then said the other: "The iron might be turned to some use": and lifting it up (as God would have it) he was so burned in the hand that he cried aloud and cast it down. When the master of the house saw this, he caught the incendiary by the cloak and cried: "Thou art the true culprit!" The man was taken before the judge, confessed his crime unwillingly, and was condemned to be broken upon the wheel.

THE KNIGHT AND THE CRUCIFIX

In the earliest version of the following story, immortalized by Burne-Jones, the hero is St John Gualbert, founder of the Order of Vallombrosa, who died in 1073. For other forms see A. G. Little, *Liber Exemplorum* (1908), pp. 155–6: but this of Matthew Paris is perhaps the most vivid narrative of all. Matthew Paris, Monk of St Albans and Historiographer Royal to Henry III, is unquestionably the greatest of the English medieval chroniclers, and has few rivals in Europe during this period. He was a man of many and various accomplishments—diplomatist, mathematician, poet, theologian, and artist, though the best authorities ascribe to other hands nearly all the beautiful drawings which illustrate the MSS. of his works. Far more extracts would have been given here, but that a complete translation of his Chronicle, uninspired but otherwise satisfactory, has been published in Bohn's Antiquarian Library. He died in or about the year 1259.

43. THE KNIGHT AND THE CRUCIFIX

A.D. 1232. In the reign of the said King Richard [I], a certain English knight who dwelt in the New Forest, and had long been wont to hunt the King's deer by stealth, was caught one day with his stolen venison and banished by sentence of the King's court. For thus had this King, most merciful in time of peace, tempered the law of deerstealing; whereas under his predecessors all who were taken in this misdeed lost their eyes, their hands, or their feet, or suffered other nameless mutilations. But to the good King Richard such a sentence seemed too inhuman, that men made in God's image should stand in peril of life or limb for the sake of beasts which are by natural law common to all men; nay, he thought that in this he would himself be more than a beast.... The knight therefore was banished as aforesaid; and he, who had before rejoiced in choice delicacies, must needs beg his bread now among strangers with his wife and children. Coming therefore at length to himself, he thought to implore the King's mercy, that he might earn the restoration of his inheritance; wherefore, coming to the King in Normandy, he found him at early morn in a certain church, whither he was come to hear mass. Into which church he entered trembling, not daring to raise his eyes to the King, who, being one of the comeliest of men to see, was yet terrible to behold at such times. The knight therefore betook himself to the crucifix, before which he bowed again and again on his knees with bitter tears, beseeching that Crucified One with all humility that He, in His ineffable clemency, might mercifully restore him to the King's grace, and that he might recover his lost heritage. The King, seeing how earnestly the knight prayed, with what tears and unfeigned devotion, beheld in him a marvel worthy of record. For as often as the knight (whom he knew to be none of his own train) bowed his knees to adore that image, the crucifix for his part inclined his head and neck most humbly to his genuflections; which the King marvelled to see again and again, and was moved to admiration. When therefore the mass was ended, the King straightway summoned that knight to speak with him, and enquired closely who and whence he might be. To whom he answered trembling: "My lord, I am your liegeman, as were all my ancestors"; and told in order how he had been caught stealing the deer, and deprived of his inheritance, and banished with all his family. Then said the King, "Didst thou ever in thy life any good deed for reverence and honour of the Holy Cross?" Then the knight, casting carefully back in his memory, told the King what he had once done in such reverence. "My father," said he, "once divided a certain village with another knight, each possessing his moiety by inheritance. My father abounded in all riches; wherefore the other, ever poor and needy, was moved by envy to lie in wait and slay him. I therefore, being then a boy, when I was come of age and had been confirmed in the possession of mine heritage, purposed immoveably to slay that knight in revenge for my father's murder; but he was forewarned, and craftily kept himself for many years against the snares which I had carefully laid for him. At last, on a Good Friday, whereon Christ Jesus suffered the cross for the world's salvation, as I hastened to church for divine service, I saw mine enemy before me and bent upon the same purpose; wherefore I drew my sword and ran after him. But he, looking behind by chance and seeing how swiftly I hastened towards him, fled to a wayside cross; for he was broken with age and unable to defend himself. When therefore I had raised my sword and would have slain him while he embraced the arms of the cross, as I was

DEATH OF MATTHEW PARIS

From MS. Royal 14, chap. vii, fol. 218b; a portrait by a contemporary monk of St Albans. The dying man has a blanket thrown over his regulation *staminea*, or woollen shirt, and rests his elbow on a book inscribed, "The Book of the Chronicles of Matthew Paris." (J. Strutt, *Horda Angel Cynnan*, plate xxv.)

even ready to scatter his brains on the earth, then he adjured me to spare his life, in His name Who hung that day on the tree for the whole world's salvation; vowing the while and solemnly promising that he would endow a chaplaincy for ever to sing funeral masses for the soul of my father whom he had slain. The sight of this weeping greybeard stirred my bowels; wherefore, overcome with pity, I returned my sword to its sheath and forbore to touch him. Thus then, for love and reverence for that life-bringing cross, I pardoned my father's murderer." Then the King answered and said, "And thou didst wisely: for now hath the Crucified made thee a full return." Then, calling the bishops and barons who were there present, he revealed to all men the vision that he had seen: to wit, how the crucifix had humbly bent his head and neck at each genuflection of the knight. Then, calling forthwith for his Chancellor, he bade him send letters patent to the Sheriff whom that knight should name, commanding him, as soon as he should have read them, to restore all his lands as fully as he had received them when the knight had been banished; and (as we believe) this merciful act of pious King Richard, with other deeds of his, freed him from the peril of damnation and released him the sooner from torment.

Odo Rigaldi (Eudes Rigaud) was of noble birth; he joined the Franciscans in 1236 and studied at their convent in Paris, where he became Professor of Theology in 1242. In 1248 he was chosen Archbishop of Rouen, a dignity which he accepted only after much hesitation. He earned the personal friendship of St Louis, whom he accompanied on his second Crusade (1269) and who named him one of his executors. Contemporary anecdotes show him not only as a saint but also as a wit. A clerical buffoon once ventured to ask him across the table, "What is the difference, my lord, betwixt *Rigaud* and *Ribaud* [rascal]?" "Only this board's breadth," replied the Archbishop. In 1274 he was one of the three great churchmen chosen by Gregory X to preside at the Ecumenical Council of Lyons, one of his colleagues being his fellow-Franciscan St Bonaventura. He died in 1275. Odo's work in his own diocese earned him the title of *The Model of Good Life*; he has left a voluminous diary of the years 1248–1269 which is the most interesting of all existing episcopal registers, and from which, even if all other documents had perished, we could reconstitute pretty exactly the inner history of a medieval diocese. See *St Francis to Dante*, pp. 289 ff. and 428 ff. (second edition), where among other data I give a full translation of his first visitation of a rural deanery. I give here his report on the next six deaneries, containing 217 parishes and one chapelry —that is, as many as small modern dioceses like Llandaff (225) or St Asaph (204), and half as many as Lichfield (456). The reports give of course only the seamy side; but I omit all Odo's threats and disciplinary measures, and also his reports on habitual incontinents, who amounted to about 15 in every 100 parishes. With his monastic visitations I hope to deal fully in another book.

44. NORMAN PARISH PRIESTS

JAN. 16, 1248–9. *Deanery of Bures.* The priest of Pomerevalle is in evil repute and still ill-famed of tavern-haunting; he confesseth not to the Penitentiary, and is drunken. *Item*, William, priest of Mesnières, is ill-famed of trading, and keepeth farms to which he goeth oftentimes, so that divine service is diminished in his church. *Item*, the priest of Lortiey weareth his cassock[1] but seldom, and confesseth not to the Penitentiary, and is drunken. *Item*, the priest of Aulayge is

---

[1] Church synods attempted constantly but vainly to compel the clergy to wear decent attire—*i.e.* a *capa clausa*, or closed cassock, reaching at least below the knees, of neither red nor green, which were specially worldly colours. Some ten years before this date, the Council of Rouen fulminated afresh against clerics who neglected their tonsure, and who went about in tabards or jackets: the offending garments were to be confiscated and given to leper-houses. Odo, strict disciplinarian as he was, shows no sign of having carried this rule into practice: the Rouen synods of 1279 and 1313 were compelled to deal again with the same matter.

grievously ill-noted of drunkenness and tavern-haunting. *Item*, we found that a certain chaplain of Meulers sang a certain mass for hire on Christmas Eve.

Jan. 18. *Deanery of Aumale.* The priest of Morville is ill-famed of drunkenness and haunteth taverns, *item* of exacting money for the marriage-benediction. *Item*, Peter, priest of St Valery, hireth land to sow. Robert de Poys, priest, is ill-famed of trading; he hath promised us to desist.

Jan. 19. *Deanery of Foucarmont.* We found the priest of Neuilly ill-famed of trading, and ill-treating his father who is the patron of his benefice; and he fought bodily with drawn sword against a certain knight, with hue and cry and the help of his kinsfolk and friends. *Item*, the priest of Bazinval haunteth taverns. *Item*, the priest of Vieux-Rouen goeth about with a sword at his side and in unhonest garb. *Item*, the priest of Bouafles weareth no cassock and selleth his corn at a dearer price on account of a certain day.[1] *Item*, the priest of Hamies is a leper, as it is thought. *Item*, the priest of Ecouis is a dicer and a player of quoits;[2] he refused to take the pledged faith of espousal from a man, because he had not restored a legacy of his father; he haunteth taverns. *Item*, the priest of Petra hath celebrated mass, though suspended from his functions.[3] *Item*, the priest of St Remy is ill-famed of drunkenness, weareth no cassock, playeth at dice, haunteth the tavern and is there oftentimes beaten.[4] *Item*, the priest of Gilemerville dwelleth not in his parish, as he should, nor weareth the

---

[1] *I.e.* makes usurious bargains out of other men's necessities, which rendered him *ipso facto* excommunicate: see Busch. in vol. II.

[2] Many most respectable games enjoyed an evil reputation in the Middle Ages on account of the gambling and quarrels which accompanied them. With regard to dicing, Odo's friend St Louis discouraged it even among the laity: in this same year 1248 Joinville tells us (§ 405), "One day he asked what the Count of Anjou was doing; and they told him he was playing at tables with my Lord Walter of Nemours. And he went thither tottering, for he was weak by reason of sickness; and he took the dice and the tables, and threw them into the sea; and he was very wroth with his brother because he had so soon taken to playing at dice. But my Lord Walter came off best, for he threw all the moneys on the table into his own lap—and they were very many—and carried them away."

[3] This again entailed excommunication *ipso facto*: see the first extract from St Bonaventura, no. 61 of this volume.

[4] *Et ibi multitociens verberatur.* It is very probable that this is a Gallicism meaning simply that he often *fights* there.

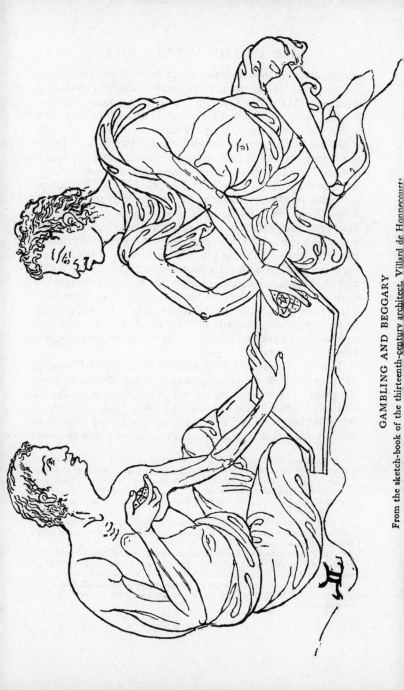

GAMBLING AND BEGGARY

From the sketch-book of the thirteenth-century architect, Villard de Honnecourt.

cassock, and sometimes he loseth his garments in taverns.[1] *Item*, Robert, priest of Campneuseville, hath no cassock. *Item*, the priest of St Martin du Bois is litigious and a wanderer (*vagabundus*). *Item*, the priest of Pierrepont is drunken, and playeth at dice and quoits. *Item*, Master Walter, priest of Grandcourt, is ill-famed of overmuch drinking. *Item*, from Robert, priest of St Mary's church at Mortemer, (whom we found grievously ill-famed of misbehaviour, litigiousness, and tavern-haunting,) we have the letters here below.[2] *Item*, the priest of Realcamp, corrected by the Archdeacon, had promised that in case of relapse he would hold his benefice as resigned *ipso facto*, and hath since relapsed, even as he sometimes also loseth his garments in taverns. We have denounced the aforesaid priest as *ipso facto* deprived of the aforesaid church. *Item*, we found that the priest of Mesnil-David, oftentimes corrected by the Archdeacon, hath relapsed, and it is said that he hath celebrated in spite of suspension, wherefore we have bidden him purge himself in form of law from these accusations, or we would proceed to an inquisition against him.[3] To which he answered that he would take counsel hereupon: we therefore have assigned him a day to answer these things.

Jan. 20. *Deanery of Neufchâtel*. Adam, priest of Neuilly, hath been corrected for drunkenness by the Archdeacon. *Item*, the priest of Sommery resideth not in his parish as he should, and rideth abroad like a vagabond. *Item*, Thomas, priest of Mesnil-Mauger, is said to buy and sell horses and to trade in other ways. *Item*, the priest of Fosse cometh not to [ruri-

---

[1] *I.e.* at dice. Cf. Cæs. Heist. *Dial.* vol. iv, p. 44, and the two parodies of Church Services in *Carmina Burana*, nos. 189, 196; and again the songs 193, 195: "When a man hath drunk his tunic. Let him dice away his shirt!" This is illustrated in the sketch-book of Villard de Honnecourt, from which the accompanying illustration is facsimiled: another similar picture may be found in Wright's *Homes of Other Days*, p. 230.

[2] From the worst sinners—for these priests of Mortemer and Realcamp were habitually unchaste also—Odo exacted letters promissory that they would resign their benefices in case of relapse.

[3] The allusion is here to the process called *compurgation*. A clerk accused in the bishop's court could clear himself by bringing a certain number of fellow-clergy (or sometimes, of neighbours) to swear with him to their belief in his innocence. This procedure was notoriously a great temptation to perjury: see Rashdall, *Universities of Europe in the Middle Ages*, vol. ii, pp. 410, 417, and *From St Francis to Dante* (second edition), p. 430.

decanal] chapters, nor to the synod. *Item*, Master Robert de Houssaye, parson of Conteville, is ill-famed of drunkenness and dilapidation [of church property]; he vexeth folk and dwelleth not in his parish. *Item*, the priest of Malacopula frequenteth assizes and lay courts. *Item*, the priest of Lucy exacteth from each woman 13 pence; even though the child die before the churching, he will not church the mother until she pay 13 pence. *Item*, the priest of Haucourt buyeth and holdeth land on farm from the abbess of Buieval. The priest of Nogent hath no cassock. The priest of Louvechamp keepeth hunting hounds. *Item*, the priests of Salicosa Mara and Beaubec have no cassocks.

Jan. 22. *Deanery of Eu.* We found the priest of Panliu ill-famed of drunkenness; he selleth his wine and maketh his parishioners drunken. The priest of Auberville resideth not in his parish as he should. The [rural] Dean is ill-famed of exacting money, and it is said that he had forty shillings from the priest of Essigny for dealing gently with him in his incontinence. The prior of Criel is ill-famed of trading: he selleth rams. The priest of St Aignan is unhonestly dressed; *item*, the priest of Berneval is a trader in cider, corn, and salt. *Item*, the priest of Bouville selleth wine, as it is said.

Jan. 27. *Deanery of Envermeu.* Renier, priest of Jonquières, is ill-famed of drunkenness; so also William and Ralph, priests of Bailly, who have been corrected by the Archdeacon. *Item*, Robert, priest of Derchigny, of trading and taking farms. *Item*, the priest of St Sulpice is drunken; *item*, the priest of Sauchay-in-the-Forest celebrates though suspended; *item*, in that parish are wakes every Saturday; we enjoined that the church should be closed at nightfall, and no man should hold wakes there.[1] *Item*, the priest of Sauchay by

---

[1] There were repeated attempts to put down these wakes in England, from at least as early as 1240 to the verge of the Reformation: see Wilkins, *Concilia*, vol. I, p. 675; vol. II, p. 706; vol. III, pp. 68, 845; Grosseteste, *Epistolae*, p. 74. Abp. Thoresby of York, for instance, ordained "since it often cometh to pass that folk assemble in the churches on the eves of holidays, who ought there to busy themselves in divine worship, or in praying for souls at the obsequies of the dead, yet who, turning to a reprobate mind, are intent upon noxious games and vanities, and sometimes worse still, grievously offending God and His saints whom they feign to honour, and making the house of mourning and funeral-prayer into a house

the Sea is drunken; so also is the priest of St Mary at Envermeu. *Item*, the priest of St Martin-en-Campagne, of selling hemp; *item*, the priest of Belleville hath ships on the sea, and haunteth taverns. *Item*, Vinquenel, chaplain of Bracquemont, is drunken. *Item*, the priest of Martin-Eglise is drunken; he hath twice been corrected and hath sworn to the Archdeacon that, if he relapsed, he would take his benefice as resigned. *Item*, the chaplain of Douvrend is ill-famed of drunkenness, and the priest of St Laurent-le-Petit of selling his sacraments. *Item*, the priest of Etrun, of trading. *Item*, the priest of Bailleul singeth not his vespers in the church.

Etienne de Bourbon is one of the many distinguished mission-preachers who arose among the early Friars. Born about 1195, he was studying at Paris when the Dominicans first arrived there. He joined the Order about 1223, preached in many places and with great effect for the crusades and against the heretics, and was appointed Inquisitor shortly after 1235. His active career seems to have ended in 1249; he died about 1261, leaving still incomplete his Preachers' Manual, of which its modern editor justly says: "Whoever wishes to grasp the moral and mental state of St Louis's time, and all that intimate side of medieval society towards which modern learning seems most willingly to turn, must henceforth study this collection of anecdotes" (*Anecdotes Historiques, etc., d'Etienne de Bourbon*, ed. by A. Lecoy de la Marche for the Société de L'Histoire de France, 1877, p. iii). Very many of the tales are taken from Etienne's personal experiences; but even those which are patently legendary throw much light on the ideas of the age.

45. PAUPER FUNERALS
(Bourb. p. 384.)

A SECOND evil thing to sell is the burial of the dead; for he who selleth it selleth their rest, [*requiem*] so far as the body is concerned. To the priest who for such a man sings Mass and the *Requiem eternam*, the Lord may say: "Rest he shall not have, for he hath sold it for money.". . . In reproof of those men's wickedness who demand money for burials, Master Jacques de Vitry used to tell how a poor man in Lorraine,

of laughter and excess, to the most grievous peril of their own souls; therefore we strictly forbid that any who come to these wakes or obsequies, especially within the aforesaid churches, should make or in any way practise wrestlings or foul sports [*turpitudines*], or anything else tending to error or sin."

James by name, lost his mother, and his priest would not bury her unless he would give money, which indeed he had not. He therefore put his mother's corpse in a sack and carried it to the priest's house, laying her on his bed and saying that in this sack he had brought for a pledge the linen and the balls of yarn which she had made. The priest felt her head and, taking it for a great ball of yarn, "Now" (quoth he) "I have a good pledge." So he went straightway to the poor man's house with his cross and his parishioners, to fetch the body. Then said the other, "You need not labour to carry her hence; for she lieth already in your house and on your bed; it is she who lieth in the sack for a pledge; you may now lay her in earth or in salt as it liketh you best."

Another man was poor in worldly goods but rich in children, one of whom died. When therefore his priest would not bury the child without money, which the poor man had not, then he brought his son's body in a sack to Roche-Scise, Archbishop Regnaud's palace of Lyon, and told the porter that it was a present of venison which he brought to his lord. Then, when he had been admitted and brought before the Archbishop, he laid the child down at his feet and declared the whole matter. The Archbishop therefore gave the boy honourable burial; after which, calling the priest, "Pay me" (quoth he) "my fee as your Vicar"; for which he forced him to pay a great sum.

46. UNSUCCESSFUL MAGIC
(Bourb. p. 317.)

WHILE I was a student at Paris, one Christmas Eve when our companions were at Vespers, a certain most noted thief entered our hostel, and, opening the chamber of one of our fellows, carried off many volumes of law-books. The scholar would have studied in his books after the feast; and, finding them not, he hastened to the wizards, of whom many failed him, but one wrought as follows. Adjuring his demons and holding a sword, he made the boy gaze upon the blade; and he, after many things there seen, beheld at last by a succession of many visions how his books were stolen by one of our fellows, his own cousin, whom he thought the most upright of our fellowship; whom the possessor of the books slandered not only among the scholars but also among his friends, accusing him that he had stolen them. Meanwhile the aforesaid thief stole other things and was detected, whereupon he fled to a certain church where he lay in the belfry, and, having been duly examined, confessed all that he had stolen, and where, and what he had done with his thefts. When therefore certain scholars who lodged hard by our hostel had found by his means a mantle which they had lost and he had stolen, then he who had lost his books could scarce rest until he had gone to enquire of this thief; who answered and told him when and where he had taken his books, and the Jew's house where he had pledged them, where also my friend found them. This I have told that ye may clearly mark the falsehood of those demons who showed the vision in the sword-blade in order that they might slander that good man and break the bonds of charity between those kinsfolk, and bring the man who believed in them to eternal perdition, both him and his.

47. ICONOCLASTIC USURERS
(Bourb. p. 365.)

It befel at Dijon, about the year 1240, that a certain usurer would have celebrated his wedding with much rejoicing; and, having been led with instruments of music to the parish church of the blessed Virgin, and standing now under the church portal that his bride might give her consent and the marriage be ratified according to custom by the promise "I do," and so the wedding might be solemnized in the church by the singing of mass and other ceremonies—while this was there being done, I say, and the bride and bridegroom should have been led with joy into the church, a certain usurer carved in stone upon the portal above, whom a carven devil was bearing to hell, fell with his money-bag upon the head of this living usurer who should have been married, and crushed and slew him; so that the wedding was turned to mourning, and their joy to lamentation, and the living man was thus shut out by the stone image from that entrance into church, and those sacraments, from which the priests not only did not exclude him but would have led him in.[1] Then the usurers, or other citizens, by dint of bribes, procured the destruction of the other graven images which stood without, on the forefront of the said portal, which I myself have seen there broken away, lest a like fate might befal them or others under like circumstances.[2]

48. THE WISE CONFESSOR

(Bourb. p. 162.)

HERE let us consider what should be the nature of true and salutary confession. . . . I have heard how a priest in the diocese of Reims had a certain woman in his parish whom he knew to be a grievous sinner, but in secret. When therefore she was justifying herself before him, nor could he press from her any confession of sin, then he shut the screened enclosure wherein she was, saying that God had given him a most precious relic such as had never been found of any woman save only the Mother of God, who was sinless! Then, ringing the bells, he called together his parishioners and told them how he would set her in a silver shrine; whereby she was brought to confusion, and confessed many heinous sins.

49. THE ANATOMY OF HERESY

(Bourb. p. 289.)

HERETICS are refuse and debased, and therefore they may not return to their former state but by a miracle of God, as dross may not turn to silver, nor dregs to wine. In the county of the Albigenses a heretic argued with a Catholic that his own sect was better than the faith of the Roman Church, since our

---

[1] By strict church law, the sacraments should have been refused to an impenitent usurer; but Etienne agrees with all others in complaining that the golden key opened this door also.

[2] Etienne tells the same story more briefly on p. 60, where he adds that this destruction was still fresh when he saw it, and that the Bishop of Cambrai held forth about it on the spot itself.

Catholics sometimes turned to heretics, but never from heretic to Catholic. To whom the Catholic answered that this was rather a sign of their utter depravity and corruption, since excellent wine may turn to vinegar, but never contrariwise, especially when it is much corrupted; and corn may turn to tares or weeds, but never back again.

50. THE IRISHMAN AND THE DEVIL
(Bourb. p. 157.)

WHILE two Friars Preachers wandered amidst the mountains of Ireland, and had lost their way, they saw hard by a little man to whom they cried. He fled from them; but they followed after him and caught him in a narrow pass betwixt the hills. Then they asked him their way, but he could scarce answer them; wherefore, when they had long insisted to know who he might be, he told them how for thirty years he had served the demons who appeared unto him in divers wickednesses, and had done them homage to perform their bidding; in sign whereof he showed them a seal impressed upon his hand, and inscribed with the letters of that homage. The friars had much ado to persuade him to come with them to the town; but when they were come thither, and one of them had preached on the abominableness of sin and on God's mercy towards the penitent, that man proclaimed his own guilt before the congregation; and, having made his confession with tears to the friar, he found the devil's seal erased from his hand. After a few days he returned, comforted and instructed, to his accustomed forest, that he might bear thence his few possessions. Here he met that same demon to whom he had done homage, scouring the mountains with a multitude of fellow-demons, and black horses and hounds. The devil asked him whether he had seen such and such a man, his runaway slave whom he had lost. At length, therefore, the man asked the demons whether they knew him not; and they said "No." "Yea," said he, "for I am the man whom ye seek!" whereupon they looked upon his hand and, finding not the seal, told him that he lied, not bearing the sign of his homage; and, believing themselves to be mocked of him, they departed. The man came back rejoicing to the friars, and abode with them. This was told me by an Irish friar who had come to the lord Pope's court at Lyons.

51. PILGRIMS' DISORDERS

(Bourb. p. 167.)

PILGRIMS should be joyful (as the Psalmist saith, "Be glad in the Lord, and rejoice, ye just") that they may sing of God, as the Germans do, and not of other vanities and foul things, as the Jews who had gone forth from Babylon, and of whom it is written that they spake in the speech of Azotus [2 Esdras xiii, 24]. Now *Azotus* signifieth *fire*. So do those pilgrims also who, when they visit holy places, sing lecherous lays whereby they inflame the hearts of such as hear them and kindle the fire of lechery; and sometimes they themselves are burned by God's hand with material flames or hell-fire, as those most sacrilegious persons who tread down the bodies of holy Christian folk in the churchyards, where they dance on Saints' eves and kindle the living temples of God with the fire of lechery, flocking to the churches on Saints' days and eves and holding dances and hindering the service of God and His saints.[1] It came to pass in the diocese of Elne that, when a certain preacher had preached in that country and had straitly forbidden this holding of dances in churches and on the vigils of saints, whereas in one of the parishes certain young folk were wont to come and ride upon a wooden horse, and to dance masked and disguised in the church and through the churchyard on the vigil of the dedication-day of that church— whereas, I say, the men had left their dances by reason of the words of that preacher and the prohibition of their priest,

---

[1] All dances, almost without exception, were anathema to the medieval moralists. Thoroughly characteristic is the following quotation from Cardinal Jacques de Vitry given by Lecoy on p. 162. The dancers joined hands and sang as they tripped round, led by one who gave time and tune to the rest, and of whom the Cardinal writes: "As the cow which goeth before the herd hath a bell at her neck; so likewise the woman who leadeth the song and the dance hath as it were the devil's bell bound to hers."

a certain youth came to his fellow and invited him to the accustomed sport. The other refused to play, telling how the priest and the preacher had forbidden it; but the youth harnessed himself, saying that the man should be accursed who should abandon the wonted sport on account of their prohibition. When therefore the aforesaid youth pranced upon his wooden horse into the church, while the congregation were keeping their vigils in peace and prayer, then on the very threshold of the sanctuary a fire caught him by the feet and utterly consumed him, horse and man. No man in that church, whether kinsman or friend, could bring him the least help to quench those flames that burned before their eyes; wherefore at length the whole congregation, dismayed by this judgment from heaven, left the church and fled to the priest's house. He arose and came to the church, where he found the youth already almost utterly consumed; from whose body rose so great a flame that it seemed to issue forth from the windows of the spire. This I heard in the parish itself, not long after the event, from the chaplain and the youth's parents and other parishioners.

52. THE SIN OF DANCING[1]
(Bourb. p. 397.)

WE should specially avoid the places wherein dances take place, and the dances themselves. The devil is the inventor and governor and disposer of dances and dancers. I have heard how a certain holy man saw the devil, under the form of a little Ethiopian, standing over a woman who led the dance, and leading her round at his will, and leaping upon her head.... The inventor of these things is Satan, leading vain folk who are like unto thistledown wafted on the blast, or the dust which the wind lifteth from the face of the earth, or clouds without water, which are carried about by winds.

Moreover, God suffereth him sometimes to vex men with a sudden tempest for this sin of dancing, and to wreak the fury

[1] It is difficult to exaggerate the unanimity with which medieval theologians condemn dancing as immoral, except under exceptional circumstances.

90

of his wrath upon them. I have heard from Brother Philip, first prior of our convent at Reims, of a certain church in the diocese of Soissons wherein dances had been made. While the priest sang mass one morning in that church, there arose suddenly a great whirlwind and uproar, and a thunderbolt fell upon the church, consuming the altar-cloth and slaying many of the congregation, but leaving the priest and the host untouched; moreover it overthrew a mill that was there and slew four men. One who fled thence saw many demons springing and leaping after the fashion of dancers over a certain ditch; by whom he was beaten to death and scarce escaped by making the sign of the cross, whereat they fled in indignation and terror. One of the demons in his wrath bit a mighty stone in the wall and carried away a great part in his mouth, leaving the marks of his teeth on the stone, as the men of that place showed to Brother Philip in testimony of the fact; and the aforesaid man who had been beaten by the demons told the tale in the presence of Master Jean des Vignes, who was in those days the greatest clerk and preacher in France.

53. A BISHOP AND HIS FLOCK
(Bourb. p. 268.)

Such as defile or violate holy places, or do injury to them... are accursed, for they incur the sentence of anathema, which is the greatest of ecclesiastical penalties.... Yet many fear more to be hurt in their purses, though it were but a small fine, than to be smitten with this sword fatal both to body and soul —for it destroyeth both and consumeth to all eternity. I have heard how a certain Bishop of Grenoble commanded his priests, when they came to the synod, to come decently in stole and alb or surplice; which they scorned to obey. Then he commanded it under pain of suspension; yet even thus they obeyed not; then he made his hand yet heavier, proclaiming at the next synod that they should come under pain of excommunication; yet few obeyed even then. Then said the Bishop: "Come to-morrow as I have bidden, under pain of five shillings." Then all the clergy, fearing this fine aforesaid, sought out albs and surplices, or even hired them; so that all came attired as they had been bidden. Wherefore the Bishop rebuked them in that synod, showing plainly how they feared more to lose a little money than to lose their souls.

54. SAINT GREYHOUND
(Bourb. p. 325.)

DISHONOURABLE to God are all superstitions which attribute divine honours to the demons, or to any other creature, as idolatry doth, and as those wretched witches do who seek health by adoring elder-trees[1] or offering to them, in contempt of the churches and the relics of saints, by carrying their children thither or to ant-hills or to other places for health's sake. So they wrought lately in the diocese of Lyons, where I preached against witchcraft and heard confessions, and many women confessed that they had taken their children to St Guinefort. Whereof I enquired, supposing him to be some true saint; and at last I heard that he was a certain greyhound who came thus by his death.

In the diocese of Lyons, near the nuns' town called Villeneuve, on the lands of the lord de Villars, was a certain castle whereof the lord had one little boy by his wife. One day that he and his lady and the nurse had gone forth, leaving the child alone in his cradle, then a vast serpent glided into the house and moved towards the child. The hound, seeing this, followed him in all haste even beneath the cradle, which they overturned in their struggles; for the dog gnawed upon the serpent, which strove to defend itself and bit him in turn; yet at last the dog slew it and cast it far from the child; after which he stood then by the bloody cradle and the bloodstained earth, with his own head and jaws all bloody, for the serpent had dealt roughly with him. Hereupon the nurse came in; and at this sight, believing that the hound had slain and devoured the child, she cried aloud in lamentation; hearing which the mother hastened to the spot, and saw, and believed, and cried likewise. The Knight also came and believed the same; where-

[1] The text has *sambucas*, but *sambucos* seems to give a better sense.

fore, drawing his sword, he slew the hound. Then, coming to the child, they found him unhurt and softly sleeping; and seeking further, they found the dead serpent all torn to pieces by the hound's teeth. Wherefore, recognizing the truth, and grieving that they had so unjustly slain this hound which had done them so great a kindness, they cast him into a well hard by the castle gate, and cast an immense heap of stones over him, and planted trees by the spot as a memorial of his deed.

But God so willed that this castle should be destroyed, and the land made desert and left without inhabitants. Wherefore the country folk, hearing of that dog's prowess, and how he had lost his guiltless life for a deed that deserved so great a reward, flocked to that place and honoured the hound as a martyr, praying to him for their sicknesses and necessities; all which came to pass at the instigation of the Devil, who oftentimes deluded them there, that he might thus lead men into error. More especially the women who had weak or sickly children were wont to bring them to that spot; and they used to take an old woman from a town that lay a league distant, who would teach them the due rites of offering to the demons and calling upon their name, and would guide them to that place. When they were come thither, they offered salt with certain other oblations, and hung the child's clothes upon the bushes around, and thrust a needle into the wood which grew over the spot, and thrust the naked child through a hole that was betwixt two tree-trunks; the mother standing on one side to hold him and casting him nine times into the hands of the hag who stood on the other side, calling with demoniacal invocations upon the hobgoblins which haunted that forest of Rimita, and beseeching them to take the child (who, as they said, belonged to the fiends), and bring back their own child which these had carried off, fat and well-liking and safe and sound. After which these murderous mothers[1] would take the child and lay him naked at the foot of the tree upon the straw of his cradle; and, taking two candles an inch long, they lighted them at both ends from a fire which they had brought thither, and fixed them upon the trunk overhead. Then they would

[1] This is evidently what Etienne means by his "*hoc facto, accipiebant matricide puerum, etc., etc.*"

withdraw so far that the candles might burn out and that they themselves might neither see nor hear the wailing babe; and thus these white-hot[1] candles would oftentimes burn the children alive, as we found there in certain cases. Moreover one woman told me how, when she had called upon the hobgoblins and was withdrawing from the spot, she saw a wolf come forth from the forest towards the child, whom he would have devoured (or a devil in wolf's form, as she said), if her motherly love had not driven her to prevent him. If therefore, returning to the child, they found him still living, then they would take him to a stream of rushing water hard by, called Chalaronne, wherein nine times they plunged that child, who indeed must needs have the toughest of bowels to escape this ordeal, or at least not to die soon afterwards. Wherefore we went to that place, and called together the folk of that country, and preached against this custom. We caused the dead hound to be dug up, and the grove to be cut down and burned together with the dog's bones; and we persuaded the lords of that country to issue an edict threatening confiscation and public sale against all who should thenceforth resort to that same place for this purpose.[2]

55. BOY ARCHDEACONS

(Bourb. p. 352.)

A CERTAIN bishop, having received a gift of a basket of pears, asked of them who sat at meat with him, to whose custody he should commit them. His young nephew, to whom he had even then committed an archdeaconry, answered and said, "I will keep the pears." To whom his uncle answered, "Thou rascal! ill wouldest thou keep them!" Then said a certain honest man who was there present, "O wretch! How hast thou dared to commit an archdeaconry of so many souls to this youth, to whom thou daredst not commit a basket of pears?" As a common proverb hath it, "The wolf waxeth fat on evil guardianship."

[1] So the text has it, *candentes*; but Etienne probably wrote *cadentes*, "falling."
[2] The editor notes that the worship of St Guinefort is still said to survive among the women of the district round Romans, though without these cruelties (for which compare Extract 14). The legend is of course a variant of that of Gelert, which can be traced to the east.

A CATHEDRAL VISITATION

I give here a typical series of documents which throw instructive side-lights on church life in the Middle Ages. The reports given here are neither the best nor the worst of their kind. The Rouen record is the earliest known to me, and that of York the latest; the Exeter visitations are, as human documents, perhaps the most vivid of all that have survived. Others almost equally interesting may be found not only in the Rouen, Exeter, and York volumes here quoted, but also in the *Visitations of South-well* (Camden Soc.), *Ripon Chapter Acts* (Surtees Soc.), *Beverley Chapter Act Book* (*Ib.*), and several episcopal registers. Archbishop Odo Rigaldi of Rouen was one of the greatest reforming prelates of the Middle Ages, and Grandisson of Exeter one of the most energetic English bishops of the fourteenth century.

56. A CATHEDRAL VISITATION

ROUEN CATHEDRAL. (19 March 1248, *Regestrum Visitationum Odonis Rigaldi*, ed. Bonnin, p. 35.)

W E visited the Chapter of Rouen, and found that they talk in choir contrary to rule.[1] The clergy wander about the church, and talk in the church with women, during the celebration of divine service. The statute regarding the entrance [of lay folk] into the choir is not kept. The psalms are run through too rapidly, without due pauses. The statute concerning going out at the Office of the Dead is not kept. In begging leave to go forth, they give no reason for so going. Moreover, the clergy leave the choir without reason, before the end of the service already begun; and, to be brief, many other of the statutes written on the board in the vestry are not kept. The chapter revenues are mismanaged [*male tractantur*].

With regard to the clergy themselves, we found that Master Michael de Bercy is ill-famed of incontinence; *item*, Sir Benedict, of incontinence; *item*, Master William de Salemonville of incontinence, theft, and manslaughter; *item*, master John de St-Lô, of incontinence. *Item*, master Alan, of tavern-haunting, drunkenness, and dicing. *Item*, Peter de Auleige, of trading.

---

[1] Great churches had generally special statutes against talking among the ministers during divine service: sometimes, however, the prohibition extends only to *too distant* conversations. At the collegiate church of Mortagne, for instance, it was forbidden to talk as far off as to the third stall, but the Cathedral statutes of Meaux (A.D. 1240) are more indulgent: "Let none speak in choir loud enough to be heard from one stall so far as to the fourth stall following in the same row." (See p. 233 of this *Regestrum*, and note 2.)

Master John Bordez is ill-famed of trading; and it is said that he giveth out his money to merchants, to share in their gain.[1] Of our own free will we have denounced these persons aforesaid to the Archdeacons of Greater and Lesser Calais; and the Chapter is bound to correct these offences through the aforesaid archdeacons, or through other officials, before the Assumption of the Blessed Virgin [Aug. 15]; otherwise (we said), we ourselves would forthwith set our hands on the business, as we have notified to them by letter; and it is for them to let us know how the corrections have been made.

57. ANOTHER

EXETER CATHEDRAL. 15 October 1330. (Mandate from Bishop Grandisson to the Dean and Subdean: *Register of John de Grandisson*, ed. Hingeston-Randolph, p. 586.)

WE have learned from the lips of men worthy of credit, not without grave displeasure, that certain Vicars and other Ministers of our Cathedral Church—to the offence of God and the notable hindrance of divine service and their own damnation and the scandal of our Cathedral Church aforesaid—fear not to exercise irreverently and damnably certain disorders, laughings, gigglings, and other breaches of discipline, during the solemn services of the church; which is shameful to relate and horrible to hear. To specify some out of many cases, those who stand at the upper stalls in the choir, and have lights within their reach at mattins, knowingly and purposely throw drippings or snuffings from the candles upon the heads or the hair of such as stand at the lower stalls, with the purpose of exciting laughter and perhaps of generating discord, or at least rancour of heart and silent hatred among the ministers (which God forfend!), at the instigation of the enemy of mankind, who (as we find by experience) knoweth and striveth to create the greatest evils not from unlawful or greater occasions only, but even from the least and most lawful. *Item*, whereas some ministers do sometimes (and, as we grieve to say, too often)

---

[1] Clerical trading was of course forbidden in any case, but in this case there was usury, and therefore mortal sin.

commit plain faults in singing or reading incorrectly, then others who know better, (and who should rather have compassion on the ignorant and bewail the defects of their brethren,) break out, in the hearing of many, into this speech of imprecation and derision in the vulgar tongue: "Cursed be he who told the last lie!"[1] *Item*, some whose heart is in the market-place, street, or bed, though their body be in the choir, seeking for their own part to hasten through God's work negligently and fraudulently, or to draw others as accomplices into the same fault,—these (I say) will sometimes cry aloud in the English tongue to the very officiant himself, or to others, commanding and enjoining them to make haste. *Item*, sometimes, commencing the service off-hand, some show no sort of shame in beginning again and again one service, while others begin another, (as for instance an Anthem or Responsory or suchlike,) with the accompaniment of quarrels and discords. There is yet another sin less of commission than of omission, which hath here become a rooted custom, and whereto in the past (if ye remember), we ourselves personally brought what we thought to be a sufficient remedy, not only by plain admonitions but by alluring indulgences, yet which hath now broken out yet worse through men's negligence: namely, that very few remain in the Choir during the Mattins of Mary, that Blessed, Glorious, and Sweetest Mother of Mercy, not considering that (though perchance some may say them more distinctly outside, as some judge of themselves, than together in the Choir, on account of the murmurs and tumult of divers and discordant voices,) yet to God and His Blessed Mother the gift of prayers offered by all together is incomparably more acceptable than the same prayers said or chanted separately in streets and corners, both as commending the unity of the Church, and also for the humble observance of the custom, statute, and precept, and on account of the presentation (as the Apostle saith) of many faces, and because it may chance that each deserveth not to be heard by himself, yet no faithful man doubteth that he may be helped by the accordant prayers of

---

[1] Cf. the *Contes Moralisés* of the contemporary English Franciscan Nicole Bozon (ed. Toulmin Smith, 1889, p. 207), where the friar tells of a son who read the lesson ill in church: "then said his father, 'In truth thou liest concerning God.'"

persons acceptable to God as there present in common with him. Moreover, if sedulous and spontaneous diligence were here brought to bear, with but a little further expense of time, those praises would be duly and distinctly and meritoriously rendered to God which can scarce be satisfactorily paid in this present fashion. Wherefore, stirring up and inciting your duty, we beseech, enjoin, charge, and command your discretion and devotion to read and expound these present letters of ours, on three separate days, in the Chapterhouse, to the Vicars and Ministers of our Cathedral; that ye may strive to admonish and induce and persuade them to abstain from the aforesaid faults and exercise themselves in good. Such as obey not must be sternly constrained first by due subtraction of their salaries; and those who still remain obstinate and rebellious, by sentence of excommunication (if they knowingly refuse to correct themselves), and lastly by actual banishment from the Cathedral; that their blood may rather be sprinkled on their own heads than be required at our hands by the Almighty Shepherd and Judge. Strive now so sedulously to fulfil this our present prayer and mandate, that ye may thereby reap up for yourselves a richer grace in the present, and everlasting glory for the future. Fare ye well.

58. ANOTHER

EXETER CATHEDRAL, 16 December 1333. (Mandate to the Subdean and Canon William de Nassyngtone: *Register*, p. 723.)

WE have learned from the lips of men worthy of credit, not without grave displeasure, that certain Vicars and other Ministers of our Cathedral, to the offence of God and the grievous hindrance of Divine Service, and to the scandal of our Cathedral Church itself, fear not irreverently and damnably to exercise disorders, laughter, gigglings, and other breaches of discipline, even with masks on their faces, by which obscene orgies of gesticulations they make vile the honour of the clergy before the eyes of the people. Wherefore we, having no small affection to the honour of God's house through the office committed to us, and willing to guard for the future against such wanton disorders, enjoin and command strictly to you, all and severally, appealing to your devotion, that, having called the said Vicars and Ministers to your presence upon receipt of these present Letters, ye do without delay publish this our mandate with all that is therein contained, and forbid them all and singly, in our name, ever again to presume to exercise the aforesaid or similar disorders, if they would fain escape from due canonical punishment.

59. ANOTHER

EXETER CATHEDRAL, with the Collegiate Churches of Ottery St Mary, Crediton, and Glasney. (Mandate dated 7 January 1360–1: *Register*, p. 1213.)

JOHN [etc.] Bishop of Exeter, to his beloved sons in Christ [etc.], wishing them health and honesty of clerical manners. It hath come to our knowledge, not without grievous amazement and displeasure of heart, that for these past years and some years precedent, at the most holy solemnities of Christ's Nativity, and the feasts of St Stephen, St John the Apostle and Evangelist, and the Innocents, when all faithful Christians are bound to busy themselves the more devoutly and quietly in praise of God and in Church Services, certain Ministers of our aforesaid Church, together with the boys, not only at Mattins and Vespers and other Hours, but also (which is more detestable) during the solemnity of the Mass, have rashly presumed, putting the fear of God behind them, after the pernicious example of certain [other] Churches, to associate together within the Church itself and play certain foolish and noxious games, unbecoming to clerical honesty:—nay, rather, to conduct detestable mockeries of Divine Service: wherein they have in many fashions defiled the Vestments and other Ornaments of the Church, to the no small damage and disgrace of this same Church and of ourselves, with spatterings of vile and drunken [. . . .].[1] By whose gestures, or laughter and derisive

---

[1] As the editor points out, there is an evident corruption of the text here: it reads *vilium scilicet scenulentorumque sparsione multipliciter deturpando*. I have taken *scenulentorumque* as a clerical error for *temulentorumque*, and assumed the loss of one or two words before *sparsione*.

gigglings, not only are the congregation (who at those times, according to Catholic custom, do most especially flock to the Church), distracted from their due devotion, but they are also dissolved in disorderly laughter and unlawful pleasures, the Divine worship is mocked, and the Service wickedly impeded: whereby that which was first invented to excite and increase the devotion of the faithful is by such disorders converted—or rather perverted—to the irreverence and contempt of God and His Saints, not without guilt of blasphemy. We therefore, no longer able to wink at such abominable abuses or pass them by without remedy, enjoin and command you, under pain of suspension and excommunication, to desist henceforth altogether from such disorders and mockeries, and to permit none such hereafter to be practised in the aforesaid Church; but rather set your minds more devoutly than usual to conduct the Divine Service, as the reverence due to those days doth itself require. And, lest henceforth any ignorance avail to excuse you in this matter, we command you, the Warden,[1] solemnly to publish these present Letters before the impending feast of Christmas, in the presence of all the Ministers, and to cause these same letters, lest they fall into oblivion, to be transcribed into four or five of the Church books most commonly used; but if any shall presume to contravene this our mandate, cite him or cause him to be cited peremptorily to appear before us on the third lawful day after the aforesaid Feasts, to answer for this so rash presumption and to receive condign punishment.

[1] Of Ottery St Mary. The same letter (it is noted in the register) was sent "with the exception of a few changes" to the Dean and Chapter of Exeter and the authorities of Crediton and Glasney.

60. ANOTHER

YORK MINSTER. A.D. 1519. In printing this last visitation in its original spelling, as a specimen of ecclesiastical English shortly before the Reformation, I have thought it best to save the reader trouble by appending a special glossary. Most of the words, however strange to the modern eye, become at once intelligible when read aloud. The Report may be found, in company with a great many others, in *York Fabric Rolls* (Surtees Soc., vol. xxxv, p. 267). The editor notes that he has omitted the frequent complaints against the characters of the officiants.

MDXIX.—ECCLES. CATH. EBOR. Imprimis at the renewynge of the sacrament there wantethe a torche, and a clerke of ye vestre in his surples for the renovation of the same. Item we fynde grete neclygense of ye decons and clerkis of ye vestre yt the mesbuke is not clasped, wherby a fayre boke is nye lost. Item how one [of] ye basyns afor the heghauter wt ij candelse afor our Lady, of the southesyde, should be lighte all tymes of serves, which is sum tyme not done. Item the goodly reyredewse is so full of dust and copwebbes that by lyklyode it shalbe shortly lost wtoute it be clensed & better keppte than it hathe bene. Item the litile awterse is so ragged and torne that it were grete shame to se suche in any uplandyshe towne. Item the sudary that the colet holdes the patan in is to shamefull to be sene about the holy sacrament in suche a place. Item the cophynse in the where, as rectors of ye where sitte, the folkes yt be pylgrams and straungers wonderse to se suche in yt place & yet yer wantes one. Item all the hangynges of ye where lyeth opynly in the presbitory, dogges pysses of thame, wax droppys of thame, & the mynysters put furthe of yer rowmes. Item ye clothe yt coverse ye reyredewse is of party colors, whiche is not honeste for straungers to luke upon. Item the bokes of the where be caduke & yll, & so false yt [they] oftyn tymes makethe the vycars to make grete dyscorde in the where. Item if the lettron in the chapitor were skowred and set in myddys of the hye where, and the roste yerne in the same where set in ye chapitour, we thynke shulde do well.

THE VESTRY. Inprimis there wantethe towelse for the ebdomadory to wype of daly. Item the lavitory in the vestry,

where we resayve our water, it is stopped, & every mane, on
efter an other, puttethe and wasshethe there crowet in a bukket
wt water, whiche by ye same maner is corrupped, and so
usethe we wt the same, and all in defawte of dressyng of ye
pullye & stoppynge of the synke whiche were sone amendyd.
Item a goodly well in the crowdes, whiche hathe bene used in
old tyme & dyde grete goode what tyme as the churche was
borned, whiche wantethe no thynge bot a pully & a rope, and
the dore of the same is kepte lokkyd & no man nor woman
can do there devotion in that place to our Lady. Item the
vestiary, there is a chest full of suspent stuffe yt will make
parores, amettes, coshyns, & to amende many usuall thynges
in ye where, and such as ye secunde forme weres nowe is all
so torne whiche tha walde amend well for every day. Item
the albys for preists, many of thame be torne & made so straite
both in the bodes and slevys, that men cannot get thame on
bot wt grete payne. Item the heghe awter is nowe served both
ix lessons and dowbill fests all in lyke, there is ordande chaunge
for bothe bot tha will not be had. Item the chylder cummethe
abowte the awter sum in one colour and some in an other, wt
vyle and unclenly albys nothynge sortynge accordynge to ye
day. Item the cause this is not amended, in amendynge of
copes, chysables, tunakles and such othere, it is not knawne
who shulde pay for thame, where John Loksmythe is unpaid
for the same amendynge, of his awn proper use, and not of the
churche coste: if it were knowne whethere ye clerk of ye
warke or the chaumberlane shuld do it we trust tha shulde be
better looked on. Item the amendynge of the dalmatykes for
ye Advent & Septuagesym myghte be done wt a litile cost,
whiche nowe mosters away & not occupied. Item the lettron
wherupon the gospell is red is moisterd away & faullyn downe,
whiche specially wold be amendid by cause it is in opyn sighte.
Item, specially, we besche youe, that ye revestre may be
keppte after ye old facion, that the dure may be kepte opyn
as hathe bene frome the begynnynge of matens unto xj of ye
cloke. Nowe, oftyn tymes, the dure is stokked, and we parsons
& vicars cannot get brede, wyne nor water, when we be redy
& makethe us to say no masse for watynge of the where.
Item we find grete faute the churche walles be full of cop-

webbys & all the pyloures of the same, whiche dothe full yll. Item we thynke it were convenient that whene we fetche a corse to the Churche that we shulde be in our blak abbettes mornyngly, wt our hodes of the same of our hedes, as is used in many othere places. Item we desyre and beseche youe that all the abbet may use there surples & ames wtowt blake abbet feriall, and othere frome Pasche to our latter Lady day, and generall processions, as tha do in other cathedrall churches, & this we desire for a special cause; oftyn it happs that the secund forme & othere that be necligent oftyn tymes cummethe in there blak abbetts, when they shulde cum in surples, & when they shulde cum in surples thay will cum in abbet, whiche wolde not be so if we did as tha do in other places cathedrall. Item we fynde the segistans gevethe not suche attendaunce of the Churche as hathe bene, for it hathe bene that one of them hathe gevyn attendaunce all ye day when there wek fel, and sawe there were no dogges nor bryborse in ye Churche, bot tha wolde rewarde thame; and also a resonable tyme betwene ye fyrst pele and the secund, and also they wolde have no (query *mo* ?) plukkes, as we thynke, than tha giff tham, for ye pelys be veray shorte. . . .

GLOSSARY

Mesbuke=mass-book; heghauter=high altar; wt=with; reyredewse= reredos; awterse=altars; uplandishe towne=remote country village; sudary=towel; colet=acolyte; cophynse=chests; where=choir; yt=that; presbitory=the part of the choir where the canons' stalls are; put furthe, etc., apparently means that the ministers are responsible for having put these hangings forth from their proper places; caduke=dilapidated; lettron=lectern; chapitor=chapter-house; roste yerne=a small iron oven used for baking the eucharistic bread; ebdomadory=the priest who has charge of the services for the week; crowet=cruet, for holding the wine and water before consecration at mass; sone=soon; crowdes=crypt; borned=burned; suspent=cast-off; parores=trimmings; amette=amyt, a mass-vestment; coshyn=cushion; weres=whereas; albys=albs; or-dande=ordained; chysable=chasuble; tunakle=tunicle; moster or mois-ter=moulder; revestre=vestry; dure=door; stokked=shut; watynge= waiting; abbettes=habits; ames=amyt; segistans=sacristans, sextons; when there wek fel= when it fell to their week of duty; bryborse=thieves, tramps; plukke=pull of a bell; pelys=peals.

Giovanni Fidanza, born in 1221 at Bagnorea in the upper valley of the Tiber, joined the Franciscans at an early age as Brother Bonaventura. He became first Professor of Theology at Paris and then Minister General of his Order. Dante has immortalized his character and genius (*Paradiso* XII); but his moderation as General rendered him unpopular with the Spirituals; and he is the unnamed Adversary who in chap. xlviii of the *Fioretti*, is represented as persecuting the saintly John of Parma. In concert with his old friend and fellow-Franciscan Odo Rigaldi (see this vol., no. 44) he led the van of the Reforming party at the Ecumenical Council of Lyons; and died, probably of overwork, before the end of the Council (1274). The following Extract is abbreviated from the treatise *Quare Fratres Minores praedicent* (ed. Mainz, 1609, vol. VII, pp. 341 ff.).

61. A SAINT'S APOLOGY

Now this is the reason why, in early days, no Religious were called or sent by the Apostolic See to the aforesaid offices of preaching and confession. When the sickness is as yet slight, it needs fewer and lighter remedies; but when it begins to grow strong and spread abroad, then we must apply more and stronger remedies lest the sick man's state become desperate. So also, now that the state of the world seems far worse than of old, it is fit that there should be more helpers, according to the text: *The harvest truly is great, but the* fit and faithful *labourers are few; pray ye therefore the Lord of the harvest that he would send forth labourers into his* vineyard. Again as it is written in Romans: *Where sin abounded, grace did more abound.* We see the harvest of people multiplied in our days, and woods hewn down for the building of towns [or villages]. We see sins invented in great numbers, and more perplexing cases [of conscience] springing up from day to day; the wicked becoming still more incorrigible from mere habit, and more hardened in their sins. Again, we see that many of the clergy by their evil example corrupt the laity both in morals and in faith; also, that few of them are experienced enough to teach as they should, or can be trusted to do so. Again, we see that they rule negligently over the souls committed to their charge, and are too closely bent upon worldly business. Again, that many of them are suspended, excommunicated, and hindered in

BAGNOREA

From the *Magazine of Art*, by kind permission of Messrs Cassell and Co.

divers manners from the performance of their duty. Again, that few rectors reside in their parishes, but the cure of souls is offered for sale among slight vicars: and that the prelates,[1] given up to temporal cares, dissemble these things, so that there is scarce any hope of correction. If, moreover, they ever wished to correct these things and remove the unprofitable persons, they have no better to put in their places. Since therefore the Church is now as a ship tempest-tossed, wherein the rowers quake for fear and the stormy billows almost cover the bark, therefore we Friars have been sent by the supreme Pilot, and supported by the authority of the Apostolic See, that we may scour the world in our little boats and snatch from the waves all such as we find in peril of shipwreck, to bring them back to the shore of salvation.

Now there is no parish that has not either a proper Parson, or one in some way insufficient, or one that is no Parson [nullum]. . . . Since therefore the parishioners of these [last two] classes both may and should confess to others, rather than to such as seem their Parsons, on account of these said defects; and since the laity have no discernment to choose better, and the vicious clergy would rather send them to others like themselves than to proper priests, and there are few indeed among the clergy nowadays who are not spotted with any of these blemishes, therefore we Friars have been sent throughout the world by the Apostolic See.[2] . . . There are other cases which sometimes make even honest persons fear confession to their own priests; because vicars are unstable and often changed, wherefore men dare not reveal their secrets to them, since they must so often have unknown confessors. Again, because many [plerique] of them are so vicious that an honest woman fears to lose her reputation if she whisper secretly with them. Again, because many [plures] of them are unknown, and men fear that they are apostates, or hindered in their priestly office,

---

[1] The *ipsi* of the text seems an obvious error for *praelati*, to whom alone the following complaints of St Bonaventura could apply.

[2] The rest of this Extract is from the second part of the treatise, the authenticity of which has lately been questioned for the first time by the Friars of Quaracchi, but without sufficient reason. Their main argument is that it is wanting in a single manuscript: another is that "it contains scarcely anything but a repetition of the first part," which is perfectly true, and may go far to reassure the less sceptical reader.

or perchance with no priestly Orders at all....Now, that it may be more plainly seen how few there are now in these parts among the rectors or their vicars who have free power of binding or loosing, or who deal well with men's souls in confession, and that ye may thus understand how sorely our Brethren are needed to supply their places, and to succour perishing souls, let these things following be considered. Every man that is suspended from his office, or irregular, or excommunicated, or who hath entered by an ill way into a cure of souls, hath no power of binding or loosing, nor aught else pertaining to the exercise of that jurisdiction which the Church hath forbidden to him: wherefore, whatsoever that man bindeth or looseth or the like, is of no validity. See therefore how very many nobles and great men, in whose gift benefices are, frequently incur the sentence of excommunication, whether by law or by judicial sentence, through their wars and other excesses, or in other ways lose the right of conferring such benefices....In like manner we see Bishops, through wars or other excesses, oftentimes fall under sentence of excommunication or suspension, or become suspended by the lord Pope, or excommunicated. Some, again, are either themselves promoted through simony or simoniacally confer cures of souls on others. Likewise certain other prelates gain their own promotion and promote others by simoniacal means; and all benefices thus conferred, or by such means, confer no legal rights on the recipients. We see rectors hire out their parishes to their vicars on condition of certain yearly pensions, and one will oftentimes supplant another by promising a greater pension, that he may thus get the parish; which is oftentimes done incautiously and with peril of simony. We see that very many undertake cures of souls contrary to canon law; as those who have no clerical Orders, or are under the right age, or of illegitimate birth, or are subject to any excommunication or irregularity, and therefore unable to receive such a benefice. Many, again, have several benefices with cures of souls, which involve certain obstacles invalidating their election or institution, as for instance the plurality of the benefices, or the like. For even though some have a Papal dispensation permitting them to take ecclesiastical revenues up to a certain yearly sum, yet by this the Supreme Pontiff doth not intend to grant any man the unconditional right of amassing so many cures of souls as to glut his ravenous appetite indiscriminately with their revenues, leaving the souls shepherdless and forsaken; but (as the best and most experienced authorities expound) such dispensations rather apply to other revenues, as prebends and other benefices which involve no cure of souls. We see again that judges oftentimes command parish priests, under pain of suspension or excommunication already pronounced, to proclaim or execute certain judgments, which these neglect and thus incur the penalty. We see that many, receiving Orders against the episcopal prohibition, incur the penalty of suspension; we see that students oftentimes strike [other] acolites in wrath and thus fall under canonical sentence, yet seek no absolution, but proceed to [Holy] Orders or take church benefices, solemnly serving churches and executing clerical duties.[1] We see that very many among the clergy are notorious fornicators, keeping concubines in their own houses or elsewhere, or sinning at large with several women. Now a notorious fornicator is defined as he whose guilt can by no equivocation be concealed, or is testified by the public which (according to some authorities) consists of ten men or women: and all such notorious sinners are *ipso facto* suspended both as to themselves and as to [their ministrations to] others. Some are also sometimes [specially] excommunicated by their own bishops or by the lord Pope's officials.... There are very many more impediments of the clergy which I omit for superfluity's sake; but by these few words it may be seen how many parish priests there are in these parts who are such in themselves, or promoted or instituted by such men, or in such ways, that they have no power to bind or loose souls; so that men may know how sorely God's Church needs the Friars to take their places, and succour souls which thus might perish.

[1] All university scholars were, in theory at least, in the lower clerical Orders, and thus enjoyed full clerical immunities. These unabsolved strikers would be *ipso facto* excommunicate; so also would all who, when suspended, went on celebrating mass; therefore the absolution they pronounced in the confessional would be as invalid as many of their other ministrations; and they themselves would thus plunge daily deeper into mortal sin.

62. THE SHEEP AND THE GOATS

(From Thomas Cantimpratanus, *De Apibus*, lib. ii, cf. 54, p. 440.)

THE sixth and last cause of joy [to the blessed spirits in heaven] will be to behold the damned on their left hand, to whom (when He hath set them on His left) the Judge will say, "Depart, ye accursed, into everlasting fire!" Concerning these, as the Psalmist saith, "The just shall rejoice when he shall see the revenge." And Esaias saith, in the person of Christ, "They" (that is the saints) "shall go out and see the carcasses of the men that have transgressed against me:... and they shall be a loathsome sight to all flesh." Yet some simple folk are wont to wonder that the saints, at the Last Judgment, will be in no wise disturbed at the sight of the damnation of their parents and friends; but all faithful souls will account this their astonishment as mere folly, seeing that they know how the saints, confirmed in their perpetual exultation, can be touched by no trouble or grief. For if, even in this present life, it is required in every perfect Christian that he should become united to and accordant with the divine justice in all things, how can we marvel if we now believe of the saints in glory that they are not grieved even at the saddest of sights among earthly men? [He then goes on to relate how the Blessed Marie d'Oignies, having been certified in a vision of her own mother's damnation, ceased thenceforth to weep for her.]

The following Extract is from the *Meditations on the Life of Christ*, generally attributed to St Bonaventura in the Middle Ages and printed in most editions of his works. It is, however, attributed in the *Conformities*, no doubt correctly, to a later Franciscan, Brother Joannes de Caulibus, who "wrote *according to* St Bonaventura," but concerning whom nothing more is known. It admirably exemplifies that graceful intermixture of Bible history and legend upon which so much of medieval art was based.

63. A CHRISTMAS PAGEANT

So when the term of nine months was approaching, there went forth an imperial decree that the whole world should be registered, each in his own city. When therefore Joseph wished to go to his own city of Bethlehem, and knew that the time of his wife's delivery was at hand, he took her with him. Our Lady therefore went again on this long journey (for Bethlehem is hard by Jerusalem, at a distance of some five or six miles). They therefore took with them an ox and an ass, and went as poor cattle-dealers. So when they were come to Bethlehem, seeing that they were poor, they could find no lodging, for many had come together on the same business. Think pitifully of our Lady, and behold her so young and tender (for she was of the age of fifteen years), wearied with her long journey and conversing with shame among those folk, seeking a place of rest and finding none, for all sent her and her companion away; and thus they were compelled to take shelter in a certain covered way, where men took refuge in rainy weather.[1] There it may be that Joseph, who was a master-carpenter, enclosed himself after a fashion. But now consider with the utmost diligence all that I shall say, more especially because I purpose to tell things which were revealed and shown by our Lady herself, as I heard them from a trustworthy saint of our Order, to whom (as I believe) they were revealed. When her hour was come, which was one Sunday midnight, the Virgin rose and leaned against a certain pillar which stood there, and Joseph sat sadly by, mourning perchance that he could not prepare all that was fitting.... And the Virgin Mother, stooping forthwith, raised her Babe and gently embraced Him, then she laid Him in her lap and, taught by the Holy Ghost, began to anoint Him all over with the milk of her breast, which was filled from Heaven; after which she wrapped Him in her own head-veil and laid Him in the manger. And now the ox and the ass bent their knees and stretched their heads over the manger, breathing through their nostrils as though they knew by the light of reason that the Babe, so miserably clad, needed their warmth at a time of such bitter cold. His mother, for her part, bowed her knees in adoration, and gave thanks to God, saying, "Lord and Holy Father, I thank Thee that Thou hast given me Thy Son; and I adore Thee, God Everlasting, and Thee Son of the living

---

[1] It is evident that the writer imagined Bethlehem built like an Italian city, with covered arcades along the streets.

God and of me." In like manner did Joseph adore Him; and taking the ass's saddle and drawing from it a little cushion of wool or rough cloth, he laid it by the manger that our Lady might sit thereon. She therefore set herself down thereon, and laid the saddle under her elbow; and thus sat the Lady of the World, holding her face over the manger and fixing her eyes with all the desire of her heart upon her dearly-beloved Son. Thus far by revelation, which after she had declared our Lady vanished away; but an Angel stayed behind and told the Brother great songs of praise which he repeated to me, who have been able neither to learn nor to write them. ...So, when our Lord was thus born, a multitude of angels stood there and adored their God; then they went in all haste to the shepherds hard by, perchance at a mile's distance, to whom they told how and where our Lord was born; after which they ascended to heaven with songs of rejoicing, announcing the glad news to their fellow-citizens also. Wherefore the whole court of heaven, filled with joy, made great feast and praise; and, having offered thanks to God, all the angels of heaven came according to their Orders, turn by turn, to see the face of their Lord God; where, worshipping Him with all reverence, and His Mother likewise, they quired unto Him with songs of praise. For which of them, hearing this news, would have stayed behind in heaven, and not visit his Lord thus humbly set on earth? No such pride could have entered into any angel's heart; wherefore the Apostle saith: "And again, when He bringeth in the first begotten into the world, He saith: 'And let all the angels of God worship Him.'" I think it sweet to meditate thus of the angels, howsoever the truth may stand.

The thirteenth-century MS. known as Carmina Burana was preserved for centuries in a special cupboard of the monastery of Benediktbeuern in Bavaria; like other volumes which have come down to us in a similar way, it contains the strangest mixture of piety, profanity, and obscenity. The piece here translated (fol. 11a, ed. Schmeller, p. 22) is the mildest specimen of the parodies in which wandering clerks delighted: it should be compared with the Monk's Martyrdom in the Franciscan MS. Harl. 913, fol. 60.

64. THE CARDINALS' GOSPEL

THE Beginning of the Gospel according to Marks of Silver. In those days said the Pope to the Romans: "When the Son of Man shall come to the seat of our majesty, say first of all, 'Friend, wherefore art Thou come hither?' And if He shall persevere in knocking and giving you nought, cast him forth into outer darkness." Now it came to pass that a certain poor clerk came to the court of the lord Pope, and cried out, saying: "Have pity on me, have pity on me, at least you the door-keepers of the Pope, because the hand of poverty hath touched me. For I am poor and in misery; wherefore I beseech you to succour my calamity and my wretchedness." But they, hearing this, were moved to indignation and said: "Friend, thy poverty perish with thee: get thee behind me, Satan! for thou savourest not the things that be of money Verily, verily I say unto thee, thou shalt not enter into the joy of the Lord until thou shalt have paid unto the last farthing!" The poor man therefore departed, and sold his cloak and his coat and all that he had, and gave to the cardinals and ushers and door-keepers. But they said: "What is this among so many?" And they cast him forth from the doors: and going forth he wept bitterly, as one that could not be comforted. Afterwards there came to the court a rich clerk, grown fat and thick and gross, who for sedition's sake had committed murder. He gave first to the door-keeper, then to the usher, and thirdly to the cardinals: but they thought within themselves that they should have received more. Now the lord Pope, hearing that his cardinals and ministers had received many gifts from this clerk, grew sick unto death: but the rich man sent unto him an electuary of gold and silver, and forthwith he grew whole again. Then the lord Pope called together his cardinals and ministers and said unto them: "Brethren, take heed lest any man deceive you with vain words. For I give you an example, that as I take gifts, so should you do also."

Berthold von Regensburg, or of Ratisbon, was born about 1220 of a well-to-do citizen family. He joined the Franciscans while still a youth, and became the favourite pupil of David of Augsburg, whose writings were often attributed in the Middle Ages to St Bonaventura. He was already famous as a preacher in 1250; until his death in 1272 he tramped from village to village, like a Whitefield or a Wesley, through Bavaria, Rhineland, Switzerland, Swabia, Austria, Moravia, Bohemia, Silesia, Thuringia, and Franconia. His fame spread all over Europe; he is enthusiastically extolled in the chronicles of Salimbene and the XXIV Generals; and Roger Bacon, speaking of contemporary preaching in words which do not err on the side of compliment, expressly excepts Berthold as one who "alone maketh more excellent profit in preaching than almost all the other Friars of either Order" (*Opp. Inedd.* R.S. p. 310). A thick volume of Berthold's sermons, translated into modern German, is in its third edition as a book of living theology (Regensburg, Manz. 1873). The text here used is that of Franz Pfeiffer (2 vols. Vienna, 1862). The abrupt changes from *thou* to *ye* are in the original.

65. PARDONERS AND HERETICS

(*Pred.* I, 393. Berthold is describing the different hindrances that keep men from God.)

HEAVEN is still below us as above us, and when the sun is in heaven below us, then it is night with us above. So the earth stands midway betwixt us and the sun; wherefore by night the earth hinders us from seeing the sun until morning, when he shall rise again in the East, as Solomon saith: "The sun riseth, and goeth down, and returneth to his place." So the earth hindereth us far and wide that we may not see the worldly sun: and this earth is a type of a certain sin which hinders us far and wide from the sight of the true sun. This sin is called covetousness for wealth—filthy lucre—and it is grown so great that no man can measure it. Alas! how many folk there are who strive for filthy lucre, and gain filthy lucre! Such are deceivers in their trade and handiwork; such are men thieves and women thieves, within the house and without; usurers, pawnbrokers, money-lenders, forestallers that they may buy cheaper, and all such as inflict violent taxes, unrighteous taxes, unrighteous tolls, unrighteous contributions; such as take on this hand and not on that hand; and penny-preachers, who are among the dearest servants that Satan hath in the world. Fie! penny-preacher, murderer of all the world! How many a soul dost thou cast with thy filthy lucre from God's own sunlight to the bottom of hell, where there is no hope more for them! Thou promisest so much indulgence for a single halfpenny or a single penny, that many thousand people trust thee and dream falsely that they have done penance for all their sins with that penny or that halfpenny, as thou babblest to them. So they will do no right penance, and go straight hence to hell where there is no more help for them. Therefore shalt thou too be cast to the bottom of hell, and all they shall be cast upon thee whom thou hast seduced away from almighty God and hast sold, every soul for a penny or a halfpenny. Thou murderer of right penitence! thou hast murdered right penitence in our midst, which is one of the seven holy things of the highest that God hath. It hath been so murdered now by penny-preachers that there are few among us who will still do penance for their sins; for they count upon thy false promises. For this penny-preacher preacheth to them so long and in such manifold words of our Lord's passion that men take him for a true messenger of God: for he weepeth in his preaching and useth all manner of deceit whereby he may coax pennies from his hearers, and their souls into the bargain. Therefore be so many led astray by their covetousness that they never see the true sun.[1] Even

[1] So also wrote the Oxford Chancellor Gascoigne, about A.D. 1450, "Sinners say in our days, 'I care not how many or great sins I commit in God's sight; for I can get with all ease and despatch a plenary remission from any penalty or guilt whatsoever through an absolution and indulgence granted me by the Pope, whose writing and grant I have bought for fourpence or sixpence, or won at a game of ball.'" Evidence of this kind is so essential to the real comprehension of medieval life, and the facts are so persistently falsified in certain quarters, that I must append here for the reader's comparison a quotation of a kind from which I have usually tried to refrain in this book. Abbot Gasquet, in his *Eve of the Reformation*, p. 437, writes, "In the literature of this period, it must be remembered, there is nothing to show that the true nature of a 'pardon' or Indulgence was not fully and commonly understood. There is no evidence that it was in any way interpreted as

in cloisters has covetousness so utterly won the upper hand that God must ever have pity to see how things go in some cloisters, with sacrilege, with simony, with possession of private property. Thou monk or nun, if but a halfpenny be found in thy possession there is no help for thy soul! (contrition and repentance, nevertheless, I refuse to no man). "Evil lay-folk, evil religious," as it is written; but that is the very devil made visible! Thus the world betokeneth covetousness. The earth is cold and dry, so also is covetousness; it is cold of true love and dry of all true contrition. Ye priests, to all men who are so cold and dry at their last end that they will not restore and give back their ill-gained wealth (so far as it is in their power, and so far as the rightful possessors are known), to such men should ye never give our Lord's Body, whether they be whole in body or sick, neither before their end nor after their end; nor shall ye ever bury them in a consecrated spot, nor shall any baptised hand ever be laid upon them. "Brother Berthold, how shall we then do?" Why, take a rope and make a noose in it and put the noose on the man's foot with a hook, and drag him out of the door. "Brother Berthold, but when the threshold is high, how shall we do then?" Then shall ye dig through the threshold and drag him through; but never shall a baptised hand be laid on him. Then tie him to a horse's tail and drag him out to the crossways where the hanged criminals and the suicides lie. Drag him to the gallows with the rest of the gallows-birds; he is scarce worth even that....

The third thing that leads us astray is betokened by the moon...that is, unbelief. Now see how many thousand men are led astray thereby, that they never see the high and true sun. Firstly, heathendom far and wide and great; and then Jews and heretics into the bargain. Now have pity yourselves, that God may be pitiful to you, for that so many men are damned through unbelief. The moon betokens unbelief, because unbelief is of so many changing forms. The heathens

a remission of sin, still less that any one was foolish enough to regard it as a permission to commit this or that offence against God." The Roman Catholic Bishop of Newport (while mistakenly limiting the period), quotes this statement under the evident impression that it is trustworthy and conclusive (*XIX Century*, January 1901, p. 170).

have so many and divers unbeliefs that there is no end thereof; and the Jews believe in one house that which they believe not in another, and they believe such simple things of God as they scarce dare repeat to their children; for they are become heretics and break their Old Testament in all points. Twelve of them came together and made a book that is called *Talmoud*, and it is a mere mass of heresy, wherein stand such accursed heresies that it is pity they should live. It saith and saith such evil things as I am loth to repeat. Ask me a Jew where God is and what He doth; then saith he: "He sitteth on the heaven, and His legs stretch down even to the earth." Alas, good God! Thou must needs have two long hosen if this speech be true! And therefore doth the moon betoken unbelief, because she is so unstable and her changes are so many. To-day she is young and to-morrow older; to-day she wanes, to-morrow she waxes; now small, now great; now riding aloft in heaven, to-morrow riding alow; now here, now there; now this, now that. Even so are faithless folk; so are the heathen, so are the Jews, so are the heretics. They have the most manifold unbeliefs that ever were heard of. They have a good hundred and a half of heresies, the one believeth not as the others.... Nevertheless, however many names they have, all alike are called *Ketzer*.[1] And that is not without cause in God's providence that they are called *Ketzer*. Now wherefore are they not called *Hunder*, or *Mauser*, or *Vogler*, or *Schweiner*, or *Geiszer*, after dogs, mice, fowls, swine, or goats? God called the creature a *Ketzer* for this cause, that he can creep secretly where no man seeth him, as doth also the cat [German, *Katze*], who can make herself most soft and secret; and there is no beast, for all her soft ways, that hath so soon done so great evil as the cat; but most of all and swiftest of all in summer. Let all folk beware of the cat! She goeth apart and licketh a toad wheresoever she may find him, under a hedge or wherever he may be found, until the toad begin to bleed. Thus his poison maketh the cat thirsty, then she maketh for the water whence Christian-folk are wont to cook or drink; and she drinketh thereof and defileth the folk so that many a man lieth half a year sick thereafter, or a whole year, or his

---

[1] *Ketzer* (corrupted from *Cathari*) is the ordinary German word for heretic.

whole life long, or taketh sudden death thereby. Oftentimes drinketh the cat so greedily that a drop falleth from her eye into the water, or that she sneezeth therein; and whosoever useth that water for cooking or drinking must taste bitter death therefrom; or she sneezeth in a dish or some other vessel wherefrom a man will eat or drink, whence he taketh great harm and sickness, or perchance two or four, or as many folk as are in the house. Therefore, good folk, drive the cat from you, for the breath that cometh from her throat is most unwholesome and dangerous. Bid the maids drive her forth from the kitchen or wherever else ye see her, for she is deadly unclean. Therefore is the heretic called *Ketzer*, because he is like no beast so much as a cat, for he goeth so spiritually to good people and speaketh such sweet words at the first and can do all as softly as the cat herself; and even so swiftly hath he defiled a man's body. Thus doth the heretic; he will rehearse to thee so sweet speeches of God and the angels that thou wouldst swear a thousand oaths he were an angel himself, yet is he a devil in human form; and he saith he will show thee an angel and will teach thee so that thou shalt see God with thy bodily eyes, and so much of this sort will he say to thee that he will soon have turned thee from thy Christian faith and there shall be no more hope for thee. Therefore he is called *Ketzer*, because his soft ways are as baneful as a cat's; yea, and far more baneful! The cat will defile thy body, the heretic defileth the soul and body, so that all hope of both is lost. So baneful is he that, had I a single sister in the whole countryside wherein there was but one heretic, I should live in fear for her sake because of that single heretic, so destructive is he. Therefore let all folk take good heed of him. I hold—God pardon the word—my Christian faith as fast as every Christian man rightly should; but before I would dwell knowingly for a single fortnight in a house wherein a heretic was, rather would I dwell for a whole year in one house with five hundred devils. What heretic! art thou perchance here in this congregation? Now God Almighty grant that none be before me here! Moreover, they go not into goodly towns; for there the folks are understanding, and mark them for heretics at the very first word. They love to creep round the hamlets and villages, and even to the children that herd the geese in the field. Formerly they went even in clerical garb, and never swore for any occasion, whereby indeed men knew them.[1] Now they change their life and their heresy even as the changing moon; now they wear sword and dagger, long hair and long garments; and now they swear oaths. There was a day when they had rather suffered death, when they said that God had forbidden to swear; and now their masters allow them to swear oaths. Say, wretched heretic, if God hath forbidden it, how then can thy master allow it? What devil hath given him such power—to a cobbler or weaver or spurrier, such as thou callest thy spiritual master? How may such an one allow what God hath disallowed? Ah, the man shall turn twelve Christian folk to heretics, and thereby shall he atone for his sinful oath! Fie, miserable heretic, rather shalt thou thyself be burned, than that thou shalt make another heretic like unto thyself!

Thomas Cantimpratanus (of Chantimpré in Brabant) was the son of a noble who had fought under our Richard I in the Holy Land. A hermit near Antioch, to whom the father had confessed his sins, warned him that some of them would keep him long in purgatory unless he bred up one of his sons to the priesthood. The child Thomas was therefore sent to school at Liège, where (as he tells us himself) he spent eleven years. At the age of fifteen he was much impressed by Jacques de Vitry's preaching. In early manhood he became a Canon Regular at Chantimpré, but passed over to the stricter Dominicans about 1231. He became a very distinguished preacher, a suffragan bishop, and a fairly voluminous writer. By far the most valuable of his works is the *Bonum Universale de Apibus*, a treatise on virtues and vices by analogy with the life of the bee, illustrated by personal and historical anecdotes. This was written somewhere about 1260; my extracts are from the Douay edition of 1597.

66. A MOTHER'S TEARS
(Lib. ii, c. liii, p. 415.)

It was my own mother who told me the story which I am about to relate. My grandmother had a firstborn son of most excellent promise, comely beyond the wont of children, at

---

[1] The avoidance of oaths, whether in common speech or in a court of Law, is recorded in inquisitors' manuals as a presumption of heresy. Many readers will remember how Chaucer's Host "smells a Lollard in the wind" so soon as the Poor Parson begins to protest against profane language. Compare Extract 12 above.

whose death she mourned and could not be consoled, partly, perchance, through a foreboding of future ills; for after him she had another son who, though he was renowned in knighthood, yet, seduced by the pomp of vain glory, became an utter prodigal and squandered his paternal inheritance. His mother, therefore, as we have said, mourned for her firstborn with a grief that could not be consoled, until one day, as she went by the way, she saw in her vision a band of youths moving onwards, as it seemed to her, with exceeding great joy; and she, remembering her son and weeping that she saw him not in this joyful band, suddenly beheld him trailing weary footsteps after the rest. Then with a grievous cry the mother asked: "How comes it, my son, that thou goest alone, lagging thus behind the rest?" Then he opened the side of his cloak and showed her a heavy water-pot, saying: "Behold, dear mother, the tears which thou hast vainly shed for me, through the weight whereof I must needs linger behind the rest! Thou therefore shalt turn thy tears to God, and pour forth thy pious and devout heart in the presence of the Sacrifice of Christ's Body, with alms to the poor: then only shall I be freed from the burden wherewith I am now grieved."

67. A STRANGE ELECTION
(Lib. i, c. ii, p. 10.)

CERTAIN canons, not being able to agree in the election of a bishop, gave up their votes to the Provost and the Dean on condition that they should choose one of the ministers of that church; after which they went their ways, leaving these others to order more freely the election of the bishop. One of the canons, unwilling to defer the hour of dinner, hastened from the Chapter-house to the nearest tavern; where, having dined, he sat down to play dice, for he was a youth of disorderly life, though excelling all the rest in mother-wit, affable to all, and eminent for his natural gifts. When therefore the Provost and Dean, having conferred together, saw that they could find none spiritual or proper for the office among all their fellow ministers, then at last they agreed to choose for the bishopric that young canon who had such excellent parts. The choice was proclaimed to the Chapter, the procession was ordained, and all moved in solemn array to the tavern. There they found the youth, who had gambled away his clothes. They dragged him weeping and struggling into the open air, carried him to the church, and set him in the bishop's seat, where in due time he was consecrated. He, therefore, as soon as he found himself a bishop, was changed into another man, and ordered all things that were proper to his office so perfectly within himself that no vestige of his former life remained, and men might have believed him to have lived all his life in this high station. He so managed the outward affairs of his bishopric that none should hinder him in the exercises of his spiritual offices. Why should we marvel? The free gift of virtue which had come upon him shaped the possibilities of his excellent nature. . . . Yet, though the choice of this youth, who had as yet been given to vanity, had in this case so good and happy an issue, yet it should by no means be made into a precedent where any safer way can be found. But what should be done in any congregation where many wise, noble, or powerful men, ungraced by a good life or manners, strive for authority over the rest, may be seen in that which here followeth. [Among the bees,] when the froward members of the hive begin to grow to maturity, then all with one consent fall upon them and slay them, lest they distract the community and incite the rest to sedition. So when such undisciplined men begin to set up their horn of liberty, they should be repressed without delay by such as are holier than they, and further advanced in virtue. They should be kept close and withdrawn from all offices of authority, lest they find any occasion of showing their malice. Against such Ezekiel crieth: "Remove the diadem, take off the crown": What then? Do I here inveigh against learned men? Do I teach my readers to abhor the noble or powerful? God forbid. Nay, if such are shown to be fit by manners that suit their station, then, as the Apostle saith, they are "esteemed worthy of double honour": But alas! in these days learning for the most part is puffed up without charity, worldly nobility is for the most part degenerate in manners; almost all are wont foully to abuse their power. Of old, the Apostle Paul, though he went round the whole world and was most learned in the law, "by the foolishness of preaching saved them that believed." Peter, by throwing out his net and leaving his ship, subdued the Roman Empire; and do our pontiffs in these days, those that hold the highest places, believe that the Church can be firmly built with the noble but lukewarm blood of infants? —that Church which was founded on the blood of robust martyrs? God forbid!

68. THE ACCURSED TALMUD

(Lib. 1, c. iii, p. 14.)

I MYSELF also have seen another Archbishop in France, a man of learning and noble birth, upon whom the following vengeance fell from God. [Saint] Louis King of France, devoutest of princes, commanded about the year 1239, at the persuasion of Brother Henry of Cologne, of the Order of Friars Preachers, that men should gather together at Paris, under pain of death, all copies of that most abominable Jewish book called the Talmud, wherein unheard-of heresies and blasphemies against Christ and His Mother were written in many places; wherefore divers copies of this book were brought to Paris to be burned. The Jews therefore came in tears to the Archbishop, who was the King's chief Councillor, and offered him untold gold for the preservation of those books. He, corrupted by these bribes, repaired to the King, whose boyish mind he soon bent to his own will. The Jews, having recovered their books, ordained a solemn yearly day of thanksgiving; but in vain, since the Spirit of God had ordered otherwise: for at the year's end, on the same day and at that very place where these execrable books had been rendered back— to wit, at Vincennes near Paris—the Archbishop aforesaid was seized with intolerable inward pains on his way to the King's council, and died that same day amidst cries and lamentations. The King with all his train fled from the spot, fearing sore lest he also should be struck by God's hand; and within a short space, at the persuasion of Brother Henry as before, the Jews' books were gathered together under pain of death and burned in very great multitudes. Now note, good Reader, that all Eastern Jews do hereticate and excommunicate their brethren who, against the law of Moses and the Prophets, accept and copy this book called Talmud; yet this Christian Archbishop defended such a book!

69. THE PLURALIST'S FATE

(Lib. I, c. xix, p. 62. The author has been complaining of pluralism and absenteeism rampant in the Church.)

I SPENT eleven years of my youth in a certain Episcopal city, where the Cathedral church was served by sixty-two Canons endowed with exceeding fat prebends of the value of almost two hundred *livres parisis*;[1] yet many of these occupied many other benefices. Lo now, what vengeance of God's I have seen against those foul occupiers of benefices! So may the Holy Trinity, the One God, testify and judge me, as I have seen few of these men die the death of other men; but all died suddenly and in reprobation: so that one of them, hearing how one of his fellows had gone to bed in sound health and had been found dead in the morning, clapped his hands and cried, "What would ye have? He hath, as ye see, died after the wont and custom of our Cathedral!" I myself have seen, within a few years, four archdeacons of that church die after this fashion: see, Reader, and marvel at the miracle! The first, falling from his great barded charger, brake his neck, and gave up the ghost. The second sat down one morning in his stall, and was found to be dead. The third fell backwards as he stood in choir, while Christ's body was being raised on high in the mass; and, losing sense and speech at once, he died on the third day like a brute beast without the sacraments of the Church. The fourth, refusing to confess or receive the sacraments, died thus and was buried in unhallowed ground.

[1] *I.e.* about £1200 modern English money. The cathedral in question is Liège.

70. THE MAIDEN'S PSALTER

(Lib. i, c. xxiii, p. 76.)

I KNEW in Brabant a woman of most holy life, the manner of whose living I will briefly narrate, that thou mayest the more easily believe that which shall follow. She was enclosed within a scanty cell of stone; she wore an iron coat of mail next to her flesh, and over the mail a hair-shirt of bristles which pricked her deeply through the mail. She slept upon the hardest cobble-stones, at broken intervals, and bare-footed; she ate only thrice a week, and then only according to weight and measure, of a bread made with equal parts of ashes and dough. This woman, in her prayers, offered daily supplications to God for many people who had commended themselves to her, that He might in His mercy defend them from all adversities. Hear now a miracle worthy of the greatest admiration: she herself told me how, at the moment when she remembered any one of these in her prayers, she felt virtue or grace go as sensibly from her, as though she had felt a bodily hurt in some joint or limb. Wherefore (as I know by most certain proof) very many were delivered by her prayers from long-standing temptations, perils, and adversities.

Concerning this woman one indubitable miracle was in all men's mouths. She was the daughter of a very poor man; and, while yet in her sixth year, some marvellous inward fervour of the spirit impelled her to beseech her father, even with tears, that he would buy her a psalter. "Nay, daughter," answered he, "how shall I buy thee a psalter, when I am scarce able to earn for thee our daily bread?" She therefore turned her supplications forthwith to the Mother of Christ, and prayed, saying: "O blessed Mary, Mother of Christ, give me this psalter which my father cannot give, and I will be thy servant to all eternity!" In this simple prayer she persevered for a whole year; when lo! the blessed Virgin Mary appeared to her in a dream bearing two psalters and saying, "Take now, my daughter, whichsoever of the two thou wilt choose." She therefore chose one hastily and with the greatest joy; whereupon the blessed Virgin disappeared; and she, awaking from

123

her dream, found nought in her hands: so that she burst into a flood of tears, complaining that the Mother of Christ had deceived her. Her father, hearing this, laughed and comforted her, saying, "Go now, on Sundays and holy-days only, to the mistress who teacheth the psalter to the daughters of rich folk; learn first to read, and then perchance the blessed Virgin will procure thee a psalter." Marvellous to relate, the maiden received his words in simple faith, came to the mistress who taught the daughters of the rich, looked upon a psalter, and read it; and thus the blessed Mary fulfilled in a far more marvellous fashion the promise she had deigned to give. When the honourable and wealthy ladies of the parish saw this, they bought a psalter for the maiden; and, in later days, seeing how eager and devout she was in the service of Christ, they hired a cell hard by the church as an hermitage for her.

71. HUGH OF ST VICTOR'S PURGATORY

(Lib. ii, c. xvi, p. 174.)

MASTER HUGH was canon of the monastery of Canons Regular of St Victor at Paris; men called him a second Augustine; that is, second in learning to St Augustine himself. Although his life was most laudable, yet in this one thing he wrought somewhat imperfectly, that he received discipline for daily faults neither in secret nor in the Chapter-house with the rest; for he had from his boyhood a most tender skin, and of exceeding delicacy. Seeing therefore that he never conquered in himself, by the exercise of virtue, this his imperfect nature, or rather habit, hear therefore what suffering befel him. In his latest moments, a certain fellow-canon who had loved him very dearly in life adjured him to appear to him in death. "Willingly," answered he, "if only the Master of Life and of Death grant me that power." In the midst of which compact Master Hugh died; and, not long afterwards, he appeared to his expectant comrade, saying, "Lo, here am I; ask what thou wouldst know, for my time is brief." Then the other, with fear indeed yet with no small pleasure, said, "How is it with thee, my dearest friend?" "It is well with me now," answered he, "yet, because in my lifetime I would not accept discipline, therefore there remained scarce one devil in hell who dealt me not some shrewd blow on my way to purgatory."

72. PRIEST AND PENITENT

(Lib. II, c. xxx, p. 290.)

WHEN I was in Brussels, the great city of Brabant, there came to me a maiden of lowly birth but comely, who besought me with many tears to have mercy upon her. When therefore I had bidden her tell me what ailed her, then she cried out amidst her sobs: "Alas, wretched girl that I am! for a certain priest would fain have ravished me by force, and began to kiss me against my will; wherefore I smote him in the face with the back of my hand, so that his nose bled; and for this as the clergy now tell me, I must needs go to Rome."[1] Then I, scarce withholding my laughter, yet speaking as in all seriousness, affrighted her as though she had committed a grievous sin; and at length, having made her swear that she would fulfil my bidding, I said, "I command thee, in virtue of thy solemn oath, that if this priest or any other shall attempt to do thee violence with kisses or embraces, then thou shalt smite him sore with thy clenched fist, even to the striking out, if possible, of his eye; and in this matter thou shalt spare no order of men, for it is as lawful for thee to strike in defence of thy chastity as to fight for thy life." With which words I moved all that stood by, and the maiden herself, to vehement laughter and gladness.

---

[1] "If any man, at the devil's instigation, incur such a guilt of sacrilege as to lay violent hands on a cleric or a monk, let him be laid under the bond of anathema, and let no bishop presume to absolve him (unless on his death bed) until he shall have come personally to the Pope and received his commands."—Decree of Innocent II in the Lateran Council (1139). A few years later, Alexander III decreed that women, children under age, etc., might be absolved from this crime by their own bishops.

73. DISCIPLINE AND HUMILITY

(Lib. ii, c. xxxix, p. 313.)

I HAVE heard, from the lips of those who knew the man, of a certain most capable Dean of the Cathedral at Reims, an Englishman by birth, who used to correct his canons severely for their faults. Now it came to pass at that time that the venerable and worthy father in God, Albert, Bishop of Liège, brother to the duke of Brabant, was banished from the empire by the Emperor Henry, whose knights slew him treacherously hard by Reims for righteousness' sake. The venerable Rotard, a man of royal blood, who was then Archdeacon of Reims but already Bishop-Elect of Châlons, came to his funeral with a multitude of nobles but without his wedding-garment. After that the sacred body had been decently laid in the Cathedral choir, then the Dean summoned all the canons to the Chapter-house, and the Bishop-Elect of Châlons with the rest. When all were seated, the Dean said unto him, "As I believe, you have not yet resigned your archdeaconry or canonry." "Not yet," answered the Bishop-Elect. "Rise therefore," said the Dean, "and make satisfaction to this church; prepare your back for discipline in the presence of the Brethren, seeing that you have violated the rule of the Cathedral by coming into the choir among the canons without your wedding-garment." The Bishop-Elect rose forthwith, fell on his face, stripped his back, and accepted a most hearty discipline from the Dean's hands; after which he clothed himself and stood upright, saying publicly to the Dean with all grace of speech, "I thank God and His most merciful Mother, to whom our Cathedral is dedicated, that I leave such an one as you in authority here. I shall ever love this place the better, and shall revere the worthy memory of this severity when I pass to mine own see." With these words he resigned his archdeaconry and canonry, verifying in his own person that common proverb: "The higher the head, the softer the neck." . . .

Hear again that which this same Dean did in the case of his erring nephew. For love and reverence of his uncle, a canonical prebend in the Cathedral of Arras was conferred upon this clerk; but after a while the clerk was punished for a lapse of the flesh by one year's suspension from his prebend. It chanced now that the Dean his uncle came to Arras upon business; where he was received by the canons with all honour due to such a man. The nephew's fault was related by his fellow-canons, together with the punishment inflicted: to wit, that he should lose his canonical portion for a whole year; but they assured him of the Chapter's willingness freely to release the nephew from this punishment, if the Dean deigned to pray for him. "Wherefore not," replied he; "for he is my sister's son." When therefore the canons were assembled in chapter, he said, "I have heard my nephew's fault, and how he hath been mulcted of his prebend for a year according to the custom of your church: I pray you therefore to submit this fault to my judgment." To this all gladly consented forthwith—for the clerk was (as the vulgar saying hath it) one of those good fellows who had never done well.[1] Then said the Dean, "For your own sakes, beloved sirs, ye have submitted my nephew's fault to my judgment. I do indeed commend and approve your custom whereby ye punish the unchaste for a year. To this year wherein ye have mulcted my nephew of his prebend I add now a second year, so that he may lose all profit of his prebend for two years: and, if he so amend himself meanwhile as worthily to deserve restoration, herein I assent to your benevolent liberality: if not, by the very fact of his misconduct let him be shut out for ever from his prebend and from the bosom of this Cathedral." The canons, hearing this, were marvellously edified by his words, and noised abroad this virtue of the Dean's throughout the whole realm of France.

74. A PSYCHOLOGICAL PROBLEM

(Lib. ii, c. xlvi, p. 352.)

I KNEW a youth in a religious Order in France, who, albeit of most slender learning and dull of wit, yet set himself earnestly to learn, and devoted himself to the study of books.

---

[1] Erat enim clericus de bonis sociis illis, quorum nec unus unquam, ut vulgo dicitur, bene fecerat.

Now he had a custom (as I learned from his own lips) of praying long and earnestly every evening and recalling all that he had learnt during the day; after which he would lie down to sleep. Then within a little while, when his ear caught the sound of the bell that roused the Brethren to the night services, that last recollection of his reading, wherewith he had lain down to rest, would come into his mind; and, taking it with him to mattins in the choir, he would stand there with his eyes shut. Then the whole series of the Scriptures[1] would appear to him as it were a vast, lofty, and long palace, of exceeding beauty; and at that hour he understood them so perfectly that no question—not even the most difficult—seemed insoluble, but he saw all the hidden things of Scripture with the greatest clearness, even as the five fingers of his own hand. If however he opened his eyes, were it but for the twinkling of an eye, then the vision would flee away, nor could he recall any but the most superficial memory of the least fragment thereof; yet, when he shut his eyes again, the vision would return forthwith. Moreover, the vision had this most marvellous character that, while he chanted his psalms with the rest, he lost no whit either of its contemplation or of its admirable sweetness; but his attention was in a fashion divided betwixt the chant and the contemplation, and he enjoyed the fruit of both to an inestimable degree.

75. THE SIN OF DANCING

(Lib. II, c. xlix, p. 371.)

THERE is also a third kind of game, namely dancing. How harmful this is, St Augustine teacheth in his book *Of the City of God*, wherein he relateth how Scipio Nasica, the most noble general of all the Romans, removed all benches from the theatre lest the citizens, who had recently triumphed in war

---

[1] This word, though of course often applied to Holy Writ in the Middle Ages, had at other times a far wider signification. Michelet has noted, in his *Italie* (chap. vi), that prolonged fasting produced on his own mind a similar rapturous clearness of intellect, from which however he could bring nothing tangible back with him into ordinary life.

over Carthage the inveterate enemy of their empire, should give themselves over to dances and the sports of Venus, whereby they would become effeminate and envious one of the other, and be moved to war by their intestine discords, even when all outward wars were at an end. This is a most plain and evident token among the dancers, that they circle round towards the left (on which side the accursed goats will be set), and will therefore lose that Kingdom which shall be bestowed by the Judge upon the blessed who are set at His right hand. But if it be better (as St Augustine truly saith) to plough on a Sunday or holy day than to dance; and if servile works, such as ploughing, are a mortal sin upon holy days, therefore it is far more sinful to dance than to plough. Yet those dances which are held at the weddings of the faithful may be partly, though not wholly, excused; since it is right for those folk thus to have the consolation of a moderate joy, who have joined together in the laborious life of matrimony. For, according to the vulgar proverb, that man is worthy to have a little bell hung with a golden chain around his neck, who hath not repented of taking a wife before the year is out.

76. A NARROW ESCAPE
(Lib. II, c. liii, p. 406.)

THERE was a certain priest, reverend in his life and his office, who had a special love for St Bartholomew, and fed more poor on his day than at any other time. Now it befel once upon St Bartholomew's day that, after the priest had sung his mass, he found a Devil standing without the church, in the form of a most comely woman in honourable and decent attire; whom he saluted and bade her to dinner with him. She accepted, and entered in, and sat down to table with the priest: yet no poor man was then invited as usual. St Bartholomew therefore, not unmindful of this priest his devotee, and of his long service to him, came and cried at his gate under the form of a poor beggar; but the servant, coming to see who cried there, forbade his entrance and bade him wait for alms until after dinner. To whom the Apostle made answer with a cheerful face, "It is well, I will wait; but meanwhile bid thy master answer and tell me what is that thing which is most marvellous of all in the world, and yet is bounded by a single foot's space." At this the servant smiled and came to his master, relating that question of the beggar. The priest was at a loss for an answer; but the lady his guest whispered in his ear, "It is a man's face, which is so various amid so great a multitude of men that none is shaped like unto another, though all be of the same nature." The priest therefore sent word of the solution of that question; which the Apostle commended and said: "Go once again and ask from me, 'What is most proper to man of all things that he hath?'" The servant therefore came back and propounded the question, to which again the priest could find no answer, until the lady whispered in his ear, "The most proper to man of all things that he hath is sin." The master therefore told this solution to the servant, who bare it back to the gate. Then again the Apostle commended the answer, and said: "Two have now been solved; I will but add yet a third, and then I will hold my peace. Go therefore and ask from me, how many miles the way stretcheth from heaven to hell?" The servant returned and propounded this third question, which again the priest knew not until the lady whispered in his ear, saying: "No man knoweth that better than he who hath often measured that road on his way to hell." When therefore the servant had received this answer and borne it to the gate, then said the Apostle: "Well indeed hath thy master answered. Go therefore and say unto him, 'Who then is he who hath oftentimes measured that road, but this foul demon who whispereth softly in thine ear under the form of a lady at meat with thee, and who would have enticed thee to sin but that I, Bartholomew the Apostle, whom thou hast devoutly served, have mercifully prevented him?'" When the servant had reported this saying, then the Devil vanished forthwith from before his face, in the twinkling of an eye. The priest started up in amazement from the table and ran to the gate that he might see his saviour: but he was nowhere to be found.[1]

---

[1] This story is told, with slight variations, by a fifteenth-century English preacher (Myrc's *Festial*. E.E.T.S. 1905, p. 9). In this case, the saving saint is Andrew.

77. WHO SUPS WITH THE DEVIL—
(Lib. II, c. lvi, p. 447.)

CERTAIN men of note in this world sat drinking in the tavern; and, as they grew warm with wine, they began to talk together of various things; and their talk fell upon that which shall be after this life. Then said one, "We are utterly deceived by those clerks, who say that our souls outlive the destruction of the body!" Hereupon all fell a-laughing; and with this there came in a tall big man, who sat down among them and called for wine, and enquired of the matter of their talk. "We spake of souls," said that fellow aforesaid; "if any man would buy mine, he might have it right good cheap, and ye should all drink away the price with me." Then all laughed again, and the newcomer said: "Thou art the very merchant whom I seek: I am ready to buy it: tell me now thy price." "So and so much," quoth he cheerfully; and they were straightway agreed concerning the price, which the buyer counted out forthwith. Then they filled up their cups again and drank with universal rejoicing, nor did he who had sold his soul show any anxiety for a time. But as evening drew on, the buyer cried: "It is time that each should return home. Give me judgment now, good fellows, before we part; if a man buy a horse tied by a halter, doth not the halter go with the horse, and pass into the buyer's possession?" To this all answered with one voice, "Yea indeed!" Then the buyer seized straightway upon the seller, who sat trembling with horror at this question and answer, and caught him up before all men's eyes, body and soul, into the air, bearing him most indubitably to hell; since he was a devil in man's form. For who else would call himself a merchant of souls, save only he in whose person it was said to Abraham, "Give me the persons,[1] and the rest take to thyself."

---

[1] The word thus translated in the Douai version is *animas*, literally *souls*.

For the Blessed Christina von Stommeln (a village near Cologne) see the *Acta Sanctorum*, June 22, and Renan's Essay in *Nouvelles Études d'Histoire Religieuse*, p. 353. Born in 1242, of a well-to-do farmer's family, she became an ecstatic from her very childhood; and at the age of ten she contracted (like the later St Catherine of Siena) a mystic marriage with Christ. Three years later, she left her home and joined the Béguines at Cologne, who sent her back to her parents at the age of eighteen. In 1267, at the height of her local reputation as an ecstatic, she made the acquaintance of a young Dominican Friar, Peter of Sweden, who afterwards achieved distinction in his Order and wrote her biography, but died before her. Peter was then studying at the Dominican Friary of Cologne, one of his brother-friars being Albert the Great, ex-Bishop of Ratisbon and master of St Thomas Aquinas. The greater part of the Life deals with her demoniac temptations (especially to suicide and infidelity in various forms), and with the personal violences inflicted upon her by baffled demons; these sufferings began when she was fifteen and ended only in 1288, a few months after Peter's death. But the narrative contains also many very touching passages; the reader may profitably compare them with the life and experiences of St Lydwine of Schiedam, which Huysmans has lately made accessible to modern readers from medieval sources.

78. THE FIRST SIGHT OF A SAINT
(Lib. 1, c. i, *AA.SS.* ed. 1743, p. 279.)

So far back as my memory can reach, from the earliest dawn of my childhood, whensoever I heard the lives and manners, the passion and the death of saints, and specially of our Lord Christ and His glorious Mother, then in such hearing I was delighted to the very marrow.... In such affections much time passed, and a multitude of days, and more than twenty years, as I think.... Then at last the Father of all mercies, visiting me in the bowels of His mercy, and seeing that my merits sufficed not [by themselves], showed me thus unexpectedly a person by whose sight and speech He brought me manifold joys, not only by their present exhibition but also through recording memory. The lady Alfrade, eminent for her illustrious marriage with a spouse of noble birth, fell sick and sent for Brother Walter, her old confessor, who, taking me for his companion, went to her on St Thomas' Eve. We came late; when therefore he had sat down and was hearing the said lady's confession, there came to me as I sat in the same house a certain Béguine named Alice, who asked whence

I had come. "From Cologne," quoth I. "Ah," quoth she, "would thou hadst been in our village, and hadst seen the marvels that are done there in a certain Maiden!"

Now it befel on the morrow, at even, that we lodged at the house of the parish priest, for so the said Walter had ordered it; where was at that time the said Maiden also, on account of the necessity of the tribulation that lay upon her; and it was to visit her that my companion, who had been her confessor almost from childhood, came to that house. As we came, therefore, I resolved to keep utter silence concerning whatsoever I might chance to see there unwonted or marvellous, not knowing how such things might be esteemed by those who were there present. So, when I entered into the said house, I found it poorly furnished, and the household sorrowful, and one Maiden, her face covered with a cloak, sitting somewhat apart. When therefore she rose to salute Brother Walter, forthwith the Demon, amid the very words of greeting, cast her backward and struck her head so heavily against the wall that the whole wall was shaken. Whereupon those present were troubled at this event, fearing still more for the tribulation that was to come, which they surely expected according to its wonted course. So while all those present sorrowed for the evil that had befallen, and feared for worse that they awaited, I alone was penetrated with an unwonted joy, and was consoled in my inmost heart, and stood in amazed suspense. . . . Wherefore, to hide my feelings, I busied myself with the household, that is with the Parson and his mother and sisters and other persons present in the same hall, wherein my companion sat somewhat apart with this Maiden, and told her divers examples of the patience of Christ and the Saints. But so strong an impression of joy came upon me, as aforesaid, that even now, eleven years later, it clings to me not only in memory but in certain presence; for in that hour, as I believe, some influence of God was impressed upon me. While I sat thus, hearing the talk of the household, and mingling serious words with jest, yet my eye dwelt all this while— not only my bodily eye, but that intention of my heart—fixed where I knew that Person to be by whose presence I thought myself already a changed man; for I knew well that this

Person, so dearly beloved in future days, was she by whose grace the Lord had already vouchsafed me so great a gift. So, while I watched closely my companion and this Maiden, I saw that the Devil cast her seven times; four times against the wall at their back, and thrice against a chest at her left hand, with such violence that the chest rang and the wall rattled even afar. . . . And, after we had sat thus awhile, I heard the said Maiden sigh, as though some sudden pain had come upon her: which the women round her heard also, and asked the cause of her sighing: whereunto she answered, "I am hurt in my feet." They sought, and found it so; for in each foot was a wound dropping fresh blood. When therefore she had thus groaned four times in succession, being moved with compassion amid the compassion and tears of those that sat by, who saw new wounds at every groan, I myself also rose and (as I think) looked the last two times, and saw wounds so recent that methinks my sight forestalled the flow of blood, as between the infliction of a wound and the issue of blood there is commonly a brief interval of delay. . . . And when we had said Compline in presence of the said Maiden, with all due rites thereunto pertaining, Brother Walter knelt and laid both hands upon the Maiden's head and recited the Gospel, "In the beginning was the Word," as a defence against the fury of our malignant enemy Leviathan. After which I besought his leave to watch that night with the household; which when he had granted I followed him to the bed, prepared for us in the house itself on account of their reverence for his age and religion; for he was a most religious man, advanced alike in age and in grace, white-headed, fair of face, and of good report among religious and worldly persons alike. Therefore, returning with his leave to this Person aforesaid, that I might comfort her and be comforted by her in the marvels of God, I found in the hall two lights which burned until daybreak, with seven persons who watched all through that night, not in turns but all together, without break or interval or lying down to sleep of any one. For it was needful to watch thus, since each of those present might well fear not only for his goods but also for his life, through the fury and malice of the demons, who raged so grievously and so far beyond the power of human sufferance. So my coming was welcomed with great solace by those that sat by; and, when at their instance I had taken the same place from which my companion had arisen, and sat there for a while in silence, then the Maiden said to me, "What is your name?" "Peter," quoth I. "Good Brother Peter," quoth she, "tell me then somewhat of God, for I gladly hear such, even though I cannot listen closely in this mine urgent need, for which I am truly sorry." So at her instance, and that of the rest, though I spake but imperfectly in the German tongue, yet I related two examples proper for edification, as I thought; the first, how the Blessed Virgin taught a certain Carthusian monk how to serve and love her; and the second, how a Friar Preacher was freed from fifteen years of purgatory through a Mass sung by a certain elder Friar his most familiar friend.

After which, I held my peace awhile: when behold! the Maiden began suddenly to groan more grievously than her wont. When therefore I had asked what ailed her, she answered, "I am wounded hard by the knee." Then, after a brief interval, wherein one might have recited a "Have Mercy on me, O God," she groaned again and withdrew her right hand through the sleeve under her garment, and brought forth an iron nail stained with fresh blood, and laid it in my hand... and I felt it hotter to the touch than any human flesh could heat it, whether one had held it in one's hand or in one's bosom. So when midnight was come (as I thought) then I went to my companion to say our Mattins in due course. And while we said the Mattins of the Blessed Virgin, and had begun the Lauds, there was so loud a murmur from the whole household that, breaking off our Mattins in amazement, and forestalling the messenger, we hastened down to the said Person and her companions, and asked what had befallen. So it was told us that the Maiden had been grievously wounded. When therefore my companion had come to her and sat down to comfort her, he found her grievously afflicted and almost fainting: yet after a while her spirits came again and, withdrawing her other hand in the manner above described, she brought forth another nail, freshly bloodstained and heated even as the first, yet far more horrible in shape; which nail she laid in my companion's hand, saying, "Behold that which hath wounded me." When therefore all considered this nail, amazed and shuddering at its horrible aspect, I prayed that it might be given to me as a great gift and a perpetual memorial; which request they granted, and I have kept the nail even to this day, making thereupon a sure sign how deep it had been fixed in the Maiden's thigh; for the flesh that clung thereto, and the blood that stained it, gave a most certain testimony of this fact...so when morning came I returned to Cologne whence I had come; but I knew not whether in my whole life until that hour I had felt my heart so well-disposed; so that I would then have done nothing more gladly than sing a Mass of the Blessed Virgin in thanksgiving for these divine gifts vouchsafed unto me: yet at this time no opportunity of such comfort was granted unto me. For it seemed to me that I might then understand that which is written, "And night shall be my light in my pleasures; but darkness shall not be dark to thee and night shall be light as the day." O happy night, O blessed night! thou wert to me the beginning of divine illuminations which know no difference of night or day.

79. THE SAINT'S FRIENDS
(Lib. 1, c. iii, p. 286.)

Besides these, Peter enumerates elsewhere (i) John, the village school-master, who helped him to write this life and afterwards studied for the priesthood, and (ii) "Sir John, Parish Priest of Stommeln...a devout man, and of so great chastity that he is said to have died a virgin" (p. 292).

Now she had a wound on the outer side of her hand also, proportionately corresponding to that on the inner side, as though a nail had pierced it through.... But, besides the things which I saw, I will narrate here also the things which I heard from her familiar friends, though I never heard her mention such things in a single word.... Now these were her chief friends: Hilla von Berg, her kinswoman, the inseparable companion of all her tribulation and consolations, whose face I never saw changed amid weal or woe, a virgin worthy of all praise, fearless in tribulation, cautious in times of gladness and prosperity, ever showing forth the maiden in her acts, her bearing and her speech. Her merriment was grave, and her gravity seemed merry, for the even temper of her words and manners. Next to Christina herself, I know not if I have ever seen so pure a maiden; for it seemed to me that she could not sin, and God Himself knoweth that I never marked in her a wanton gesture or sign or word, although (as will be seen hereafter) I conversed often and long with her in all familiarity. The second friend was Gertrude, sister to the parish priest, eminent herself also for honesty of manners, of whom we shall speak again. The third was the blind girl Alice, who had lost her eyes, it is believed, by weeping [in prayer], and who murmured not at their loss; moreover, she had lain seven years in bed and shown a marvellous patience in this failure of all bodily forces; her virtues cannot be expressed in writing, especially to one who knew her in person, for to such her deeds must needs appear above all praise. The fourth was a little maiden of good promise, still wearing the worldly habit, yet bound by a willing and hearty vow of chastity. With all these persons devoted to God . . . I conversed singly and separately, and all with one voice told the same tale concerning the aforesaid miracles.

80. SACRED LOVE

Letter of Christina to Peter, then studying at Paris (A.D. 1270, lib. II, c. iv).

To her most beloved Brother in Jesus Christ, Peter the Swede, dwelling at Paris, Christina his daughter or sister in Stommeln, sendeth greeting and whatsoever he may desire of best or most profitable in the Lord. Dearly beloved, you must know that I am inwardly solicitous on your behalf; and, though I have often written to you, yet I cannot refrain from writing still to say how great is my yearning for you, (that is, to have your presence, which was so sweet to me,) and how I long for you in the bowels of Jesus Christ, and how I desire that we may see one another in the Kingdom of our God. Wherefore I beseech you instantly that, if by any means you can procure it, you may dwell some time at Cologne. Moreover, I can never suffice to thank you for the consolation sent to me in your letters, which was so sweet to me that I pray God may reward you to all eternity. Again, concerning that which you lately wrote to me, how you have long desired to know of my state, and that it should be noted in the book,[1] you must know that I purpose this so far as I can, and herein you have the first claim, for I could do this well for none [other] under heaven. Wherefore I promise you this, for I trust in you who have been wont to keep me in all my ways as carefully as I have kept myself. Above all these things, most faithful friend, I beseech you to procure me as many intercessors as you may, and do you intercede for me, as I have confidence in your prayers; for sore distress lieth on me, for every night I am in such suffering that I scarce know how to live; for I am afflicted with such weariness of soul that meseemeth worldly folk have a better life than mine, and I despair of God, though that be pain and grief to me. Wherein I am more tormented than I care to write to you at present; and I strive against it, by God's help, even to the shedding of blood from my nose and mouth: yet I take delight in no good, wherefore have pity upon me! I am sick in the body, in the breast, in the head; yet I have had no outward pain since Christmastide. On the fourth day after the First Sunday in Lent, a multitude of demons came into my chamber and (for I heard all from the beginning) one began telling the other how much harm they had done me, and in which temptations they had conquered, and in which they had been conquered, and what had been their punishment. At length they departed and left there fragments of a fur garment which they had burned.[2] I beseech you from the bottom of my heart, write me often of your own state; for if you knew what a joy it would be to me to see your letters, you would do this gladly. My father and my mother salute you. I beseech you, as they beseech you through me, pray for them.

---

[1] Christina kept a sort of journal of her experiences.
[2] Like very many other visionaries, Christina was always haunted by illusions of fire and wounds.

81. THE ANSWER

To this Peter wrote two letters in reply, the second of which follows here.

To Christina his dearest sister in the bowels of mercy of Christ Jesus, and worthy of especial love, Brother Peter sendeth greeting, by profession a Friar Preacher, but in fact and deed a vile and humble sinner, and prayeth that she may happily purchase to herself eternal salvation in the spirit of saving grace, and sweetly meditate thereon, finding continual sweet consolation therein and thereby. You asked me to send you word of my state; nay, but your very prayer hath pierced to the inmost recesses of my heart; wherefore I give you to know that, albeit by your presence I was once inwardly comforted and revived to my very marrow by God who dwelleth with you, and enlightened to the very inmost recesses of my heart, if I may so say, and inflamed with fire from heaven; yet I confess, and thank God in confessing it, that sometimes, though perchance too seldom, the memory of you brings me that profit which your presence was wont to bring; yet so much the less by all the difference that there is between memory and presence, between a similitude and the thing itself which it represents! Yet (to satisfy your prayer) know that at Paris we have most devout novices, most learned students, most religious Brethren, and most kindly Prelates, among whom, as stones of fire, beautiful men, I myself converse as the reproach of men and the outcast of the people; so that, as they are such of whom the world is not worthy, I am one who is not worthy of the world. O therefore, dearest Virgin of Christ, Christina, who preachest the love of Christ by thy very name and showest it forth in thy manners, have pity upon me, who am arid amidst this exceeding devotion of such holy men, cold amidst the burning love of so many, remiss amid their so strenuous conversation, lax beside their strict religion, yet who fear not to converse with them. If therefore there be in you any consolation of mind, if any compassion, if any bowels of mercy, if any affection of charity, pray to God that He may deign by His grace to awaken me from this torpor of insensibility, this lukewarmness of negligence, this loitering drowsiness of mine.

Such then is my daily round, my quotidian fever, my most dolorous misery. Yet, though my heart be hardened, my senses blunted, my affections chilled, yet am I compelled (as the Apostle saith) to rejoice with them that rejoice, or at least to put a joyful face over my sorrow of heart. Know therefore that, though my hours of sunlight be rare and fleeting, yet the serener day doth sometimes shine upon me, a healthier air breathes round me, a more cheerful sun breaks forth, a sweeter devotion is felt in my heart, and especially when I handle and bear in my hands the Sun of Righteousness so often as the bodily sun ariseth. For then my heart warms a little, and my eyes grow moist, and my understanding clear, and the world vile; every earthly delight vanishes, every temptation is dumb, all inordinate affection is at rest. "Then," (as saith the Poet) "a new race is sent down from the height of heaven, then returneth the Virgin also."[1] Alas, beloved, what word have I said? and what do I remember? for all these things have passed away like a shadow, leaving scarce a memory behind, and altogether withdrawing their presence. O how sweet and how joyful it would be to linger amid such delights, to be sated with such feasts, to revel in such banquets, were it not that sloth impedes, negligence holds back, and the multitude of sins stands between! Yet I hope that these and the like hindrances to devotion, whereof I mourn to feel so many in myself, will vanish by your compassion.

[Extract from a letter of one of Peter's fellow-students first at Cologne and now at Paris, lib. v, c. i.]

82. AN UNDERGRADUATE'S LETTER

To the devout Virgin of Christ, and his own dearly-beloved in the Lord, Christina of Stommeln, Brother Maurice, student in the convent of the Friars Preachers at Paris, wishes health and the consolation of the Holy Ghost. To write to you is no

[1] Virgil, *Ecl.* iv, 6, 7, slightly misquoted to give it a Christian sense.

ungrateful task, but one truly full of joy, since I delight in speaking with you as with mine own heart. But, since I had no matter of writing, fearing the perils of the journey for letters, especially when directed to women, and distracted by divers business and occupations, I have so long omitted to answer your letter.... Now of mine own state—your special friend, but in secret "for fear of the Jews"—know that, passing through fire and water, and suffering many tribulations in body and soul, (as I think you have heard from the Brethren) I came to Paris on St Maurice's day, where by reason of the mutation and novelty of my way of life I have never remained in one stay, but have been vexed with divers infirmities all winter through until after Easter; from all which, by God's grace and loving care of me, I was fully freed and cured before the Feast of the Ascension; and now I am fully wont to eat our eggs, more corrupt and fewer in quantity than those eggs of the Eifel which are supplied to our Brethren in Cologne;[1] more anxious in this care, thinking over the fresh eggs and pot-herbs, when we were wont to sit beside the fleshpot, and see, and eat thereof. Oftentimes indeed I go down (though not in body) to see your Egypt of Stommeln; and, if I might, even in body would I come down, and would oftentimes have come down, and many other companions with me, even though the village were ten good miles further from Paris than it is from Cologne! But enough of this! I pray you, vouchsafe to let me know of your state, and that of your brethren—and you, Sir Parish Priest,[2] of your own and your mother's and your household's—as soon as ye may, that I may send word to Brother Peter; for I have messengers, as I believe, who will be going to Sweden. Fare ye well ever in the Lord, remembering me in your prayers (according to your promise, and the confidence which I have in you), when you speak secretly in the bed-chamber to Jesus Christ your Spouse. Salute from me your father and mother and sisters, etc. I would not that you should show this letter to any, lest through sinister interpretations any blame should

---

[1] Some readers will remember Erasmus' description of Paris university eggs.

[2] It is evident from many indications that Christina wrote not with her own hand, but through the Priest and the Schoolmaster.

fall on the writer. Bid the lady Beatrice make ready fresh eggs for the Brethren returning from the General Chapter, and her condiment of new cheeses,[1] and that she should remember me when it is well with her among the Béguines. Given on the day of Saints Vitus and Modestus. Farewell, and pray for me.

83. TROUBLES AND TRIALS

Christina to Peter, who has now come back to Sweden and stands high in his Order (A.D. 1272, lib. II, c. vi, p. 320).

To her dear, her dearer, her dearest Brother Peter, Lector of Skenninge, his own Christina von Stommeln sends salutations in Him Who is our true Salvation. After your departure, being long without my Beloved, I was so affected that great gouts of blood, as many saw, came from my mouth. I complain now of my friends, in whose trouble I am afflicted. You must know my grief in the matter of my well-beloved lord the Prior of Braunweiler, who died after the Assumption of the Blessed Virgin, committing himself to me in his last sickness with such pitiful words as I cannot relate without weeping. This same Prior desired me to write that you also might intercede for him; and I too beg for him that, even as I am confident you would do for me if I were to die, so you should do the same for his soul; for you know not how much good he did for me in his lifetime. After this, [my confessor] Brother Gerard von Greifen departed and was made Prior at Coblenz, to heap up the measure of my sorrows; and thus almost all my friends have left me.

Moreover there hath been other and most grievous trouble with my remaining friends and my parents, who are fallen into such poverty that my father, by reason of his standing surety between Jews and Christians, hath lost all that he had; where-

[1] To this the learned Jesuit editor notes "above the word *cheeses* is written *cherries*, from which our Flemish peasants make a most excellent condiment which they keep a whole year; meanwhile I note so clear a difference of style and spirit between this letter and Brother Peter's, that I do not wonder how Christina, so earnest and so intent on divine things alone, should be less pleased with the former than with the latter."

fore he dares not stay here, but is departed from the village three months since. Consider therefore, my well-beloved, how great was my tribulation when my father, who had done me so much kindness, was thus stripped of all his goods and departed! And when he was at Cologne, I must needs cumber myself with his business and go to him; and when I saw his affliction I shed many tears. On Innocents' Day, when my mother must needs go to Cologne to see my father, she fell from the cart and broke her arm and took a grievous wound in the head, and so is departed to Cologne. This again was a grievous tribulation to me; for she must needs keep her bed a long while and spend much money; and with all this she had a sharp fever, and your Brethren anointed her; moreover she broke out in boils and blains so that no man knew her face. There then she stayed seven weeks long in all these afflictions; wherefore I myself went to Cologne immediately after Christmastide, though I could not put on my shoes by reason of my green wounds, in bitter cold and in great torment of body and mind.[1] And when at last I returned, I found our farm and house deserted; and here I dwelt like a poor outcast wretch, finding nothing in the place; and so I must needs go hither and thither in all pain.

Such are the pains with which I am filled to-day, and I await still worse; yet I must needs cumber myself with business, and all day long I expect a separation between us. Wherefore, dearly beloved, I instantly beseech and warn you, that you may vouchsafe to intercede for me and on my behalf: (for, as you now already know, grievous necessity is laid upon me), that God may vouchsafe to keep me without sin in these tribulations, nor any the more withdraw His grace by reason of my distraction; that my tribulation may at last be changed to joy which no man can take from me. This Lententide, wherein I write you this letter, you must know that all grace hath been taken away from me, and all delight in prayer, and withal I have a grievous temptation of heart. Moreover,

---

[1] During the Advent weeks, the devil had more than once pierced her feet with green withies, plaited them together, and hung her naked by night on a tree in the garden! "That same tree" (notes Peter with solemn reverence) "I have seen with mine own eyes."

when I pray, then cometh the Devil in the likeness of a great spider, as great as an egg, flying in my face and molesting me. Already he hath set boils in my finger, whereof I fear I shall suffer yet more from this spider. Dearly beloved, again I beseech you, if so it may be, vouchsafe now to see me as soon as you may; for I need your counsel and would gladly see your face. Farewell in the Lord Jesus Christ.

Meanwhile, among other diabolical temptations, Christina was some-times tormented by visions of trusted friends who came and told her lies; of letters from Peter, brought by devils who grinned and vanished with horrible sounds or smells (380, 444). At last in 1279 (hearing how the house had suddenly fallen down about Christina's ears, and how she herself suffered grievous tribulation from the parish priest's mother, who accused her of embezzlement) Peter obtained leave from his Provincial to go to Cologne.

84. BALM IN GILEAD

(Lib. II, c. 1, § 4.)

So with God's help, and further reinforced (as I most certainly hope) by the merits of Christina, all my purposes fell out prosperously; and I found by experience that the Poet saith true: "Importunate love conquers everything."[1] ... At length, on the Octave of the Nativity of the Blessed Virgin, we came to Stommeln, the place for which we had yearned, fair in God's sight with many gifts, and specially for the devotion of those that dwelt there. As we drew near the village, we saw from afar how the people came away from Mass, for it was the sixth day of the week; and at last we saw two Béguines, and I said to my companion Folquin, "See where Christina goeth!" for he also yearned to see her. Now Christina could be discerned from the rest; for, even as she was more religious in her manner of life and devouter in her aspect, so also was she graver in her walk, and, to be brief, from every act of hers, or gesture, or motion, or step, there shone forth a certain special grace, so that whosoever devoutly

---

[1] *Amor omnia vincit improbus*, parodied from Virgil. Many similar passages were borrowed and adapted from the heathen poets by the medieval mystics. It will be remembered that Chaucer's Prioress bore on her brooch *Amor vincit omnia*.

considered her manners could not doubt that God's grace and presence was with her and in her. So when we had come to the parish priest's house, to get the things necessary for our Mass, there stood the wife of the bell-ringer and looked hard at me, and said at last, "What is your name?" "Peter," quoth I. "Whence come you?" "From Sweden." Then she leapt forth into the street and began to cry with a loud voice, "Christina, Christina! come back, if you would fain hear a Mass." We too therefore went out into the street and met Christina returning. When I had saluted her, she stood as it were in stupor of heart, scarce knowing what to answer. At last she said, "Whence come ye?" and I answered, "The Lord God hath sent me hither." And so, when my companion and I had said our Masses, we ate with Christina in the inner room, by the hospitality of Master John [the schoolmaster], a most devout man: but the parish priest also bare us company. On the morrow, after Vespers, when at Christina's prayer I had preached on that text, "Good measure and pressed down and shaken together and running over shall they give into your bosom," she herself fell into such a transport of mind that she could neither sup nor speak.... At length, when she was somewhat recovered, Master John and Alice led her to her own lodging; and once, when I went by her side, she asked who I was: and they told her how I was Brother Peter. Then she said, "Brother Peter, if thou wilt speak of God, thou art welcome; otherwise, thou mayest quickly do thy business and depart; for otherwise we shall soon wax weary of thee."[1] So she remained all that night in this devotion: but on the morrow, those who had heard this began to repeat it to her, as it were complaining that some one had insulted me. Whereunto she replied, "Truly, whosoever said that was over-bold": for she had no recollection of that which she had said the evening before. We therefore were three days in Stommeln, and thus we came to Cologne, much edified and comforted by Christina's presence.... Here I dwelt wellnigh a month...and here I procured nine heads of the [Eleven Thousand] Virgins, and one of the Theban Legion,

[1] The Devil had more than once come to her in the form of Peter or other spiritual friends, seeking to dissuade her from mortifications and special devotions.

by the kind offices of the Brethren at Cologne, and with the help of Brother Folquin.

[About Michaelmas we paid another visit to Stommeln.] On the fourth day of the week, when all the Béguines of Stommeln were come together, and had made an excellent dinner for Brother Folquin and me, (at which the parish priest was present, and Gerard the Advocate's son, and Master John,) and when after dinner I had made a discourse concerning spiritual joy on the text, "Rejoice, O Jerusalem," then I began to talk specially with Christina in the church, in the presence of many others, concerning a certain miracle told by Brother Folquin, how the Priest espoused St Agnes with a ring,[1] and her image accepted it and held forth its finger from the wall, whereon the ring abideth still unto this day; for when this was told I saw in Christina evident signs of joy, and heard her saying: "I was glad and overjoyed to hear that instance"; and, when I had enquired what this speech might signify, she added: "Because I know that there is in our case some similitude of this thing." Wherefore I earnestly insisted upon her, and after many words she said: "I will tell thee a secret which I have never yet revealed to living man. From my very infancy I have known you[2] in the spirit, and discerned your face and voice, and loved you more than all men, so that I have vehemently feared lest some tribulation of temptation might arise hence for a time. For never in my prayers could I separate your person from mine own intention, but needs pray as much for you as for myself; and in all my tribulations I have ever had you for my fellow. When therefore I for a long time sought the cause thereof with supplications before God, to know whether it were of Him, then on St Agnes' day I was certified of this matter;[3] for in my Communion a ring was given visibly unto me, and signed upon my finger. And when you first saluted me, and I first saw you, then I discerned thy voice and recognized thy face clearly, and was sore amazed

---

[1] The story is in the *Golden Legend* (Temple Classics, vol. II, p. 251).

[2] Here and elsewhere I follow the *thee* and *you* of the original.

[3] It must be remembered that this day and its eve were among the traditional times at which village girls hoped to dream of their future husbands; this idea would be in the air among the worldly folk of Stommeln at the time.

and rejoiced when the Lord appeared unto me. . . . There are very many proofs of this thing, given me from God, which I cannot for shamefastness reveal unto thee; for I have often received the figure of a ring in assurance thereof." Now I will here insert what I have heard from others concerning this ring. John, the parish priest, of pious memory, said that the figure of a ring was not painted on her finger, but inscribed on her flesh with sundry ornaments. For at times it had on its boss the figure of a cross, at other times it was marked in with the most glorious name of Jesus Christ, now in Hebrew letters, now in Greek, again in Latin. Master John told me the same. And when I said to her, "Methinks you had the ring on that same finger whereon I have a token of our mutual love," she besought me most humbly never to speak thereof to Master John.[1] Here therefore our colloquy ended, for we parted in mutual comfort, and were certified of that whereof we had doubted before. Whereof I know not how to speak or to write, save by praising God for all the good things which He hath vouchsafed to us. . . . So on the evening of the day before our final departure from Stommeln, while Christina was saying her vespers and commending our journey to God, she received much consolation, so that she could not conceal it; for at supper she was more joyful than her wont. When therefore after supper I had enquired of the cause, she said, "For these two days past I have been most grievously afflicted for your departure; and even now, as I said Vespers under a certain tree, and commended you to God in much bitterness of heart, then said the Lord unto me, 'Be not troubled; I was with Brother Peter in his coming, and I will be his guide in returning'; and He said more to me, whereby I am consoled, adding among other things, 'I have planted your mutual love in Myself, and there will I keep it.'" Wherefore I took this occasion and began to speak of the sweetness of divine love; and Christina fainted so sore in her devotion that she withdrew from me and was rapt altogether from her senses, and lay

---

[1] One day she had a vision of Peter sitting by her side, with a resplendent ring on his finger, "on which was written: 'Jesus Christ is your [*vestrum*, plural] eternal faith [or troth]': but what was written on the inner side of that ring she would not divulge." p. 442, § 51.

without motion, stiffened in all her limbs. But early on the morrow, the feast of SS. Crispin and Crisipinian, we said our Masses and ate our dinner; and then, when I had delivered a discourse on the text "Turn, O my soul, unto thy rest, for the Lord hath been bountiful to thee," we bade farewell to Christina and her fellows and went on our way, each commending the other to the Lord.

The Letters continued, and Peter probably revisited Christina once more in 1287, on his way back from the Chapter General at Bordeaux. He wrote from Louvain (June 1): "Though importunate Love conquers all, yet he worketh not without labour and sorrow, as I find in myself at this present time. For on this long pilgrimage, not less perilous than wearisome, undertaken for your love, I have suffered manifold labours and no small bodily pain in divers members....I hope to God, though I halt sore of my left foot, to see you next week, and I pray that you may be as well in health as I desire." The next letter, probably written in 1288, is from Folquin, announcing briefly how 'that reverend father of ours, Brother Peter, late Prior and Lector of our convent, migrated in Lententide to the Lord; whose soul I commend most earnestly to your holy prayers." The letters end here: but a contemporary life of the Saint gives us a few more particulars.

85. LAST DAYS
(*AA.SS.* June, vol. IV, ed. 1707, p. 454.)

F O R a whole year and a half she ate nothing but ginger, which was about the time of the battle of Woringen, between the lord Siegfried, Bishop of Cologne, and John Duke of Brabant; in which battle the Lord of Berg escaped death by this Virgin's intercession...moreover she interceded for certain lords of Luxemburg and very many others, who at her prayers and intercession escaped the pains of hell by God's mercy. These innumerable and incomprehensible kinds of torments which I have above written, she had obtained grace from the Lord to suffer for the sake of those men and others; for in those days, for a whole year and a half, the demons salted[1] her like a fish that is to be baked; after which she had issues of blood, and pain, so that at least two linen cloths daily were soaked

[1] If we may read *salsabant* for the *saltabant* of the text. Otherwise I suppose we must interpret *saltabant* as some frying or grilling operation, like *sauter* in modern French.

through and through with her blood.... This was the last pain which the demons inflicted upon Christina, the Spouse of Christ: so that after the battle of Woringen all persecution of the Devil ceased altogether.

At this time she was in her 47th year, and had no doubt learned the death of Peter, whose naïve admiration had hitherto encouraged the hysterical excesses of her earlier mysticism. The advanced age to which she lived (70) tends to corroborate the biographer's assurance that her later years were tranquil.

The following are from the collection of *Latin Stories* published by T. Wright for the Percy Society in 1842. They are from preachers' manuals of the thirteenth and fourteenth centuries, to be used as illustrations in sermons.

86. GRIN AND BEAR IT

(p. 24.)

A CERTAIN woman complained to a witch of her husband, that he ill-treated her contrary to her deserts. The witch said: "I will give thee a remedy: take with thee cheese, wine, and a penny, and go lay them down in yonder forest, saying thus:

> So wist I the broom
> That is me for to do'n!
> I have the worst husband
> That is in any land.

Whereunto the witch, hid among the thorn-bushes, answered thus:

> If thy husband is ill,
> Hold thy tongue still!

87. PSALM-SKIPPERS

(p. 44.)

A CERTAIN holy father, seeing the devil sore laden with a sack that was well-nigh filled, adjured him to say what he bore there. "I bear," said he, "the syllables cut off from the reading and the verses of the psalms which these clergy here stole last night." Then said the saint, "What is thy name?" "Tity-villus," answered the demon. Wherefore the saint made that verse:—

Fragmina Psalmorum Tytyvillus colligit horum.[1]

88. THE BLASPHEMER'S REWARD

(p. 66.)

IN the town called Château en Brie, two ribalds played at hazard in the church porch, wherein was a great image of the Blessed Virgin with the Child Jesus on her lap, all carved in stone. One of these fellows, therefore, losing at the game, blasphemed the Blessed Virgin, omitting none of her members, but enumerating all both outward and inward. When therefore he lost all the more, then he dishonoured still more this Mother of Mercy and Shamefastness with his affronts, daring to call her a harlot, and to invent unheard-of lies against her. At last, having lost all, he fell into a fury, and, rising to his feet, seized a stone which he hurled at the image, and broke the left arm wherewith she held her Child. Then, as the Boy seemed about to fall, she stretched forth her right arm by the marvellous power of God, and caught her Child. Moreover, blood flowed in abundance from her left arm, which men and women caught and laid up with all diligence. But the sacrilegious wretch was seized with a devil; and, seeing that he had blasphemed the bowels of the spotless Virgin, therefore in that same place, and in the eyes of all the people, his own bowels gushed foully forth as a worthy end to his unworthy life.

[1] The poem of which this verse forms part is given in *Reliquiae Antiquae*, vol. I, p. 287. It runs in English, "These are they who wickedly corrupt the holy psalms: the dangler, the gasper, the leaper, the galloper, the dragger, the mumbler, the forskipper, the forerunner, and the overleaper: Tutivillius collecteth the fragments of these men's words."

89. THE HOST MALTREATED
(p. 133.)

At Pinchbeck in Holland [Lincs.], in the year of our Lord, 1343, it befel that a certain woman went to market with two bushels of corn; on which day she could get but twelve pence for her corn, whereas she would fain have had fourteen pence; wherefore she left the corn in a friend's house until another day. On that day she came again into the market, and then she could but get ten pence for her corn. Then she said: "O Lord God, this hast Thou done to me! the other day I might have had twelve pence, and to-day no more than ten; I will do Thee as much evil and shame as Thou hast brought loss upon me!" So at Eastertide she came to church to take Christ's Body; which she let fall from her mouth into her hand, so that none might see or know; then she laid it in her chest and took a loathly toad and laid him on the Host, and shut down the chest. That night, as her husband came to bed, he heard in his room the wailing of a child, and said to his wife: "I hear a child crying." "Nay," said she, "but it is a fantasy of thine own brain": and so she fell asleep. The man awoke in the morning; and, hearing the wails as before, he said: "In truth there is a child in the room": and again she denied it. The man sought all round the house; and, coming at last to the chest, he seemed to hear the wailing from thence. He required the key; but she (as she said) knew not where it might be. Then he brake the chest, and found a little wailing child therein with a toad; and whensoever the toad drew near to the child, he cried aloud and waved it away with his hand. Then the man, being amazed, straitly questioned his wife, who told him the truth; wherefore he sent for the priest, that he himself might confess all and receive [the communion], after which it returned to its former shape. But she said that she could not find it in her heart to take the communion heartily; nevertheless, at her goodman's prayer, she took it into her mouth; and, when the priest offered Christ's Body to her lips, a coal-black toad leapt in instead, and her body was turned to blackness, and she gave up the ghost, and her husband let burn her forthwith. So therefore, after this morsel, Satan entered into her [as into Judas].

The following three stories are from a *Liber Exemplorum*, or book of illustrations for sermons, recently edited by Prof. A. G. Little for the British Society of Franciscan Studies. The author, who wrote about 1275, had been a fellow-student of Roger Bacon at the Franciscan friary in Paris: "it is perhaps not irrelevant to point out that his only two references to his student life in Paris are concerned with stories of magic." He was apparently a Warwickshire man, and had passed some years in Irish friaries: several of the anecdotes are drawn from his own experiences.

90. TIT FOR TAT
(p. 30.)

ONE more instance of the loving-kindness of the glorious Virgin I found in an ancient sermon, and certainly it should not be despised. A certain poor woman loved the Blessed Virgin, decking her image with roses and lilies and such ornaments as she could find. It befel that her son was taken and hanged. The woman, in the bitterness of her soul, went to the image of the Blessed Virgin and besought her to restore her son; and, seeing that she recovered not her son as soon as she wished, she said: "Is this then the price of service to thee, that thou succourest me not in my need?" Then, as though maddened by the excess of her grief, she said: "If thou restore me not my son, I will take away thy Son." And, as she reached out her hand impetuously to bear away the image of the little Babe, behold! her son stood by her and seized her cloak and cried, "What dost thou, Mother? Hast thou lost thy senses? Behold, the Mother of God hath restored me to thee." So the mother rejoiced to recover her son.

91. VENGEANCE DEFERRED
(p. 65.)

A CERTAIN great lady being left a widow by the death of her husband, and wooed by many in marriage, one of her many suitors was comely to see, doughty of his body, practised and renowned in arms, but poor. When, therefore, he besought her instantly, seeking to bend that lady's mind to consent to the marriage, seeing also that his body pleased her while his poverty (according to the way of the world) displeased her, she gave him one day the following answer: "Beloved sir, how could I, being such a lady as I am, take thee who art so poor a man and of so slender substance? Not thy person displeaseth me but thy poverty; if thou hadst a fief I would gladly take thee." Hearing which the noble departed, and laid wait in a certain public way whereby the merchants were wont to pass; until, finding a merchant that went by with great riches, he slew him and carried away all his goods. Thus he came to sudden wealth and, being raised from his poverty to glory, he went to the lady, showed her his wealth, and besought that she would deign to receive him. She, amazed at his so sudden fortune, asked him how he had come to so great riches; nor would she admit his prayer until he told her the truth. So sore was he pricked with love for this lady that he dared not offend her in anything, but clean confessed the whole matter. She, having heard his tale, bade him go to the place where the dead man lay, if he would have her hand, and watch there one whole night long. He did according to her bidding; and, as he kept earnest watch, he saw how in the silence of the night a storm arose, and the dead man sat up and stretched out his hands to the heaven and prayed to the Lord, saying, "Lord, Who art the just judge of all, Thou knowest how unjustly I died! If it be Thy will, do justice now." Then from above there came a rushing mighty voice that said: "This day thirty years, thou shalt be avenged." With that the dead man fell back again to the earth; and the murderer went back and told his lady all that he had seen and heard. But she, thinking within herself that she would atone for the deed by penance before the time appointed, took him for her husband; and from thenceforth they grew daily in wealth and worldly glory. They waxed and increased with many happy children, and bound their family by marriages to the noblest of their neighbours. So when the time began to glide by, year by year, the lady solicited her husband many times to do his penance; but he, blinded by the glory of this world, put it off so long that year after year stole away, and at last the thirtieth came. When therefore the appointed day of vengeance was at hand, then that nobleman made great preparations in one of his castles, and invited all his friends for that day to a feast. When therefore they were all assembled, he saw to it that none should enter from whom he might fear aught. So, while all feasted and made merry, a fiddler came to the door and besought admittance after the wont of such men. The porter, daring to admit no man without leave, announced the fiddler to his lord, who cried: "Let him in!" So he came in, and in due time would fain have done his office, and tuned his fiddle to a song: but one crept up in jest and greased the strings of his fiddle-bow with lard or some other fat. Then the fiddler caught up his bow and would have drawn it over the strings; but all was dumb, for the grease smothered the melody. What then could the poor fiddler do? Utterly confounded, he thrust his viol into the bag, rose from his seat, and hastened forth from the castle. He was already gone some distance from the spot, when he was aware that he had lost one of his gloves; and, looking anxiously around, as we do at such times, he turned by chance towards the place whence he had come: when lo! he saw naught there but the level earth. Amazed at the sight, he retraced his steps to the place where that castle had been; yet here again he found a level flat, and in the midst a fountain, by the side whereof lay his glove: for the castle and all that was therein had been swallowed up by the earth. In truth the Lord showed plainly by this example that He is a patient payer; if therefore, while time glideth by, vengeance draweth near by God's just judgment, then "delay not to be converted to the Lord, and defer it not from day to day."

This example was preached by Brother Hughde Sutton in the parts over sea;[1] who told how he knew it by hearsay; and, when he had thus told the story with that reservation, then said one of his congregation: "Brother, you may tell that story without misgiving; for I know the very place where it came to pass."[2]

---

[1] This phrase generally means "in Palestine."

[2] For two curious Welsh parallels to this story see Rhŷs' *Celtic Folklore*, pp. 73 and 403, or the summaries printed by Prof. Little in his note. The whole story is told, with slight variations in Mirk's *Festial* (E.E.T.S. 1905, p. 88).

92. A SHORT WAY WITH ALL DEVILS
(p. 85.)

F O R the commendation of faith and the buffeting of infidelity or infirm belief, methinks that example is most pertinent which was told me by Brother Thomas O'Quinn, of our Order, a good and faithful man of great learning, who was even chosen to the bishopric of Cloyne, after that he had served God sedulously for very many years in poverty and humility with true and edifying exhortation.[1] When he was already a bishop, he told me a story of his own life, saying: "In the days when I worked as a Preacher in our Order, I went once to preach in Connaught. And behold! in those days there was a marvellous and miserable plague in the diocese of Clonfert; for, when men went to their ploughs or walked elsewhere in the fields or the forests, then (as they told me) they were accustomed to see whole armies of demons that passed by and sometimes fought one with another. Such as saw these visions were forthwith smitten with sickness and disease, languishing and taking to their beds with all weakness of body; and many died miserably. When I heard this" (quoth the Bishop) "then I called the people together in no small multitude, and preached the word of God, saying among other things: 'Ye have now this great plague among you, and it is caused by the demons whom very many of you see oftentimes in these parts. Know ye wherefore the devils have power to bring such evils upon us? This is certainly for no other cause than for your want of faith. For ye fear their power too sore, not believing or thinking or trusting that the Lord will defend you and guard you against all hurt of theirs. Therefore doth the Lord suffer them to have this power of doing you the evil which they now work. If ye had stout faith, and if ye believed firmly that the devils have no power but in so far as the Lord suffereth, and if ye would amend your lives, beseeching God instantly to defend you from their wilds, then ye may be sure that they

[1] Prof. Little notes that, already in 1244, O'Quinn had been proposed for the bishopric of Elphin, but not elected. Being the son of a priest, he had to procure a papal dispensation before he could accept the bishopric of Cloyne; he died in 1279.

would have no power to hurt you.' 'Why!' quoth he, 'Ye see and know that we friars are the men who do most in this world against the devils, and say most harm of them; and here stand I, saying and preaching all this evil of them; and I say to them now, I wish they would come to me and do unto me even as they may! Let the demons come if they dare,' quoth he; 'let them come all at once! Wherefore is it that they come not? What are they about? Where are they? I defy and insult them in these words, over and over again, in the ears of the whole people.' And behold! from that time forth the demons vanished, so that they never appeared again in that land, and forthwith that plague ceased which had so long and so miserably raged among the people. Ye see how little the devils can do in the face of firm faith, when all their efforts were baffled by the defiant challenge of a single poor friar, backed up by an unshaken belief."

93. THE RESOURCEFUL JONGLEUR

Jean de Beaume was a Dominican friar who died about 1312. The following anecdote from one of his sermons is recorded in the *Histoire Littéraire de la France*, vol. xxvii, p. 154.

IN my country there was a jongleur named Roland, who grew old and lost favour, so that his tricks ceased to divert. Yet he repaired to all the feasts; and, when the old man appeared at a wedding, the women would laugh and say, "Hold out thy bowl, Roland, and we will give thee somewhat": whereat he would hold his bowl and they would give him alms. Now it befel one day that a silver cup was lost, and the men of the household accused him of the theft, saying: "There is none here whom we can suspect, for all are rich; but we accuse thee, who alone art poor." As Roland swore that they accused him falsely: "Then," cried the others, "thou must prove thine innocence by the ordeal of hot iron." "Yea, let heat the iron." The bar heated, they proffered it to the jongleur, who held out his bowl to receive it, saying, "lay it there." "Nay," said they, "but thou must needs touch with thine hand, since thou claimest to be innocent." To which he replied, "Ye therefore swear likewise to your innocence, and if ye will that I believe you, touch the iron first; I will touch after you, but by no means before!" Thus is it with the preacher who would fain persuade his hearers to gain salvation by works of charity; he must first grasp the iron—that is to say, not only speak well but do well: otherwise they will have no faith in him.

The *Grandes Chroniques de St Denis*, according to the learned and enthusiastic Paulin Paris, are "perhaps the most beautiful, the most glorious historical monument which was ever raised in any language or among any nation, except that Book *par excellence*, the Holy Bible." At least, none reflects the spirit of its age more clearly than this. It was a book of very gradual growth, begotten of successive attempts to set before the laity, in their own tongue, the historical treasures hitherto accessible only in Latin, more especially among the archives of the royal monastery of St Denis. It owed its inception to the command of Philip the Bold—unless indeed this monarch was here only carrying out the instructions of his father St Louis. A monk of St Denis, named Primat, was commissioned with the work, which was presented to the king in 1274. This was the first version, which attained something like its final form in about 1310, except that successive generations constantly added fresh matter to bring it up to date. From 1350 onwards, these additions have no further connection with St Denis, but are purely secular. The text here used is that of Paulin Paris. 6 vols. 1836.

94. THE LAY-BROTHER AND THE DEVIL

(Vol. v, p. 157.)

THIS same year [1303], on the Saturday before Christmas, a Lay-Brother of Vaux-Cernay, of the Order of Cîteaux, whose name was Adam and who was warden of a Grange named Croches, hard by Chevreuse—this Adam, I say, awoke on the Saturday aforesaid, before daybreak, yet believing indeed that it was day, and set out on horseback with a servant on foot by his side. When therefore he had ridden forward a little space, he was aware of the Devil in visible shape under four or five forms, at some distance from the Grange aforesaid. For, as he rode along, saying his accustomed prayers in lieu of mattins and hours, he saw before him as it were a great tree in the road whereby he went, which said tree (as he thought) came hastily to meet him. Then his horse fell a-trembling and became half-crazy, so that he had much ado to guide him in the right way; and his servant, for his part, began to shudder, and the hairs of his head stood on end, and he was smitten with so great an horror that he could scarce stand on his feet or follow after his master. Then that same tree began to draw near unto the Lay-Brother aforesaid; and, when it was come nigh, it seemed dark and as it were covered with hoar-frost. Seeing this, he would fain have ridden by without touching it; but there issued therefrom a hideous stench of corruption. Then that Lay-Brother knew how this was the Devil, who would have done him harm; wherefore he set himself to cry upon the most Blessed Virgin Mary as devoutly as he might. So, after that he had recommended himself to our Lady, he began to ride very slowly, as one in sore dismay; then again he saw the Devil riding behind him on his right side; and the fiend seemed in human form, some two feet distant from the Brother aforesaid; yet no word did he say. Then the Brother took heart of grace and spake unto the Devil, saying: "Evil one, how art thou so bold as to assail me at this hour, while my Brethren sing their mattins and lauds, praying for me and for the other absent Brethren to God and the Blessed Virgin Mary, to whom this blessed day of Saturday is hallowed? Get thee hence, for thou hast no part or lot in me, who have vowed myself a servant of the Virgin." Then the Devil vanished away; nevertheless again for the third time he appeared in the form of a man of great stature, yet with a small and slender neck, standing there hard by. And then the Lay-Brother, being in grievous indignation to be so let and hindered of the Devil, took a little sword that he bore at his side, and began to smite manfully; yet were his strokes as vain as though he had smitten a cloth hanging in the air. Again, for the fourth time this Devil appeared to the said Brother Adam, in the garb of a black man, neither too great nor too small, even as it had been a black monk of St Benedict, with big and gleaming eyes like unto two copper cauldrons newly furbished or newly gilt. Then the said Brother, who was now sore wearied and troubled with the vexation that this Devil made upon him, thought within himself to smite him in one of those eyes: whereunto he aimed his stroke to smite; but therewith his cowl fell over his eyes, and so he lost his stroke. Then again the Devil came in shape as a strange beast, having great ears like unto an ass. Then said the servant unto the Brother his master, "Sir, I have heard say that whosoever maketh a great circle, setting the sign of the cross in the midst and all round about, then the Devil is never so hardy as to come near. This Evil One vexeth you too sore; wherefore I counsel you to do as I say." Then the Brother took his little sword that he wore, (which sword had a blade sharp on either side) and made therewith a circle; in the midst whereof, and all around, he made the sign of the cross; and within he set his horse with his servant. Then he went to meet the Devil on foot, and began to assail him with many injurious and reviling words; and at length he spat in his face. Then the Devil changed his great ears into horns, and it seemed as though he were a horned ass: seeing which, the Lay-Brother would have cut off one of his horns; but his stroke leapt back as though he had smitten upon a marble-stone, for it did the Devil no harm. Then cried the servant to his master, "Sir, make upon yourself the sign of the cross." Then the said Brother signed himself: whereupon the Devil went suddenly thence, in shape of a great rolling barrel, towards a town called Molières that lay hard by; and that Brother saw him no more. Then he set out again on his way, for it was now clear day, and came as best he might to his Abbot, who was at one of the Granges with other Abbots of that Order; to which Grange the Abbot had bidden that Brother to dine with him. Thither he came, early in the morning, and told them of the adventure that had befallen him: thus therefore doth he testify who wrote this chronicle, and who was there present when that said Brother pledged his faith by oath before the Abbot of this Order, that whatsoever is here above written did indeed befal him, in the form and manner wherein he told it. And thereunto again beareth this present writer witness, that he knoweth that place well, and that he saw the very horse; which before then had been peaceful and debonnair, yet thenceforth he was ever impetuous and as it were half-crazy. All which things were confessed and testified upon oath by the said servant who was with the Brother when these things came to pass. And we must needs strip that Lay-Brother of the frock that he had worn, (so pestilent was the stench thereof,) and clothe him with one of the other Brethren's frocks.

95. WITCHCRAFT EXTRAORDINARY
(Vol. v, p. 269.)

MOREOVER, it befel in this year [1323] that an abbey of the Cistercian Order was robbed of a marvellous great sum of money. So they managed by the procuration of a man who dwelt at Château-Landon and had been provost there (for which cause he was still called Jean Prévost) that an agreement was made between him and an evil sorcerer, that they should contrive to discover the thieves and compel them to make restitution, in the fashion here following. First, the sorcerer let make a chest, with the help of the said Jean Prévost, wherein they clapped a black cat; and this they buried in a pit in the fields, right at a cross-way, and set three days' meat for the cat within that chest, to wit bread steeped and softened in chrism and consecrated oils and holy water;[1] and, in order that the cat thus interred might not die, there were two holes in the chest and two long pipes which rose above the earth thrown over that chest, by which pipes the air might enter therein and suffer the cat to breathe in and out. Now it befel that certain shepherds, leading their flocks afield, passed by this cross-way as had ever been their wont; and their dogs began to scent and get wind of the cat, so that within a brief while they had found the place where she lay. Then began they to scratch and dig with their claws, for all the world as it had been a mole, nor could any man tear them away from that spot. When the shepherds saw that their dogs would by no means depart thence, then they drew near and heard the cat mew, whereat

---

[1] In the face of such abuses of things consecrated, the church Councils of the Middle Ages constantly insisted that the Pyx, the Chrismatory, and the Font must be kept under lock and key in all churches. The neglect of these precautions is one of the points most frequently noted by official visitors.

they were much amazed. And, seeing that the dogs still scratched without ceasing, one who was wiser than the rest sent word of this matter to the justice, who came forthwith to the place and found the cat and the chest, even as it had all been contrived; whereat he was much astonished, and many others who were come with him. And while this provost of Château-Landon pondered anxiously within himself how he might take or find the author of so horrible a witchcraft, (for he saw well that this had never been done but for some black art; but whereof or by whom he knew not) then it came to pass, as he thought within himself and looked at the chest which was newly-made, that he called all the carpenters of that town, and asked them who had made this chest. At which demand a carpenter came forward and said that he had made it at the instance of a man named Jean Prévost; "But so help me God," quoth he, "as I knew not to what purpose he had bidden me make it." Then within a brief space this Jean Prévost was taken upon suspicion, and put to the question of the rack: upon which he accused one Jean Persant as the principal author, contriver, and inventor of this cursed witch-craft; and afterwards he accused a monk of Cîteaux, an apostate, as the special disciple of this Jean Persant, and the Abbot of Sarquenciaux [Serquigny?] of the Order of Cîteaux, and certain Canons Regular,[1] who were all abettors of this wickedness. All of whom were taken and bound and brought before the Official of the Archbishop of Sens and the In-quisitor at Paris. When they were come before them, men enquired of them—and of these more especially of whom they knew by report that they were masters in this devilish art—wherefore they had done this thing. To which they answered that, if the cat had dwelt three days long at those four cross-roads, then they would have drawn him forth and flayed him; and from his hide they would have made three thongs, which they would have drawn out to their fullest extent and knotted together, so that they might make a circle within the compass

---

[1] Canons bound to the lifelong observance of a Rule; the best known are the Austin Canons and the Praemonstratensians. They were in fact practically monks, and are often so-called by medieval writers, though modern pedantry sometimes ignores this. Cf. Chaucer, *Canon's Yeoman's Tale.*

whereof a man might be comprised and contained. Which when they had done, he who was in the midst of the circle would first nourish himself in devilish fashion with the meat wherewith this cat had been fed; without which these invocations would be null and of none effect. After which he would have called upon a devil named Berich, who would presently have come without delay, and would have answered all their questions and discovered the thefts, with all those that had been principal movers therein and all who had set their hands thereunto; and in answer to their questions he would have told them all the evil to be done. Upon the hearing of these confessions and downright devilries, Jean Prévost and Jean Persant, as authors and principals in this accursed witchcraft, were adjudged to be burned and punished with fire; but while the matter was drawn out and delayed, Jean Prévost chanced to die; whose bones and body were burned to ashes in detestation of so horrible a crime, and the other, to wit Jean Persant, was bound to the stake with the cat around his neck, and burned to ashes on the morrow of St Nicholas' day; after which the Abbot, and the apostate monk, and the other Canons Regular who had administered the chrism and other matters to this witchcraft, were first degraded and then, by all rules of law, condemned and put into prison for their lives.

Moreover there was in this same year a monk of Morigny, an abbey hard by Etampes, who by his curiosity and pride would fain have revived and renewed that condemned heresy and sorcery which is called in Latin *ars notoria*: but he had thought to give it another title and name. Now this science is such that it teacheth to make figures and impreses,[1] which must be different from each other and assigned each to a separate science; then they must be contemplated for a certain while spent in prayers and fasting; and thus, after this steady contemplation, that science was spread [into the student's mind] which, by that contemplation, he would fain have and acquire. But it was necessary to call upon certain unknown names, of which names men firmly believed that they were devils' names; wherefore that science deceived many, for none had ever practised it who had drawn any good fruit therefrom.

[1] Quasi-heraldic personal insignia, with motto; cf. *Richard II*, Act iii, Sc. 1.

Nevertheless that monk revived this science, inasmuch as he feigned that the Blessed Virgin had oftentimes appeared to him as if to inspire him therewith; in whose honour he had let paint many images of her in his books, with many prayers and characters, very piteously and in fine colours, saying that the Virgin Mary had revealed all this unto him. Which images being applied to each science, and contemplated after the prayers duly said, then should a man receive the science that he coveted, and more withal; for, if a man would fain have riches, honours, or delights, then he had them [through this book]. Seeing therefore that the book promised such things, and that a man must needs make invocations and write his own name twice in the book, and let write the book for his own proper use alone, which was a matter of great cost, otherwise it would be worth nothing but if the book were written at his own cost and expense—therefore, I say, the said book was judged at Paris and justly condemned to be burned in the fire, as false and evil and contrary to Christian faith.

96. A PRECOCIOUS MIRACLE-WORKER
(Vol. v, p. 335.)

I N this same year [1329] in the diocese of Paris and the town of Pomponne, there was a boy of eight years old or thereabouts, who was said to heal sick folk by his word only; wherefore it came to pass that the sick flocked to him from divers parts. So it befel that some were healed and others not; moreover, he had no semblance of truth in his deeds and words; but, when men came to him with fevers or other such evils, then he would bid them eat meats that were contrary to their health. Wherefore prudent folk, seeing the manner of his conversation, paid no heed to it, for it seemed to them that this was but vanity and error. Then within a while it befel that the Bishop of Paris, seeing clearly how this was naught but error, sent for the father and mother of the said child and commanded them to suffer him no more to do such things; as also he forbade to all the folk of his diocese, under pain of excommunication, that none from thenceforth should resort unto this boy.

97. THE BEATIFIC VISION

(Vol. v, p. 347, A.D. 1331.)

ON the first Sunday in Advent, Pope John XXII must needs
preach publicly at Avignon, that the souls of such as die in
grace see not yet the Divine essence, nor are in perfect bliss,
until the resurrection of the body: wherefore many who heard
those words and that opinion were sore scandalized. Yet we
must believe that the Pope uttered those words according to
his opinion, and not for certain truth; for that would have been
heresy, and whosoever would affirm such a thing must be
judged an unbeliever and an heretic.... Again, in this year
[1333] when the sermon which Pope John had preached at
Avignon, concerning the Beatific Vision, as aforesaid, seemed
as it were to have been brought to nought, though some held
it as true for favour of the Pope, and many more for fear [of
him], then it came to pass that a Friar Preacher delivered a
sermon asserting the true doctrine and gainsaying the Pope's
opinion.[1] When the Pope knew this, he caused the said Friar
to be put in prison. Then were two Friars sent from the Pope
to Paris, one a Minor and the other a Preacher.[2] So the Minor
came and preached plainly, in full congregation of the University, that the blessed souls see not God face to face, neither
before nor after the Day of Judgment [sic]; whereupon a great
murmur arose among the scholars who were there present.
Then all the Masters of Theology at Paris judged this opinion
to be false and full of heresy. When the Friar Preacher had
heard how great a scandal had arisen among the Scholars at
Paris, by reason of this Friar Minor's preaching and determining concerning the Beatific Vision, then he made ready
to return to Avignon and speak with the Pope: yet before his
departure he excused the Pope in a public sermon, saying how
his Holiness had said all this not for certain truth, but according
to his own belief. So this news came to the King's ears, and

[1] This was an Englishman, Thomas Wallis. The whole dispute was partly due
to jealousies between the Dominican and Franciscan Orders; the Pope's view had
been first mooted among the Franciscans.

[2] See note to vol. IV, no. 19.

the Friar Minor who had preached as aforesaid knew that the King was ill-pleased with him. Then the said Friar sought the King's presence and greatly desired to excuse himself; but it was the King's will that he should speak thereof in the presence of clerks. Therefore the King sent for ten Masters in Theology, amongst whom were four Friars Minor; of whom he asked, in the presence of this Friar aforesaid, what they thought of his doctrine which he had freshly published at Paris. Then these Masters made answer with one voice that it was false and evil and stuffed full of heresy; yet, for all that they said or showed to that Friar, he would not budge one whit from his sentence or his opinion. Then the King called straightway together to his castle of Vincennes all the Masters of Theology, all the prelates and all the abbots who could then be found at Paris, before whom the said Friar was summoned, and the King asked two questions of him in French: to wit, first, whether the souls of the saints see God's face forthwith, and secondly, whether this vision which they have at present of God's face will fail at the Day of Judgment, so that another vision must come. Then the Masters answered affirming the first to be true, and the second doubly [false]; for the vision will abide perpetually and will thus be the more perfect. To which the said Friar Minor consented, as it were by constraint. After which, the King required that letters should be drawn up concerning this matter. Then three pairs of letters were made, containing the same form, and sealed singly and separately by twenty-nine seals of the Masters who were there present. One of these the King sent to the Pope, requiring him to give a fuller approval to the sentence of the theologians concerning the Beatific Vision (as justice required), than to that of the jurists; and demanding that he should correct all such as maintained the contrary, for this would now be his duty. Moreover, this same year [1334], on the fourth of December and in the 19th year of his reign, Pope John gave up the ghost; and on his deathbed (as men report) he revoked this error which he had so long held concerning the Beatific Vision....

And in the year 1350, King Philip died...to whom men gave several surnames. Firstly he was called Philip the

Fortunate. . . . Secondly, Philip the Happy. . . . Thirdly, Philip the Most Christian. . . . Fourthly, Philip the True Catholic; for, as is written of him, he showed this both in word and in deed during his life. . . . In deed he showed it when, during his reign (to wit, in the year 1331), Pope John had publicly preached at Avignon a grievous error concerning the Vision of God, which error had finally been preached in the city of Paris by two Masters of Theology.

This strange story of the dispute concerning the Beatific Vision will be found fully related in Rashdall's *Universities of Europe*, vol. I. pp. 529 ff., and Fleury, ann. 1331-4. The Pope relied upon the authority of Saints Augustine and Bernard; his reply to the King's letter "is as humble and apologetic as if he were a young student at Paris in danger of losing his Bachelor's degree for heresy. He apologizes for venturing to express an opinion upon a theological question when he was not a Doctor of Divinity, denies that the Franciscan General's utterances were inspired by him, and declares that he had in his sermon only explained the two views taken on the subject by different Fathers without positively committing himself to either side of the question. He refused, however, to condemn the opinion to which he personally leaned." In another letter, he expressed himself even more humbly: "Moreover, we add that if any person say that we have spoken against the aforesaid [truths], in any certain article or articles, then are we ready to hear that person with benignity, even though it were a child or a woman; and, if that person could prove us thus to have spoken, we offer ourselves as prepared to revoke those words, specially and expressly, in all due form" (H. Denifle, *Chartularium Universitatis Parisiensis*, t. 2, p. 983). The genuineness of his deathbed Bull of Revocation has been seriously contested; it is admitted by all that he did not seal it, and that the earlier printed versions of it were garbled in the orthodox interest; but the mere fact of this garbling seems to imply the genuineness of the slightly less edifying form of the document as enrolled in the Papal Registers. How great a storm this event raised throughout Christendom may be seen from the large number of references collected in Baluze's *Vitae Paparum Avenionensium*; and from Villani's account (see next Extract). It is probable that the recollection of this, as much as anything else, dictated the frank admission of St James of the Mark, that "certain Popes" have in fact died in heresy (Baluze-Mansi, *Miscellanea*, vol. II, p. 599, written in about 1449).

Giovanni Villani, perhaps the most brilliant of all medieval historians next to Froissart, was a Florentine merchant of good family. He was a Prior of the Republic in 1316, played an important part in politics for many years, was ruined with many others by our Edward III's repudiation of his debts, and died of the Great Plague in 1348. He had been inspired to write his book by the sight of the pilgrims from all Europe who flocked to Rome for the first Jubilee of 1300, as Gibbon was inspired to write his *Decline and Fall* by the sight of the Capitol. An excellent volume of selections from Villani's Chronicle has been published in English by Mr P. H. Wicksteed and Miss Rose Selfe, and is indispensable to all Dante readers who cannot get at the original. This selection, ending in 1321, necessarily omits the following important extract, which is from the last chapter of the tenth book. After telling briefly the story of John XXII and the Beatific Vision the Chronicler goes on:

98. THE BEATIFIC VISION AGAIN

THIS opinion of his he proved and argued by many authorities and sayings of the saints; yet this question displeased the greater part of the Cardinals; nevertheless he commanded them, and all Masters and Prelates at his court, under pain of excommunication, that each should study this same question of the Vision of the Saints and should make his report to him thereof, according as each was of the same or the contrary opinion; protesting always that he had not determined on one side or the other, but that whatsoever he himself said and proposed was by way of disputation and exercise, to discover the truth. Yet with all his protestations it was certainly said and seen in fact that he thought and believed the said opinion; seeing that whensoever any Master or Prelate brought him any authority or saying of the saints favouring in any measure this opinion of his, then he received him gladly and rewarded him with some benefice. Then the Minister General of the Friars Minor, who was of the Pope's native city and a creature of his, preached this opinion at Paris: wherefore he was reproved by all the Masters of Divinity at Paris and by the Dominican and Austin and Carmelite Friars; and King Philip of France sore rebuked this said minister, saying that he was an heretic and that, if he recognized not his error, he the king would burn him as an heretic, for he suffered no heresy in his realm; moreover he said that, even though the Pope himself had set forth this false opinion and would have maintained it, he would rebuke him for an heretic, saying as a faithful Christian layman that we should pray in vain to the saints, and hope vainly for salvation through their merits, if our Lady the Blessed Virgin Mary and St John and St Peter and St Paul and the other saints could not see the Deity or have perfect beatitude in the life eternal until the Judgment Day; and that, if this opinion were true, then all indulgences and pardons granted of old by Holy Church, or to be granted in future, were vain; which thing would be a great error and mischief to the Catholic faith. And it was agreed that, before the said Minister departed, he should preach the contrary of that which he had said, saying that whatsoever he had preached was only by way of question, and that his own belief was such as Holy Church was wont to believe and preach. Whereupon the King of France and King Robert [of Sicily] wrote to Pope John rebuking him courteously; for (as they said) notwithstanding that he propounded the aforesaid opinion only by way of question to seek out the truth, yet it became not a Pope to raise suspected questions against the Catholic faith, but to cut off and extirpate such as should raise them.

From an inventory of 1346, dealing with a single chapel, the *Chapelle du Marché*. When the list comes to the Virgin's flower and Gabriel's window, the modern editor notes: "This article and those like it, curious testimonies to the credulity of that epoch, have been marked off in this and the following inventories, on the occasion of the successive revisions to which they were subjected. In proportion to the more recent date of these revisions, we find marginal notes such as 'naught'; 'it is false'; 'worthless'; 'not to be found'; and at last these more than suspicious relics end by disappearing from the lists, leaving room for objects certainly more worthy of public veneration" (*Mém. Hist. de la Soc. des Ant. de la Morinie*, t. VI, pt. II, pp. xl ff.). The inventory is written on "a parchment roll several yards long"; the printed list is therefore far from exhaustive; but it is given here as it stands.

99. RELICS AT ST-OMER OF JESUS CHRIST AND HIS PASSION

A PIECE of the Lord's sign of the Cross, of His lance and His column. Of the manna which rained from heaven. Of the stone whereon Christ's blood was spilt. Item, another little cross of silvered wood, containing pieces of the Lord's sepulchre and of St Margaret's veil. Of the Lord's cradle in a certain copper reliquary.

GIVEN BY THE LORD DEAN [BOCHEUX].

In a certain crystal vessel, portions of the stone tables whereon God wrote the law for Moses with His finger. Item, in the same vessel, of the stone whereupon St James crossed the sea. Item, of the Lord's winding-sheet. Item, of Aaron's rod, of the altar whereupon St Peter sang mass, of St Boniface; and all this in a glass tube.

OF ST MARY

Of the hairs of St Mary; item, of her robe; item, a shallow ivory box without any ornament save only a knob of copper, which box containeth some of the flower which the Blessed Virgin held before her Son, and of the window through which the Angel Gabriel entered when he saluted her. Item, of the Blessed Mary's oil from Sardinia. Item, in the same place, of the blessed Mary's sepulchre in [the vale of] Jehoshaphat, in a certain leaden case enclosed in a little ivory casket. Item, of the wax which was miraculously given to the play-actors, in a certain box with a glass cover.

OF THE MARTYRS

Of the tunic of St Thomas of Canterbury, Archbishop and Martyr; of his hair shirt, of his dust, of his hairs, of his cowl, of his seat; again of his hairs. Again of his cowl and of the shavings of his crown. Again of his hairs, of the blanket that covered him, of his woollen shirt; again of the aforesaid St Thomas's hair-shirt, in a certain pouch contained in an ivory box. Item, of the blood of the same saint Thomas of Canterbury. Item, the staff of the aforesaid St Thomas the Martyr, Archbishop of Canterbury.

The *Gesta Abbatum S. Albani* is a chronicle of the Abbots of that great house compiled about 1350 by Thomas Walsingham, precentor of the Abbey and last of the great English chroniclers. The writer had access to the wide collection of documents in his Abbey; the *Gesta* extends from 793 to 1349, and Walsingham's own *Historia Anglicana* goes down to 1422. The edition of the *Gesta* here used is that published in the Rolls Series; it is brilliantly summarized by Froude in one of his Short Studies (Annals of an English Abbey).

100. HERMITS AND AN HERMITESS

(Vol. 1, p. 97.)

In the days of this Abbot [Geoffrey, 1119–1146] flourished Roger...who was indeed one of our monks, but lived in an hermitage under the obedience of his Abbot. The hermitage wherein he dwelt may be seen by the wayside on the right hand as you go from St Albans to Dunstable, hard by the village which in these days is called Markyate; and our Roger had taken this spot by God's gift, having been led thither by the ministry and revelation of angels....Never, as I think, did the cunning fiend send sharper temptations, or set more snares, for any man; but he, armed with the virtue of the Cross, conquered the first by God's grace, and avoided the second with the utmost discretion....His devoted disciple was the Blessed Christina, a virgin born at Huntingdon, who for the love of chastity had left her ample possessions, and the home of a wealthy father. Yet he never consented to see the virgin's face, though for four years and more she was shut up in his cell. Now there was a building adjoining the oratory of the said Roger, with which it made an angle. This [angle], having a board before it, might so be concealed as to lead the outside beholder to suppose that no man was in this space, where there was only [   ].[1] In this prison Roger placed the joyful Christina, and set for a door a proper oaken plank which was so heavy that the anchoress could by no means move it either to or fro. Here the handmaiden of Christ sat crouching on the hard cold stone until Roger's

[1] This sentence, as Riley points out, is corrupt as it stands. It runs: "Is, antepositam habens unam tabulam, poterat ita celari, ut de foris aspicienti nullum interius haberi persuaderet, ubi tantum plus palmo semis inesset." But the general sense is sufficiently plain.

death, that is for more than four years, unknown to the five hermits and to all who dwelt together with Roger. Oh, what discomforts she there endured from heat and cold, hunger and thirst, and daily fasting! The place was too narrow for her to wear the clothing needful for cold weather; while in the heat this close-fitting closet allowed her no refreshment. Her entrails were shrivelled and dried up by long fasting; and at times, for her burning thirst, clots of blood boiled up from her nostrils. Only at eventide could she go forth........; since she could not open the door for herself, however great might be her need, and Roger was customably slow; so that she must needs sit motionless in her place, and suffer torment, and hold her peace; for if she would have had Roger come to her, she must call to him or smite upon the door, and how could the hidden virgin do this, who dared not to utter even half a sigh? For she feared lest some other than Roger might be near, who at the mere sound of her breath might discover her hiding-place; and she would rather have died in her prison than make herself known at that time to any person outside.

To all these sufferings were added many and terrible diseases; but she bore all her tribulations meekly for the love of Christ. Yet Roger, the friend of God, would teach her now with words, now by example, and taught her almost incredible things of the secrets of heaven; for he showed himself such that his body alone seemed to remain on earth, while his whole soul conversed among heavenly things. And Christina profited so much by Roger's doctrine that the Lord Jesus Christ, fairer than the sons of men, appeared as she sat in her cell, bearing a golden cross which He gave for her comfort, bidding her not to fear, and saying that all who would fain go to Jerusalem must needs bear this cross: which, (as He promised,) He would soon take away from her; after which He vanished from her eyes. This vision she related to Roger, who began to weep for joy, saying in the vulgar tongue, "Rejoice with me, *myn gode Sonendayes doghter*" (which is, being interpreted, *my good daughter of the Lord's Day*)[1] ."for your tribulation will soon

---

[1] *Sunday's child* is still a German phrase for a lucky person; cf. the English rhyme:
Sunday's child is full of grace,
Monday's child is fair of face, etc., etc.

be ended"; and it came to pass as the man of God said. Roger therefore, taking his hope from the multitude of graces which he had proved Christina to possess, thought to leave her as heir of his hermitage after his death. But she, having been warned in a vision and comforted by the Virgin Mary, knew that she would succeed to Roger's dwelling.

In those days Thurstan, Archbishop of York, a lover and cherisher of chaste pursuits and a faithful and devoted friend to Roger for his sanctity's sake, came to these parts; to whom Roger told of Christina's purpose, beseeching that he would deign to grant her his help. The Bishop therefore bade that he should send the virgin to him, wishing to speak with her privately concerning her purpose. Roger therefore, having sent for Godescal of Cadingdon and his wife, who were devoted friends of his, besought them to return on the morrow and bring Christina to Redbourn, whither the Archbishop intended to repair. When therefore they had gladly consented, then said the man of God: "Go home in peace, for I will pray for you, and it may be that ye will not repent of the travail which ye undergo for this handmaiden of God." They departed therefore, both content with the single horse which had borne them hither; and as they leaned forward[1] on their horse uphill through the winding woodland paths, saddle and riders rolled suddenly to the ground, for the girths had broken. It was already night: the horse had fled, and the infirm old folk had no attendant, nor could they have followed the beast even in daylight. What was to be done? At last they left the saddle, since it was too heavy to carry, and began to stumble forwards on foot through the dark, groping their way as best they could; and, in their trouble at this mishap, they complained "Where now is the promise of the man of God?" Scarce had they spoken, when lo! the horse stood by them, bridled and saddled and in his right mind; and by his side was the stump of a felled tree which seemed left there as a mounting-block for these servants of God: seeing which, they rendered hearty thanks to God and His servant Roger, mounted the beast, and came safely home. On the morrow, Godescal returned to Roger and

---

[1] The text has, *nitentesque jumento contra ascensum*, etc.; but perhaps we should read *nitente*, and translate, "as the horse was struggling up-hill, etc."

brought Christina to the Archbishop, who was lodging at Redbourn. The Prelate, having bestowed salutary counsel upon the virgin, sent her back to Roger, with whom she remained in his hermitage until the day of his death, serving God in chastity and innocence, in humility and patience, according to his doctrine, until she had attained to the summit of all virtues. At last Roger, leaving this world at the call of the God whom he served, went the way of all flesh; his body was borne to St Albans Abbey, where it was buried with all due honour in an arched tomb built into the south wall of the church, hard by the choir of the brethren. After his death, when Christina had borne many and almost unendurable temptations, both from man and from the devil, and had always stoutly resisted them, then the Lord Jesus Christ appeared to her in the shape of a babe, coming to the arms of His spouse and remaining all day long with her, plain both to touch and to sight; and thenceforth all temptations left her so utterly that she never feared any trial again. Then, by God's grace, she began to shine forth in the spirit of prophecy and to become a worker of miracles, so that the fame of her was spread abroad throughout the whole country round.

Here follows a record of commonplace miracles, which may be conveniently told in Mr Riley's summaries: "Alured, a deceased monk of St Albans, appears to Christina and discloses to her a certain intention of Abbot Geoffrey. The Abbot refuses to give credit to Christina, but is soon made to repent of his unbelief. His vision. Abbot Geoffrey affords aid and countenance to Christina, his spiritual adviser. Abbot Geoffrey founds a Nunnery at Markyate, for Christina and her fellow devotees. Miraculous appearance of Christina to Abbot Geoffrey, in a vision. Through the intercession of Christina, Abbot Geoffrey is twice excused from going to Rome. Her 'Life' preserved at Markyate. The Abbot consults her before repairing to court."

On such occasions the Abbot was wont to frequent Christina's company. She for her part revered the Abbot; and so great was the affection of mutual charity between them that, unless the whole multitude had well known how holy both were, it may be that evil suspicion would have arisen from so great a love. He who would learn more of the life and merits of this holy virgin, may find it at the convent of Markyate in the more fully-written Book of her Life.

In the days of the same Abbot Geoffrey flourished the anchorite Sigar, who dwelt in the hermitage at Northawe [near St Albans]...of him it is reported that, having once been much disturbed in the tenour of his prayers by the singing of a nightingale, he bowed his knees to God and prayed Him to remove all birds of this sort, lest he might seem to rejoice rather in the warbling of birds than in the devotions whereunto he was bounden before God. And it befel according to the prayers of the holy man; so that not only while he yet lived, but even to the present time, birds of that kind avoid the place of his habitation, not only never presuming to sing, but never even appearing, for the distance of a whole mile round it. He, buried in our church, lieth in the same coffin as Roger the Hermit; whose tombs not the common people only, but even Kings of England were wont to visit, offering there precious brocades of Bagdad, wherewith they desired that the tombs might be covered.

101. A MIRACULOUS STATUE

(Vol. ii, p. 335.)

At this same time [1335–49] there arose a great strife and contention betwixt our Infirmarer, Brother John of Redbourn, alias Pyk, and William Puff, Vicar of St Peter's in the town, concerning a certain petition that was claimed to be unjust, and the taking of certain offerings and oblations at a cross lately erected in the churchyard of St Peter's. This cross had been most devoutly carved by the very hands of Master Roger de Stoke, clockmaker [*horologiarius*], who had set it up in the place where he had chosen to be buried. And many men say that he carved his cross on Fridays only, on which days he is said to have fasted on bread and water. When therefore the said cross had been set up, then stupendous miracles of God began to be wrought in that spot, which within a brief space brought pilgrims to worship at this cross from far and near. When therefore the pilgrims flocked thither and the oblations increased, then arose the aforesaid contention between the said Infirmarer and Vicar. The cause was brought into the Consistory Court; where, after much dispute, the said Vicar was lawfully condemned for the unjust detention of these oblations, and was sentenced to pay the said Infirmarer, as Rector of his church, forty shillings (to which sum the oblations made at the said cross and taken by him were said to amount); moreover, he was condemned to pay the expenses incurred by the said Infirmarer in that cause.

An extremely close parallel to this may be found in the Chronicle of the Abbey of Meaux in Yorkshire (*Chronicon de Melsa*, R.S. vol. III, p. 35).

102. ANOTHER

THE aforesaid Abbot Hugh [1339–1349] caused a new crucifix to be made in the choir of the Lay-Brethren; whereon the sculptor carved no specially comely or notable lineament save upon Fridays only, on which days he himself fasted on bread and water. Moreover, he had a naked man before him to look at, that he might learn from his shapely form and carve the crucifix all the fairer. When therefore this crucifix was set up, the Almighty constantly wrought many solemn and manifest miracles through it; wherefore we thought that, if women might have access to the said crucifix, the common devotion would be increased and it would redound to the great profit of our monastery. Wherefore we petitioned the Abbot of our Mother House at Cîteaux, who granted us his special license to admit men and women of good repute to the aforesaid crucifix, provided only that the latter should not enter through our cloister or dormitory or other domestic buildings, excepting only our patroness, or the wife or daughter of our patron; yet even these might not spend the night within the abbey precincts nor enter before Prime nor stay beyond Compline; if this prohibition were broken, then the license should be null and void forthwith and for ever. Under pretext of which license women flock frequently to the aforesaid crucifix, yet only to our own damage, since their devotion is but cold, and they do but come to gaze at our church, and increase our expenses by claiming hospitality.

103. THE LITTLE RED MAN

(Walsingham, *Hist. Ang.*, A.D. 1343.)

AT that time there befel a marvel in the northern parts, in the matter of a certain youth who had been of the household of the Baron of Graystock. He, riding one day through a rye-field, and marking how the rye rippled like a sea, suddenly saw a little red man raise his head from the corn; who, as the youth gazed upon him, seemed to grow bigger and bigger in stature. Then this apparition drew nigh and caught his bridle, and led him against his will into the rye, to a place where it seemed to him that a lady was seated, of wondrous beauty, with many maidens like unto herself. Then the lady bade them take him from his horse and tear his skin and flesh, and at last she commanded that he should be flayed alive. Then the said lady cut his head through the midst and (as he thought) took out his brain and closed up the empty skull; after which she bade them lift him upon his steed and dismissed him. With that he straightway lost his senses and began to rave and play the mad-man. When therefore he was come to the nearest town, then a certain maiden came and cared for him, who had been of the same lord's household and had loved him well; and, lest he should harm those who waited upon him, she let him be bound in chains. Thus she led him to many saints beyond the sea for the restoration of his health; until, seeing that all was vain, she brought him back to England. All this while that red man with the red hair ceased not to haunt him, but stood everywhere before his eyes, even as he had first appeared to him; and, even though men bound him with three or four chains, he was ever wont to loose them. At length, after six years of this misery, he was wholly cured at the shrine of St John at Beverley; where, falling into a quiet sleep, he seemed to see that comely lady cleave his head once more and replace the brain even as she had first taken it away. Therefore, finding himself restored to health, he wedded that same maiden who had led him from shrine to shrine; by whom he had fifteen sons. After her death he took Holy Orders, and was made a priest, and received the benefice of Thorpe Bassett. While therefore he sang Mass with much devotion, and raised the Body of Christ in his hands, according to custom, for the people to see, then that same red man appeared to him and said: "Let Him whom thou hast in thy hands be thenceforward thy guardian, for He can keep thee better than I."

John de Grandisson was one of the most notable English bishops of the fourteenth century. He was born in 1292, the second son of an English baron who was descended from the lords of Granson near Neuchâtel, and therefore nearly connected with some of the greatest families on the continent. One of his cousins was the Sir Otho de Granson, "flower of them that make in France," to whom Chaucer did the honour of translating three of his *balades*. In later life, the bishop himself inherited the barony (1358). His second sister was the famous Countess of Salisbury of the *honi soit qui mal y pense* legend. At seventeen he was a Prebendary of York; he studied in Paris under the future Pope Benedict XII and became chaplain to Pope John XXII, who "provided" him in 1327 to the See of Exeter. Grandisson ruled this diocese with great vigour until his death in 1369.

104. A POPULAR MIRACLE

A.D. 1340. (*Register*, p. 941, Mandate from the Bishop to the Dean, the Subdean, and another, dated Feb. 12.)

THOUGH the news be brought by complacent public report, yet we have heard not without anxious and doubtful amazement how, on this Sexagesima Sunday [Feb. 11], all the bells of our Cathedral Church were rung at morning out of due course, before the ringing for the Mass of the Blessed Virgin, as though for a miracle there wrought by God's hand; which as we cannot easily prove either plainly or distinctly, so also we must not lightly believe, lest (which God forbid!) the people committed to our charge should perchance fall into idolatry or err from the path of Truth and the Catholic Faith; as we have often known it befal in several places, both in our own days and in the writings and acts of the Saints, through mad and false illusions and feigned superstitions of devils or of false Christians who are members of the devil, and sometimes for vain glory's or filthy lucre's sake. Wherefore we forbid you all and singular, in virtue of holy obedience and under pain of the Greater Excommunication against all rebellious persons, and of sentence of suspension to be laid upon the Chapter, and interdict upon the aforesaid Church,—and through you we prohibit all and singular the Ministers of our Cathedral, of whatever rank or condition they be—and we command you never in future, for any occasion or cause not first approved by ourselves, to ring, or cause or permit to be rung, the aforesaid bells, nor offer or make, nor let them offer or make, solemn or public prayers, or solemn adorations or worship of any sort soever in honour of any who are not yet canonized by the Holy See, in the said Church or elsewhere, after any fashion whatsoever, to the prejudice of orthodox faith; nor shall you or they proclaim or assert as a miracle any deed hitherto wrought in the aforesaid Church, or in future to be wrought, until we have been informed of the circumstances of this deed, and have thought fit to declare first that it is of God and not of any artifice; *item*, that it is against the course of nature; *item*, that it hath befallen by the merit of man and to the confirmation of the Faith. For since, before canonization, such solemn worship may not legally be paid even to proved miracles (which however are wrought both by good and evil persons, as may be more fully read and noted in the chapters *Teneamus* and *Prophetavit* [of Gratian]), every wise man must plainly see how much more blameworthy we must think it thus to worship where the miracles are not proved to be true. Yet we intend not hereby to prohibit you and others of our subjects to offer prayers in secret to any dead man whom ye and they believe to have been and to be a Saint. [The Bishop then cites the object of the alleged miracle, and his parents, to appear and give evidence at his Manor of Chudleigh by February 25th. He also probably saw to the matter himself; for already on February 13th he writes again:] Ye should not have forgotten how, even as the angel of Satan, (for so the Apostle teacheth us,) is wont to transform himself into an angel of light, and the crafty fox's cunning under a cloke of simplicity will baffle the hunter's wiles, so ye should not easily believe every spirit. In truth, after our late letter to you, since we wished to inform ourselves concerning the circumstances of a certain deed which the simple have reputed miraculous, wrought in our Cathedral of Exeter on Sexagesima last, a certain man who called himself John le Skynner, in whose person this was said to have come to pass, was set before us in the Chapel of our Manor of Chudleigh, in the presence of several Notaries Apostolic and no small press of other folk. Although at first he strove pertinaciously to defend his error, and to colour it with many shifts and oaths, wavering and vacillating hither and thither; yet at last, led by a better spirit, he confessed that he had feigned this deed for worldly lucre's sake and to relieve his poverty, admitting that for the last seven years he hath lacked the sight of one eye, and lacketh it still, and that he seeth with the other no better now than before; but that, deceived by the devil's wiles, he had cloked his assertions and oaths under colour of the blindness of the one eye and the sight of the other, which is even now as then. Wherefore, since we must proceed most cautiously where the danger is greatest, and on another occasion, (as Holy Scripture witnesseth,) the unbelief of Thomas was of more profit to Faith than the belief of the other disciples, therefore we bid you, guarding yourselves in future against such trifles, and especially against vile and unknown strangers, never to make or suffer to be made any solemnities in our Cathedral of Exeter on the strength of any assertions or oaths (not to say perjuries) of this kind, until the deed be first discussed and proved true with prudent care; lest ye be less circumspect than the Jews, who called the parents and acquaintances of the man born blind, that by many witnesses the truth might be established. Moreover, seeing that true miracles are often made vile by such feigned superstitions, to the peril of the purest truth of Orthodox Faith, we bid you expound the aforesaid to the people in our Cathedral on this next Quinquagesima Sunday, with such caution that no matter for scandal may flow therefrom, nor the indevotion of the faithful wax abundant, nor the Faith be imperilled, nor dangers arise to men's souls.

105. ANOTHER

A.D. 1361. Letter of Bishop Grandisson to his Commissary in the Arch-deaconry of Cornwall, demanding an enquiry: *Register*, p. 1232.

It hath come to our ears, through a growing rumour, not without vehement wonder and amazement, that—albeit according to the Apostolic and Canonical Institutes no man is permitted, even though he work miracles, to venerate them publicly as actually wrought, without the authority of the Roman Church—yet certain impudent sons of this our Church of Exeter, not considering that we must not believe all spirits, (nay, rather seduced, perchance, by diabolical illusion and by a false superstition spread abroad by members of Satan,) commonly ascribe the title of Saint to Richard Buvyle formerly rector of the parish of Whitstone in our diocese, (who was slain, according to various opinions, either by those who envied him or by his own hand) venerating and worshipping him for a Saint, to the offence of the Catholic Faith and Canon Law. Wherefore all the inhabitants of the parts adjoining, and oftentimes foreigners also, flock in crowds as pilgrims to the spot where his body is said first to have been buried, and there make solemn oblations; and every week, on Saturdays, they hold there to a late hour, and through the whole night, watchings or wakes, wherefore victuals and other things are at such times brought thither for sale, and are sold as at a market; under colour and pretext whereof the sins of gluttony and drunkenness are there committed, and unhonest conventicles are held, with perpetration of things unlawful and abominable, which it beseemeth us not here to express. We therefore, (willing so far as in us lieth to restrain such wanton disorders and superstitious abuses, as we are bound to do in virtue of our own pastoral office, treading close in the footsteps of the Sacred Canons,) do now strictly enjoin and command you to publish this present mandate in all Chapters by you to be presently held, expounding it intelligibly in the vulgar tongue, and peremptorily prohibiting once, twice and thrice to all our subjects whatsoever, under pain of the Greater Excommunication—and cause to be likewise prohibited to their parishioners by all

Curates within the boundaries of the said Archdeaconry—and through you also, in virtue of these present Letters, we prohibit—that none presume to hold there such watchings or wakes, nor to be present thereat, nor to worship or venerate the said defunct as a Saint, until perchance, his own merits demanding full enquiry, and having been declared in due course, he may be enrolled on the list of canonized Saints. And, seeing that miracles are oftentimes attributed not only to good but also to evil men, therefore we strictly enjoin and command you, as above, to enquire diligently and prudently concerning the persons who are said to have been healed at that spot, and whether they are known or unknown, and of what condition in life: concerning their infirmities and diseases also, what and what kind they were, and of how long duration, taking full and sworn evidence from men worthy of credit in those parts. And, if you find that aught was there done which could be done by no fiction, art, device, or natural means, then cite peremptorily, or cause to be cited, that person or those persons who have received this grace of healing, and witnesses through whom the truth may be more clearly proved in this matter, to appear before us, at a certain competent place and time to be fixed by yourself, that they may depose to the truth which they know, and act further as required by Canon Law.

[The Archdeacon convened a jury in the parish church of Wyke St Mary, consisting of three neighbouring vicars, three chaplains (*i.e. curates*), and six laymen, whose evidence he reports as follows.]

They say that the daughter of a certain William Ludlou of the Parish of Launcells, who was born blind and suffered from such blindness four weeks or more, was brought to the place of the first burial of the aforesaid R. Buvyle and there received her sight, and henceforth could see, as they say. Moreover a certain Cornishman whose name and surname they know not, lame and bent, who went on his knees with two low crooks in his hands, was cured of his infirmity at the said spot about the Feast of the Holy Trinity 1359, and, leaving the said crooks there as an offering, departed whole and upright. Moreover a certain smith of Winkleigh, whose name they know not, who had his left hand so contracted and so long closed that the fingers of the said hand made as it were holes therein, was cured of this said infirmity, as they say, in the Church of Whitstone, after that the corpse of the said defunct was moved thither from its first place of sepulture. Moreover, a certain Joan Gyffard, of the parish of Hartland, who for two years before the death of the aforesaid Richard Buvyle lay in a palsy, and was so grievously sick that she could neither rise from her bed nor raise food to her own mouth, was taken to the first place of sepulture of the said Richard Buvyle on a certain pallet of her

A CRIPPLE

From a fourteenth-century MS. in T. Wright's *Homes of Other Days*, p. 338.

own, and on the Saturday next following the Feast of the Holy Trinity last past two years agone, about midnight following the aforesaid day, was there healed of her aforesaid infirmity. Moreover a certain Roger Hennygan of Bodmin, blind in and of both eyes, on the Saturday next following the Feast of St John Baptist last past, in the aforesaid Church of Whitstone, after the removal thither of the body of the said defunct, was healed of the blindness of his left eye, and saw, and henceforth was able to see therewith; how long he had suffered blindness in both eyes they know not, as they say. Moreover a certain Thomasia, wife of Arnulph Coke of the Parish of Great Toriton, lame of her right leg, and so crooked therein that she could not set down her right foot lower than to her left knee, on the Sunday next after the Feast of the Blessed Virgin Mary last past, in the aforesaid Church of Whitstone wherein the body of the said defunct lay buried, received there the grace of healing for the said infirmity. Moreover a certain woman of the parish of Northam, whose name they know not, furious and crazy of her mind, was brought tied and bound to the said Church of Whitstone after the removal hither of the body of the said defunct; and this same woman, though so vexed with madness that she tore the wax tapers in the said Church with her teeth, and would have torn down and broken the images therein, about the Feast of the Nativity of St John Baptist last past one year agone, was cured of this furious sickness; since when certain of the aforesaid inquisitors have seen the said woman, in her right mind, coming to the said Church for the sake of pilgrimage and devotion, and there saying her prayers and supplications, as they say. Moreover a certain woman of the parish of Clovelly, whose name they know not, lame and grievously sick, was brought in a certain horse-litter to the said Church of Whitstone after the burial there of the aforesaid defunct; and this same woman, about the Feast of St Peter called *Ad Vincula* last past one year agone, was there cured of the said infirmity. Moreover a certain man of Woodford in the parish of Plympton, whose name they know not, but who had for two years lost the sight of his right eye through a blemish called *cirrhus*, came to worship and pray at the aforesaid Church of Whitstone after the burial there of the said body; and there, about the Feast of the Assumption of the Blessed Mary last past, he recovered the sight of the said eye. Moreover a certain Lavinia Stolloke, of the parish of Whitstone, having a great and horrible hump [*gibbum*] on her left foot, and being lame for a month, in Easter week last past two years agone, was brought on horseback to the first place of sepulture of the said defunct, to pray for his soul, having heard before that the body of the said defunct should be removed from thence; and there, after that she had said a Paternoster with an Ave Maria for the soul of the said defunct, she received the grace of healing for the aforesaid infirmity, and returned thence whole to her own home.

[Here the records end: we may therefore presume that the Bishop did not think the evidence sufficient to justify any petition for the late Rector's canonization.]

106. A BISHOP *IN PARTIBUS*

Bishops *in partibus infidelium* first became common towards the close of the thirteenth century, when the final failure of the Crusades and expulsion of the Christian clergy threw numbers of unemployed eastern bishops upon the European dioceses. These merely titular bishoprics were, however, regularly filled up; some of the Bishops *in partibus* were useful as Papal commissioners, while others were employed as suffragans by overworked or absentee prelates. They were nearly always friars, with too little dignity or responsibility to command very much respect or popularity. In a well-known passage of *Piers Plowman* the author complains of

> prelates that [the Pope] maketh,
> That bear bishops' names, of Bethlehem and Babylon...
> That hop about England to hallow men's altars,
> And creep amongst curates and confessen against the law.[1]

The following articles of accusation by Grandisson against such an intrusive Friar-Bishop are entered in his Register under the year 1347, p. 1028. They should be compared with the Extract given in my second volume from the Limburg Chronicle, *an.* 1386.

IMPRIMIS, ye must know how formerly the Austin Friars, of their own wayward will, took a certain site in the town of Dartmouth, (which is within the parish of Tunstall, united and appropriated to the Abbot and Monks of the Praemonstratensian house of Torre in the said diocese,) and there began to erect a chapel in spite of various inhibitions of the said Lord Bishop of Exeter,...[whereupon followed long legal proceedings, ending in a definite judgment from Rome against the Friars]....After which, on the 14th day of March in the year 1344, there came to the aforesaid town of Dartmouth the said Brother Hugh, secretly and almost suddenly, in habit as a layman with long sword and buckler, clad in a close short coat with buttons, giving himself out at his first coming as a servant and fiscal officer of the Lord King, sent to arrest ships in that port; after which, entering the said Friary, he there put off the aforesaid coat and clad himself in the dress of an Austin Friar, and forthwith took a pastoral staff in his hand and set a mitre on his head, and summoned the parishioners

---

[1] B. xv, 537: it is noteworthy that the parallel passage in C-Text alters the titles of the bishops: "that bear name of Naphtali, of Niniveh and *Damascus*." (C. xviii, 261.)

of the said church of Tunstall in a great multitude; whereupon he publicly asserted and claimed that he was Bishop of Damascus, sent to the aforesaid Friary by our Lord Pope and all the Lord Cardinals, to consecrate the Chapel of his Brethren there, and that the said Friars had gained all their will and won the victory at the Roman Court against the said Abbot and Monks; and he sprinkled [holy] water and went round the aforesaid Chapel. After which, he granted to the said parishioners and others Indulgences even of a hundred days,[1] confirmed babes and children and anointed them on the forehead, heard confessions of the said parishioners, and absolved certain men excommunicated under the Canon *Si quis suadente Diabolo*[2] on account of violent assault committed even in the said town, as he said, and granted letters to those whom he had thus absolved. After which he repaired to many taverns in the said town and drank therein, showing to men and women his hand with a certain ring which he wore, and saying that the Lord Pope had given him this with his own hands. And, when men asked why and how he could do such things in a diocese not his own, pleading how the Lord Bishop of Exeter had to dedicate churches in his diocese, and confirm children, and absolve, and perform other such offices, and not another man unbidden by him, then this same [Brother Hugh] answered and said that he cared naught for the said Lord Bishop, and wrought and said other abusive things, to the scandal and ignominy of our Lord Pope, and the Lord Cardinals of the Apostolic See, and the See of Exeter.

Grandisson, therefore, excommunicated the intrusive Bishop—or rather Archbishop—who finally submitted, excusing himself in writing

---

[1] The Bishop himself seldom gave so much: *e.g.* to all who would contribute to the Leper-house at Exeter, or worship at Clotworthy chapel, 20 days (*Reg.* pp. 376, 378), to those who performed certain ceremonies in Exeter Cathedral, 30 days (p. 389), to those who attended the sermons of a preacher from Yorkshire, 40 days (p. 390). The culprit, in his answer, pleads that he gave Indulgences of only 40 days.

[2] "If any, at the Devil's instigation, incur such a guilt of sacrilege as to lay violent hands on a cleric or a monk, let him be excommunicated, nor let any bishop presume to absolve him, except on his deathbed, until he present himself before the Pope and receive his commands" (Gratian, *Decretum*, p. II, c. xvii, q. iv, c. 29, from a decree of Pope Innocent II). The Pope, however, commonly deputed such powers of absolution to the Diocesan bishop: see Extract no. 72.

to the Archbishop of Canterbury. The following is the gist of his apology, apart from some rather lame denials of special points.

As for the first article...of coming by stealth to Dartmouth, this the aforesaid Lord Archbishop confesseth, as also that he came in lay dress, wearing a sword, (but no buckler as is asserted,) and clad in a close buttoned short coat. Yet he saith that from the beginning of his journey at Cambridge as far as Exeter he went in the habit of his Order, with two brother-friars in his company: in which city (as he saith) he was informed by certain friends of his Order that he must needs pass through a certain town in the domain of the Abbot of Torre; and, because it was noised abroad that a Bishop was to come and consecrate the cemetery of the Austin Friars' Chapel at Dartmouth, such ambushes were prepared, (as the said friends reported,) that, if he had been known to come for that cause, he would have incurred peril of his own body; for which cause, and no other, he took and put on a lay dress for that journey.... Again, as to the article that he heard confessions of the aforesaid parishioners and absolved certain excommunicate under the Canon *Si quis suadente Diabolo*...he denieth it; but he saith that a certain shipman, calling himself a native of St Albans, whose name (as he saith) he knoweth not, ran upon him as he wore his pontifical dress, and smote him on the arm with a certain bow which he carried, thinking (as he said) that he was the Abbot of Torre, come to expel the Friars from their said Friary: and the said Archbishop affirmeth that this same shipman, with many others his aiders and abettors, threatened him savagely [*intulit ei minas feroces*] that, unless he would absolve him, he should never leave that town alive; whereupon he, moved with fear (which might fall even upon a man of constant spirit), absolved him and drew up Letters for him regarding this absolution aforesaid.[1] Yet he first said that to himself pertained only forgiveness of the injury, and that absolution pertained to the Diocesan Bishop. As to the article that he went to taverns in the said town and drank there, he saith that at the invitation of William Smale, then Mayor of

---

[1] It will be noted that this happened when Chaucer was not yet in his teens; if only it had been a little later, we might have been tempted to find in one of these aiders and abettors the immortal Dartmouth Shipman of the Canterbury Tales.

the town of Dartmouth, and William Bakon, burgess of the said town, he entered into their houses and drank with them in their hall and principal chambers, and not elsewhere in the said town. With regard to his showing to men and women his ring and saying that the Lord Pope gave it to him with his own hands, he denieth it. . . . As to the consecration of the said cemetery, he saith that the Brethren of his Order told him how they had a Papal Privilege wherein it was indulged to them that, if the Diocesans should refuse to consecrate their cemeteries, churches, or oratories, or should show themselves difficult in that matter, then the said Brethren might cause this to be done by any Catholic bishop willing to do them the service: yet he saith that he saw no such Privilege. And, being asked whether he had never been cited by the Bishop of Exeter to answer to him concerning the aforesaid complaints to be made in virtue of his office [as Diocesan], he said that, on his way back from Dartmouth to Exeter, as he was at dinner, a servant came to him bearing a wand and asserting himself to be the apparitor of the Bishop of Exeter, and said to the Lord Archbishop, "My Lord, I summon you to appear before my Lord Bishop of Exeter (at a certain place and hour then expounded by the said servant) and to answer to the aforesaid complaints to be made against you in virtue of his office." Yet (as this Archbishop said) this citation seemed to him unlawful, because the said servant showed not his commission, nor expounded the articles whereupon he cited him; wherefore (as he said) he appeared not on the day assigned him to appear before the Lord Bishop of Exeter. . . .

The Bishop of Exeter then removed his excommunication, and the Archbishop of Damascus promised to appear personally at Lambeth and accept the Primate's decision on the matter.

Eustache Deschamps, Chaucer's French contemporary and panegyrist, is a voluminous poet who, without much inspiration, gives many vivid pictures of contemporary life. This *balade* is all the more significant because Deschamps represents ordinary orthodox lay opinion, and his murmured complaint was repeated a generation later by the great Gerson. The edition quoted is that of the *Société des Anciens Textes Français*.

107. GRAVEN IMAGES

(Vol. VIII, p. 201.) Balade.

That we should set up no graven images in the churches, save only the Crucifix and the Virgin, for fear of idolatry.

TAKE no gods of silver or gold, of stocks or stones or brass, which make men fall into idolatry; for it is man's handiwork wherein the heathen vainly believed, adoring false idols from whose mouths the devils gave them doubtful answers by parables; warned by their false beliefs, we will have no such images.

For the work is pleasing to the eye; their paintings (of which I complain), and the beauty of glittering gold, make many wavering folk believe that these are gods for certain; and fond thoughts are stirred by such images which stand around like dancers in the minsters,[1] where we set up too many of them; which indeed is very ill done, for, to speak briefly, we will have no such images.

The Cross, the representation of Jesus Christ, with that of the Virgin alone, sufficeth fully in church for the sanest folk, without this leaven of wickedness, without believing in so many puppets and grinning figures and niches, wherewith we too often commit idolatry against God's commandments; we will have no such images.

[1]   "Telz ymages qui font caroles
                         Es moustiers ou trop en mettons."

Carole was often used of any circlet, or series of objects arranged in a ring; also it was the ordinary word for a round dance, accompanied (as nearly all medieval dances were) with song. The *Metrical Life* of St Hugh of Lincoln applies the same simile to the slender marble shafts with which the plain stone core of each column is ringed; the thirteenth-century architect Villard de Honnecourt uses it of the colonnade round a semi-circular apse; see his *Album*, ed. Lassus, p. 121, and J. Quicherat, *Mélanges d'Archéologie*, vol. II, p. 272.

GRAVEN IMAGES

L'ENVOY

Prince, let us believe in one God only, and we shall have Him perfectly in the fields, everywhere, for that is reason; not in false gods of iron or adamant, stones which have no understanding; we will have no such images.

Geoffrey de la Tour-Landry fought in the Hundred Years' War at least as early as 1346 and as late as 1383. He wrote in 1371, for the instruction of his daughters, a book which became the most popular educational treatise of the Middle Ages. This "Book of the Knight of the Tower" was translated into German, and at least twice into English; it had passed through seven editions in the three languages before 1550. After Caxton's edition of 1483 there was none in English until it was reprinted in 1868 by T. Wright for the Early English Text Society, from a MS. of Henry VI's reign. It is from this edition that the following extract is taken.

108. GOSSIP IN CHURCH
(p. 41.)

YET will I tell you what befel at the mass of the holy man, St Martin of Tours, and as he said mass there holp him St Brice, the which was his clerk and godson, that after St Martin was Archbishop of Tours, the which Brice took up a great laughing, and St Martin perceived it. And when the mass was done, St Martin asked him why he laughed, and he answered, that he saw the fiend write all the laughings that were between the women at the mass, and it happed that the parchment that he wrote in was short, and he plucked hard to have made it longer with his teeth, and it scaped out of his mouth, and his head had a great stroke against the wall, "and that made me to laugh." And when St Martin heard him, he knew that St Brice was an holy man. And he preached this to the women, and how it was a great peril and sin to speak and counsel of worldly matters at the mass or at God's service, and that it were better not to be there than to have such language and clattering. And yet some clerks sustain that none should not speak no manner thing while they be at mass, and especial at the gospel, nor at the "per omnia";[1] and therefore, daughters,

---

[1] Part of the Canon of the mass, designated by its first words.

mektin chantant baxe seruoit·· Et se xpoit en ung toucquet·
Voyant que se diable escripuoit De deux comexes se cacquet··

ST MARTIN'S MASS

From the famous tapestry at Montpezat, dating from about 1500 (Didron, *Annales Archéologiques*, vol. III, p. 95; cf. vol. II, p. 268). Note the statue of Moses with his horns under the niche on the altar. The same scene is represented on the carved screen of St Fiacre in Brittany.

here is an example how ye shall hold you humble and devout in the church, and for no thing have no jangling with nobody while ye are at the mass, nor while ye serve God.

The British Museum Royal MS. 6, E. VI, is a great theological dictionary in two volumes, compiled at the beginning of the fourteenth century from many earlier authors of repute. The book illustrates in many passages the ideas of Dante's age: *e.g.* on fol. 37 b the friars are spoken of in much the same terms as *Par*. XII, 112 ff., and the author refers to the damnation of Pope Anastasius for heresy (fol. 360 b, cf. *Inf.* XI, 8).

109. CHAUCER'S ARCHDEACON

(fol. 132 b, rubric *Archidiaconus*.)

AND, seeing that God Almighty, Whose are all things, demandeth not money for sin, yet certain judges, who altogether ignore this, or who scorn it presumptuously and of set purpose, remit for a small money-fine the spiritual or corporal penalties fixed by the Canons for sin, and (which is yet worse) in violation of repeated Canons and Constitutions, take payments of money from the delinquents for mortal and notorious sins, and such as breed scandal . . . (135 b). And, albeit they are at fault in many things, yet these are their besetting sins. First, they impose unlawful taxes upon the priests of their archdeaconries. . . . Secondly, that they must needs take the white cow or some other worldly chattel for the ceremony of institution. . . . Thirdly, that they suffer the clergy to live in their sins, for the sake of the moneys which they extort from them. . . . Eighthly, that, to the detriment of their own good name, they must needs have light women in their houses.

From a MS. volume of English Sermons, written at the latter end of the fourteenth century, sometime in the library of St Martin's-in-the-Fields, London, now Brit. Mus. MS. Add. 24,202 (*Reliquiae Antiquae*, II, 45). The preacher is arguing against those who defend miracle-plays.

110. A SERMON AGAINST MIRACLE-PLAYS

BUT here-against they sayen (1) that they playen these miracles in the worship of God, and so diden not these Jews that bobbeden Christ. (2) Also oftentimes by such miracle-playing be men converted to good living, as men and women seeing in miracle-playing that the devil by their array (by the which they moven each other to lechery and to pride) maketh them his servants to bring themselves and many others to Hell, and to have far more villainy hereafter by their proud array there than they have worship here. And seeing furthermore that all this worldly being here is but vanity for a while, as is miracle-playing, wherethrough they leaven their pride and taken to them afterwards a meek conversation of Christ and of His saints; and so miracle-playing turneth men to the belief and not perverteth. (3) Also oftentimes by such miracle-playing men and women seeing the passion of Christ and of His saints be moved to compassion and devotion, weeping bitter tears. Then they be not scorning of God but worshipping. (4) Also profitable to men and to the worship of God it is to fulfillen and seeken all the means by the which men may see sin and drawen them to virtues. And sith as there be men that only by earnestful doing willen be converted to God, so there be other men that willen be converted to God but by games and play; and nowadays men be not converted by the earnest doing of God nor by men nor of men; then now it is timely and skilful to assayen to converten the people by plays and games, as by miracle-playing and other manner mirths. (5) Also some recreation men must have, and better it is or less evil that they have their recreation by playing of miracles than by playing of other japes.[1] (6) Also since it is lawful to have the miracles of God painted, why is not as well lawful to have the miracles of God played, since men may better readen the will of God and His marvellous works in the playing of them than in the painting? and better they be holden in men's minds and often rehearsed by the playing of them than by the painting, for this is a dead book, the other a quick.

(1) To the first reason we answeren saying that such miracle-playing is not to the worship of God. For they be done more to be seen of the world and to pleasen to the world than to be seen of God or to pleasen to Him, as Christ never ensampled them, but only heathen men that evermore dishonouren God, saying that to the worship of God that is to the most villainy of Him; therefore as the wickedness of the misbelief of heathen men lieth to themselves when they sayen

---

[1] Jests.

that the worship of ther maumetry[1] is to the worship of God,
so men's lechery nowadays to have their own lusts lieth to
themselves, when they say that such miracle-playing is to the
worship of God.......(2) And as anents the second reason
we say that, right as a virtuous deed is otherwise occasion of
evil, as was the passion of Christ to the Jews, but not occasion
given but taken of them, so evil deeds be occasion of good deeds
otherwhile, as was the sin of Adam occasion of the coming of
Christ, but not occasion given of the sin but occasion taken
of the great mercy of God; the same wise miracle-playing,
albeit that it be sin, is otherwhile occasion of converting of
men, but as it is sin it is far more occasion of perverting of
men, not only of one singular person but a whole country, as
it maketh all the people to be occupied in vain, against this
behest of the Psalter-book that saith to all men, (and especially
to priests that each day readen it in their service,) "Turn away
mine eyen that they see not vanities," and again, "Lord, Thou
hatest all waiting [on] vanities." How, then, may a priest
playen in interludes or given himself to the sight of them,
sithen it is forbidden him so expressly by the aforesaid behest
of God? especially, sithen he curseth each day in his service all
those that bowen away from the behests of God: but, alas!
more harm is, priests nowadays must shrewen[2] themselves, and
all day, as many that all day crien "What, shrew!" shrewing
themselves. Therefore, miracle-playing, sithen it is against
the behests of God that biddeth that thou shalt not take God's
name in idle, it is against our belief, and so it may not give
occasion of turning men to the belief but of perverting, and
therefore many men weenen that there is no Hell of everlasting
pains, but that God doth but threaten us and not do it indeed,
as be playing of miracles in sign and not in deed.[3] Therefore

---

[1] Idolatry; our medieval ancestors imagined Mohammedans to be idolaters.
[2] Curse.
[3] Such freethought was common already in the thirteenth century, as Berthold
von Regensburg testifies (ed. Pfeiffer, vol. I, p. 386; cf. vol. II, p. 227). "Some
men say 'the man who is used to hell is more at his ease there than elsewhere.'
That is a great lie: for no man can ever be used to hell. Master Cain was the first
to go down thither; yet his torments are as sore, and the fire is as hot for him at this
hour as on the first day: and if a man is to grow used to hell at all, then Cain might
well be so used after these seven thousand five hundred years. Others again say

such miracle-playing not only perverteth our belief but our very hope in God, by the which saints hopeden that the more they abstaineden them from such plays the more meed they then should have of God; and therefore the holy Sara, the daughter of Raguel,[1] hoping her meed of God, saith: "Lord, thou wottest that never I coveted man, and clean have I kept myself from all lusts: never with plays y-mingled me myself." And by this true confession to God, as she hoped, so had she her prayers heard and great meed of God; and, sithen a young woman of the Old Testament, for keeping the bodily virtue of chastity and for to worthily take the Sacrament of Matrimony when her time should come, abstained her from all manner idle playing and from all company of idle players; much more a priest of the New Testament, (that is passed the time of childhood, and not only should keep chastity but all other virtues, not only ministering the sacrament of matrimony but all other sacraments, and especially sithen him oweth to minister to all the people the precious Body of Christ) ought to abstain him from all idle playing both of miracles and else. . . . . . . (3) By this we answeren to the third reason, saying that such miracle-playing giveth none occasion of very weeping and needful; but the weeping that falleth to men and women by the sight of such miracle-playing, as they be not principally for their own sins nor of their good faith within sorry, but more of their sight without, [therefore their] sorrow is not allowable before God but more reprovable. For, sithen Christ Himself reproved the women that wepten upon Him in His passion, much more they be reprovable that weepen for the play of Christ's passion, leaving to weepen for the sins of themselves and their children, as Christ bade the women that wepten on Him. (4) And by this we answeren to the fourth reason, saying that no man may be converted to God but only by the earnestful doing of God and by none vain playing. For

(I have heard it even from learned folk) that our Lord maketh for some men a house and a mansion in hell, that no torment may come nigh them. That again is a lie and a heresy."

[1] Tobias iii, 16, 17, which runs thus in the Douay version, "Thou knowest, O Lord, that I never coveted a husband, and have kept my soul clean from all lust. Never have I joined myself with them that play: neither have I made myself partaker with them that walk in lightness."

that which the word of God worketh not, nor His sacraments, how should playing worken, that is of no virtue but full of default? Therefore, right as the weeping that men weepen oft in such play commonly is false,—witnessing that they loven more the liking of their body and all prosperity of the world than liking in God and prosperity of virtue in the soul; and therefore, having more compassion of pain than of sin, they falsely weepen for lacking of bodily prosperity more than for lacking of ghostly, as doen damned men in hell;—right so oftentimes the converting that men seemen to be converted by such playing is but feigned holiness, worse than is other sin beforehand. For if he were verily converted he should haten to see all such vanity, as bidden the behests of God, albeit that of such play he take occasion by the grace of God to flee sin and to follow virtue. And, if men sayen here that if this playing of miracles were sin, would God converten men by the occasion of such playing? hereto we sayen that God doeth so for to commend His mercy to us; that we thinken entirely how good God is to us that, while we be thinking against Him, doing idleness and withstaying Him, He thinketh upon us good and sendeth us His grace to fleen all such vanity.... Therefore the priests that sayen themselves holy, and busien them about such plays, be very hypocrites and liars. (5) And hereby we answer to the fifth reason, saying that very recreation is not unlawful occupying in false works, but more ardently working greater works; and therefore such miracle-playing nor the sight of them is no very recreation but false and worldly, as proven the deeds of the fautours[1] of such plays that yet never tasten very sweetness in God, travailing so much therein that their body would not sufficen to bearen such a travail of the spirit; but as men goeth from virtue to virtue, so they go from lust unto lust, that they more steadfastly dwellen in them; and therefore as this feigned recreation of playing of miracles is false conceit, so is it double shrewdness, worse than though they playen pure vanities. For now the people giveth credence to many mingled leasings,[2] for [the sake of] other mingled truths, and maken weenen that to be good which is full evil; and so oftentimes less evil it were to

---

[1] Favourers, abettors.   [2] Lyings.

playen ribaldry than to playen such miracles. And if men axen what recreation men shoulden have on the holiday after their holy contemplation in the church, we sayen to them two things; one, that if he had throughly occupied himself in contemplation before, neither would he ask that question nor have will to see vanity; another, we sayen that his recreation should be in the works of mercy to his neighbour, and in delighting him in all good communication with his neighbour as before he delighted him in God, and in all other needful works that reason and kind axen. (6) And to the last reason we sayen that painting, if it be very, without mingling of leasings, and not too curious to much feeding men's wits, and not occasion of maumetry to the people, they [the paintings] be but as naked letters to a clerk to readen the truth. But so be not miracles-playing, that be made more to delighten men bodily than to be books to lewd[1] men. And therefore, if they be quick books, they be quick books to shrewdness more than to goodness. Good men therefore, seeing their time too short to occupyen them in good earnest works, and seeing the day of the reckoning nighen fast, and unknowing when they shall go hence, fleen all such idleness, hasting that they weren with their spouse Christ in the bliss of Heaven.

John Gower, Chaucer's friend, was probably a London merchant and a country squire: the reader should consult G. C. Macaulay's admirable essay on him in the *Camb. Hist. Eng. Lit.* vol. II, chap. vi. His poems are frankly satirical, but gain much force as evidence from his frequent protest that he simply voices what the public is saying around him. The following Extract is from his *Mirour de l'Omme*, ed. Macaulay, ll. 25,213 ff. and 26,077 ff.

III. AH, CONSTANTINE!

The author will now speak partly of the estate of such as govern this world, and firstly of the Court of Rome.

To speak of these Prelates who are as it were ambassadors of God, with the clergy appertaining to them, these are become advocates of Sin to plead in law against the Soul; moreover, to

---

[1] Unlearned, common.

speak of Kings, they so rob their people daily that all men complain, both high and low. And if we go on to speak of men of law and merchants, I see peril in all estates.

I firmly believe that the authority of him who is Head of Holy Church under God, if he govern himself by right, is set above all others; but nowadays that ordinance is changed; for that which was once Humility is now Pride, and we see how the largess of old times is now turned to covetise. Whether Chastity dwell there nowadays or no, I know not whether it be for me to say; wherefore I hold my peace on that matter. Whatsoever I think to write here is not of mine own self, for it is the murmur, the complaint, the voice and the cry of all Christian folk. What they all say I unsay not:—that the Court of Rome is ruled in our days by simony of gold and silver, so that the poor man's cause shall never be heard for all his clamour: he who bringeth no gifts thither shall never meet with justice or charitable mercy. . . . By papal law it is established that thou shalt not espouse thy cousin, and other cases are forbidden more than I will here relate; and they say that whosoever doth these things hath done mortal sin. Then I would have thee ask whether, for the gold that thou shalt give them, thou mayest find mercy at that Court? Assuredly, if thou doest thus, the purse that thou shalt bear will make the Pope thy friend. But if it be so mortal a sin as they say, why then are they willing to grant a dispensation for it beforehand? For the God of Heaven, who is more upright than the Pope, cannot do so; on the contrary, I know well that it would be vain to beg God's leave to break to-morrow the law and precept which He hath established; but the Pope of Rome, if my purse be full of gold, will be more courteous and complaisant to me. "The fowler," (quoth he) "the wider he stretches his nets, the sooner are the birds caught; so likewise the more divers sins we have imposed by Our decrees, the sooner will ye be found transgressing, and much more will ye be subject to Our power. For such sins may be redeemed in Our court for money; and We will that Our table may be all the heavier laden with meat, Our stables the more crowded with great palfreys. . . . Render to Caesar that which is Caesar's, and to God that which is God's: but We would fain have both, for

We bear the estate of both in this world. We have God's full power, wherefore We Ourselves desire to receive outright such part of His possessions, as that none shall take his share with Us, unless We may surely see that it shall be repaid to Us twofold. So do We make God Our profit, as to leave naught of all the gold that We can get, neither great nor small; for prelates and cowled monks, curates and vicars, are so subject to Us, that they dare not gainsay Our will. They must render gold at Our pleasure without murmuring, or their sanctuary shall be interdicted by Our decree. But We now bear Caesar's office, from whom We have inherited the city of Rome, where it is Our will to take due tribute from all folk; nay, the very Jew in his degree, and the common prostitute, shall not be quit of their payment;[1] thus have We found what Caesar in his days forgot, that vices are current for ready money. I trow that, when Constantine first gave to the Pope of Rome full possession of earthly power, the King of Glory in His foresight bade a celestial voice cry aloud from the heights of heaven, saying that the condition of Holy Church, with all her priests, would never be so good and Christian as that of their forefathers had been, for the venom that must needs grow from these their earthly possessions."

---

[1] The medieval Popes nearly always protected the Jews; but contemporaries relate this only with indignation, for it was a highly profitable policy, commending itself to money-loving and far-sighted rulers of every kind but scandalizing all their subjects. Gower is not the only satirist to point out that prostitutes enjoyed the same toleration in Rome as Jews, and for a similar consideration.

The best introduction to the history of the fifteenth and sixteenth centuries would be to compile a catena of passages in which churchmen of the five preceding centuries express their despair of their own times. Such a catena would fill a whole volume of this size: for in the Middle Ages pessimism is not confined to a Carlyle and a Ruskin here and there; it is the prevailing tone of all, or practically all, who pause to pass any judgment on the world around them. Mr C. F. G. Masterman, M.P., reviewing my *From St Francis to Dante* in the *Speaker*, deplored that I had quoted so much from writers who took a dark view of their own generation. I replied by challenging him to name a few medieval writers who express any more hopeful view; no such name was suggested. Yet the recognition of medieval facts is absolutely essential to the comprehension not only of the Reformation period but of our own age; Mr Masterman's *Condition of England* and Dr Gairdner's *Lollardy and the Reformation*, with all their ability and learning, are vitiated by a false perspective of history. In spite of all that is sordid and depressing in our own age, in spite of all the wickedness and unrest that were let loose by the great religious revolution of the sixteenth century, it must still be borne in mind that the past had been even worse; and that, if we face the facts of the Middle Ages as frankly as we are often compelled to face those of our own time, we shall recognize man as an improving animal—or, in other words, we shall see that God was not mistaken in judging His creation to be good. A few examples will here suffice; but these few at least are necessary to mark the significance of the epoch which gave birth to the modern world. The most damning complaints of all, as to the general immorality of the clergy, are omitted as much as possible here because I have already emphasized them sufficiently elsewhere.

Pope Gregory X held an ecumenical Council in 1274 for the reform of Christendom. As a preliminary, he wisely requested some of the most distinguished churchmen of the time to send in a formal statement of matters requiring correction. Two of these have survived: (i) by Humbert de Romans, Minister General of the Dominicans (Labbe-Mansi, *Concilia* XXIV, 109 ff.), and (ii) by the Bishop of Olmütz (Raynaldus, *Annales*, 1273, § vi). Both give substantially the same picture; I quote briefly from the former as the greater man and the more explicit writer.

112. A PROGRAMME OF REFORM

WITH regard to divine service, it would seem wise to enact that men should not be compelled to keep new feast-days beyond the authority of the Roman Church; and that, except on the greater holy-days, instituted by the Church, men should be permitted to work after divine service, both because sins are the more multiplied on holy-days at the bidding of wicked sloth, in taverns, dances, and brothels; and also because the work-days are scarce enough now for the poor to earn their daily bread....Fourthly, that divine service should be so abbreviated that it might be said and heard from end to end, and devoutly. Fifthly, that in great churches there should be a sufficient number of clerics at every service....

In the parishes, the first thing blamable seems to be that some are too poor for any good parson to take. Secondly, the rich parishes are given to such as will not or cannot reside. Thirdly, vicars are put in, not of the best, but of the cheapest who will do the work. Fourthly, they are not given for God's sake to the best, but to unworthy men, sometimes for money from hand to hand, or for promises, or for services done. Fifthly, that [clergy] of evil fame are not corrected, but are oftentimes suffered to sin freely for the sake of bribes. Sixthly, some manual should be written for the instruction of the ignorant and unlearned in the duties of their office, seeing that they know not the Scriptures. As to the common run of the clergy, many of them are possessed with gluttony, lechery, vainglory, wastefulness, idleness, and many other evils, which should be corrected for the scandal that they give to the laity. Pardoners defile the Church with lies and filthiness, and render it a laughing-stock. Secondly, they bribe the prelates, who therefore suffer them to say whatsoever they will. Thirdly, in their briefs or cartels they lyingly feign so many indulgences, and expound them so ill, that scarce any man believeth. Fourthly, they gain much money, yet send little to headquarters; and they deceive the people with false relics.

In 1311 Clement V pursued the same policy for his Ecumenical Council of Vienne. The reports of two distinguished bishops have survived: (i) Guillaume le Maire of Angers (*Mélanges Historiques. Choix de Documents*, t. II, 1877), and (ii) Guillaume Durand of Mende (*Tractatus de Modo Generalis Concilii habendi*, Paris, 1671). Both are very lengthy documents, and most unflattering on every page.

113. A SECOND
(Le Maire, p. 477.)

I n many parts of the kingdom of France there has grown up an irreligious custom—nay rather, an abominable abuse—

namely that, on Sundays and other principal holydays dedicated to the Majesty of the Most High, whereupon Christian folk should cease from servile work, come to church, spend their time in divine service, and receive the food of the word of God which they need so sorely, from prelates and others who have commission to preach—on such days they keep markets and fairs, pleas and assizes. Whence it cometh to pass that the faithful, savouring more of the flesh than of the spirit, leave the church and her services, and flock to such places, where they pursue their trades or their lawsuits. Wherefore on those holy days, whereon God should above all be worshipped, the Devil is worshipped instead; churches stand empty; law-courts, taverns and workshops ring with quarrels, tumults, blasphemies; perjuries and crimes of almost every kind are there perpetrated. From this it followeth that God's law, the articles of faith, the other things pertaining to the Christian religion and the salvation of souls are almost utterly ignored by the faithful: God is blasphemed, the Devil is revered, souls perish, the Catholic Faith is wounded; wherefore it is most needful to apply some salutary remedy to so great an error and abuse.

114. A THIRD

(Durand, p. 133.)

THAT none feast within the Churches, nor hold lawcourts therein; and that the gilds wherein both clergy and layfolk swill together [*se ingurgitant*] be abolished: and that whatsoever is there spent be given to the poor. . . . (296) The whole Church might be reformed if the Church of Rome would begin by removing evil examples from itself, and then gradually from the prelates and the rest: by which evil examples men are scandalized, and the whole people are as it were infected, and (as Esaias saith) they that rule over them suffer God's name to be blasphemed for this. . . . (300) To the same effect are these defraudings of alms, this restriction of hospitality, the diminution of ecclesiastics deputed to divine service, and the wandering abroad of prelates and parish priests who flee from their cities or their parishes on feast-days and other church solemnities.... For in all lands whereunto the sound of the Apostles hath gone forth, the holy Church of God, and especially the most holy Church of Rome, is in evil repute; and all cry and publish it abroad that within her bosom all men, from the greatest even unto the least, have set their hearts upon covetousness. For, since covetousness is grown in the churches, as it grew in the Roman Empire, the law hath perished from the priest, and the seeing of visions from the prophets, as Jerome saith.... (309) That the whole Christian folk take from the clergy pernicious examples of the sin of gluttony is clear and notorious, since the said clergy feast more luxuriously and splendidly, and with more dishes, than kings and princes.... (316) The sin of sloth and negligence is most deeply rooted in God's Holy Church, and all Christian folk take an evil example therefrom. For there are few among the clergy who are not called, or who could not be called, negligent in the offices which pertain to them, and for which stipends or church benefices were founded.... (318) The negligence of learning and the plague of ignorance might be remedied;... in the conferring of all sacred Orders and ecclesiastical ministries enquiry should be made whether the candidate be of mature age, steadfast morals, and knowledge of letters.... (319) We might remedy the neglect of learning among parish clergy if we obeyed the Council of Toledo, wherein it was decreed that, when a priest is ordained to a parish, he should receive from his bishop an official booklet, containing all that pertaineth to the cure of souls, in order that such clergy may be instructed before they approach their appointed parishes, lest they offend through ignorance of Holy Scripture.... (325) Let the first [clerical] tonsure be conferred upon no man unless he know how to read and chant competently.... (326) And if all were certain that they could not otherwise come among the clergy, then all would strive better to learn, and their parents and kinsfolk to provide for them [in the schools]: especially if they were certain that they could not attain to ecclesiastical benefices unless they had sufficient learning; from which study and laborious attention they are now discouraged, seeing how by the favour of the authorities, of their parents, and of rich folk, young men insufficient and illiterate are unduly preferred to those who surpass them in literature and merit, through the disordered ambition of rectors and prelates; and it would be better for the Lord's priesthood and clergy to have a few sufficient ministers who might worthily perform God's work than to have many and innumerable of the unprofitable sort; who, according to St Clement, bring a grievous burden and confusion upon God's holy Church.... (329) There is also a manifest negligence concerning the cure of souls herein, that the Roman Church giveth dispensations to many, without evident necessity or utility, that they may hold a plurality of cures of souls, and that they shall not be bound to reside personally for any very long time; and men with such cures of souls—nay, even prelates—are detained for long times at the Roman Court, and in divers manners absent themselves from the churches committed to them and to their care.... (330) This negligence of cures appeareth manifestly herein, that not only simple cures of souls, but even double cures (and, which is more detestable, prelacies) are committed to men who, through defect of age or of learning or other causes, are notoriously and publicly known among the laity and others to be incapable of such cure of souls; for the perdition whereof (though souls be more precious than all earthly and corruptible possessions) they seem to care little; so that, by a general abuse on the part of prelates, churches are committed to such men. ...Such men cry not aloud, nor preach, nor warn the people of their crimes, nor hear confessions, nor meddle in the least with the cure of souls, but only with gathering their revenues. ... (334) Another neglect of correction is this; that grievous, (nay, most grievous) offences and crimes perpetrated by churchmen, when indeed they are punished at all, are punished in money; although such criminals should justly be committed to a lifelong prison; ... the remedy whereof would seem to be that these pecuniary fines which are received by the Church for crimes and from ecclesiastics, should be applied to pious uses, as some Doctors say that they should in justice be applied [even now].... (335) This neglect [of divine service] appeareth but too plainly in the clergy, both in the Head and in the Members; and would that the word of Esaias were not true of the clergy, when he saith, "This people honoureth Me with their lips, but their heart is far from Me"!...(337) There are few of the said prelates and higher clergy who come to say or hear God's service solemnly and without [other] occupation or conversation; but they say it amidst other occupations, and sometimes without chant, undevoutly and with omissions of syllables and insufficiently.... Moreover the canons and ecclesiastical dignitaries, while divine service is proceeding, frequently hold conversations together, or sleep, or disturb the service; and some, leaving the choir during the worship of God, walk about the church lest they lose their distribution, mingling with the talk of men and women, with their jests and laughter and applause....(338) And many princes, while they cause the solemnities of mass to be celebrated in their presence, give an almost continuous audience to men in other matters, or busy themselves with other things, paying no attention to the service nor saying their prayers.[1] Some of the nobles, great men, and others of the people, do indeed come to church while Christ's Body is to be elevated, and withdraw in haste when this hath been done, scarcely saying a *Paternoster* within the church walls: [*he goes on to quote councils which had vainly forbidden this abuse*]. (340) Moreover, divine service and worship are neglected; for holy days and Sundays are not celebrated or kept as the laws bid... and sometimes on those days more sins are committed than in the whole week; nor doth the people seem to care for divine things, but only for songs, jests, dances, caperings, or foul and unhonest chants, even within the churches or churchyards, busying themselves day and night with such vanities....(346) Another negligence concerning divine service is the matter of church ornaments; for in many parish churches, (and especially in such as are in the presentation, collation, or disposition of exempt Religious,) there is a general defect of vestments and priestly garments; as also of books, chalices, and other church

---

[1] At Strasbourg the civic authorities regularly gave business audiences and heard law-cases in the Cathedral during mass. Even more significant is the fact that St Louis is praised for having *very seldom* done this, and that Pope John XXII, in a private letter of advice to Edward II, recommended him not to fall into this habit (*Acta Sanctorum*, August 25th, § 38; *Lanercost Chronicle*, Appendix, p. 420).

ornaments. And in some churches the vestments are so vile and sordid that they raise disgust [*abominationem inducunt*]. In some churches the celebrants lay their sacerdotal vestments over their tunic or jacket or tabard, under the people's eyes, without a rochet or Roman shirt. In others, the ministrants or servers wear no surplice or clerical habit; and in some Religious Orders the lay-brethren serve the priests; and, in the general confession which is made by the priest before the Introit of the mass, the said laymen or clerklings or boys answer the celebrant like another priest, thus in a manner absolving him from the sins which he hath generally confessed, though they have no such power [of absolution].

Durand's and Le Maire's complaints probably contributed a good deal to the decree *Gravi nimirum* issued by Clement in this Council, which sets forth how "many church ministers, casting away the modesty of their Order,...presume to say or sing the Canonical hours with undue haste, and skipping of words, and frequent intermingling of extraneous, vain, profane, and unhonest talk, coming late into choir and often leaving the church without reasonable cause before the end of service, sometimes bringing hawks with them or causing them to be brought, and leading hunting-dogs." The decree goes on to speak equally strongly of the indecent dances and songs in churches and cemeteries, the sordid vestments and furniture, and the offence to God; but its inefficacy is proved by countless documents of the fifteenth and early sixteenth centuries. See Peter Schott's letter in this volume, no. 126.

Chaucer's Good Parson, "full loth were him to cursen for his tithes," may be better understood by a perusal of the rhymed *Instructions for Parish Priests* written about 1420 by John Myrc, a Canon Regular of Lilleshall (E.E.T.S. 1868). In the following Extract (p. 21 ff.) the author is compelled by the exigences of his subject to lapse into prose. In the long list of crimes which earn this grisly curse, that of withholding tithes is emphasized by threefold repetition.

115. PULPIT CURSING

THE great sentence I writë here,
That twice or thricë in the year
Thou shalt pronounce, withouten let,
When the parish is together met.

Thou shalt pronounce this hideous thing,
With cross and candle and bell-knelling.
Speak out clearly, fear not thou wound,
That all may thee understond. . . .

(In this manner should the sentence be pronounced:)

By the authority of the Father and of the Son and of the
Holy Ghost and of our Lady Saint Mary God's mother of
heaven, and all other Virgins, and Saint Michael [and all other
Angels, and St Peter] and all other Apostles and Saint Stephen
and all other Martyrs, and Saint Nicholas and all other Confessors and of all the holy Saints of heaven; we accursen and
bannen and departen from all good deeds and prayers of Holy
Church, and of all these Saints, and damn into the pain of hell,
all those that have done these articles that we have said before,
till they come to amendment: we accursen them by the authority of the court of Rome, within and without, sleeping or
waking, going and sitting, standing and riding, lying above
earth and under earth, speaking and crying and drinking; in
wood, in water, in field, in town; accursen them Father and
Son and Holy Ghost! accursen them Angels and Archangels
and all the nine Orders of Heaven! accursen them Patriarchs,
Prophets and Apostles and all God's Disciples and all holy
Innocents, Martyrs, Confessors, and Virgins, Monks, Canons,
Hermits, Priests and Clerks! that they have no part of mass
nor matins nor of none other good prayers that be done in holy
church nor in none other places, but that the pains of hell be
their meed with Judas that betrayed our Lord Jesus Christ!
and the life of them be put out of the book of life till they come
to amendment and satisfaction made! *Fiat, fiat. Amen.*

Then thou thy candle shalt cast to ground,
And spit thereto the samë stound.   [*hour*
And let also the bellës knell
To make their heartës the morë grill.   [*afraid*

Myrc wrote also the *Liber Festivalis*, a book of sermons for the use of parish priests. Caxton printed a free version of this in 1483, and Pynson reprinted it in 1502. The following sermon for the dedication day of a church (the German *Kirchweih*) is taken from Pynson's edition, with a few corrections and additions from the MS. published in 1905 by the Early English Text Society.

116. THE HOUSE OF PRAYER

GOOD men and women, such a day [naming the day] ye shall have your dedication day, that is your church holy day, ye shall come to church and hear divine service in the worship of God for three causes the which the church is hallowed for; that is, for the church cleansing, for devout praying, and for the dead bodies burying. The first is for the church cleansing. The church is ordained for all the people that come thither should be in perfect charity and there meet with God, for God is ever there present. And when all the people come so together at this assignment, it pleaseth God much to hear them and hear good words in that place: but when the fiend seeth any man busy thereto, he is full sorry, and seeketh all the ways that he can or may to let him from the church, for they should not come to the presence of God. Then when holy fathers knew the malice of the fiend, they ordained the church to be hallowed, and so by good prayers the fiend is driven out, but if any cursed liver bring him in again that is out [of] charity or in deadly sin, [who] is with the fiend and the fiend with him. But, how the fiend is driven away by the hallowing, I will tell you by ensample that is written in *Legenda Aurea*. Saint Gregory saith in a book that is called [Dialogus]: On a time as a church was on hallowing, a swine ran among the people to and fro, and so ran out of the church door; and that was a fiend that ran away. But yet, the next night after, he came again and made such a noise as though all the church should have fallen down, and then came never more again. But there be many lewd people that say their prayers, they were as good at home as at church, but they err foul against the faith of holy church. For if there be any man or woman that hath a matter to speak with his good friend, and would fain have his intent, he will go home to his house goodly and lowly in hope to speed the better. Right so if any man would pray God devoutly he should come to church. There is God, for he that is in clean life and prayeth to God, he speaketh with Him; for many of you wot not how ye should pray. The setting of the church giveth you knowledge, for the church is set in the east; and so, when ye pray, set your hearts in the east, [thinking that Paradise is in the east, and] praying heartily for mercy with perfect charity; though ye be put out of your heritage by malice of the fiend that is enemy to your souls, for that we should not have the joy of paradise that he was in, and lost it by his pride. Also we lost it by our father's trespass, Adam. Let us think that Christ died in the east, and therefore let us pray busily into the east, that we may be of the number that He died for. Also let us [think] that He shall come out of the east to the doom; wherefore let us pray heartily to Him and busily that we may have grace of contrition in our hearts of our misdeeds, with shrift and satisfaction; that we may stand that day on the right hand of our Lord Jesus Christ, and so be of the number that shall be saved and come to everlasting bliss and joy, and that we may escape that horrible rebuke that shall be given to all them that shall be damned and go to everlasting pain, that will not be sorry and repent them and ask mercy in this world.

And thus for devout prayers holy church was ordained to be hallowed. For God saith thus, *Domus mea domus orationis vocabitur*, "Mine house is called a house of prayers," but it is now made an house of rowning,[1] whispering, crowing, clattering, scorning, tales and simple speaking, moving of vanity and many simple words and lewd. We read how St Gregory was at mass on a time and St Austin was his deacon and bade the people turn to the pope's blessing. Then he saw two women rowne together in the pope's chapel, and the fiend sat in their necks writing a great roll, and it lacked parchment, and he drew it out with his teeth; and so it fell out of his claws, and St Austin saw it and went and took it up. Then the pope was wroth and asked him why he laughed him to scorn; and he showed him what the fiend had written of the women. And

---

[1] Muttering.

then he came to the women and asked them what they had said all the Mass-time: and they said, "Our *Pater noster*." Then the pope bade read the roll to them that the fiend had written; and St Gregory read it, and there was never a good word therein. Then they kneeled down and asked mercy, and besought the pope to pray for them, and so he did, and brought them out of the fiend's books. Also holy church [is hallowed for the long resting]; for, when a man is dead, he is brought to the church to his rest. Sometime the people were buried at home, as poor people, and the rich were buried on the hill tops, and some at the foot of the hill in tombs made of rocks. But the savour was so great and grievous [to them that lived], that holy fathers ordained churchyards to bury the people in, for two causes. One is, to be prayed for as holy church useth. And another is, for the body shall lie there without travail; for the fiend hath no manner of power to anything within Christian burials, but if so be that the body be not worthy to be buried in such holy ground. For, as John Beleth telleth that, there should none other body be buried in the church, but if it be the patron that defend it from bodily enemies, or the parson, vicar, priest or clerk that defend the church from ghostly enemies with their prayers; for some have been buried there and cast out again on the morrow, and all the clothes left still in the grave. An angel came on a time to a warden of a church, and bade him go to the bishop and bid him cast out the body that he had buried there, or else he shall be dead [himself] within xxx days; and so he was, for he would not do as he was bode.

Also we read *in Gestis Romanorum* that an angel told an holy bishop [Eucharius] how that Charles the king of France was damned, for he took away the right of holy church that good people had given tofore; and bade him go and open his tomb and see it. Then the bishop took with him other people and opened the tomb, and there came out a great dragon and flew forth and left the tomb brenning within as it had been an oven mouth: and thus to bury in holy places is but little avail to them that be damned. Also there be many that walk on nights when they be buried in holy places, but that is not along of the fiend but of grace of God to get them help, and some be guilty and have no rest. It happened also beside the abbey of Lilleshall that four men stale an ox of the abbot's of the same place to their larder. And the abbot did a sentence cursed therefore, with the abbey; so three of them were shriven and asked mercy and were assoiled, but the fourth died and was not assoiled and had not forgiveness. So, when he was dead, the spirit went by night and feared all the people about, that after sun going down durst no man walk. Then, as the parish priest, [Sir Thomas Wodward,] went on a night with God's body to housel a sick man, this spirit went with him, and told him what he was and why he went, and prayed the priest to go to his wife, and they should go both to the abbot and make him amends for his trespass, and pray him for the love of God of forgiveness, and so to assoil him; for he might have no rest. Anon the abbot assoiled him, and he went to rest and joy for evermore. To the which joy and bliss bring us all He that died for us on the rood-tree. Amen.

Mr Shaw's brilliant play has attracted fresh attention to Joan of Arc and the Inquisition. His presentation of this latter subject, however interesting, will scarcely be taken as final; and readers may welcome fresh opportunities of judging for themselves.

Johann Nider studied at the Universities of Vienna and Cologne, became professor at Vienna, and prior of the Dominican convents at Nuremberg and at Bâle. He distinguished himself as preacher and as inquisitor. In 1431 he was called as a representative to the General Council of Bâle, and entrusted later with an important embassy on behalf of that Council. His *Formicarius* and *Preceptorium* show him as a learned, pious, and naturally kind-hearted man; but he was also a zealous witch-finder. I subjoin here his account of St Joan and of other unnamed visionaries of his time; they are of great interest as showing the ideas of a German inquisitor, who had far better sources of information than most of his contemporaries, as to the action of his fellow-inquisitors in France. Both Extracts are taken from the edition of *Formicarius* published at Douai in 1602. Nider wrote the book between 1431, when he joined the Council of Bâle, and his death in 1438; St Joan was burned in May 1431.

116 A. JOAN OF ARC
(p. 385.)

PUPIL. In your opinion, have some good men been deceived by sorceresses or witches in our own day?

Master. In what here follows, I suspend my judgment;

but I will tell you what is repeated by public rumour and report. We have in our days the distinguished professor of divinity, brother Heinrich Kaltyseren, Inquisitor of Heretical Pravity. Last year, while he was exercising his inquisitorial office in the city of Cologne, as he himself told me, he found in the neighbourhood a certain maiden who always went about in man's dress, bore arms and dissolute garments[1] like one of the nobles' retainers; she danced in dances with men, and was so given to feasting and drink that she seemed altogether to overpass the bounds of her sex, which she did not conceal. And because at that time, (as, alas! even to-day) the see of Trèves was sorely troubled by two rivals contending for the bishopric, she boasted that she could and would set one party upon the throne, even as Maid Joan, of whom I shall presently speak, had done shortly before with Charles king of France, by confirming him in his kingdom. Indeed, this woman claimed to be that same Joan, raised up by God. One day therefore, when she had come into Cologne with the young count of Württemberg, who protected and favoured her, and there, in the sight of the nobles, had performed wonders which seemed due to magic art, she was at last diligently scrutinized and publicly cited by the aforesaid inquisitor, in order that she might be examined. For she was said to have cut a napkin in pieces, and suddenly to have restored it whole in the sight of the people; to have thrown a glass against the wall and broken it, and to have repaired it in a moment, and to have shown many such idle devices. But the wretched woman would not obey the commands of the Church; the count protected her from arrest and brought her secretly out of Cologne; thus she did indeed escape from the inquisitor's hands but not from the sentence of excommunication. Thus bound under curse, she quitted Germany for France, where she married a certain knight, to protect herself against ecclesiastical interdict and the sword. Then a certain priest, or rather pimp, seduced this witch with talk of love; so that she stole away with him at length and went to Metz, where she lived as his concubine and showed all men openly by what spirit she was led.

[1] Fifteenth-century moralists are always severe, and not altogether without reason, upon the prevailing fashion of doublet and hose.

Moreover, there was lately in France, within the last ten years, a maid of whom I have already spoken, named Joan, distinguished, as was thought, both for her prophetic spirit and for the power of her miracles. For she always wore man's dress, nor could all the persuasions of any doctors [of divinity] bend her to put these aside and content herself with woman's garments, especially considering that she openly professed herself a woman and a maid. "In these masculine garments," she said, "in token of future victory, I have been sent by God to preach both by word and by dress, to help Charles, the true king of France, and to set him firm upon his throne from whence the king of England and the duke of Burgundy are striving to chase him"; for, at that time, those two were allied together, and oppressed France most grievously with battle and slaughter. Joan, therefore, rode constantly like a knight with her lord, predicted many successes to come, was present at some victories in the field, and did other like wonders, whereat not only France marvelled, but every realm in Christendom. At last this Joan came to such a pitch of presumption that, before France had been yet recovered, she already sent threatening letters to the Bohemians, among whom there were then a multitude of heretics. Thenceforward layfolk and ecclesiastics, Regulars and Cloisterers began to doubt of the spirit whereby she was ruled, whether it were devilish or divine. Then certain men of great learning wrote treatises concerning her, wherein they expressed not only diverse but also adverse opinions as to the Maid. But, after that she had given great help to king Charles, and had confirmed him for some years upon his throne, then at last, by God's will, as it is believed, she was taken in arms by the English and cast into prison. A great multitude were then summoned, of masters both in Canon and in Civil Law, and she was examined for many days. And, as I have heard from Master Nicolas Amici,[1] Licentiate of Theology, who was ambassador for the University of Paris, she at length confessed that she had a familiar angel of God, which, by many conjectures, and proofs,

---

[1] This seems a scribal error for Nicolas Midi, who is among the Parisian masters named in the proceedings of May 12th, May 23rd, etc.: *e.g.* T. Douglas Murray, *Jeanne d'Arc*, pp. 119–121.

and by the opinion of the most learned men, was judged to be an evil spirit; so that this spirit rendered her a sorceress; wherefore they permitted her to be burned at the stake by the common hangman; and the king of England gave a like account of this story, at great length, in a letter to our emperor Sigismund. At this same time two women arose near Paris, preaching publicly that they had been sent by God to help Maid Joan; and, as I heard from the very lips of the aforesaid Master Nicolas, they were forthwith arrested as witches or sorceresses by the Inquisitor for France, and examined by many Doctors of Theology, and found at length to have been deceived by the ravings of the evil spirit. When therefore one of these women saw that she had been misled by an angel of Satan, she relinquished that which she had begun, by the advice of her masters, and, as was her duty, abjured her error forthwith. But the other abode in her obstinacy and was burned.

Pupil. I cannot sufficiently marvel how the frail sex can dare to rush into such presumptuous things.

Master. These things are marvellous to simple folk like thee; but they are not rare in the eyes of wise men. For there are three things in nature, which, if they transgress the limits of their own condition, whether by diminution or by excess, attain to the highest pinnacle whether of goodness or of evil. These are, the tongue, the ecclesiastic, and the woman; all these are commonly best of all, so long as they are guided by a good spirit, but worst of all if guided by an evil spirit.

116B. TORTURE AND EVIDENCE
(p. 226.)

Master. Hear, therefore, what befel a certain woman whom I saw at Regensburg in the days of this present Council of Bâle [*i.e.* after 1431], and whom I helped to examine. She was an unmarried girl, nor had she ever a husband, nor was she suspected of incontinence; but she had often changed her abode from city to city, from house to house, and this had gone on for very many years. Then, at the age of about fifty-three, she came to Regensburg, where she uttered certain very incautious words concerning the Rule of the Faith; on which account she was accused before the vicar of the bishop of Regensburg, who clapt her into prison. Meanwhile there came the lord John de Polomar, archdeacon of Barcelona, as envoy of the said General Council in the matter of the Bohemian [rebellion]; a man full of all devotion, and singularly learned both in Canon and in Civil Law; I was his companion and colleague in those days upon the same mission. Therefore we were called in to the examination of the said woman, wherein she was daily proved, and found to be in many errors; yet she seemed to have no hurt in her brain that would cause defect of reason, for she answered very astutely to each objection made against her, and, when we questioned her, she answered with great deliberation and caution to avoid contradicting herself. For she said that she had had a spirit of God, or divine revelations; she refused obedience to the pope in matters which he had ill disposed; she affirmed herself more blessed than the chiefs of the Apostles had been in this present life; she believed herself inerrant or impeccable, and, in short, she asserted both in word and by signs of her head that she was the mother of the whole Church of Christ, which was represented at this Council of Bâle. I therefore, and many who were present, strove by persuasive words from Holy Scripture to get these wayward thoughts out of the woman's head; but there we profited nothing; for she answered boldly that she knew she was in no error with regard to the aforesaid matters, but rather that her examiners erred; and thus she showed herself ready to go through fire in defence of her own truth. When we saw this, the above-mentioned archdeacon said unto the Doctors both of Divinity and of other Faculties, whereof there were many present: "Ye shall see that *vexation alone shall make* her *understand* [Is. xxviii, 19]; wherefore it is necessary that she be racked by the torture of public justice, somewhat slowly in proportion as her sex may be able to endure it; but you" (this he said secretly to me and to my companion in the [Dominican] Order, a certain very devout and learned Lector) "show in this woman's sight that you will not be present at her torture, and, if you please, absent yourselves, in order that her goodwill towards you may the more endure, and thus, when she hath been humbled by torture, you will then be the better fitted to convert her." So we did, and all things were done as I have described. And they asked of her, while she was being tortured, from whom she had learned her errors and whether she had any disciple or accomplice therein; for on these points she had never before given anything but denial, saying that no man had taught her these errors, nor had she taught any woman, but that she had believed them silently in her own heart, taught (as she said) by an angel or by the Spirit of God. Therefore, having been tortured for a little while, she added nothing new, confessed no man's guilt but her own, and abode constantly by her assertions. And I think she spake truth; yet she was much humbled by the vexation of her limbs; wherefore she was brought back to her prison-tower and, at the archdeacon's bidding, my companion and I visited the wretched woman that same evening. She could scarce stir for pain; but when she saw us she broke into loud lamentations, and told us in good faith how grievously she had been hurt. So we, considering that she had been humbled, and that she had a good opinion of us, told her many stories to show how many eminent and learned men had been deceived by incautious revelations and misled by the angel of Satan; and we adduced many citations from Holy Scripture to show how frail is the female sex when unaided. Then, by Christ's grace, she began to change her mind for the better, and to promise that she would follow me and my companion in all things. Therefore she believed herself to have been deceived, and of her own accord she made sacramental confession to me of all that she had done from her youth up, and showed herself ready to revoke her error publicly and to repent. Thus on the third day after, before the whole city of Regensburg, while many wept for joy and compassion, she performed all that I have said.

LIFE IN THE MIDDLE AGES

No mere extracts can do justice to St Bernardino's mission-sermons, yet no book of this kind could be complete without some specimens. The following are taken from the course of 45 sermons preached in the great public square of his native Siena during August and September of the year 1427, and in the 48th year of his age. How these sermons were recorded, the writer of the *Prologue* tells us himself.[1] "Moreover, how well-pleasing and acceptable to God were the labours which the Saint endured for His honour and to the profit of his fellows, is shown among other things by this present Book, which, as it setteth a new style and rule for preachers, so God hath willed that, (as it were beyond all fashions hitherto established,) these sermons should be collected and written for the love and increase of devotion. Wherefore the great and mighty God inspired one Benedetto di Maestro Bartolomeo, citizen of Siena and shearman of cloth; who, having a wife and many children, few worldly goods and much virtue, and leaving for that time his daily work, gathered and wrote these present sermons word by word, not omitting a single word which he did not write even as the Saint preached it....And, that ye may note the virtues and graces of this shearman Benedetto, as he stood at the sermon he would write with a style on waxen tablets; and then, when the preaching was ended, he would return to his workshop and commit to paper all that he had already written on the aforesaid tablets: so that on the same day, before setting himself to his own work, he had twice written the sermon. Whosoever will take good heed of this, shall find it as marvellous in performance as generous in conception, that within so brief a space he should have written so full a matter twice over, not leaving one syllable unwritten—nay, not the slightest—of all that fell from that sacred mouth, as may be manifestly seen in this present Book."

The reporter does in fact note even the preacher's interjections, the occasional protests of his hearers, and the casual interruptions natural to these open-air sermons—"You there, by the fountain, selling your wares there, move off and sell them elsewhere! Don't you hear, you there by the fountain?"—"Let us wait till that bell has stopped."—"Give it to that dog! send him off! send him that way! give it him with a slipper!... That's it; when one dog is in trouble all the rest fall upon him! Enough now, let him go" (II, 270; III, 305, 405).

Many brief extracts from the sermons are given in Paul Thureau-Dangin's entertaining biography (*St Bernardin de Sienne*: not very adequately translated into English by Baroness von Hügel). Those which I give here are as continuous as possible, from the five sermons on Marriage and Widowhood, which not only show the saint at his best as a stylist, but perhaps throw more light on medieval conditions than any others.

[1] See page 4 of *Le Prediche Volgari di San Bernardino da Siena*. Ed. L. Banchi (3 vols., Siena, 1880). A far greater number of Latin skeletons for sermons, drawn up by the saint himself, may be found in his collected works (ed. Père de la Haye. Paris, 1636, and Lyons, 1650). These also are full of significant passages, of which I have room here for one only.

117. WIVES AND WIDOWS

(Extracts from Sermons XVIII–XXII, *Thou shalt love thy neighbour as thyself*. Luke x, 27.)

WE have to speak this morning of the love and affection that the man should bear to his wife, and she to her husband.... She who is wise hath brought her daughter to this morning's sermon: she who is but so-so, hath left her in bed. O! how much better hadst thou done to bring her to hear this true doctrine! But to the point.

Let us see this morning the three foundations of my discourse. The first is called *Profit*, the second *Pleasure*, and the third *Honesty* or *Virtue*, which is all one....

Let us begin with the first, with Profit. If a thing be of little profit, thou lovest it little.... See now the world's love: do two vicious folk love each other?—Yea indeed.—Why then?—for some profit that they find. O worldlings, if the profit be small, small shall be the friendship betwixt you! Thou shopman, doth such and such an one come and get him hosen at thy shop?—Yes—Lovest thou him?—Yes—Wherefore? for thine own profit, I say. For, were he to go to another shop, thou wouldst have no more profit of him, and no more friendship. So also with the barber: take away the profit, and thou hast taken the friendship. Why, if one be a barber, and another go to be shaven of him, and the barber flay his cheek, be sure that he would lose all love for him, and go thither no more. Why then? Because the man is neither profitable in his eyes, nor pleasant, nor honest. I knew a man who was at a barber's shop for the shaving, and who cried, "Ha, what dost thou?" "What do I?" quoth the barber; "why, I shave thee." "Nay," (quoth the other) "thou flayest me rather!" Let this suffice for the matter of Profit.

Now let us add Pleasure to Profit, as with the man who entertaineth a mistress that keepeth his house, washeth for him, cooketh for him, layeth his table and so forth; and with all this profit he hath also the pleasure of the flesh: all the more is their friendship. Yet if she be of swinish nature, unkempt, unwashed, careless of her household, then is the love and friendship so much the less. Well and good for a while; but presently, if she fall sick, to the hospital she goeth! Why shouldst thou make bile for her sake? gone is all thy love, for thou hast neither pleasure nor profit from her.... This is no true love: true love should be riveted by the three corners: true love is as God's love, which hath in itself Profit and Pleasure and Honesty to boot.... Moreover, each should seek above all for goodness [in his spouse], and then for other advantages; but goodness first, goodness first of all. Consider now and think of such as choose their wives for other reasons; for example, of such as take a wife for her good dowry's sake; if then they be affianced, and the dowry come not, what (thinkest thou) shall be the love betwixt them both? A love stuck together with spittle! Nay, even though the dowry come in due time, yet is this an inordinate love, for thou hast not looked to the true aim; many a time hath money driven men to do many things whereof they have afterwards bitterly repented. Wherefore I say to you, lady, take not for thine husband the man who would fain take thy money and not thy self; take rather him who would take thee first and afterwards thy money with thee; for if he love thy money more than thee, thou art in evil case.... Behold! I am neither Pope nor Emperor; would that I were! This I say, for that I would proclaim a custom, if I could, that all women should go dressed in one fashion, even as the Roman women who all go dressed in linen; for their magnificence they all wear white linen, on back and head, the wives of princes no less than other women. And when they go mourning, they go all clad in sombre colours; there, truly, is a fashion that pleaseth me well. When they go to pardons, they go in light attire: no labour of drawn thread in their garments, no spoiling of the stuff with snippings and slashings, no such spoiling of good cloth to make their bravery! Wherefore I say to thee, lady, take no husband who loveth thy stuff more than thy body.... Hath the man gotten the stuff without other goodness or virtue?—Yes—Then, when the woman cometh to her husband's house, the first greeting is, "Thou art come in an evil hour"; if she hear it not in word, yet at least in deed, for the man's one thought was to have her dowry.... Wherefore, ye ladies who have daughters to marry, see to it that they have the dowry of virtue to boot, if ye would have them beloved of their husbands.... Are the occasions of love but slender? then shall the love itself be slender. Dost thou know their nature? for example, knowest thou the nature of mine host's love for the wayfarer? The traveller cometh, and saith: God save thee, Host!—Welcome, sir—Hast thou aught to eat?—Yea, truly—Then cook me a cabbage-soup and two eggs—The meal is eaten and paid, the traveller goeth on his way, and no sooner is his back turned than that friendship is forgotten: while the eggs are yet in his belly, that friendship is already past. For it was riveted at no corner; such friendships are as frail as a pear-stalk: shake the tree, and the pears will straightway fall; there is no strong bond of love to hold them. If the friendship be frail, small is the love; if the pleasure be small, small again the love; if there be little virtue, slight love again!...

Wherefore I bid you all, men and women, follow virtue, that your love may be founded on these three things, Profit, Pleasure, and Honesty; then shall true friendship reign among you. And when ye have these three things, hear what David saith of you; "Thy wife shall be as a fruitful vine, on the sides of thine house." Lo! all these three things are here. First, Honesty: *thy wife*—thine own wedded wife. Secondly, Pleasure; *as a vine*—how delightful a thing is a vine at the door of a house! Thirdly, Profit, *a fruitful vine*—rich in grapes and profitable; from which three things groweth and endureth true love between man and woman conjoined by the sacrament of Holy Matrimony: whereof I know twelve reasons, four to each point. See now, and learn them. Four, I say, are the reasons under honesty, and four under pleasure, and four under profit.

The first four, of honesty, ye shall learn to-morrow, when I shall speak of the sacrament of marriage; and I believe that, when I shall have preached to you of the right deeds of matrimony, seeing that ye have not done them, ye shall all shrive yourselves again; for ye have committed many sins which ye have never confessed. To-morrow, therefore, thou shalt see whether any bag of sins be left, and thou shalt hear into what sins I shall enter, as a cock goeth upon his dunghill. Have ye ever noted the cock when he cometh upon the dung? how daintily he goeth, with his wings spread aloft far from defilement, that he may fly to his post! So will I do; as a cock upon the dunghill, so will I enter thereupon; wherefore I bid you bring your daughters to-morrow, for I promise you that I believe ye have never heard a more profitable sermon. I say not [only] that your married daughters should come, I say all, both married and to marry; and in my sermon I will speak so honestly as to avoid all defilement; even the very least!—I misdoubt me sore of you; I believe so few are saved among those who are in the married state, that, of a thousand marriages, nine hundred and ninety-nine (methinks) are marriages of the devil. Ah me! deem not that Holy Matrimony is an asses' affair; when God ordained it, He ordered it not that ye should wallow therein as the swine wallow in the mire. Thou shalt come to-morrow and know the truth.—But to my subject again, and to my first four reasons; take them with discretion; 'tis a sacred matter. And I say that there are many friars who say "would that I had taken a wife!" Come to-morrow, and thou shalt say the contrary of this. I say then, there are four reasons that make for the honesty of this God-ordained marriage. Hast thou noted, when the pack sitteth ill [on a mule] and the one side weigheth more than the other? Knowest thou that a stone is laid on the other side that it may sit straight? so I say of matrimony: it was ordained that the one might aid the other in keeping the burden straight. And mark me, women, I hold with you so far as to say that ye love your husbands better than they love you.

First reason: the spouse thou hast is the spouse ordained for thee by God. Second reason: she is espoused to thee by plighted faith. Third reason: thou shouldest love her after Christ's example. Fourth: for her own tried virtue.

First, she hath been ordained for thy spouse by God, Who ordained this from all eternity [Genesis ii, 18 and i, 28; Matt. xix, 6]. . . .

Secondly, espoused by plighted faith. Seest thou not that, when thou consentest to matrimony, a sign is given thee, to last thy whole life long? Thou, woman, receivest the ring from thy spouse, which ring thou bearest on thy finger, and thou settest it on that finger which hath a vein running straight to the heart, in token that thy heart consenteth to this marriage; and thou shouldst never be espoused but for thy consentient *Yes*....

Thirdly, marriage is love. What saith Paul in the fifth chapter of his epistle to the Ephesians?—"Husbands, love your wives as Christ also loved the Church."... Wouldst thou have a faithful wife? Then keep faith with her. Many men would fain take a wife and can find none; knowst thou why? The man saith: I must have a wife full of wisdom—and thou thyself art a fool. This sorteth not: he-fool sorteth well with she-fool.—How wouldst thou have thy wife?—I would have her tall—and thou art a mere willow-wren; this sorteth not. There is a country where women are married by the ell-yard. It came to pass that one of these people wanted a wife, and would fain see her first: so the girl's brothers brought him to see her, and she was shown to him without shoes or head-gear; and, measuring her stature, he found her tallest of all the maidens, and he himself was one of those puny weaklings! In short, they asked of him, "Well, is she to thy mind?" "Yea, truly, she pleaseth me well." But she, seeing how miserable was his presence, said, "Yet art *thou* not to *my* mind." Lo, was that not right?—But to my point again. How wouldst thou have this thy wife?—I will have her an honest woman— and thou art dishonest: that again is not well. Once more how wouldst thou have her?—I would have her temperate—and thou art never out of the tavern: thou shalt not have her! O, how wouldst thou have this wife of thine?—I would not have her gluttonous—and thou art ever at thy *fegatelli*:[1] that is not well. I would have her active—and thou art a very sluggard. Peaceful—and thou wouldst storm at a straw if it crossed thy feet. Obedient—and thou obeyest neither father nor mother nor any man; thou deservest her not. I would not have a cock —well, thou art no hen. I would have her good and fair and wise and bred in all virtue.—I answer, if thou wouldst have her thus, it is fitting that thou shouldst be the same; even as thou seekest a virtuous, fair and good spouse, so think

---

[1] Slices of pig's liver, wrapped in the fat of the caul, and roasted brown.

likewise how she would fain have a husband prudent, discreet, good, and fulfilled of all virtue. . . .

And now to my second head, of Pleasure. . . . Read Paul in the fifth chapter of his *Ephesians*; "he that loveth his wife, loveth himself."—How may this be?—Have I not already told thee that she was made of his own flesh, and by God's hand? . . . Wherefore, in the teeth of all filthy revilers, I hold with the women, and say that woman is cleaner and more precious in her flesh than man; and if a man hold the contrary, I say that he lieth in his throat, and will prove it against him. Wilt thou see? Why, tell me, did not God create man out of clay? —Yes—then, O ladies, the reason is as clear as day! For woman was made of [Adam's] flesh and bone, so that she was made of more precious things than thou. Lo! thou mayest see a daily proof how the woman is cleaner and daintier than thou. Let a man and a woman wash as well as they can or may; and, when they are thus washed, let each take clean water and wash again, and then note which of the two waters is the dirtier, and thou shalt see that the man's is far fouler than the woman's. Why is this? Why, wash a lump of clay and see the water that cometh therefrom, and see how foul it is. Again, wash a rib with the flesh thereunto appertaining, and the water will indeed be somewhat foul, yet not so foul as that wherein thou hast washed the clay. Or, to put it better, wash an unbaked brick and thou shalt make nought but broth: wash a bone, and thou shalt make none such. So say I of man and woman in their nature and origin: man is of clay, but woman is of flesh and bone. And in proof of the truth of this, man, who is of clay, is more tranquil than woman, who is of bone; for bones are always rattling.

For ye women—shame upon you, I say—for while I say my morning mass ye make such a noise that methinks I hear a very mountain of rattling bones, so great is your chattering! One crieth: Giovanna! another, Caterina! another, Francesca! Oh, the fine devotion that ye have to hear mass! To my own poor wit, it seems sheer confusion, without devotion or reverence whatsoever. Do ye not consider how we here celebrate the glorious Body of Christ, Son of God, for your salvation? Ye should therefore sit here so quiet that none need say *hush*! But here cometh Madonna Pigara, and will by all means sit in front of Madonna Sollecita.[1] No more of this! first at the mill, first grind: take your seats as ye come, and let none come hither before you.—Now to my point again....

CONJUGAL AMENITIES

From a MS. of 1456 in A. Schultz, *Deutsches Leben*, fig. 344.

Now to my third division, of Profit, under four heads.... Firstly, the preciousness of fruit. O how precious are the fruits of a good woman, as the Scripture saith: *By their fruits you*

[1] *I.e.* Mrs Slow and Mrs Worry. The whole scene is a vivid commentary on Chaucer's *Prologue*, 449, and *Cant. Tales*, B., 3091. For the Proverb, see Wife of Bath's Prologue (*C.T.*, D., 389).

shall know them: . . . Many consider not the value of a boy or a girl, and many folk who have them hold them of little worth, and when their wife brings forth a little girl, they cannot suffer her, so small is their discretion! Why, there are men who have more patience with a hen, which layeth a fresh egg daily, than with their own wedded wife: and sometimes the hen may break a pipkin or a drinking-vessel, and the man will not strike her, all for love of her egg and for fear of losing the profit thereof. O madmen thrice worthy of chains! that cannot bear with a word from their wife, who beareth such fair fruit, but if she speak a word more than he thinketh fit, forthwith he taketh the staff and will beat her; and the hen, cackling all day long without end, thou hast patience with her for her paltry egg's sake; yet the hen will perchance do thee more harm in broken vessels than she is worth; and yet thou bearest with her for her egg's sake! Many a cross-grained fellow, seeing perchance his wife less clean and delicate than he would fain see her, smiteth her without more ado; and meanwhile the hen may befoul the table, and he will suffer it. Dost thou not consider thy duty in this matter? Dost thou not see the pig, again, squeaking and squealing all day long, and always befouling thy house? Yet thou bearest with him until he be ripe for the slaughter. Thou hast patience with him, only for the profit of his flesh, that thou mayest eat thereof. Consider now, wicked fellow, consider the noble fruit of the woman, and have patience; not for every cause is it right to beat her. No!—There, enough now of this first point. . . .

The third point is the remembrance of her necessity. . . . Wherefore, as thou seest that thy wife endureth travail on every side, therefore thou, O husband, if she fall into any need, be sure thou help her to bear her pain. If she be with child or in childbirth, aid her so far as in thee lieth, for it is thy child also. Let all help her whereinsoever they may. Mark her well, how she travaileth in childbirth, travaileth to suckle the child, travaileth to rear it, travaileth in washing and cleaning by day and by night. All this travail, seest thou, is of the woman only, and the man goeth singing on his way. There was once a baron's lady who said to me: "Methinks the dear Lord our Master doth as He seeth good, and I am content to say that

He doth well. But the woman alone beareth the pain of the children in many things—bearing them in her body, bringing them into the world, ruling them, and all this oftentimes with grievous travail. If only God had given some share to man— if only God had given him the child-bearing!" Thus she reasoned; and I answered: "Methinks there is much reason on thy side."—Now to our point again!

Some men say, "What need have I to take a wife? I have no labour; I have no children to break my sleep at night; I have the less expense by far. Why should I undertake this travail? If I fall ill, my servants will care for me better than she would." Thus thou sayest, and I say the contrary: for a woman careth better for her husband than any other in the world. And not him alone, but the whole house, and all that needeth her care. Hear what Solomon saith: "He that possesseth a good wife, beginneth a possession."—"Well," saith another, "I will not take a wife, but rather keep a mistress; then at least I shall be cared for, and my house and my household."—Nay, I tell thee: for thus the woman will be set on laying up for herself alone: all her study will be of stealing; and, seeing things go ill, she careth not, but saith within herself: "Why should I pain myself to look so closely into every little matter? When I am grown old, I shall no longer be welcome in this house." . . . Wherefore, I say, it is better to take a wife . . . and when thou hast taken her, take heed to live as every good Christian should live. Dost thou know who knoweth this? That man knoweth it who hath her, the good housewife, that ruleth the whole household well. She seeth to the granary, she keepeth it clean, that no defilement may enter therein. She keepeth the jars of oil, and noteth them well:—This jar is to use, and that jar is to keep. She guardeth it, that naught may fall therein, and that neither dog nor other beast come nigh it. She setteth all her study and all her care that the jars be not spilt. She ordereth the salt meats, first in the salting and afterward in the keeping, she cleanseth them and ordereth them:—This here is to sell, and that there is to keep. She seeth to the spinning, and then to the making of linen cloth from the yarn. She selleth the bran, and with the money she buyeth yet more cloth. She giveth heed to the wine-casks, lest their hoops should break or the wine leak at any point. She provideth the household with all things. She doth not as the hired servant, who stealeth of all that passeth through her hands, and who careth not for the things as they go away; for the stuff is not her own, therefore she is slow to pain herself and hath no great love for them. If a man have neither wife nor other to rule his household, knowest thou how it is with the house? I know, and I will tell thee. If he be rich, and have plenty of grain, the sparrows and the moles eat their fill thereof. It is not set in order, but all so scattered abroad that the whole house is the fouler for it. If he have oil, it is all neglected and spilt; when the jars break and the oil is spilled, he casteth a little earth on the spot, and all is done! And his wine? When at last he cometh to the cask, he draweth the wine without further thought; yet perchance the cask showeth a crevice behind, and the wine wasteth. Or again a hoop or two is started, yet it may go its way for him; or the wine turneth to vinegar, or becometh utterly corrupt. In his bed, knowest thou how he sleepeth? He sleepeth in a pit, even as the sheets chance to have been tumbled upon the bed; for they are never changed until they are torn. Even so in his dining-hall; here on the ground are melon-rinds, bones, peelings of salad, everything left lying on the ground almost without pretence of sweeping. Knowest thou how it is with his table? The cloth is laid with so little care that no man ever removeth it till it be covered with filth. The trenchers are but sparingly wiped, the dogs lick and wash them. His pipkins are all foul with grease: go and see how they stand! Knowest thou how such a man liveth? even as a brute beast. I say that it cannot be well for a man to live thus alone—Ladies, make your curtsey to me....

The next sermon is on the same text and the same subject: though specially intended for the daughters, it is still more outspoken than its predecessor.

My beloved, seeing that we showed yesterday the love which ought to be between wife and husband, yet we showed it not fully: for sometimes their love of each other will become carnal and displeasing to God. Wherefore we will speak this morning of the manner in which each ought to love the other. . . . For ignorance excuseth not from sin. . . . So for example of a priest who undertaketh to do his priestly work, that is, to consecrate the Lord's Body, and knoweth not the manner nor the words of consecration, how wouldst thou hold this man excused? Nay, verily, he sinneth even in that he doeth not as he should. Hear now what befel once upon a time; for this is to our present point. There were two priests who spake together, and the one said unto the other, "How sayest thou the words of consecration for Christ's Body?" "I" (quoth the other) "I say *Hoc est corpus meum.*" Then began they to dispute one with the other: "Thou sayest not well"—"Nay, it is thou who sayest ill"—and, as they disputed thus, there came another priest to whom they told the whole matter, and who said: "Neither the one saith well, nor the other, for the true words are: *Hoc est corpusso meusso*": and proceeded by demonstration: "Thou seest how he saith *corpusso*, wherefore the adjective should be *meusso*; therefore (I say) henceforth say ye nought else but: *"Hoc est corpusso meusso."* To which speech the others consented not: wherefore they accorded together to ask a parish priest hard by, going to him of set purpose and laying the case before him. Then the parish priest answering said: "Ha, what needeth all this ado? I go to it right simply; I say an *Ave Maria* over the Host!"—Now, I ask thee, are those men excused? Seest thou not that they make men adore as God a mere piece of bread? Be sure that each of them committeth a most deadly sin, seeing that it was their bounden duty to do after the manner which Jesus Christ hath ordained to Holy Church. So I say also that, whatsoever a man doeth, it is his bounden duty to know all that pertaineth to that thing. . . . But the mother sinneth more than the daughter, if she teach not as she ought. I say that the mother should teach her under pain of mortal sin; for otherwise she setteth her daughter in grievous peril, together with her husband. . . . Moreover, ye confessors, whensoever such folk come into your hands, take heed that ye admonish them shrewdly. For whence cometh this?—from not knowing that which they should know. In old days, this sacrament was wont to be held in the greatest devotion, and no girl went to her husband without confession and communion. Men had much more devotion to the sacraments than they have in these days. . . .

Moreover I say, thou art not excused by thine evil purpose: for there are some men and women who say they love not to hear such things in public sermons.—Why wilt thou not hear? —Because I would fain do after mine own fashion, and mine ignorance will hold me excused—That is as the prophet David saith: "He would not understand that he might do well": he would not hear, that he might do after his own will.—Oh (quoth he) I do it not through unwillingness to do well! These things are not lawful matter for sermons, therefore I will not hear—What! how then, if they are lawful to do, how (I say) is it not lawful for me to admonish thee? A hit, a palpable hit, in thy teeth! Knowest thou what? Thou art like unto Madonna Saragia.[1] Lo! I will tell thee what befel once upon a time in Siena. There was a lady called Madonna Saragia, who loved well those great cherries of the Mark. She had a vineyard that lay out there—you know, out towards the convent of Munistero. One May, therefore, when her farmer-bailiff came to Siena, Madonna Saragia asked him: "Hast thou then no cherries yet in the vineyard?" "O," quoth he, "I waited till they should be a little riper." And she: "See then that thou bring them on Saturday, or come not hither to Siena again!" The bailiff promised; and on the Saturday he took a great basket of cherries and came to Siena and brought them to the lady. When therefore she saw him, she made much of him, and took the basket. "Thrice welcome! Oh, how much good thou hast done me!" and, taking the basket apart into her private chamber, she began to eat the cherries by the handful; (they were fine and large, they were cherries of the Mark!) To be brief, she took a skin-full of the cherries. Then, when her husband came home to dinner, the lady took a little basket of these fruit, and laid them on the table, and said: "The bailiff is come, and hath brought us a few cherries." And when the meal was finished, she took these cherries and began to eat thereof, in the bailiff's presence. And as she ate,

---

[1] *I.e. Mrs Cherry.* Such nicknames are still common in Italy: one well-known citizen of a little Southern town has lately earned the singular gastronomical sobriquet of *Ceci (chick-peas).*

she took them one by one and made seven bites of each cherry; and in eating she said to the bailiff: "What eating is there of cherries out in the country?" "Lady," quoth he, "we eat them as ye ate even now in your room: we eat them by the handful!" "Ugh! la!" cried she, "How saith the fellow? fie on thee, knave!" "Lady," quoth he again, "we eat them even as I have said." . . .

Hereupon the saint goes on to comment on Rom. i, 27, 1 Thess. iv, 4, 1 Cor. vii, 4, Exodus xx, 14, and Ezekiel xviii, 6.

118. MEDIEVAL FREETHINKERS
(Bern. Sen. *Opp.* ed. de la Haye, vol. i, p. 83, 1.)

THE first pit of slime [Genesis xiv, 10] is incredulity or default of faith. For very many folk, considering the wicked life of monks and friars and nuns and clergy, are shaken by this—nay, oftentimes fail in faith, and believe in naught higher than the roof of their own house, not esteeming those things to be true which have been written concerning our faith, but believing them to have been written by the cozening invention of man and not by God's inspiration; having no faith in the divine Scriptures or in the holy Doctors, even as the Prophet testifieth concerning the unfaithful Christians of this present time, saying: "Nor were they counted faithful in his covenant." From hence it followeth that they believe not in the power of the keys, despise the sacraments of the church, hold that the soul hath no existence, neither shun vices nor respect virtues, neither fear hell nor desire heaven, but cling with all their hearts to transitory things and resolve that this world shall be their paradise. All floweth from this one source of incredulity; since they cannot distinguish betwixt the office of prelates and priests, and their vices. For albeit the life of many clerics be full of crimes, yet there resideth in them a holy and venerable authority, as will appear in my sermon next following.[1]

[1] Compare the complaint of Benvenuto da Imola, who was a professor at Bologna about the time of St Bernardino's birth. Commenting on Dante's mention of Priscian (*Inf.* xv, 106), he says "he was a monk and apostatized in order to gain greater fame and glory, as we oftentimes see now in the case of many men

Johann Busch was born at Zwolle in 1399. He showed brilliant scholarship as a boy; but as a youth he chose to join the same congregation of Austin Canons to which his contemporary Thomas à Kempis belonged. In 1440 he became Subprior of Wittenburg, and began his long and arduous career as reformer of monasteries under a commission from the Pope and the Council of Bâle. In this work he attained more success than any of his contemporaries except the distinguished Cardinal Nicolaus von Cusa. His chief writings were (i) a charming chronicle of the monastery of Windesheim, and (ii) the *Liber de Reformatione Monasteriorum*, a minute and often very humorous record of his life's work. The edition here used is that of K. Grube (Halle, 1887). A translation of it was begun, but never completed, in the *British Magazine* for April, 1841, etc.; and the reader may there find some strange things for which there is no place here. Miss Eckenstein's account of these visitations in her *Woman under Monasticism* is quite worthless; she takes it at second-hand from a not always trustworthy monograph by Karl Grube. See Eileen Power, *Medieval English Nunneries*, Camb. Univ. Press, 1922, pp. 670 ff.

119. A DETERMINED PREACHER

SIR GERARD DEBELER, my own preacher at Halle, whom I brought thither from Hildesheim, was a man of exceeding zeal for the people of God and well-beloved of them; oftentimes he preached to the people that they should keep God's commandments. For he preached three or four sermons on a single precept of our Lord, until all in his parish of St Mary the Virgin at the City Market should keep it effectually. And when some showed themselves too slow to begin keeping it, then he said publicly to all the folk of both sexes in congregation, "Wherefore are ye so slow to begin keeping this precept of God? Perchance ye may say: 'My father and mother were good folk, just and truthful and good Christians; I know that they have gone long since to the Kingdom of Heaven; why then are we now compelled so strictly to keep God's precepts, beyond what they then did?' Hear what I answer thereunto. Hast thou sealed letters to show that thy parents, who were so good, went indeed to heaven? I would gladly see them; but I trow ye have none such. Now I say to thee: If thy parents

who speak ill of the Faith that they may seem great philosophers; as though they believed that saying of Galen, that the Christians have few men of any account because they are involved in many errors" (*Comentum*, ed. Lacaita, vol. 1, p. 522). Janssen's implication that such freethought was born of Bible translations in the later Middle Ages is demonstrably false.

lived as thou now livest, and kept not God's commandments, then I have sealed letters to show that they are now burning in hell fire; and my letters are the missals that lie on the altar, wherein are written gospels which our Lord God Jesus Christ sealed as true with His own blood. For therein is written: *If thou wilt enter into life, keep the commandments;* and again, *If any one love Me, he will keep My word,* and many suchlike. Now such transgressors of God's commandments as died and deceased in their wicked sins are now in hell, as the Catholic Faith holdeth, and as Jesus Christ's gospel saith; but those who kept His commandments in this life, though their bodies be dead, yet in soul they now live with God in heaven, and at the resurrection of the dead they shall possess eternal life in body and soul, with God and the holy angels and all the saints. Think therefore where are now your parents who seemed to you so good according to this world; think thereon, and amend your lives!"

How much good that preacher did among the people at Halle by his notable sermons, I have told more fully above in the Reform of the Monastery of Neuwerk. He did not quote much of Scripture,[1] but went straight to the point and made it plain to all men's eyes, saying, "Thou with the long cloak and the parti-coloured hosen—thou Rathsherr there—thou rich man—thou poor man—what wilt thou say to these things when thou liest on thy back breathing forth thy ghost? Think these things over now beforehand, that thou mayest study to amend thy life and keep God's commandments strictly with all thy might."

120. EXORCISM BY COMMON SENSE
(*Lib. Ref.* III, 21, p. 701.)

ONCE as I went from Halle to Calbe, a man who was ploughing ran forth from the field and said that his wife was possessed with a devil, beseeching me most instantly that I would enter his house (for it was not far from our way) and liberate her from this demon. At last, touched by his prayers,

[1] A term which included not only the Bible, but Church Doctors, etc.

I granted his request, coming down from my chariot and following him to his house. When therefore I had looked into the woman's state, I found that she had many fantasies, for that she was wont to sleep and eat too little, whence she fell into feebleness of brain and thought herself possessed by a demon; yet there was no such thing in her case. So I told her husband to see that she kept a good diet, that is, good meat and drink, especially in the evening when she would go to sleep; "for then" (said I) "when all her work is over, she should drink what is called in the vulgar tongue *een warme iaute*, that is a quart of hot ale, as hot as she can stand, without bread but with a little butter of the bigness of a hazel-nut. And when she hath drunken it to the end, let her go forthwith to bed; thus will she soon get a whole brain again."

One of the Preacher's Manuals which became so popular in the later Middle Ages was entitled *Dormi Secure*. This brief appellation is explained by the sub-title of the book, which runs thus: "Sermons for Saints' Days throughout the year, very notable and useful to all priests, prelates, and chaplains. Which sermons are called *Dormi Secure*, or 'Sleep Without Care,' seeing that they can easily be incorporated without great study and preached to the people." There is a companion volume of *Dormi Secure* sermons for the regular Sundays of the year, with practically the same sub-title. The author was a Franciscan named John of Verden or Werden, who flourished according to Wadding in 1330 or, if we are to believe more recent students, a century later. The following Extract is from fol. xxi a of the edition published by Jehan Petit (Paris, 1517); the book passed through at least thirty editions.

Although the Church refused for centuries to pronounce upon the Immaculate Conception of the Virgin Mary, and the great schoolmen of the thirteenth century were against it, and the learned Dominican Order combated the doctrine almost to the last, yet the current of opinion among the masses ran more and more strongly in its favour, and this Extract exemplifies how popular preachers explained away the contrary decision of great Saints and Doctors in the past. The Preacher has just been attempting to show that even Mohammedans hold the doctrine of the Immaculate Conception, supporting this assertion by texts from the Koran which, even if genuine, are of course utterly beside the point. He then proceeds:

121. A SAINT IN PURGATORY

VERILY I say that the Virgin Mary was conceived without original sin; for this is confirmed by examples; and in especial by three examples which came to pass in the case of three great Doctors of holy Mother Church; to wit, Master Alexander Neckam,[1] the lord Cardinal Bonaventura, and St Bernard. First then this doctrine was confirmed and proved by a miraculous example which came to pass in Master Alexander Neckam's case; of whom we read that thrice in succession he proclaimed how he would determine [in the Schools] that the Blessed Virgin had been conceived in original sin; yet was he ever prevented by sickness. At length he purposed and promised finally to declare and determine this conclusion; yet once again, the night before, he fell into great sickness and suffering. Then he called upon the Blessed Virgin to succour him; in virtue of which invocation she came by night when all was wrapt in silence and only Neckam watched, saying unto him: "This sickness is fallen upon thee for that thou strivest to prove that I was conceived in original sin." Then she took a knife from her handmaiden and cut from the Master's side a great and foul inward ulcer; after which she took her needle and sewed up the whole wound with silken thread. Then, when the Blessed Virgin was gone, the Master found himself whole and sound; wherefore he called to the scholar who slept with him in his room, and learned more fully and perfectly how the matter stood. Therefore he afterwards put away that impious opinion of his, and wrote a great book how the Virgin had been conceived without any original sin. In which book he expounded of the Blessed Virgin Mary that text of the fourth Chapter of Solomon's Song, "Thou art all fair, O my love, and there is not a spot in thee," as showing that she had no spot either of original or of actual sin.

Secondly, the doctrine was proved by a miraculous example in the case of the lord Cardinal Bonaventura, because it is still maintained in Book III, Dist. IV, Quest. 2, r. 3 [of his Commentary on the Sentences] that the Virgin Mary was conceived in original sin. Wherefore there is related of him an event

[1] A distinguished English scholar who became Abbot of Cirencester and died in 1227. A MS. formerly in possession of the Earl of Arundel had the following entry: "In the month of September 1157 Prince Richard was born to Henry II at Windsor; and that same night saw the birth at St Albans of Alexander Neckam, whose mother suckled Richard at her right breast and Alexander at her left." Bonaventura is of course the Saint, who was only canonized in 1482.

which befel at Paris. A certain devout friar of the Brethren Minor[1] prayed frequently and devoutly every night in the choir. As he was thus in prayer, he heard a buzzing as it were of a fly, and marvelled what this might be, and what might be portended by such a sound at so unwonted a time. Then he listened more carefully; and for many nights he ever heard that same sound over the altar of the Virgin Mary. When therefore he had oftentimes heard this with much wonder, then he cried: "I adjure thee by our Lord Jesus Christ, tell me who thou art." Then he heard a voice saying, "I am Bonaventura." Whereunto he made answer, "O most excellent Master, how is it with you and wherefore make ye such a sound?" Then the other made answer, "It shall be well with me, who am of the number of such as shall be saved; nevertheless, seeing that I held that conclusion that the Blessed Virgin was conceived in original sin, therefore I endure this my purgatory and pain over the altar of the Blessed Virgin; and, after that I shall have been purged, I shall fly up to heaven." Wherefore Bonaventura may say that word of the Psalmist: "For this conclusion we are mortified all the day long."[2]

Thirdly, it hath been proved by the example of St Bernard's case, who held that the Blessed Virgin Mary was conceived in original sin. . . . Wherefore it is related of him that, after his death, he appeared to a certain man with a stain, and told how he bare that blemish for that he held the conception of the Blessed Virgin in original sin. Wherefore it hath been plainly proved by three examples that the glorious Virgin was conceived without original sin. For to this effect it is well said in St John's first epistle, the fifth chapter, "There are three that bear witness in heaven," to wit, in favour of the Virgin Mary, that she was conceived without original sin. And again in the third chapter of Daniel, "These three as with one mouth praised God," to wit, because He preserved His Mother from original sin.

[1] The Franciscans in general soon decided in favour of the popular opinion, and it was their support which did much to secure its final victory. It was all the more distressing to them that their great Doctor should have already pledged himself to the doctrine of St Bernard and other great theologians of an earlier time.

[2] Psalm xliii, 22, Vulg. The preacher has taken the liberty of altering *propter te* into *de illa conclusione*.

The Blessed James of the Mark—Beatus Jacobus de Marchia—was born in 1391 and died in 1476. After brilliant studies, he joined the Franciscans at the age of nineteen, was raised to the rank of Preacher in his Order, and preached almost daily for forty years, during thirteen of which he traversed the greater part of Europe, even as far as Scandinavia and Russia. In 1460 he was appointed Inquisitor; later on, he refused the Archbishopric of Milan. His missionary tours into outlying mountain villages brought him into contact with the Fraticelli—heretics bred of the persecutions to which the stricter Franciscans had been subjected by their laxer brethren —and, in spite of his naturally merciful disposition, he became their conscientious and relentless persecutor. The two following Extracts are from his voluminous Answer to an Open Letter which the Fraticelli had written in their own defence, and in which they insisted much on the grave suspicion of heresy against John XXII (see Extracts 96–7 above). The letter of the Fraticelli is published in the *Scelta di Curiosità Letterarie* (Bologna, 1865); the Answer of St James is in Baluze-Mansi, *Miscellanea*, vol. II, pp. 595 ff.: it was written after 1449, but probably not long after.

122. POPES AND HERESY
(p. 599.)

A N D again I say unto thee, [O heretic], that albeit certain Supreme Pontiffs have died in unfaith, yet thou shalt ever find that, when one Pope died in heresy, a Catholic Pope immediately succeeded him. Wherefore it cannot be found, in the whole series of the list of Supreme Pontiffs, that any two Popes were successively and immediately heretics; and thus it is not said that faith hath failed without qualification [*simpliciter*] in the order of Popes; since, when our Lord said to Peter, "I have prayed for thee, that thy faith fail not," he said it not only for him but for the whole Church. But ye short-sighted Michaelists[1] hold as heretics all the Popes who have succeeded the aforesaid John [XXII] and all who favour, believe in, or adhere to him; wherefore ye deceive yourselves and have become heretics.... (p. 601). Yet, supposing that a Pope were heretical, and not publicly condemned, still bearing his office; supposing that a simple person, not a public person, enquired of that Lord Pope concerning the unity of the faith, and the Pope then instructed him in that heresy which he himself held for

[1] Michael of Cesena, Minister-General of the Franciscans, had played a leading part in the revolt against John XXII.

a truth; then the man thus instructed, if he be not made conscious [of his error] from some other quarter, is not to be adjudged an heretic, seeing that he believeth himself to be instructed in the Catholic faith. If therefore the simple Brethren, and the rest of the clergy and laity who hear Pope John [XXII] proclaiming his own decrees [concerning the Poverty of Christ] as catholic,—even supposing that they were heretical—if these men, I say, have believed in them, they are not to be condemned as heretics, especially since they are considered by all to be in the majority; thou therefore, being a Michaelist, art thou not an heretic? For in a matter so weighty the Michaelists ought to have looked to the determination of the Holy Church, and more especially of the Roman Court,[1] to which it specially pertaineth to decide such points as concern the essentials of faith; but these [Fraticelli], with the rashness habitual to heretics, refer to themselves and to their own knowledge, thus plunging into heresy and apostasy.

123. THE ODOUR OF HERESY
(p. 600.)

BUT I desire thee to be won over to thine own salvation; wherefore know for certain that it is a property of the Catholic faith, which was in St Peter, to grow under persecution and oppression, and to wax more worthy. But the sect of Michaelists faileth and groweth more debased under persecution. For all Catholic Doctors attribute to the true Faith that it waxeth ever in tribulation and oppression, as is clear from the times of the martyrs, when a hundredfold more were converted than those who were slain; and the more the Church was oppressed, the more glorious she rose up again; wherefore that most excellent Doctor Hilary saith: "This is proper to the Church, that she conquereth when she is hurt; when she is rebuked, then she understandeth; when she hath abandoned, then doth she obtain." And Cassiodorus: "The Church of God hath this quality in especial, to flourish under persecution,

---

[1] *I.e.* the Pope in conjunction with his cardinals, to which latter body the writer has just before attributed the primary duty of correcting the Pope in case of error.

to grow in oppression, to conquer under injury, and to stand
all the firmer when men deem her overcome." So also Augustine (*De Civ. Dei*, cap. 71) and Gregory (*Moralia*, xviii,
13). Moreover it is yet more marvellous, as the aforenamed
Doctors assert, that the Church unresisting subdueth her persecutors, and prevaileth more without resistance than when
she withstandeth her adversaries; but this sect of Michaelists
had at first most mighty and powerful defenders; yet now it
hath but gross boors. Especially mayest thou see how all other
rites which do and did exist have taken their source and origin
from St Peter and his successors, but with the lapse of time
they have grown in riches by the dignity, wisdom, virtue, and
multitude of their adherents; while all other rites which were
not [founded] in St Peter and his Catholic successors have so
dwindled that no man is left in them who knew his own rite
and could defend it and was able even to expound it. . . . Therefore the Greeks, and all other sects which have departed from
the faith of Peter, have dwindled in wisdom, honour, and
power; and all other heretical sects (which up to St Augustine's time numbered two hundred, as he himself saith in his
Book of Heresies) have failed, and have all ended in lechery . . .
(610). Moreover, in God's Church there are always holy men
through whom God worketh many miracles; for ever [*apparent lacuna in text*] even as now at this present time God
hath raised twenty-three dead men through St Bernardino of
the Friars Observant of our Order, as approved by the com-
missaries deputed by the supreme Pontiffs of the Holy Roman
Church; thrice, at three different times, hath the Holy Roman
Church enquired into the miracles aforesaid, and innumerable
others which God worketh through His servant Brother Bernardino, as they have been received and approved by the Holy
Roman Church, and as I have seen with mine own eyes; as
appeareth also by the [votive] images of gold and silver that
hang in testimony of his miracles within the church of St
Francis at Aquila; so also of many other saints who have been
since John XXII, but whom ye condemn together with the
whole Church. And it is marvellous indeed that in the case
of all heretics and schismatics, since they have withdrawn from
the Church, God hath wrought no miracles among them (for

miracles, as Riccardus and Scotus say, are wrought by God for confirmation of faith in Him); but it is never found of you who make a church of your own, nor hath it ever been heard of that any of you have wrought any miracle, except that in burning they stink like putrid flesh.[1] Whereof ye have an example in Fabriano, while Pope Nicholas V was there; some of these heretics were burned, and the whole city stank for three days long; and this I know because I smelt the stench of them for those three days even in my convent; and—whereas I had persuaded them all to come back to the faith, all of whom returned and confessed and communicated, and wept tears of compunction, and were thus justified even though they had relapsed—yet one who was called Chiuso of Fabriano, the treasurer of those heretics, would never return. I testify before God that he never called upon God to help him, or the Virgin, or any Saint; nor did he pray that God would forgive his sins; but as one desperate and withered he continued saying: "The fire cannot burn me!" and I bear witness before God that he burned for three days long, while men brought fresh wood again and again! [The Saint goes on to accuse the Fraticelli of the same crimes which they themselves laid to the charge of the orthodox clergy.]

124. ENGLISH TAILS

(Caxton's *Golden Legend*, Temple Classics, vol. III, p. 201.)

AFTER this, St Austin entered into Dorsetshire, and came into a town whereas were wicked people who refused his doctrine and preaching utterly, and drove him out of the town, casting on him the tails of thornbacks, or like fishes; wherefore he besought almighty God to show His judgment on them, and God sent to them a shameful token; for the children that were born after in that place had tails, as it is said, till they had repented them. It is said commonly that this fell at Strood in Kent, but blessed be God at this day is no such deformity.[2]

---

[1] The *corrumpuntur* of the text is an evident slip for *comburuntur*.

[2] For this curious and widespread legend of English Tails, and the different causes assigned for the phenomenon by foreigners, see Dr George Neilson's *Caudatus Anglicus* (Edinburgh, 1896).

Johann Geiler, born at Kaisersberg near Schaffhausen in 1445, became Doctor of Theology at Bâle and Freiburg, but accepted, at the invitation of Bishop and Chapter, the Cathedral Preachership at Strasbourg (1478). Here his spiritual fervour, his hatred of abuses, and the raciness of his style, raised him to a unique position among contemporary preachers. He died at his work in 1510, looking forward to an impending catastrophe from which his strict orthodoxy shrank, while he fully recognized its necessity. Preaching before the Emperor Maximilian, a few years before his death, he cried: "Since neither Pope nor Emperor, kings nor bishops, will reform our life, God will send a man for the purpose. I hope to see that day...but I am too old. Many of you will see it; think then, I pray you, of these words." See L. Dacheux, *Jean Geiler*, Paris, 1876.

125. PROPHETS WITHOUT HONOUR

(Geiler, *Peregrinus*. Strasbourg, 1513. Mos. XVII.)

THIS much is certain, that all who would live piously in Christ Jesus suffer persecutions, (2 Thess. iii:) which is true of all Religious, Clerics, and Layfolk. Religious, I say; for if anyone in a monastery would fain keep the Rule, would fain be chaste, live continently, obey, and keep the ceremonies, then he is mocked by the rest.[1] "Lo!" say they, "our pietist would fain be wiser than all others; while so many learned men and luminaries of the world live thus, he alone striveth against them!" I confess indeed that these are luminaries of the world, but such as shine for themselves and their followers to everlasting damnation; 'tis great pity that any such should perish!...They say against such a pietist, in the words of the second chapter of Wisdom, "Come, let us lie in wait for him, because he is not to our turn and he is contrary to our doings!" Truly they say thus; for they stand round him as he sitteth among them like an owl among the birds, or Daniel among the lions, or Stephen among those that stoned him. Nor is it only there [in monasteries] but among clerics also it is the same, if any of the number wear the proper garments and tonsure, living without covetousness, content with a single benefice, chaste, avoiding the company of women, an almsgiver, charit-

---

[1] This is a frequent complaint in the later Middle Ages. The lax Religious, says St Catherine of Siena, "fall upon such as would fain keep their Rule, as ravening wolves upon lambs, scoffing and scorning them" (*Dialogo*, c. 125; cf. c. 162).

able, temperate, keeping his fasts, no frequenter of banquets, gentle, peaceful, not vindictive, ready for divine things, reading masses and praying and chanting, and so forth. Such a man, I say, is a laughing-stock. "Lo, here is our daily fellow! he sticks in the choir like a nail in a tile!" All inveigh against him, even as the birds flock together and chatter round an owl; each will have his peck at him. "Oh!" quoth they, "this fellow was ever singular!" O holy singularity! many are called, but few are chosen: broad is the way to damnation, and many shall go thereby; narrow is the path to life, and few are they that find it. So also are laymen and laywomen mocked if they betake themselves and their friends to church on Sundays, and to confession in this season of Lent, or if they clothe themselves and their wives and children in becoming garb; and why should I make a long story? It is truly written in the 12th chapter of Job: "The simplicity of the just man is laughed to scorn; the lamp, despised in the thoughts of the rich, is ready for the time appointed"; for which see St Gregory's *Moralizations upon Job*. (He who will, let him here extend this discourse throughout all the deadly sins, as we have done above in speaking of clerics.) Wherefore halt not nor go thou backward for all their derision, but go ever forwards, seeing that this is no new thing, but hath flowed down to us from ancient days, and all men are in the same case.

Strasbourg had followed from time immemorial the common medieval custom of denying Communion and Christian burial to condemned criminals. Geiler attacked this custom; the magistrates and all the Religious of the city, except one, defended it. The Bishop tried to settle the dispute by consulting his clergy: here again opinions were divided. At last, in 1482, the Papal Nuncio consulted the University of Heidelberg, which decided in Geiler's favour. Yet it was not until 1485 that Geiler won his point, with the help of his pupil Peter Schott, himself a distinguished patrician of the city. For the whole negotiation see L. Dacheux (*Jean Geiler*, pp. 45 ff.), who adds: "When Strassburg was incorporated with France, the condemned were again denied Communion, according to the custom of the Gallican Church." In Sicily, they were even refused spiritual help of any kind until the middle of the sixteenth century. (Th. Trede, *Heidentum*, u.s.w. Gotha, 1890, pt. III, p. 349; cf. G. G. Coulton, *Five Centuries of Religion*, vol. I, 1923, App. 13.) The following Extract is from Peter Schott's letter to the Nuncio, printed in his rare *Lucubratiunculae* (Strasbourg, 1497). After a preface defending Geiler against the slanders of those who were interested in upholding the ancient abuses, Schott proceeds (fol. 116):

126. KNOTTY PROBLEMS

FIRST, as to the criminals led to execution, whereas ye desired to know the opinion of the Heidelberg Doctors, if ye had put off your departure for four days, ye might have seen the concordant opinions both of the theologians and of the jurists, that the Sacrament of the Eucharist should by no means be refused to such persons, if only they show signs of repentance and desire it. But there are other points also, though they have not as yet given rise to such open conflict, whereof this eminent Doctor [Geiler], stirred by the same zeal for God's glory, prayeth that he may be confirmed and strengthened by men of learning and great authority with a more settled and certain mind, lest the truth be again gainsaid when it is thus constantly preached in public as need requireth. These then, *inter cetera*, are the chief points of doubt. One statute of the city of Strassburg ordaineth that whoso entereth into a Religious Order, however wealthy he be, may not bear into the monastery more than 100 pounds (or 200 gold pieces of the Rhine); the rest he is compelled to leave to his heirs as though he were intestate. Another statute ordaineth that a citizen of Strassburg who slayeth a stranger or foreigner (that is, a non-citizen) is free of all penalty on payment of 30 pence (or about three Rhenish florins); yet if the same should steal from a foreigner, though it were but a little, he should be hanged. If again any man, even a citizen, should slay a citizen, albeit in self-defence and without undue violence, he is slain. Again, it is ordained by statute that naught may be left by will or by deathbed gift, even to holy places and pious uses. We would know, then, are the makers or enforcers of such statutes in a state of salvation? Again, they give public warranty or safe conduct against justice, so that the man thus privileged need not abide by the law. Again, they exact promiscuously from the clergy taxes and imposts and tolls, even upon the necessaries of life such as wine and corn.

Again, they have set on high in the cathedral a certain boorish image under the organ, which they thus misuse; On the sacred days of Whitsuntide themselves, whereon folk from all parts of the diocese are wont to enter the Cathedral in procession with relics of saints and devotions, singing and chanting glad songs to God's praise, then a certain buffoon hideth behind that image and, with uncouth gestures and loud voice, belcheth forth profane and indecorous canticles to drown the hymns of those that come in, grinning meanwhile and mocking at them; so that he not only turneth their devotion to distraction and their groans to rude laughter, but impedeth even the clergy in their chants of God; nay, in the case of the divine solemnities of the mass (for such are sung not far from that spot), they inflict abominable and execrable disturbance, far and wide, upon such as are zealous for the worship of the Church, or rather of God. Moreover, the Bürgermeister hath his own place in the Cathedral, wherein he is wont promiscuously to make answer and give audience to parties called before him; moreover, he hath been accustomed to talk with others there, even at times when masses are being sung by priests in the vicinity, who are troubled by so great murmur and noise. Moreover, they commit other irreverences also in the holy places, buying and selling in the church porch, though that too be a consecrated spot, and bearing fowls or pigs or vessels through the church, even in times of divine service, by which walking they obey the devil rather than God. Moreover, especially between the Feast of St Nicholas and the Octave of the Innocents [Dec. 6 to Jan. 4] a boy is clad in episcopal ornaments and singeth collects in the church; he bestoweth public benedictions, and a masked crowd troubleth all right and justice in the churches. Moreover, the Lord's Day is thus belittled by a corrupt abuse; for there is a statute that on that day and no other the bakers from without the city shall bring together a great mass of bread, and offer it for sale only at that time whereat the people should be the more intent upon divine worship. Again, whatsoever holy day falleth on a Friday, even though it be that of the Blessed Virgin, yet the public market is not forbidden. Seeing that all these things stir the wrath of our zealous man, he would fain first be informed what he must think of these things. Are all who do such in mortal sin, or all who, (having the power,) hinder them not? Secondly: Should those hold their peace or speak against these things, who have been commissioned to preach in the bishop's stead?

127. PAUL'S WALK

Guillaume Pepin, Prior of the Dominicans at Evreux, was a famous preacher who died in 1532 or 1533. His works were reprinted in a collected form at Cologne in 1610. The following is from his *Sermones de Imitatione Sanctorum* (Venice, 1594, fol. 106a).

NOTE that many come into the Temple (that is, to Church) in the spirit indeed, but not always in a holy or good spirit. Here we must mark that some come thither in divers spirits. First, in the spirit of covetousness and greed, as many prebendaries who come to the canonical hours and to the funeral services in order to receive distributions [of money], and who would not otherwise come at all. How then do these? certainly, for the most part, they are present only at the beginning and end of the service; for the rest of the time they wander about the church, spending the time in many confabulations and levities with layfolk or other persons. Yet this abuse is strictly forbidden [in two separate passages of Canon Law]. Again, those enter the Church in the spirit of greed who procure ordination or promotion for the sake of benefices and dignities, that they may thus live in greater comfort and ease. The same may be said of such as enter into endowed Religious Orders, and similar fraternities. A second class come thither in the spirit of ambition and pride, as many do who stalk in pompously on feast days, that they may be seen and honoured, or praised for the magnificence of their dress; in which pomp and abuse women are more excessive than men. . . . The third are those who come in the spirit of fornication and lechery, of which kind are many incontinent, vagabond and inconstant women, who wander about the church and the holy places to see and be seen; who pollute the holy temple, at least in their hearts. The fourth come to the temple in the spirit of surfeiting and drunkenness, as do many countryfolk who keep certain gild commemorations, in honour whereof (as they say) they come together on certain days of the year and hold their feasts within the church,[1] perchance because they have no houses large enough to hold so large a company; and thus with their surfeiting and drunkenness, with their filthiness and clamour, they profane and pollute the sanctuary of God. Wherein they resemble those Corinthians of the early church, who, after taking the revered Sacrament of the Altar, feasted magnificently within the church: and whom St Paul reproveth (1 Cor. xi, 22), saying, "What, have you not houses to eat and to drink in? Or despise ye the church of God: and put them to shame that have not?" For [as it is written in Canon Law], the church is no place for meetings or assemblies, or for the tumult of bawling voices. Enough in this place. [He repeats the same complaints more briefly in another sermon, *Fer. 2a post 4, Dom. Quad.*]

---

[1] These are of course the *Church Ales* which the puritan party among the Reformers laboured so hard to put down. In many English parishes *Church Houses* were built for these feasts.

ABUSE DESTROYETH NOT USE

More's English Works (as Principal Lindsay writes on p. 17 of the third volume of the *Camb. Hist. of Eng. Lit.*) "deserve more consideration than they usually receive." Yet he vouchsafes them no further consideration; and later on Mr Routh mentions one of them only to disparage it (p. 80). Since they are practically inaccessible to the general reader (for the folio costs from £25 to £50 according to its condition) I give in these volumes some stories which show him at his best as a raconteur, and of which the first is doubly interesting for the use that Shakespeare made of it. In the *Dialogue* More is arguing in his own person against a disputant of quasi-heretical leanings, generally alluded to as the *Messenger* or *your Friend*.

128 ABUSE DESTROYETH NOT USE

(p. 198. More speaks in his own person.)

IN some countries they go a-hunting commonly on Good Friday in the morning for a common custom. Will ye break that evil custom, or cast away Good Friday? There be cathedral churches into which the country cometh with procession at Whitsuntide, and the women following the cross with many an unwomanly song, and that such honest wives as that, out of the procession, ye could not hear to speak one such foul ribaldry word as they there sing for God's sake whole ribaldrous songs, as loud as their throat can cry. Will you mend that lewd manner, or put away Whitsuntide? Ye speak of lewdness used at pilgrimages: Is there (trow ye) none used on holy days? And why do you not then advise us to put them clean away, Sundays and all? Some wax drunk in Lent of wigges[1] and cracknels, and yet ye would not, I trust, that Lent were fordone. Christmas, if we consider how commonly we abuse it, we may think that they take it for a time of liberty for all manner of lewdness; And yet is not Christmas to be cast away among Christian men, but men rather monished to amend their manner, and use themselves in Christmas more Christianly.... Now touching the evil petitions, though they that ask them were (as I trust they be not) a great people, they be not

[1] Or *wig*, a dry, crisp biscuit. More either means that these biscuits were ordinarily washed down with strong drink, or perhaps anticipates the modern ironical excuse which attributes certain irregularities of behaviour to "the salmon."

yet so many that ask evil petitions of saints as there be that ask the same of God Himself. For whatsoever they will ask of any good saint, they will ask of God also. And commonly in the wild Irish, and some in Wales too, as men say, when they go forth in robbing, they bless them and pray God send them good speed, that they may meet with a good purse and do harm and take none. Shall we therefore find a fault with every man's prayer because thieves pray for speed in robbery?

PART II

CHRONICLES, SCIENCE AND ART

Vincent of Beauvais was born about 1190, and died probably shortly after 1260. He was a Dominican Friar, Lector and Librarian to St Louis, to whose queen he dedicated his treatise on the education of princes. His *Speculum Majus*, or *Bibliotheca Mundi*, the greatest of medieval encyclopaedias, was republished even as late as 1624 by the Benedictines of Douai. The following extract is from chapter viii of the *Prologue* to that book.

1. DIFFICULTIES OF THE MEDIEVAL ENCYCLOPAEDIST

MOREOVER I am not ignorant that Philosophers have said many contradictory things, especially concerning nature. For example, some have judged the air to be naturally hot, as Aristotle and Avicenna; while others, as Seneca, have pronounced it to be cold. Some also assert that a serpent's venom is frigid, as doth Isidorus; others again will have it to be ardent, of whom is Avicenna. Seeing however that in these and suchlike matters either part of these contradictories may be believed or disbelieved without peril to our Faith, therefore I admonish the reader that he abhor not this book if perchance he find such contradictions in many places, and under the names of divers authors; the more so as I have herein undertaken not the office of a composer but that of a compiler. Wherefore I have taken small pains to reduce the sayings of the Philosophers to concord, striving rather to repeat what each hath said on every matter, and leaving the reader to put faith in one or the other judgment after his own choice. For, seeing that even many physicians seem to dissent one from another in their judgment of the complexion, degree, or quality of simple medicines, we must reflect that the very complexions of men and animals and fruits of the earth differ according to the diversities of regions, so that one of the same kind may be here an antidote, there a poison. For (to cite an example) the black poppy is written in physicians' books

I

for a poison; yet in our parts men take it for food. Likewise Avicenna and Rhasus count the stag's tail as venomous; which, however, is constantly denied by physicians in our country.

Ralph Higden, a monk of Chester, died in 1364. His *Polychronicon* is not only a digest of such chronicles as the author could get hold of, but also a popular encyclopaedia: it has no original merit, but is most valuable as showing a learned man's outlook on the world during Chaucer's boyhood. The book was translated in 1367 by John Trevisa, chaplain to Lord Berkeley, for whom see *Camb. Hist. Eng. Lit.* vol. II, p. 71. Higden's Latin and Trevisa's English are printed on alternate pages in the Rolls Series: the extracts in this and other volumes are little modernized except in the spelling.

2. THE SAME

(Vol. I, p. 17.)

THOUGH feigning and saws of misbelieved and lawless men, and wonders and marvels of divers countries and lands be y-planted in this book, such serve and are good to be known of Christian men. Virgil sought gold of wit and wisdom in the fen of Ennius the poet; and the children of Israel, in their going into the Land of Behest, spoiled the Egyptians. That which is in other books y-written well-wide, and parcel-meal y-planted, here it is y-put together in rule and in order; so mirth to sadness and heathen to christian, ever-each among other, that strange stories be so abridged, shorted and y-lengthened that the story is whole, in soothness nought y-changed. Nevertheless more certain some is holden than other. For Augustinus, *De Civitate Dei*, saith: "We shall trow and worship the miracles of God and not them disprove by disputation." Wonders be not all to be untrowed: for Hieronymus saith: "Many wonders thou shalt find that thou wouldest not believe, and yet they be full sooth: nature may not do against God, Lord of nature." Also of many things that seemeth full sooth, nevertheless skilfully we doubteth. Isidorus saith: "If reason is uncertain of the building of the city of Rome, what wonder though men be uncertain of the building of other cities and towns? Wherefore we shall not blame makers and writers of stories, that diversly speak and write; for long passages of time and elde of deeds maketh them unknown and writers to err." Therefore Hieronymus saith: "It is seemly to trow their saws that withsayeth not our belief nor soothness that is known."

Wherefore in writing of this history I take not upon me to affirm for sooth all that I write here, but such as I have seen and y-read in divers books, I gather and write without envy, and [make] common with other men. For the Apostle saith not: "All that is written to our lore is sooth," but he saith: "All that is y-written to our lore it is y-written."[1]

The monastery of Novalese, under Mont Cenis, was founded A.D. 726; its well-known *Chronicle* was compiled by one of its monks in the first and second quarters of the eleventh century. References are to Pertz's smaller edition (*Chronicon Novaliciense*, Hanover, 1890).

3. THE EARLIEST RECORDED ALPINE CLIMB

(*Chron. Nov.* p. 11.)

To the right hand of this monastery [of Novalese] is Monte Romuleo, the loftiest of all the mountains near. In this mountain dwelt one Romulus, a most gigantic king [*rex elefantiosissimus*] from whom also it took its name, on account of the refreshment and pleasant nature of the place or of the lake thereon. This mountain, therefore, surrounds on the right hand, as I have said, the aforesaid monastery; and at the roots thereof runs the road to Burgundy. On this mountain, as also on Mont Cenis, the common folk say that several sorts of wild beasts live—bears, chamois, wild goats, and others

---

[1] Dr Gairdner (*Lollardy and the Reformation*, vol. 1, p. 212) is mistaken in quoting this passage as a proof of medieval freedom from that bibliolatry which beset the Reformers. Higden is obviously apologizing, not for historical errors in Holy Writ, but for the unequal historical value of the different authors from whom he has compiled. Even if this were not plain enough in the context, it is clinched by the chapter immediately following, which is headed "Names of the Authors quoted in this work." Then follows a list of 40 names, from Josephus and Hegesippus down to Florence of Worcester, but with no mention of the Bible.

good for hunting. There also rises a stream, falling through the dizzy heights of those rocks, wherein it is said that a spring of salt water arises and runs mingled with the other; so the chamois and goats and tame sheep are wont, for the love of the salt, oftentimes to flock to this stream, that is, through the gorge of the river-bed at the point where it opens into the plain. Now men say that the aforesaid Romulus had amassed a vast hoard of money on this Monte Romuleo when he dwelt there; to which mountain no man can ever climb, howsoever fervently he desire it; but this old man, who told me so much of the same place, told me how at a certain season he had marked the exceeding clearness of the sky; at which time he rose at early dawn with a certain Count named Clement, and they two hastened with all their might to ascend the aforesaid mountain. But, when they were now hard by the summit, its peak began to be covered and darkened with thick clouds which, growing little by little, came even to them as they climbed; wherefore, finding themselves within the dark cloud and groping their way with their hands, they escaped with much difficulty through this darkness; for it seemed to them (as they said), that stones were hurled down upon them from above; and they report that the like had happened to others also. Now on that summit nought is to be seen on one side but the wild forest; but men say that on the other side is a lake of vast extent, and a meadow. This same old man was wont to tell of a certain most virtuous marquis, named Arduin, who, having often heard the countryfolk tell of the treasure heaped up on that mountain, was kindled with the fire of covetousness and bade forthwith that certain clerks should hasten to ascend with him to the summit. These, therefore, taking a cross and holy water and royal banners and singing their litanies, went on their way; yet before they had reached the summit of the mountain they must needs turn back with shame, even as the others.

Alpinists may be interested to compare this with two other extracts illustrative of early mountaineering. No. 4 is from Vincent of Beauvais (*Speculum Historiale*, lib. i, c. 84); and no. 5 from the *Chronicle* of Brother Salimbene, who died in 1288 (*Mon. Germ. Hist. Scriptt.* vol. XXXII, p. 598).

AN ALPINE CLIMB

4. ANOTHER

PETRUS COMESTOR [died A.D. 1198] saith that Mount Olympus riseth even to the clear aether, wherefore letters written in the dust on the summit of that mountain have been found unchanged after the lapse of a whole year. Neither can birds live there, by reason of the rarefaction of the air, nor could the Philosophers who have ascended it remain there even for a brief space of time, without sponges soaked in water, which they applied to their nostrils and sucked thence a denser air.

5. ANOTHER

THIS King Peter of Aragon,[1] was a man of magnificent heart and a strong man armed and skilled in war . . . as may be seen also from this example which I here subjoin. On the confines of Provence and Spain rises an exceeding high mountain called by the men of those parts Mont Canigou [*Canigosus*], and which we may call Mount Murky [*Caliginosus*]. This is the first mountain which seafarers mark at their coming, and the last which they see at their departure, after which they see no more land. On this mountain no man dwells, nor had any son of man dared to climb it on account of its enormous height and the difficulty and travail of the way; but around its roots men dwell. When therefore Peter of Aragon had purposed to climb this mountain, wishing to learn by the sight of his own eyes what was on its summit, he called two knights who were his familiar friends, and whom he loved with all his heart; to whom he expounded that which he proposed to do. They rejoiced and promised him not only to keep his purpose secret, but also never to leave him. Wherefore they took provisions and all fit weapons, and (leaving their horses at the foot of the mountain, where are the dwellings of men) they began to climb little by little on foot. When,

---

[1] Pedro III, of Aragon, died in 1285. He was the rival of Charles of Anjou, and is placed by Dante in the Valley of Flowers (*Purg.* vii, 112–125).

therefore, they had climbed far higher, there they began to hear horrible and most dreadful thunderclaps: moreover, flashes of lightning burst forth, and tempests of hail came down, whereat they were all dismayed and, falling to the ground, were as it were bereft of life for fear and expectation of what had come upon them. But Peter, who was brave and more vigorous than they, and who wished to fulfil the desire of his heart, comforted them, lest they should faint amid those afflictions and terrors, saying that this labour should yet redound to their honour and glory. So he gave them to eat, and himself ate with them; and, after this rest from the weariness and travail of the way, he exhorted them again to go up valiantly with him. Thus he said, and thus they did, many times over. But at last these two companions of King Peter began to faint, so that they could scarce breathe for utter weariness of the way and for fear of the thunderbolts. Then Peter asked them to await him there until the morrow at eventide; and then, if he came not back, to descend the mountain and go whithersoever they would. So Peter went up alone with great travail of body; and, having come to the top of the mountain, he found there a lake, into which he cast a stone. Then a monstrous dragon of loathly aspect issued therefrom, hovering round in the air until the face of heaven was darkened with the vapour of his breath; after which Peter came down to his companions and told them fully of all that he had seen and done. And, as they went down from that mountain, he bade them publish this abroad to whomsoever they would. Methinks that this achievement of Peter of Aragon may be reckoned with those of Alexander, who would exercise himself in many fearful deeds and works, that he might earn the praise of posterity.

VIVISECTION

Guibert de Nogent, from the first publication of his works in the seventeenth century, has been known as one of the most interesting autobiographers of the Middle Ages: his *Treatise on Relics* and *God's Dealings through the Franks [in the Holy Land]* are no less interesting. His style, especially in his *Own Life*, is involved and obscure, quite apart from corruptions of the text; but he was one of the most honest and learned writers in an age of great intellectual activity; and, though he took St Bernard's side against Abelard, he shows a critical acumen which can seldom be paralleled in any period of the Middle Ages. Born near Beauvais in 1053, of noble blood, he lost his father in childhood and his mother at the age of twelve by her retirement to a convent. His old master having at the same time become a monk, Guibert ran wild for a few years. At last, through his mother's and master's influence, he took the vows at St Germer, that magnificent abbey-church which may still be seen between Gournay and Beauvais. The regularity of his life and his fame as a student earned him the honourable position of abbot at Nogent-sous-Coucy. After playing a conspicuous part in the Church politics of 1106 and succeeding years, he retired again to the peace of his abbey, wrote several books of great value, and died between 1121 and 1124. More specimens of Guibert's work would be given here, but that his life and writings have been admirably treated in a monograph by a scholar of great promise whose early death has aroused much sympathy (Bernard Monod, *Le Moine Guibert*, Hachette, 1905).

6. VIVISECTION

(Guibert's *God's Dealings*, col. 798.)

BALDWIN [afterwards King of Jerusalem] had been wounded in battle while he rescued a footsoldier of his army, with whose bravery he was much delighted. The leech whom he summoned feared in his foresight lest the cataplasm outwardly applied might film over the wound, which (as he knew) had pierced deep into the prince's body; he feared therefore lest, while the skin grew smooth over the wound, it might rankle inwardly with a mass of putrid matter. This he foresaw in his wondrous skill, partly by a most praiseworthy conjecture, and partly from past experience. He therefore besought the king to command that one of the Saracen prisoners (for it would have been wicked to ask it of a Christian) should be wounded in that same place, and afterwards slain; whereby he might enquire at better leisure in the dead man's body— nay, might clearly perpend from its examination—how it was with the king's wound at the very bottom. From this however, the prince's loving-kindness shrank in horror; and he repeated that ancient example of the Emperor Constantine, who utterly refused to become the cause of any man's death, even of the basest, for so small a chance of his own safety. Then said the doctor: "If indeed thou art resolved to take no man's life for the sake of thine own cure, then at least send for a bear, a beast that is of no use but to be baited; let him stand erect on his hinder paws with his fore-feet raised, and bid them thrust him with the steel; then, by inspection of his bowels after death, I may in some degree measure how deep that wound is, and how deep thine own." Then said the king, "We will not strain at the beast, if need be: do therefore as thou wilt." Whereupon it was done as the leech bade; and he discovered from this proof of the wild beast how perilous it would have been for the king if the lips of the wound had become united before the matter had been drawn forth and the bottom had grown together. Let this suffice concerning the king's pitifulness.

Extracts 7 and 8 are from the *Life* of St Stephen of Obazine in Baluze-Mansi, *Miscellanea*, vol. 1, pp. 161, 154–6. St Stephen, with a few like-minded companions, founded, near Limoges, in the then desert spot of Obazine, a monastery of which he became abbot. About 1148 he procured the incorporation of his abbey into the Order of Cîteaux, then in its full glory. This *Life*, written by a disciple and fellow-monk, is full of interesting information upon twelfth-century monasticism in its strictest forms.

7. "WHO BUILDS GOOD CHURCHES MUST HIMSELF BE GOOD"

(Vol. 1, p. 161.)

AMONG other changes [involved in the incorporation with Cîteaux] the use of flesh-food for the sick was introduced, according to the Cistercian Rule. This so deeply grieved the holy man that, seeing one of the animals being slaughtered for the sick monks, he was moved in spirit and said: "Ye have brought your butcher's shambles into the House of God!" When the Chapter of the Rule concerning the sick was quoted to him, he held his peace, since he could neither

like the clause itself nor mislike the authority of the Rule.
For when our abbey-church was a-building, before the
Brethren were yet made monks (as I was told by one who was
present and heard and saw it), the hired workmen, impatient
of so long an abstinence from flesh, bought for themselves a
pig, cooked its flesh, and ate thereof in the forest; the rest
they brought back and hid in their lodging, that they might
consume it secretly next morning. When this was told to the
Abbot, he was moved to grievous indignation; and, taking
some of the Brethren, he began to go round the workshops,
until, coming to the masons' lodge, he found the flesh hidden
between two barrels, even as he had heard. Seizing it therefore, and looking round upon his companions, he asked what
should be done with this stuff. Some judged that it should be
given to the poor; others, that it should be returned to the
workmen, lest they should be grieved and depart; whereupon
he answered, "Not so, my Brethren, not so; but rather let
us send it on the road which it must so soon have taken":
saying which, he bade them cast it into the draught, and returned by the way he had come. By this time the workmen
were set again to their work; who, hearing of this deed, and
moved to furious indignation, cast away their tools, left their
labour, and began to rage against the Man of God with
murmurs and mad words of wrath. He for his part went to
pacify them; but when with soft words he began to soothe
their vexation, then they attacked him with reviling and
curses, threatening that neither they nor any others would
thenceforward work in his service, who had done them so
great an injustice. Then, making light of their threats, he
began to reproach them with their infirmity and their stealthy
repasts; adding that, if they abandoned God's work for the
allurements of their belly, he would not fail to find the builders
necessary for the Lord's house, and such as, without carnal
indulgences, would rear it better than they. Nay, even though
none such could be found, it were better (as he said) that God's
house should never be built than that the habitations of His
servants should be defiled with unclean meats: whereupon he
would have departed. But they, pricked to the heart, followed
him and fell at his feet, praying forgiveness for their words of

folly; which when they had obtained, they came back forthwith to their work, corrected and amended to their own profit and to the health of their souls.

Glimpses of medieval architects or masons at work are so rare that the reader will perhaps be glad to have two extracts describing the work, apparently at a later stage when the Brethren had learned to do their own building.

8. ARCHITECTURAL MIRACLES
(*Ib.* pp. 154, 156.)

In the daytime [the Brethren] worked busily in the fields. . . . Moreover, they built their own habitations, trimming with hammers the stones hewn from the mountain, and carrying them on their own shoulders to the builders' yard. It was marvellous to see huge stones, which many men could not have carried, borne by four of the Brethren, who went so nimbly that they seemed to bear no load at all. . . . When the Man of God came back from his visit to the Chartreuse, as the Brethren increased in number, he purposed to increase likewise the buildings of the monastery, which were but small. Beginning first with the sanctuary, he began to build a church in honour of Mary, the holy Mother of God, after the model of the Chartreuse. But as the Brethren were building it, one of the great men of that land feared lest it should become a refuge for his enemies and a cause of ruin to himself, wherefore he came with a great band of followers to stop them; by whose threats the Brethren were so terrified (for the Man of God was absent) that for wellnigh two days they continued the work after a feebler fashion than they had begun, and without proper cement. When, therefore, he returned and found the walls bound not with cement but with slime, and thus not only defiled but weakened, then he rebuked the Brethren and soon brought the work back to its first model in matter and in form. . . . And when the building itself rose higher, and the Brethren that went upon the scaffolding were carrying an immense stone in their stretcher, then the scaffold began to yield under the weight, groaning and bending and threatening ruin. The Saint, seeing this from afar, ran up quickly and, making the sign of the cross, set his shoulders to the load; whereby he supplied such virtue that the scaffold was confirmed in the twinkling of an eye, while the Brethren were so fortified that they went as though they felt no load.

The main story of Abelard's life is too well known to need repetition here. After his separation from Héloïse he became a monk at St Denis; but here he roused his fellow-monks to fury by throwing doubt upon their claim to possess, in their patron saint, no other than Dionysius the Areopagite of Acts xvii, 34. After Abelard had suffered some persecution at St Denis, the abbot was persuaded by his protectors to suffer his retirement to a solitude near Nogent-sur-Seine, where he finally founded a monastery as related in the following extract. He died in 1142 at the age of sixty-three: his last years had been spent at Cluny under the protection of Peter the Venerable.

9. THE RELIGION OF LEARNING

I THEREFORE withdrew to a solitary spot that I knew of in the country of Troyes. Here I received the gift of some land whereon, with the assent of the Bishop of that diocese, I first built a little oratory of reeds and straw, which I dedicated to the name of the Holy Trinity. Here I lived in hiding with a certain clerk for my companion, and could with truth chant that psalm to the Lord, "Lo, I have gone far off flying away; and I abode in the wilderness." When the scholars heard of this, they began to flock together from all parts, leaving their cities and towns and coming to live in my wilderness. Here, instead of spacious houses, they built themselves little tabernacles; for delicate food they ate nought but herbs of the field and rough country bread; for soft couches they gathered together straw and stubble, nor had they any tables save clods of earth. They seemed in very truth to imitate those ancient philosophers of whom Jerome thus wrote in his second book against Jovinian: "Through the senses, as through windows, vices creep into the soul. . . . Impelled by such reasons, many philosophers have left the press of cities and suburban gardens, where the fields are pleasantly watered and the trees thick with foliage; where birds chirp and living pools mirror the sky, and the brook babbles on its way, and many other things entice men's ears or eyes; lest through the luxury and abundance of plenty a soul's strength be turned to weakness, and its modesty be violated. For indeed it is unprofitable to gaze frequently on that whereby thou mayest one day be caught, and to accustom thyself to such things as thou shalt afterwards scarce be able to lack. For the Pythagoreans also, avoiding such frequented spots, were wont to dwell in the wilderness and the desert." Moreover Plato himself, though he was a rich man, whose costly couch Diogenes once trod under his muddy feet, chose the Academe, a villa far from the city, and not only solitary but pestilent also, as the fittest spot for the entire study of philosophy; that the assaults of lust might be broken by the anxiety and frequent presence of sickness, and that his disciples might feel no other delights save in those things that he taught them. Such also is the life which the sons of the prophets are said to have led, who clung around Elisha, and of whom, as the monks of those days, this same Jerome writeth in his letter to the monk Rusticus, saying among other things: "The sons of the prophets, who (as we read in the Old Testament) were monks, built themselves little lodges hard by the river Jordan, and, leaving towns with their multitudes, lived upon coarse meal and wild herbs." Such then were my disciples who, building their little lodges there beside the river Arduzon, seemed rather hermits than scholars. Yet, the greater was the press of scholars flocking thither, and the harder the life which they suffered to hear my teaching, the more glorious did my rivals think this to me, and the more ignominious to themselves. For, after having done all that they could against me, they grieved now that all things should work together to me for good; wherefore (to cite my Jerome again) "though I had withdrawn far from cities, market-places, quarrels and crowds, yet even so (as Quintilian saith) envy found me in my hiding-place." For these fellows, complaining within themselves and groaning with envy, said, "Behold the whole world hath gone after him; we have profited nought in persecuting him; nay, we have rather added to his renown. We have sought to extinguish his name, and have kindled it the more. Lo, these scholars have all necessaries at hand in their towns; yet, contemning the delights of the city, they flock together to the penury of this wilderness, and are miserable by their own choice." Yet it was then my intolerable poverty more than aught else that drove me to become a master of the schools; for I could not dig, and to beg I was ashamed; wherefore, falling back upon the art which I knew, I was compelled to employ my tongue instead of the labour of my hands. My scholars, of their own accord, provided me with all necessaries, not only in food and raiment but in tilling of the fields and defraying the cost of the buildings, so that no household care might withdraw me from my studies. Seeing then that my oratory could no longer hold even a small portion of them, they must needs extend it, building it more solidly with stones and wood. Though then it had been founded and hallowed in the name of the Holy Trinity; yet, because I had there found a refuge in mine exile and some small share of the grace of God's consolation had been breathed into my despair, therefore in memory of that lovingkindness I called it the Paraclete.

Side by side with the few men of genius like Abelard and Roger Bacon, who saw clearly the weakness of the traditional learning, and with the many medieval writers who, like Guibert de Nogent and Matthew Paris, brought a wide experience and some real critical acumen to the examination of the reports which they transmitted to posterity, there were many others who thought far more of "edification" than of objective truth. We have seen (vol. I, no. 7) how Guibert complained that this fatal indifference to facts was fostered by the rivalry existing between different churches and monasteries, each of which claimed greater antiquity and a more glorious collection of relics than its fellows. There were similar rivalries between different cities, each proud of its own legends; cf. the amusing extract quoted from the Shillingford Letters (A.D. 1444) in Mrs Green's *Town Life in the XVth Century*, vol. I, p. 342: the Mayor of Exeter claiming that Vespasian had besieged that city "soon after the Passion of Christ...and then he with Titus besieged Jerusalem and obtained and sold thirty Jews' heads for a penny, as it appeareth by the Chronicles." A still more instructive example may be found in the following extract from the *Chronicle of Tournai*, compiled by Heriman, Abbot of St Martin there, and published in vol. II of the *Corpus Chronicorum Flandriae*. The young canon Henry was born about 1125 (*Hist. Litt. de la France*, t. XII, p. 245). The story may be compared with Extract 7 (vol. I) from Guibert de Nogent.

10. HISTORY BY REVELATION

(p. 480.)

CONCERNING the building and destruction of this [city of Tournai] there is a book in our possession: the contents of which, never before seen or heard-of by us or our ancestors, nor ever found in any written record however cursorily composed, were lately revealed in the most unhoped-for fashion to a single youth of Tournai, a clerk, after the manner here following.

A certain youth named Henry, our fellow-canon, on the twenty-first of April, which was a Monday in Eastertide, chanced to go alone at nightfall through the new building of the Cathedral of Notre Dame, without the least fear in his mind; when he suddenly heard voices as of a mighty multitude rushing towards him with fearful vehemence; and he saw a torrent of flame coming upon him, which burned part of his garment and of his arm beneath it, close by the wrist. At this he was sore afraid, and fell forthwith to the ground; and, being forthwith ravished as if in an ecstasy, he saw many men whom he knew now to be dead, but whom he had known in life, coming towards him and speaking one with another. After which it seemed to him that he was in a field full of roses and lilies with all sweet and fragrant flowers, wherein he halted awhile. Then the horror of his first fear vanished away, and the exceeding sweetness of that vision so cheered him that he felt altogether refreshed and as it were a new man. Presently he was aware of four men clad in white garments, who came towards him with candlesticks and censers in their hands; after whom came three honourable men adorned with episcopal robes, with crozier in hand and crowned with golden mitres, whereon each one's name was graven. On his mitre who went in the midst was graven *Eleutherius, Saint and Bishop*; on his of the right hand, *Eloy, Saint and Bishop*, and on his of the left hand, *Achaire, Saint and Bishop*. After these followed Sir Gerard the priest, a religious man, who had been a faithful Almoner to the Cathedral, clad in his sacerdotal vestments. St Eleutherius therefore, drawing nigh unto the young man, cast his maniple over him as though he caressed him; after which he showed him the book of his own life that he bore in his hand, and bade the youth read it in his presence. When therefore he had read it through, then the Saint returned it into his own bosom and went back to the place wherein he had stood before. Then St Eloy came to the youth and offered him the book of his life, which the youth would not read, saying that he knew it well enough already. Then St Achaire showed him these words written on his right hand: *By me was a man raised from the dead in Jesus' name*. Then they departed in the same order wherein they had come; and the youth, coming to himself from this ecstasy, rose from the ground and returned to his father's house and lay sick all that night upon his bed. When morning was come, he prayed to be sprinkled with Holy water; and, thus refreshed, he showed how his garment had been burned and the flesh melted beneath, and related some of the things that he had seen. On the Saturday following, he secretly summoned William the Dean and confessed his past sins; then he received absolution and the penance enjoined, and took the Lord's Body; after which he recalled that aforesaid Book of the Life of St Eleutherius, (which he had read six days before[1] in his ecstasy,) and began to read it in the hearing of all as fluently as though he were reciting the Lord's Prayer. Struck by the strangeness of the event, we came together in wonder and began to dispute and conjecture much concerning so marvellous a vision. For, albeit some maintained that the youth, being a skilful composer in verse and prose, might himself have composed this life, yet we, who knew not his knowledge, did know very well that he had never been practised in this manner of composition; and, indeed, even though he had composed it, yet he could by no means have committed it so exactly to his memory and read it so fluently by rote. Wherefore, after taking counsel of religious men, we transmitted this vision in writing to our lord Samson, Archbishop of Rheims, and to the lord Bernard, Abbot of Clairvaux, who were gathered together at Sens with the king of France and other bishops and abbots, on the octave of Pentecost, to hear and discuss the books of Master Peter Abelard.[2] With them we consulted as to what they might think best to be done in the matter; and they sent us word that we should await thenceforth the issue of God's will. Behold, therefore! after a few days, the aforesaid youth, foreboding by certain signs that St Eleutherius would again reveal himself to him, made his confession at early dawn, heard mass, took the Lord's Body, and then entered in with a few others to pray in the secret place wherein the Saint's shrine was laid. There he fell suddenly to the ground; and, when those that were without heard thereof, very many pressed in, among whom were we ourselves. Here we found him lying on the ground like a dead man, with closed eyes, whereat we wondered, awaiting the end of that matter. Then, behold! within a brief space we heard him read concerning the enshrining of the body of St Eleutherius, and marvelled at his answers to many questions which we put to him; after which he came back from his ecstasy and wrote down that which he had read. Wherefore, being assured by this vision

---

[1] The text has *scite*; but this seems an obvious error for *ante*.
[2] This council was held in 1140: see vol. iv, no. 15.

which we had seen, of the truth of that youth's own vision whereat no man had been present, we prayed God with one accord that, if the matter were from Him, this might be manifested yet again for the third time. Then the aforesaid youth, before forty days had elapsed, feeling that the third vision would soon be upon him, on the Saturday before the Feast of St Lawrence, confessed and heard mass again at daybreak; after which, strengthened by the reception of the Lord's Body, he went with a few companions to pray in the secret place aforesaid. Within a brief space we who stood without heard that he had fallen, and ran in, where we found him as before, with closed eyes, lying like a corpse on the ground. Scarce had the fourth part of an hour elapsed, when lo! we heard him read certain miracles of St Eleutherius; and, to our amazement, he answered very many questions, amidst which he foretold publicly that the cathedral of Tournai should, within a brief space, have its own bishop and be restored to its former dignity.[1] Moreover, he read from the book of St Eleutherius the story of the first foundation of the city of Tournai; which he kept by heart and communicated to be written and read by us; and all of which, together with the Book of his Life, is kept in our library. If perchance, by reason of so novel a matter, somewhat less authority or faith be given to this book, yet there remaineth in confirmation Julius Caesar's story of the Gallic War; in the second book whereof the description of the devastation of the Nervii, (to wit, of the territory of Tournai at its most flourishing time;) by that same Julius, would seem to accord with the Book aforesaid. We, however, thinking it superfluous to write the whole story in this work of ours, have only borrowed such as might display the foundation or desolation of the city in ancient times.

[1] This was a burning question of the moment, and doubtless contributed much to the enthusiasm created by the clerk's visions. The chronicler relates lower down (p. 505) how these enlisted the sympathy of St Bernard, who persuaded Simon, Bishop of Noyon (to whose diocese Tournai now belonged), to suffer the erection of a separate see: the separation was presently ratified by Innocent II. One of the pleas which most moved Bernard and the Pope was that the diocese of Noyon was too cumbrous to be ruled by one man; it was admitted that, out of a population of 900,000 in the Tournai district, more than 100,000 had died unconfirmed within the last ten years. No doubt both these numbers are subject to the usual medieval exaggeration; but this would not affect the proportion of one to the other.

The author goes on to tell how Tournai was founded 143 years after Rome and about the time of Nebuchadnezzar, by Tarquinius Priscus, who called the city "Second Rome," or "Lesser Rome"; how it was afterwards called Tournai after Turnus and Aeneas, etc., etc.

Abbot Haimon, of St Pierre-sur-Dives in Normandy, wrote to the prior of his dependent cell of Tutbury, in Staffordshire, an account of the religious associations formed to assist in church-building. Medieval chroniclers often notice briefly certain waves of enthusiasm which impelled whole populations, rich and poor, to labour together upon the town walls in times of danger, or upon some favoured church at a moment of livelier faith. The substantial accuracy of Haimon's description, apart from obvious exaggerations, is proved not only by brief notices under the year 1145 in French and English chronicles, but also by a contemporary letter from Hugh, Archbishop of Rouen, to Thierry, Bishop of Amiens, printed by Mabillon in his *Annales Benedictini*, t. VI, p. 392. The archbishop describes the origin of this devotion at the cathedral fabric of Chartres in 1145, its rapid spread first to Dives and then throughout Normandy, the religious enthusiasm and the miracles, in language which bears out all the main particulars of Haimon's narrative. The full text may be found in the *Bibliothèque de l'École des Chartes*, 1860, pp. 120 ff. After the general description here given, there follows a long catalogue of miracles of the type familiar to readers of medieval documents.

11. THE RELIGION OF CHURCH-BUILDING

BROTHER HAIMON, the humble servant of the servants of the Blessed Mother of God at the monastery of Dives, desireth to his most sweet Brethren and fellow-servants in Christ that dwell at Tutbury that consolation which is promised to those who love God. Rejoice with us, Brethren, rejoice and exalt in the Lord; for the dayspring from on high hath visited us, not indeed by our own merits, but by His abundance of grace and wonted compassion; He hath poured forth upon us the bowels of His mercy, nor withheld in wrath the gifts of His loving-kindness. Oh, how great is the superfluity of His sweetness that hath been shown in our times to a world sick with sin, wounded with crimes, desperate with the enormity of its wickednesses; to a world in short which was already almost godless, because by sin it had become estranged from God: for the wickedness of man had come to such a pitch that, unless that loving dayspring from on high had quickly visited the world, unless it had mercifully succoured our falling race, He would by no means have found faith when He came to the earth. But, where sin abounded, grace also did much more abound. The loving Lord hath looked down from Heaven upon the children of men, because there was none who understood and sought God; almost all were gone aside from him and had become abominable in their iniquities; and there was none who thought in his heart and said, "What have I done?" Then He drew to Himself those that started away from him, and recalled the wandering, and taught them a new manner of seeking Him, a manner new, I say, and un-heard-of in all ages. For who ever saw, who ever heard, in all the generations past, that kings, princes, mighty men of this world, puffed up with honours and riches, men and women of noble birth, should bind bridles upon their proud and swollen necks and submit them to waggons which, after the fashion of brute beasts, they dragged with their loads of wine, corn, oil, lime, stones, beams, and other things necessary to sustain life or to build churches, even to Christ's abode? Moreover, as they draw the waggons we may see this miracle that, al-though sometimes a thousand men and women, or even more, are bound in the traces (so vast indeed is the mass, so great is the engine, and so heavy the load laid upon it), yet they go forward in such silence that no voice, no murmur, is heard; and, unless we saw it with our eyes, no man would dream that so great a multitude is there. When, again, they pause on the way, then no other voice is heard but confession of guilt, with supplication and pure prayer to God that He may vouchsafe pardon for their sins; and, while the priests there preach peace, hatred is soothed, discord is driven away, debts are forgiven, and unity is restored betwixt man and man. If, however, anyone be so sunk in evil that he will not forgive those who have sinned against him, nor obey the pious admonition of the priests, then is his offering forthwith cast down from the waggon as an unclean thing; and he himself, with much shame and ignominy, is separated from the unity of the sacred people. There at the prayers of the faithful ye may see the sick, and those that are vexed with divers diseases, arise whole from the waggons on which they had been laid; ye may see the dumb open their mouths to God's praise, and those who are vexed by demons come to a sounder mind; ye may see the priests of Christ set each above his own waggon and exhorting all men to confession, to lamentation, to the resolution of better life, while the people fall to the ground, whereon they lie outstretched and kiss the earth again and again; old men and young men, with children of the tenderest age, cry unto the Mother of God, to whom especially they uplift their sobs and sighs from the inmost recesses of their heart with the voice of confession and praise: for this work is known to be specially hers next to her gentle Son. She more especially commended herself in this work after Him; she adorned first the Cathedral of Chartres and then our church dedicated to her with so many and so great signs and wonders that, if I would express all that it hath been vouchsafed to me to see, even in a single night, my memory and tongue would utterly fail me. For these miracles would seem to exceed both number and faith, yet I will tell of them below as truly as I may, so far as the strength which God hath given me will permit.

When, therefore, the faithful people (to return to my purpose) set on their way again with bray of trumpets and waving of banners borne before, then, marvellous to relate, the work went on so easily that nothing hindered them on their way, neither steep mountains nor deep waters rolling between, but (as we read of the ancient Hebrews that they entered Jordan in their bands), so one by one, when they came to cross the river, these suddenly entered without delay into the waters that stood over against them, under the Lord's guidance, so that even the waves of the sea at the place called St Marie du Port, while the whole company were crossing on their way to us, are credibly said to have stood away from them on their passage. Nor can we wonder that the older and more aged undertook this burdensome labour for the multitude of their sins; but what urged boys and children to this work? Who brought them to that good Teacher who hath perfected His praise in the mouths and works of children? Hath perfected, I say, that by all means the work begun among the elders may be proved to have been completed by the children;

for you might see them, with their own little kings and leaders, bound to their laden waggons, and not dragging with bowed backs like their elders but walking erect as though they bore no burden, and (more wonderful still) surpassing them in nimbleness and speed. Thus went they in a fashion far more glorious, holy, and religious, than any words of ours could express.

When they were come to the church, then the waggons were arrayed around it like a spiritual camp; and all that night following this army of the Lord kept their watches with psalms and hymns; then waxen tapers and lights were kindled in each waggon, then the sick and infirm were set apart, then the relics of the saints were brought to their relief, then mystical processions were made by priests and clergy, and followed with all devotion by the people, who earnestly implored the Lord's mercy and that of His blessed Mother for their restoration to health. If, however, the healing were but a little delayed, nor followed forthwith after their vows, then all might have been seen putting off their clothes—men and women alike, naked from the loins upward, casting away all confusion and lying upon the earth. Moreover, their example was followed even more devoutly by the children and infants who, grovelling on the ground, not so much crept from the church porch upon their hands and knees, but rather dragged themselves flat upon their bodies first to the high altar and then to all the others, calling upon the Mother of Mercy in this new fashion of prayer, and there extorting from her surely and forthwith the pious desires of their petitions; for what— (I will not say could they not *obtain*, but)—could they not *extort* by this fashion of prayer, this affection of piety shown in their groans, their sighs, their tears, and therefore ascending even to the divine ears of the Mother of all Pity? Who indeed would not be moved, nay rather, whose stony heart would not be softened as he watched that pious humility of the innocent children dragging their naked ribs on the bare ground? Who would not be pricked to tears by those lamentable voices crying aloud to Heaven? Who, I ask, would not be bent by those tender hands and arms stretched out to be beaten with rods? For it did not suffice them (though that surely were admirable at so tender an age!) to cry so long with the voice of weeping; it did not suffice that so many tears should be shed, but of their own accord they must needs add bodily affliction also, to obtain the healing of these sick folk. The priests stood over them, shedding tears while they beat with their scourges upon the tender limbs thus exposed, while the children besought them not to spare their stripes nor withhold their hand in too great mercy. All voices echoed the same cry, "Smite, scourge, lash, and spare not." There might be seen more than a thousand hands outstretched to the scourge; nay, they exposed their very ears and eyes and tongues, saying, "Let these hands be smitten which have wrought iniquity; let these ears be lashed which have listened to vanity, these eyes which have seen it; this tongue and these lips which have uttered idle and lying words!" Here I ask with assurance, who is so hard-hearted that he is not moved to tears? Who is so fierce and merciless that he is not moved forthwith to pity at this pious sight? Truly the Mother of Mercy is moved without delay to pious compassion on those who afflict themselves before her, and showeth by the immediate efficacy of her healing hand how nearly she is touched and how truly she hath heard their cries; for soon all the sick and infirm leap forth healed from waggon after waggon, casting away the staff whereupon they had hitherto leaned their crippled limbs, and hastening without support to render thanks at her altar. Blind men see, and thread their way with ease; the dropsical are relieved of their grievous load and lose their fatal thirst. What say I? Why should I enumerate one healing after another, when they are innumerable and more than man can tell? After each miracle a solemn procession is held to the high altar, the bells are rung, praise and thanks are rendered to the Mother of Mercy. This is the manner of their vigils, these are their divine night-watches, this is the order of the Lord's camp, these are the forms of new religion, these the rites, the heaven-taught rites, in their secret watches. For here nothing carnal is seen; nothing earthly of any kind; all is divine, all is done as in Heaven; heavenly altogether are such vigils, wherein nothing is heard but hymns, lauds, and thanks!

FATHER, FORGIVE THEM!

The three following passages are here put together as illustrating the too common attitude of the medieval Church towards the Jews. Popes did indeed often protect the Israelites, but (if we are to believe their contemporaries) mainly for the same causes which moved so many lay lords to protect them, as profitable beasts of commerce. Saints like St Bernard might also protest against massacres of the Jews; but the mass of the clergy, and especially of the monastic clergy, were among their hottest persecutors. No. 12 is from the *Chronicle* of Prior Geoffrey, printed in Dom Bouquet's *Historiens*, t. XII, p. 436. No. 13 is from the *Life* of St Théodard, Bishop of Narbonne (Duchesne, *Scriptores*, vol. III, p. 430). No. 14 is from the *Chronicle* of Adhémar de Chabannes (ed. Chavanon, p. 175).

12. FATHER, FORGIVE THEM!

RAYMUND TRENCHAVAL, viscount of Béziers, returned from Jerusalem in the year of Grace 1152, whereupon he received money to release the Jews from the affliction which they suffered from the Christians in the week of our Lord's Passion. I will narrate the matter at length to such as may be ignorant of it. Many Jews have dwelt in the town of Béziers from time immemorial; on Palm Sunday the bishop, having preached a mystic sermon to the people, was wont to exhort them in many words to the following effect: "Lo! ye see before you the descendants of those who condemned the Messiah, and who still deny that Mary was the Mother of God. Lo! here is the time wherein our heart echoes more often to the injury done to Christ. Lo! these are the days wherein ye have leave from the prince to avenge this so great iniquity. Now therefore, taught by the custom of your ancestors and fortified with our benediction after that of the Lord, cast ye stones against the Jews while there is yet time, and, in so far as in you lieth, atone manfully for the evil done to our Lord." When, therefore, the bishop had blessed them and (as in former days) the prince had given them the customary leave, then they would batter the Jews' houses with showers of stones, and very many were oftentimes wounded on either side. This fight was commonly continued from Palm Sunday until Easter Eve, and ended about the fourth hour; yet none were permitted to use other arms but stones alone. All this, as we have said, was forgiven to the faithless Jews by this Raymund.

The Jews were accused of having betrayed Toulouse to the Saracens; therefore, when the city was recaptured by the citizens, all were condemned indiscriminately to death; but at length Charlemagne had mercy on them, and contented himself with the execution of the actual traitors.

13. THE SAME

NEVERTHELESS, they who had assented to, but had not been present at the aforesaid treacherous compact were suffered to live and dwell in the city only on condition of submitting to the following punishment. On the day of the Lord's Birth, on the night of His Passion, and on that of His Ascension to Heaven, one of these Jews themselves, or one of their descendants, was chosen yearly to be buffeted before the porch of the Cathedral Church, receiving one blow only from some strong man, and having first offered a tribute of three pounds of wax.

This "so holy and so just condition" was solemnly registered under the king's seal and that of many bishops, in order that whosoever presumed to break it "might know that he must be condemned to eternal vengeance and have no part in the Kingdom of Christ and God." Under Carloman the Jews attempted to shake this off; a conference was held between them and the bishops in the king's presence, the Jews in vain pleading that the sons should not bear the iniquity of their fathers. They were not only non-suited, but the court accepted St Théodard's suggestion that in future the victim should confess before the blow that he had justly deserved this as the descendant of those who had smitten Christ: in default of which confession "let him be smitten seven times, that the words may be fulfilled which are written in their law: 'I will increase your pains sevenfold, turning My face against you.'"

14. THE SAME

IT came to pass on the Good Friday of this year (1020), after the adoration of the Cross, that the city of Rome was imperilled by an earthquake and an exceeding great whirlwind; and forthwith a certain Jew brought word to the lord Pope that at that hour the Jews in their synagogues were wont to make a mock of the image of the crucified Lord; which Benedict VIII carefully sought out and, finding it to be true, he presently condemned the authors of that crime to death. No sooner had they been beheaded than the fury of the winds ceased. At this same time Hugh, chaplain to Aimery, viscount of Rochechouart, passed his Easter at Toulouse with his master, where he gave the customary buffet to the Jew at Eastertide, with which buffet he suddenly smote the brain and eyes from the fellow's faithless head and scattered them on the earth; whereupon the dead man was taken forthwith from the church of St Stephen to the Jews' synagogue and there buried.[1]

Petrus Cantor, "Peter the Precentor," was also Rector for many years of the Cathedral School at Paris—*i.e.* of perhaps the busiest centre of learning in Europe. In 1191 he was chosen Bishop of Tournai; but the election was contested, and he willingly withdrew his claim; soon afterwards he entered a Cistercian monastery, and died in 1197. Cardinal Jacques de Vitry, who had known him personally, described him as "a lily among thorns, or a rose among thistles....A man mighty in word and in deed...whose uprightness of life added weight and gravity to his doctrine." The following extract is from his *Verbum Abbreviatum* (Migne, *Pat. Lat.* vol. 205).

15. THE EIGHTH LAMP OF ARCHITECTURE
(C. lxxxvi, col. 255.)

EVEN as, in the superfluity and curiousness of raiment and food, the labour of nature is perverted and the matter falleth into wrong if it be without art, so also is it in the superfluity, curiousness and sumptuosity of buildings. For behold how far we are departed from the simplicity of the ancients in this matter of buildings. We read that Abraham, in the first days of faith, dwelt in tabernacles, possessing on this earth not even whereon the sole of his foot might rest: for he pitched his tent between Bethel and Ai, not as a citizen, but like unto a stranger and pilgrim that hath no abiding habitation; and under this roof-tree—that is, under his thatched hut—he had the angels for guests. So likewise Lot and Noah abode in

---

[1] The editor notes that this deed is attributed by other chroniclers to Aimery himself, and referred to the year 1102.

tents; as some of the ancients dwelt in rocky caverns, others under the bark of hollow trees, so that, being seen to issue thence, they were fabulously believed by some to be born of stones and trees. Elisha had no dwelling of his own, but (by the charity of a widow) a little chamber under another's roof, where he had his little chamber, his little table, his little bed and his candlestick.... Moreover, seeing that not only in stature but even in length of life we [moderns] are abridged by reason of our manifold superfluities and our sins; seeing that the end of the world and the consummation of all things are come upon us, what madness and excess is it that we should be so solicitous concerning the bigness and curiousness and costliness of the buildings that we make, as though such works would never perish! More especially seeing that the ancients —to whom God granted longer lives, and who, born at the very birth of the world, were far removed from its end— cared for no such things, believing rather that at the end of the world all the foundations of the earth shall be moved; to wit, that she shall be purged even to her inmost bowels, so far as the works of sinful men have gone downwards, and so far as their works have risen upwards into the air. Wherefore said a certain clerk of Reims, "If these builders believed that the world would ever come to an end, no such lofty masses would be reared up to the very sky, nor would such foundations be laid even in the abysses of the earth.[1] Wherein they resemble those giants who built the tower of Babel, rearing themselves up against the Lord: wherefore let them fear lest they themselves also be scattered abroad from the face of the earth (that is, from God's Church), and be then confounded in the fires of hell." Moreover, this superfluity and costliness of buildings and stone walls is a cause why we have in these days less pity and alms for the poor; since we are not rich enough to feed them while we spend also upon such superfluous expenses. Let us remember also what Esaias saith: "Heaven is my throne, and the earth my footstool; what is this house that you will build to me? and what is my place

---

[1] Peter wrote during that wave of architectural enthusiasm described above in Extract 11. It is probable that the rebuilding of Notre Dame, his own cathedral, as we see it to-day, was already planned at this moment, if not actually begun.

of rest?" Moreover, Jerome saith, "I know that there is a people, to wit the men of Megara, who build as though they would live for ever, eating meanwhile and drinking as though they must die on the morrow; for they say, 'Let us eat and drink, for to-morrow we die.'" Moreover, Paul the first hermit dwelt in a crypt, that is in a cave under the earth; and an angel fed him with half a loaf [daily]: wherefore St Anthony, archimandrite and father of the hermits, hearing of his sanctity, came to visit him and knocked at his door: whom Paul supposed to be a wild beast or a wolf.... Moreover he asked very many questions of Anthony, among which he enquired whether the idolatry [of the heathen] and the obstinacy of the Jews were yet removed, and whether the Christian religion imitated the Gentile worship in the costliness of its edifices, saying: "Do the towers and bulwarks still rise to heaven, with the palaces, and all those so lofty and costly buildings of Rome?" "Yea," quoth Anthony: whereat the other bewailed this superfluity even with tears, mourning that men were given up to such vanities, whereas Christians ought rather to exhort each other saying: "We have not here a lasting city, but we seek one that is to come."...As one prelate said to another, "What meaneth this loftiness of your buildings? Wherefore have ye towers and bulwarks withal? Thou shalt not thereby be better defended against the Devil, but all the nearer to him." Moreover this lust of building is testified by the palaces of princes, reared from the tears and the money wrung from the poor. But monastic or ecclesiastical edifices are raised from the usury and breed of barren metal among covetous men, from the lying deceits and deceitful lies of hireling preachers;[1] and whatsoever is built from ill-gotten gains is in much peril of ruin: for, as Ovid saith, "A sordid prey hath no good issue." For example, St Bernard wept to see the shepherds' huts thatched with straw, like unto the first huts of the Cistercians, who were then beginning to live in palaces of stone, set with all the stars of heaven. But oftentimes to the Religious themselves, as to other men, their own offence becomes an instrument to punish them for this disease of building: for the construction of comely and ample

[1] See Guibert de Nogent, in vol. I, no. 7.

houses is an invitation to proud guests. Even the granges of the monks are oftentimes castellated in self-defence; and Religious oftentimes conceal the truth and leave God's righteousness, lest they should lose such granges, not daring to murmur against princes, since they have lost their old freedom whereof the poet spake: "The traveller that hath no money in his purse will sing in the robber's presence." This (I say) they have lost for the sake of rich granges and lands, suffering robbers and usurers to build them dormitories and refectories, for a sign and an eternal memorial of their covetousness; though they should not have suffered this even had the money pertained to good men, but should rather have bid them apply such moneys to the feeding of the poor and the redemption of captives. Men sin even in building churches; for, seeing that their heads should be more lowly than their bodies for the mystery's sake (since our Head, which is Christ, is more lowly than His Church), yet they are now built higher.[1]

For Higden, the author of the *Polychronicon*, and Trevisa, his translator, see preface to Extract 2.

16. THE EARTHLY PARADISE

(R.S. vol. i, p. 67, *Of the Provinces of the World, and first of Paradise*, chap. x.)

FOR the knowledge of earthly Paradise three points must be i-knowe. Wherefore three questions are asked: the first question asketh, If any such place is on earth? The second asketh, Whitherwards or where is Paradise in earth? The third asketh, What country or what place is Paradise in earth? For the first four manner witnesses we have that Paradise is in earth; first, stories that liken Sodom, before it were overturned, to Paradise; the second witness is of them that assayed and wrote and said, that they had seen that place; the third

[1] Peter apparently refers here to the east end of the church, called in French *chevet*, or head. The reconstruction of cathedrals often began at this end, and the lofty choir would then contrast strangely with the old nave, as in the well-known case of Cologne Cathedral for more than five centuries after the completion of the choir in 1322.

witness is the four rivers, that run out of Paradise; for the head of these rivers is not found in the sea, neither in fresh water, neither in land wherein men live, though kings of Egypt and many others laboured well oft and sought there-after.... Basilius, in *Hexameron*, Isidorus, *Eth. lib. quarto decimo*, and Josephus, in his first book, say that waters falling from the greatest hill of Paradise make a great pond, and out of that pond (as it were from a well) the four rivers spring.... The most certain author, Salustius, saith, that there cometh a well out of Cerauneys, the hills of Armenia, and springeth out at the foot of the hill that is yclept Caucasus; and that well is the head of two rivers of Tigris and Euphrates, the which two rivers sometimes are parted asunder and sometimes mingled together, and oft-times they are swallowed into the earth, and eft spring up again, and long after they go about Mesopotamia that land, and downward into the Red Sea. And though men read in books that Nilus cometh out of Paradise, yet some men affirm and say that Nilus springeth in the west side of the land of Ethiopia, not far from the hill that is yclept Atlas, and goeth about Ethiopia and downward by Egypt. (Seek the property of Nilus in the chapter *Egiptus* [of this book].) The fourth witness and proof, that such a place is in earth that is y-clept Paradise, is old fame and long-during; for men shall trow old fame, that is not withsaid; but fame of Paradise hath y-dured without withsaying six thousand year and more; for from the beginning of the world anon to our days it hath endured. And fame that is false dureth not so long, for it falleth out of mind, or is disproved by soothness y-knowe. Of the second question, that asketh in which side of the world and in what place Paradise should be; though short-witted men and little of assay say that Paradise is a long sailing-journey from earth that is habitable, and also departed from the earth and is high as the moon, [yet] it is not to be believed; for kind and reason both withsay. For if Paradise were departed asunder from the earth that men live in, neither water nor air might bear such a burden. Also the fire occu-pieth all the middle space between the air and the moon, then Paradise is not there; for then nothing might live therein. Also if Paradise were so high, sometime it should bereave the light, and make the eclipse of the moon; but of such eclipse heard we never. Also if Paradise were so high, and parted asunder from every other land and earth, how should the four rivers that spring out of Paradise pass by the air and the wide sea and come into lands that men dwell in? And if men say that Paradise is so high and in one place continued to the earth that men dwell in, then must the earth be even-long and not round all about, as wise men describe it; but that may not stand: for it is y-known by experience and assay, that in every eclipse of the moon the earth maketh a round shield. Therefore the earth, with all his parts, must needs be round. And so wise men conclude that Paradise is in the uttermost end of the east, and that it is a great country of the earth no less than Ind or Egypt; a place large and convenable for all mankind to dwell in, if mankind had not y-sinned. Of the third that asketh of Paradise, what manner place it should be, Isidore saith, *libro quarto decimo, capitulo tertio*, that this name Paradise y-turned out of Greek into Latin is to-meaning *an orchard*. But Paradise in Hebrew is yclept *Eden*, that is to-meaning *liking*; the which twain put together maketh *an orchard of liking*. No wonder, for in that place is all thing that accordeth to life. There is health, for the air is in temper neither too hot nor too cold, so that nothing that liveth may die therein: that witnesseth Enoch and Elias, that yet be there on live. [As saith] Johannes Damascenus, that place hath fair weather and mirth, for it was the cellar and place of all fairness: no manner of tree loseth there his leaves; no flowers there wither; there is mirth and sweetness; of fruit and trees that grow there, in Genesis, *secundo capitulo*, it is y-written: Every tree therein is sweet to eat and fair to sight. Therein is sikernesse and surety, for the place is high. Petrus [Comestor], *capitulo tertio decimo*, saith that the water of the great flood came not in Paradise. Though some men say that Paradise is high as the moon, that is not sooth in words and in deed; but that speech is y-saved by an excusacioun of speaking, that is yclept yperbolica: so that they that so speak would mean, that Paradise in height passeth all other lands. (*Trevisa;* So we praise a worldly man Jordan or John, and say that he was the best man that ever was; and yet he was never so good as Christ.

So in words that subtle men will divine, the meaning is true and good.)[1] But alas, as Isidore saith, *libro nono, capitulo primo*: Our way to Paradise is fast y-stopped by cause of the sin of our former father; it is y-closed all about with a fiery wall, so that the burning thereof reacheth to heaven, as some men would ween. Paradise is y-closed with that wall to hold out mankind; angels stand on that wall to keep well Paradise, that none evil ghosts may come therein.[2]

17. RICHARD I AND THE JEWS

(R.S. vol. VIII, p. 83.)

KING HENRY is dead at Fontevraud, and his son Richard was king after him and reigned ten years.... This king ordered readily his things beyond the sea, and came into England for to be crowned. After his coming prisons were opened and he was crowned at London of Baldwin, Archbishop of Canterbury, the third day of September, the which is accounted an evil day by the vain belief and usage of misbelieved men, as it is y-cleped in the calendar *dies Egipciacus*, and *dies malus*, an evil day by the vain belief, as it were a day of boding of evil haps to the Jews; for the Jews of England had evil haps that day. Many Jews came to this solemnity lest the wealth that they had under the old king should be withdrawn in the new king's time. But the king hight and commanded that the Jews should not come into the church while he were y-crowned, neither into the palace while he were at meat. But while the king was at meat some of the Jews pressed among other and came within the palace gate, and one of them was y-smitten with a man's fist. Then the rabbish people weened that the king had so bidden, and up with staves, bats, and stones, and laid on the Jews and made

[1] The translator often, as here, intercalates a remark of his own, with his own name to distinguish it.

[2] There is a similar, but much briefer, description of the Earthly Paradise in Vincent of Beauvais, *Spec. Hist.* lib. L, c. lxiii. For a fourteenth-century legend, see vol. IV, no. 53.

AN AUTO-DA-FÉ OF JEWS

From a fourteenth-century MS. of the Chronicle of Abbot Gilles li Muisis, figured in *Corpus Chronicorum Flandriae*, vol. 1, p. 348.

them to flee. Hereof sprang liking tidings[1] into all the city, as though the king had bidden, and up with staves to destroy the Jews. And the people, raving and crying, brake up the house where the Jews were y-flown for dread, and burned and spoiled and took what they might, and would not leave for the king's sending....At the last the Jews had peace granted.... Also without the mischief and woe that Jews suffered in their body and chattels at Lincoln and at Lynn, yet at York after a long siege and great mischief and woe, Rabbi, master of Jews, for-cut the veins of four hundred Jews, and his own veins also, and his wife's throat. Also at Stamford Jews were y-beaten, y-slain, and y-spoiled. And one John, most hardy of Christian men, came to Northampton with many great preys; there his hosteller slew him privily by night for covetise of money that he had y-brought, and threw the body by night without the city, and fled away as a thief should. Then old wives dreamed, and there were seen wonder false sights and false tokens, and the silly men bare on hand that it was for the holiness of that man, that they held a very martyr, and worshipped the sepulchre of the dead man with solemn watches and gifts; but wise men laughed them to scorn; but clerks of the place were well-pleased therewith, for they had profit thereby. This was told the bishop, and anon he forbade the doing of simple men upon the pain of cursing, and the great boast of covetous men and of their false martyr.[2]

Roger of Hoveden (R.S. vol. III, p. 12) gives further details as to this massacre. "So while the king sat at meat, the chief of the Jews came with gifts for him; but, because the populace had been forbidden the day before to come to the king's court on his coronation day, therefore with eye of pride and with an insatiable heart they fell upon the Jews and despoiled them and beat them and thrust them forth from the court of the palace. Among which Jews was Benedict, a Jew of York, who, having been thus persecuted by the Christians, and so grievously wounded that he despaired of life, was baptized by William, Prior of St Mary's Abbey at York, in the church of the Holy Innocents, and was named William, and thus escaped from peril of death and from the hands of those that persecuted

[1] This is Trevisa's translation of Higden's *gratus rumor*, "tidings which gratified them."

[2] Trevisa has here misunderstood his original, which runs, "he profaned the insignia of this false martyr, which had been maintained by the zeal of simple and covetous folk."

him. When, therefore, the citizens of London heard this, they fell upon the Jews of the city and burned their houses and slew them; yet a few escaped by the kindness of their Christian friends. So on the morrow of his coronation the king sent his servants and took those evil doers who burned the city—not for the Jews' sake, but for the sake of the houses and goods of Christians which they had burned and despoiled also—and some of them he hanged. And on that same day the king sent for the aforesaid William, who had been made Christian, and asked him, 'Who art thou?' And he answering said, 'I am Benedict, thine own Jew of York.' Then the king turned himself to the Archbishop of Canterbury and the rest who had told him how the said Benedict had become Christian, saying, 'Did ye not tell me that he is a Christian?' And they made answer, 'Yea, Lord.' Then said he, 'What therefore shall we do with him?' To whom the Archbishop of Canterbury, less circumspectly than his duty required, answered in the fury of his spirit, 'He will not be a Christian; let him be the Devil's man!' for he ought to have said, 'We demand the judgment of Christian folk upon him, even as he was made a Christian and now saith nay.' But, because there was none to resist, the said William returned to his Jewish pravity; and within a little while after he died at Northampton and was a stranger to the common burial-ground of the Jews, even as of the Christians; both because he had been made a Christian and because, like a dog to his vomit, he had returned to his Jewish pravity.'

18. BISHOP AND POPE

(*Ib.* p. 241.)

ALSO that year [1253] died St Robert Grosseteste, bishop of Lincoln, the ninth day of October. He was cunning in all the liberal arts, and specially he expounded many things in logic, ethics, and astrology. He sent to the fourth Pope Innocent an epistle sharp enough that beginneth in this manner, "Our Lord Jesus Christ." He sent that epistle for that the pope grieved the churches of England with taxes and with payments undue and uncustomable. Also, for that he had given his little nephew a canonry which first voided in the church of Lincoln. And this Robert would not receive the child, but he wrote to the pope and said that he neither would neither should put such to the cure of souls that could not rule himself.[1] Therefore this Robert was summoned to the [Pope's]

[1] Cf. vol. i, no. 29.

court and accursed; then from Innocent's court he appealed to Christ's own throne. Then after Robert his death, it happed in a night that the pope lay in his bed for to rest, a bishop appeared to him arrayed as a bishop, and spake to the pope and said, "Arise, wretch, and come to thy doom"; and smote him with his cross in the left side right to the heart; then on the morrow the pope's bed was found bloody, and the pope dead; therefore, though Robert was a noble man, and did often miracles, the court suffered him not to be canonised.

Lambert, parish priest of Ardres, describes in his chronicle how, about A.D. 1200, Arnold II, Count of Guisnes and Ardres, fortified the latter town for fear of his enemy the Count of Boulogne. The accompanying illustration shows clearly the state of these earthworks in the early seventeenth century.

19. FORTIFYING A TOWN

(*M.G.H.* vol. XXIV, p. 640.)

A T the advice of his father, and of the peers and burgesses of the Town (for it was in the very navel and midst of the land of Guisnes, and was already waxing richer than the other towns and cities of the said territory, wherefore it was more obnoxious to his furious adversaries, and he himself was the more carefully bent on its defence) the Count shut it in, and surrounded it himself with a most mighty moat after the fashion of the moat at St Omer, such as no hand had conceived hitherto in the land of Guisnes, nor no eye had seen. Wherefore no small multitude of workmen came together to make and dig this moat aforesaid; who, howsoever vexed by the hardships of the season and pinched by the great famine and afflicted by the labour and heat of the day, yet chattered together and lightened their labour oftentimes with merry words, whereby their hunger was appeased. Moreover, many oftentimes came together to see these great earthworks; for such poor folk as were not hired labourers forgot their penury in the joy of beholding this work; while the rich, both knights and burgesses and oftentimes priests or monks, came not daily only, but again and again every day, to refresh their bodies

Ardres

Grand Eglise   Maison de Ville   S! Bernard

THE EARTHWORKS OF ARDRES

From a seventeenth-century view in Zeiller's *Topographia*.

and see so marvellous a sight. For who but a man stupefied and deadened by age or cares, could have failed to rejoice in the sight of that Master Simon the Dyker, so learned in geometrical work, pacing with rod in hand, and with all a master's dignity, and setting out hither and thither, not so much with that actual rod as with the spiritual rod of his mind, the work which in imagination he had already conceived?—— tearing down houses and granges, hewing to the ground orchards and trees covered with flowers or fruit, seeing to it with the utmost zeal and care that the streets should be cleared, on workdays even more than on holidays, for all convenience of traffic, digging up kitchen-gardens with their crops of potherbs or of flax, treading down and destroying the crops to make straight the ways, even though some groaned in the indignation of their heart, and cursed him under their breath? Here the peasant folk with their marl-waggons and dung-carts, dragging loads of pebbles to be laid upon the road, cheered each other to the work with strokes and hearty blows on the shoulders. There, again, laboured the ditchers with their shovels, the hoe-men with their hoes, the pickers with their pick-axes, the beaters with their wooden mallets, the shavers with their shaving-irons, and the stone-layers and wallers and rammers and paviours with their proper and necessary gear and tools, the load-men and hod-men with their hods, and the turfers with their oblong sheets of turf, cut and torn at the master's bidding from all the meadows around; the catchpolls[1] too, with their rods and knotted clubs, rousing the labourers and busily urging them to their work; and ever in the forefront the masters of the work, weighing all that was done in the scales of their geometrical plan; moreover, all these labourers were driven and constrained to this work through a continual time of travail and grief, of fear and pain.

[1] Officers, constables.

Jacques de Vitry studied at Paris, was ordained priest in 1210, and devoted himself to preaching by the advice of the Blessed Mary of Oignies, whose *Life* he also wrote. After her death in 1213 he preached the crusade first against the Albigensians and then against the Saracens. In 1214 he was elected Bishop of Acre; here he worked many years with his accustomed zeal, until at last, disheartened by the vices and failures of the crusaders, he resigned in or about 1227. Next year he was made a cardinal, and in 1239 elected Patriarch of Jerusalem; but the Pope was unwilling to spare him. He probably died in 1240. A passage from one of his letters, recording his enthusiasm for the newborn Franciscan Order, may be found in Sabatier's *St François d'Assise,* c. xiii, p. 261. His *Historia Occidentalis* and *Historia Orientalis* describe the age in language even more unfavourable than that of Roger Bacon and others quoted in this book; but the main human interest of his works is contained in the *Exempla,* or stories for the use of preachers, published by Prof. Crane for the Folk-Lore Society in 1890. A good many of these had already appeared anonymously among T. Wright's *Latin Stories.* Prof. Crane's edition, though of very great value, contains a good many misreadings which I have been able to amend by collations procured from the Paris MS. References are to folios of the MS. Lat. 17,509 of the Bibliothèque Nationale, and to pages in Crane's edition.

20. NATURAL HISTORY

(Fol. 63, p. 128.)

SOME, though they are fervent at the beginning of their conversion, grow lukewarm in the middle and utterly cold at the end, like unto the bird which the French call *bruer*.[1] This bird is at first of great honour, taking larks and partridges like a noble fowl; in his second year he taketh sparrows and small birds; in his third year beetles, mice, flies and worms; and thus he declineth ever to the worse, until at length he becometh so slothful as to suffer himself to die of hunger.

(Fol. 77, p. 129.)

Some [Christians] are like unto the boy whom the French call *chamium* [changeling], who draineth his nurses dry of milk and yet profiteth not nor cometh to any increase, but hath a hard and inflated belly; yet all the while his body thriveth not.

(Fol. 151, p. 122.)

The mother of the roe-deer fawn, when she goeth forth

---

[1] *Coq de bruyère*, capercailzie.

to seek her food, smiteth him with her foot and maketh a sign that he should not wander forth nor leave that place. The fawn is so obedient that, even when men find him, he stirreth not from that place but suffereth himself to be taken, becoming obedient unto death. How much more should we obey God our Father, and our Mother Church, and devote the flower of our youth to the Lord.

The Lateran Council in 1215, and the growing influence of the Friars, undoubtedly made for a somewhat stricter standard among the parish clergy. In the great Synod of Oxford, held by Archbishop Stephen Langton in 1222, archdeacons are bidden "to see on their visitations that the canon of the mass is amended, and that the priests can properly pronounce at least the words of the canon and of baptism, and that they rightly understand this part [of the service books]." Similar decrees were repeated by English Church Councils down to the Reformation. It was the same in other countries: *e.g.* the Council of Béziers in 1233 provided that none should receive the clerical tonsure who could not read and sing. The following actual examinations of priests will help to illustrate these decrees and throw light on the details of medieval grammar teaching; they should be compared with one of the extracts (no. 57) from Grandisson's *Register* in vol. I, and with St Bonaventura's description of the parish clergy at this time (vol. I, no. 61). This extract is from the *Register of St Osmund*, R.S. vol. I, p. 304 (Dean and Chapter Livings).

21. CLERICAL EXAMINATIONS

ACTS of the Chapter held by William, dean of Salisbury, at Sonning, in the year of our Lord 1222, on the Friday next before the Feast of St Martin.... Vitalis, a priest, perpetual vicar of Sonning, presented the chaplain [*i.e.* curate] named Simon whom he has with him, and whom he lately engaged until Michaelmas. This Simon, examined as to his Orders, said that he was ordained subdeacon at Oxford by a certain Irish bishop named Albin, then suffragan to the Bishop of Lincoln, from whom also he received deacon's orders; and those of priest from Hugh [of Wells] now Bishop of Lincoln, four years past. He was examined in the Gospel of the first Sunday in Advent, and was found insufficient, and unable to understand what he read. Again he was tried in the Canon of the Mass, at the words *Te igitur, clementissime Pater*, etc.[1] He knew not the case of *Te*, nor by what word it was governed; and when we bade him look closely which could most fittingly govern it, he replied: "*Pater*, for He governeth all things." We asked him what *clementissime* was, and what case, and how declined; he knew not. We asked what *clemens* was; he knew not. Moreover, the said Simon knew no difference between one antiphon and another, nor the chant of the hymns, not even of the hymn *nocte surgentes*, nor did he know by heart aught of the service or psalter. Moreover, he said that it seemed indecent that he should be examined before the dean, since he was already in Holy Orders. We asked him where he was when he received his priest's Orders: he answered that he had forgotten. He is amply illiterate. [*Sufficienter illiteratus est.*]

Wokingham is served by Philip, a chaplain, who hires that chapel on farm for ten marks, and the chapel of Sandhurst for a mark, but he takes two marks from the priest who is there. He was not examined, since he is of approved life and good testimony. Where ordained...[*hiatus in MS.*].

John of Hurst presented his chaplain, Richard by name, born at Ross [? *Rosam*]....He is a youth, and knoweth nothing. He saith that he received the subdiaconate at London, from Bishop William; the diaconate six years ago from Peter Bishop of Winchester; and the priesthood that same year from William bishop of Chester. Examined on the Advent collect *Excita quaesumus Domine* [Stir up, we beseech Thee, O Lord] he said that he would answer naught of this matter: likewise also when we tried him in the Canon; (for, after his priest had left the church first after the examination, and had joined the rest, then all fell to one accord that they would not answer; yet some, at the earnest instance of the Dean, answered afterwards in detail.) Having been questioned afterwards, he would not be examined at the end of the Chapter and remained suspended [from his office].

---

[1] The canon is the most sacred part of the mass, beginning with the prayer which the priests are here asked to construe: "We therefore humbly pray and beseech Thee, most merciful Father," etc., etc. The whole canon would occupy about a page and a half of this book in print.

John of Arborfield presented his chaplain Reginald, born at Windsor. He was, as he saith, ordained to the subdiaconate at Salisbury, the diaconate and priesthood at Winchester, four years now past. Examined in the prayer, "*Excita*," etc. and the passage of the Canon *Te igitur*, etc. he utterly refused to answer. Afterwards he came and offered himself for examination, and knew nothing, whether of reading or of singing.

The chaplain of Sandhurst, John of Sherborne, saith that he was ordained subdeacon at Chichester, deacon at Winchester by the bishop Godfrey in Ireland... [*hiatus in MS.*], and hath now served the aforesaid chapel four years. Examined in the prayer *Excita* and in *Te igitur*, he knew nothing to answer. Examined in chant, in the Advent Sunday anthem *Ad te levavi*, he could not chant it.

Again Vitalis, priest, presented for the chapel of Ruscombe the priest Jordan, born at Shatton in Dorset, ordained subdeacon and deacon (as he saith) at Salisbury by Bishop Herbert, and priest by the Bishop of Rochester, Gilbert de Glanville, before the General Interdict [of 1208]. Examined, like the rest, in *Excita* and *Te Igitur*, he knew nothing. A book was given him to chant from: he would not. We commanded Vitalis to find good chaplains for this place and for Sonning, or the Dean will take the benefices into his own hands.

At Arborfield also was an old man in the [priest's] house named Richard Bullock, a priest of Reading; and when the Dean examined him whether he could see and could pronounce the words completely, it was found that he could not completely pronounce a single word of the Gospel or the Canon.[1] Wherefore the Dean bade John of Arborfield suffer him no longer to minister in that chapel.

---

[1] He need not have been illiterate; he was perhaps simply inarticulate with age. It must be remembered that the Host cannot be effectually consecrated unless the four words *Hoc est Corpus Meum* are fully and correctly pronounced.

From the *Regestrum Visitationum* of Odo Rigaldi, Archbishop of Rouen, 1248–1275 (see preface to no. 44 in vol. I), pp. 787, 159, 173, 217, 332, 395.

22. ANOTHER BATCH

IN the year of our Lord 1252, at [our palace of Mont] Ste-Catherine, (in the presence of Masters William, Archdeacon of Eu and Simon, Archdeacon of the French Vexin, Master Peter, Official of Rouen and Canon of Cambrai, William of Salomonville and Stephen of Lorey canons of Rouen; Brothers Hardouin and Peter, Friars Minor and our companions; Masters Peter of Aumâle and Robert of St-Germain, William son of Jordan, John Baston, William of Plassay, Everard, and Stephen priest of Bleneau,) we examined John, a priest presented to the church of Bernetot, in the lessons for St Cecilia's Day: *Dixit Valerianus*, etc. Asked the signification of the words *tertio miliario* he first answered "the third miler" [*le tierz miller*] and afterwards "I know not." Item, when we asked how *transeuntibus* was declined, he said *hic et hoc transeunt*. Item, asked to decline *transire*, he said *transio, transis, transivi, transire, transiundi, transitrundo, ansiundum, transimus, transior, transiris*; beyond which he would say nothing more. Asked to parse *omni* he said it was an adverb. Asked the signification of *optime*, he said "much," and again "very." Examined in the word *conscius*, what figure and species, he said "simple figure[1] and primitive species." Asked to conjugate *perferam* he did well as far as the supine, for which he said *perfertum, perfertu*.

Again, he was examined at our bidding by Master Simon, Archdeacon of the French Vexin, in the presence of Stephen Gordian of the Friars Minor of Rouen, and Nicholas of Haqueville, Master Baldwin, priest of Dieppe and Dean of Christianity at Rouen, and Master William Jordan, on the 31st of May, in the lower hall next the chapel of our manor of Déville, upon the exposition of the gospel for the Con-

---

[1] He was wrong here: the examiners were driving at the fact that *conscius* is a *compound* adjective: see Donatus, ed. H. Keil, p. 53. The second answer is apparently right, meaning that the word was, in modern terminology, of the 1st declension of adjectives.

version of St Paul: *Quia dilectissimi fratres annuam Beati Pauli*, etc. Asked the meaning of *annuam* he answered "annual"; asked again what "annual" was, he said "many times"; asked "how many times?" he said "every day." Again, having been examined as to the signification of these words: *restat ut aliquid vobis de sancti ewangelii lectione intimare studeamus*.... [1]

For the rectory of Petiville there was presented to us one Richard of Fontbois, priest, whom we rejected because we found him insufficiently lettered [*insufficientis litterature*].

May 30, 1253 [at our manor of Déville]. On this day, the Tuesday before Whitsunday, we examined Geoffrey, a clerk, presented to the rectory of St Richard de Harcourt, on the Scripture words *omnia autem aperta et nuda sunt eius oculis*.[2] Asked what part of speech *aperta* was, he answered "a noun"; asked whether it might be any other, he said "Yes, a participle." Asked from what verb it came, he said from the verb *aperio, aperis, aperii, aperire, aperior, aperieris*, et cetera. Asked what *compati* was formed from, he said from *cum* and *pateo, pates, patui, patere, patendi, patendo, patendum, passum, passu, patiens, passurus, pateor, pateris, passus, patendus*. Asked what *pateo, pates* signified he said, "to open or to suffer." Asked to parse *absque* he said "a conjunction": asked of what kind, he said "causal." Examined in chant, he could sing nothing without solfeggio or note. We therefore, both because of this his insufficiency, and because after due inquisition he was found to be ill-famed of incontinence and quarrelsomeness, thought fit not to admit him to the said rectory. Those present were Brother Osmund, Brother Walter de Minières, Brother Roger his cousin, all Friars

---

[1] The rest of this passage is blank in the MS. It is evident that the first examination left the archbishop still uncertain; and he may very possibly have been driven to accept John even after this second; it was a serious matter to "plough" a priest who had been already passed and ordained by another bishop, though the next paragraph shows us that Odo did not shrink from this when necessary. It was this somewhat inconvenient zeal, together with his work side by side with St Bonaventura at the Council of Lyons, which earned him among his contemporaries the surname of "the Pattern of Good Life."

[2] "All things are naked and open unto the eyes of Him with Whom we have to do." Note that this Geoffrey was not yet a priest; this was one of those frequent cases where a clerk in lower orders had been presented to a benefice.

Minor, Ralph the priest of Déville, Master Maur our physician; Master Peter of Aumâle, Stephen, priest of Bleneau, and Everard son of the Count, our clerks.

Nov. 20, 1253. This day, at Déville, was examined William de Wardres, presented to the rectory of Ancourt, in the lessons for the Feast of the Purification, beginning *illa namque salus*; and he construed thus. *Illa* this is, *salus* salvation, *generata* engendered, *de Virgine Maria* of the Virgin Mary, *hoc est* that is, *die* the day, *quadragesimo* of the space of forty days, *Maria* O thou Mary, *genetrice* mother, *hodie* to-day, *ab ipsa* from her, *deportata* carried, *ad templum* to the temple, *ipsius* of him, *ut ipse* that he, *redemptor noster* our father, *sit* may be, *presentatus* presented, *sic* in such a fashion, *cum substancia nostre carnis* in the substance of our flesh, *etiam* further, *adimplet* he fills, *ipsam* her. Being asked what this signified in French, he said that he understood not the sense well. Asked what part of speech is *adimplet* he said "A verb" and conjugated it well. Asked what was the word *urnis* which had been omitted, he answered "paps."[1] Again, being asked to parse *genetricis* he said "noun" and declined it thus:

N. hic genetrix
G. huius genetricis
D. huic genetrici
Ac. hanc genetricem
V. genetrix
Ab. ab hoc genetrice.

He said that it had no plural. Present at this examination: Master Simon, archdeacon of Eu, Stephen his clerk, Masters Peter of Aumâle and Hugh of Courtrai, Canons of Rouen; Sir Hugh the almoner and Everard the lord Archbishop's clerk. [William is mentioned no more in the Register, so we may hope that he passed.]

June 12, 1255. [At Bondeville] we examined Geoffrey de Tonneville, clerk, presented to us by Thomas de Pavilly, esquire, for the rectory of St Mary at Pavilly, who, beginning at the words *Factus autem cum filii Dei venissent quadam die* (Job ii, 1) when he came to *circuivi terram et perambulavi*,

---

[1] There is very likely a slip here in Bonnin's transcription: *ulnis* would mean "in her arms," and a reader who caught occasional glimpses of the sense might well interpret this "at her breast."

being asked to decline *circuivi* replied *circuo, circuis, circuivi, circuere, circuendi, circuendo, circuendum, circuitum, circuitu, circuens, circuiturus, circuor, circueris.* Asked what conjugation, answered "third." Asked to parse *coram* said "A preposition." Asked again to parse *stetit* he said, "a verb." Asked how it was declined, said *sto, stas, steti, stare, standi, stando, standum, statum, statu, stor, staris, status sum, stari.* Asked to parse *factum* said "a participle"; asked of what tense, said "Past." Asked of what signification, said "neuter."[1] Asked to derive it, said "from *facio, facis.*" Asked to conjugate it, replied *facio, facis, feci, facere, faciendi, faciendo, faciendum, factum, factu, faciens, facturus, fio, fis, factus sum, fieri, fictus, fiendus.* Again, being examined in the passage beginning *Jurat Valerianus,* he read very badly [*pessime*] and construed thus: *Valerianus* Valerian, *jurat* swears, *sponsus* thou O spouse, *prodere* to put forth, *nulla* nothing, *detegere* to discover, *Illa ait,* etc. [In the absence of further record, we may hope that Geoffrey also satisfied the examiners.]

Feb. 22, 1258 [at Paris]. On this day we examined one William, a priest, presented to us for the rectory of Rothoirs, in the presence of [4 assessors]; and he was examined in a lesson from the book of Genesis, namely *Ade vero,* etc. (Gen. ii, 20). Asked to construe and expound it in the French tongue, he said thus: *Ade* Adam, *vero* certainly, *non inveniebatur* did not find, *adjutor* a helper, *similis* like, *eius* of him. Asked how *inmisit* is conjugated, he said thus: *Inmitto, -tis, -si, -tere, -tendi, -do -dum, inmittum-tu, inmisus, inmittendus -tor-teris, inmisus -tendus.* Again he construed: *Dominus* our Lord, *inmisit* sent, *soporem* encevisseur[2] in Adam...[hiatus]. Again, being asked to conjugate *replevit* he said thus: *reppleo -ples, -vi -re, reppleendi -do -dum, repletum -tu, replens, repleturus, repleor -ris -tus, repleendus.* Again we made him divide *repleendi,* and he said: *Re-ple-en-di.* Again, he was examined in chant at the anthem *Voca operarios,* and knew not how to chant.

[1] The words are "requisitus cuius significationis, respondit quod neutri (sic) significationis."

[2] Even Prof. Léon Clédat acknowledges himself unable to explain this word; it only seems certain that it does not mean *sleep,* which the candidate should have said.

March 13, 1258. An appeal [to the Pope] was lodged against us by Master Nicholas of Condé, clerk and proctor of the Abbot of Fécamp, in the name of that Abbot and monastery...to which appeal we thought right not to defer, since the said Robert of Courcelles [priest, presented by them to the living of All Saints, Fécamp] was twice examined by our counsellors and found to be insufficiently lettered.[1]

March 16, 1259–60 we examined Nicholas called Quesnel, clerk, presented to us for the church of St Mary at Wynemerville, in the Lesson *In principio creavit Deus celum et terram* (Gen. i, 1) and he construed: *Deus* God, *creavit* created [*cria*], *celum* the heaven, *et terram* and the earth. We made him decline *Deus*, which he did well enough except that, in the accusative plural, he said "*Deos* or *Dos*." Again we asked him to parse *inanis*: he replied "a noun," and yet he said that there were two parts of speech, and declined it thus: Nom. *hec inanis*, Gen. *huius inanis*, Dat. *huic inani*, according to the 3rd declension, except that in the vocative plural he said *O inane*; he said that *inanis* signified "an evil thing." He answered fairly well concerning the accent of the middle syllable. Then we asked him to parse *ferebatur*: he said it was a verb, and translated it "he carried": then he conjugated *fero, fers*, up to the supine, where he omitted the supine, for he said there was none;[2] for participles he gave *ferens, ferturus*, and said that the verb was neuter, and in the conjunctive mood, and past perfect. Moreover he conjugated fairly well the word *dixit*. Again he thus conjugated the verb *fiat*: *fio, fis, fui, esse, fiendi-do-dum, factum-tu, fiens, facturus*. We asked him whether it had a passive, and he said: "No, for it is neuter." We asked him the sense of the words *et vidit lucem quod esset bona* (Gen. i, 4) and he said "it was a good thing to do." Again, he thus conjugated the verb *divisit*: *divido*,

---

[1] This shows that these records of examinations in Odo's diary are not exhaustive, since there is no other record of this Robert, unless the following refers to him: "Oct. 2, 1257/8. We caused to be inspected the enquiries made at our bidding by the dean of Valmont concerning the life, morals, and conversation, etc., of Robert de Ros, priest, presented to us for the living of All Saints; wherefrom it appears that the said priest had received his sacerdotal Orders from an extraneous bishop, without licence from his own bishop: therefore we would not admit him to the aforesaid benefice."

[2] Or perhaps "did not say any": the text runs "nullum dixit."

dividis, divisi, dividere fairly well until the passive, when he said *divideor, divideris*, with a long middle syllable. We asked him which kind [*cuius generis*] it was; he first said the third, and then the fourth, saying that he knew the fourth because it made its genitive in *i* and its dative in *o*.[1] Again, he declined *hic vesper* according to the third declension, and made the vocative *o vespere*. He would not chant, and said that he knew nothing of chant.

At the same place and time he put forth the following words: "Seeing that you, reverend Father, by the Grace of God Archbishop of Rouen, will not admit me Nicholas called Quesnel as rector of the church of St Mary at Wynemerville, or even confer the said benefice upon me, because you think me insufficiently lettered, although I Nicholas have been presented to the said church by the true patron, and it is vacant and free; and because you would have your enquiry made into the aforesaid matters, and especially concerning my morals, honesty and life, and the truth and lawfulness of the patronage was fully proved to you; therefore I the aforesaid Nicholas, feeling aggrieved herein, by the authority and will of John called Quesnel, patron of the said church, appeal in writing to the Apostolic See, and pray that you will give and seal me letters apostolic,[2] which if you refuse to give and seal for me, again I appeal in writing to the same Apostolic See, submitting myself and the aforesaid church, by the authority of the said patron, to the Pope's protection." To which appeal we thought not fit to defer, seeing that we found him in our examination to be of utterly insufficient learning, as for example he knew neither to read competently, nor to construe, nor would he chant. Present at the aforesaid examination and appeal [here follow the names of five assessors. There are no more entries on this subject; the appeal probably failed, for Odo was in high personal favour both with St Louis and with the Pope].

[1] According to Donatus (ed. Keil, p. 139) his answer is hopelessly wrong from the first, as it certainly is at the last. But the examiners do not seem always to have followed the terminology of Donatus.

[2] Letters dimissory, permitting a cleric to leave his diocese in order to appeal to the Papal Court, or for other reasons.

47

Compare with these an extract from the last book which Erasmus wrote, within a few months of the Dissolution of the monasteries in England (*Ecclesiastes*, in *Opp*. vol. v, col. 808, Leyden, 1704). It was from this same bishop that Erasmus had received his own orders.

22 A. CLERICAL IGNORANCE

I T will not be out of place here to relate what befel the late bishop of Utrecht, David, son of duke Philip the Good [of Burgundy]. He was a man of conspicuous learning and an excellent theologian, which is very rare among nobles, and especially among bishops of that province, who are burdened with worldly power. He had heard that, among so many who were promoted to Holy Orders, very few were really educated.[1] He resolved to get nearer to the truth; and had his own throne placed in the hall to which the candidates were admitted. He himself propounded questions to each, in proportion to the dignity of the Order which they sought; easier questions to candidates for the subdiaconate, somewhat harder for the deacons, and theological for the priests. Do you ask what happened? He rejected all the candidates but three. Those who usually managed these matters felt that it would be a terrible disgrace to the Church if three only were ordained out of three hundred. The bishop, a man of fervid enthusiasm, answered that it would be a greater disgrace to the Church if they admitted, instead of men, creatures that were more foolish than asses. He was urged to moderate his sentence, by those who reaped a certain profit from this affair; let him consider that these days no longer produce saints like Paul and Jerome, and that we must receive men of the sort that the age produces. The bishop persisted, saying that he did not require Pauls or Jeromes, but that he would not admit asses for men. This compelled them to produce their last argument. It was brought forward; and what was it? "If" (said they) "you are resolved to persist in this purpose, then you must increase our salaries; otherwise, without these asses, we shall starve." That was the battering-ram which beat down the bishop's lofty spirit. Yet this ram

[1] Paucissimos esse qui literas scirent.

might have been rebutted in many ways: "Your salaries are not given for luxury and ambition but for temperate living; and what we give is enough for this." But this might perchance have been retorted upon the bishop, whose ecclesiastical income is given for plain living, and not for a noisy crowd of retainers. It would have been nobler, therefore, to say: "If you lack anything for your use, it shall be patched up in some other way, or from my revenues, provided only that the Church be not defiled by such ministers." Skilful generals would rather lead a moderate troop of good fighting-men than a numerous crowd of useless soldiers. What does it matter whether the Church has very few priests, well fitted for ecclesiastical functions, or a numberless crowd of useless folk who rather burden than support her?...Nowadays, in some regions, every house has its private chapel and priests; and, everywhere, just as suffragan bishops are created to be hired by any bishop who wishes, so priests are consecrated with no fixed income, but such as even any leathermonger's wife may hire, to escort his mistress to church, and kneel thrice at her feet before he hands her book, and bring her home again with like ceremony. Moreover, they are created for these purposes *per saltum*,[1] as the phrase goes, and before the lawful age, provided only that they pay a fee....Now, in some places, if the corpse of some rich and ambitious man is to be buried, what a crowd of priests we see! Hundreds flock thither to sing the dirge and celebrate the funeral-feast. If the Gospel is to be preached, how few there are! You shall scarce find one.

[1] That is, taking two, or often more, orders simultaneously, instead of waiting for the intervals prescribed as safeguards by Canon Law.

Matthew Paris, monk of St Albans and Historiographer Royal to Henry III, is unquestionably the greatest of the English medieval chroniclers, and has few rivals in Europe during this period. He was a man of many and various accomplishments—diplomatist, mathematician, poet, theologian, and artist, though the best authorities ascribe to other hands nearly all the beautiful drawings which illustrate the MSS. of his works. Far more extracts would have been given here, but that a complete translation of his *Chroncle*, uninspired but otherwise satisfactory, has been published in Bohn's Antiquarian Library. He died in or about the year 1259.

23. THE WANDERING JEW

I N this year [1228] a certain archbishop of Armenia came on a pilgrimage to England that he might visit the relics of our English saints and the holy places, as he had done in other kingdoms. He showed letters from the lord Pope commending his presence to men of religion and prelates, that he might be received by them with due reverence and honourably treated. Coming at length to St Albans that he might pray to the first martyr of England, he was received with all reverence by the abbot and brethren; and, being somewhat wayworn, he tarried awhile with us for refreshment of himself and his men, during which time he enquired much through his interpreters of the rites and religion of this country and our manner of life, relating still more marvellous things concerning the eastern countries. . . . When we enquired of him, among other things, of that Joseph of whom men often spake (who was present at the Lord's Passion and spake with Him and liveth still in proof of the Christian faith), asking whether he had ever seen him or had heard aught of him, then the archbishop answered and told us the whole story in order, and after him a certain knight of Antioch, who was in his train and served as his interpreter (who also was known to a certain servant of our abbot named Henry Spigurnel), expounding his master's tale, said in the French tongue: "Well doth my lord," said he, "know that man; and, not long before he set out on his journey to these western parts, this same Joseph ate at my lord archbishop's table in Armenia, whom my lord had oftentimes seen, and heard his speech." When therefore we enquired of all that had passed between our Lord Jesus

Christ and this same Joseph, he answered: "At the time of our Lord's Passion, when He had been taken by the Jews and brought into the judgment hall before Pilate the governor, to be judged of him, the Jews constantly accused Him; but Pilate, finding in Him no cause of death, said to them: 'Take ye Him and judge Him according to your law.' Yet at length, when the clamours of the Jews increased, Pilate released Barabbas at their petition and delivered Jesus unto them to be crucified. So when the Jews drew Jesus out of the Judgment Hall, as He came to the door, then Cartaphilus who was door-keeper of that hall and of Pontius Pilate, as Jesus went through the door, smote Him in scorn with his fist upon the back, and said mockingly: 'Hasten, Jesus! Why tarriest Thou?' Jesus, therefore, looking round upon him with a stern eye and threatening mien, said: 'I go, and thou shalt await My return': as if He had said with the Evangelist: 'The Son of Man goeth indeed as it is written of Him, but thou shalt await My second coming.' This Cartaphilus, therefore, waiteth still according to the Lord's word. At the time of the Passion he was about thirty years old; and ever, when he is come once more in process of time to the age of 100 years, he is seized as with an incurable sickness and rapt into an ecstasy, after which he recovereth and is brought to life again at that same age of thirty years which he had at our Lord's Passion, so that he might say in truth with the Psalmist: 'My youth shall be renewed like the eagle's.' When therefore the Catholic Faith spread abroad after the Lord's death, then was this same Cartaphilus baptized by Ananias (who also baptized the Apostle Paul), and was called by the name of Joseph. He dwelleth oftentimes in both parts of Armenia and in other eastern regions, living among bishops and other prelates of the church, a man of holy conversation and religion, of few and circumspect words, for he saith nothing unless he be first asked by the bishops and men of religion, and then will he speak concerning all things of old time and all that was done in our Lord's Passion and Resurrection, and of the witnesses to the resurrection, that is to say, those who rose again with Christ and came into the Holy City and appeared unto many. He will tell also of the Apostles' Creed and how they separated and how they preached; and all this without laughter or any levity of speech, without any note of blame or rebuke, as one who is rather busied with weeping and the fear of the Lord, ever hearing and ever bearing in mind the coming of Jesus Christ with fire to judge the world, lest he may find Him wroth at that Last Day of trial, Whom as He hastened on to His Passion he mocked and provoked to that merited vengeance. Many come to him from the farthest parts of the world, delighting to see him and speak with him; and if they be trustworthy men he will briefly solve their questions on doubtful matters. He refuseth all gifts offered to him, contenting himself with moderate food and raiment. Therein lieth ever his hope of salvation, that he erred in ignorance; seeing that the Lord said and prayed: 'Father, forgive them, for they know not what they do.' For Paul, after sinning in ignorance, obtained grace, and likewise Peter also, who denied his Lord through frailty, that is, through fear; but Judas, who betrayed Him through the iniquity of covetousness, hanged himself with a rope and his bowels burst forth, and he ended his unhappy life without hope of heaven. Upon such reasons does this Cartaphilus set his hope of indulgence, and thus doth he defend his error." Again we enquired of the aforesaid archbishop concerning Noah's ark, which is said still to rest on the mountains of Armenia, and of many other things. He said that this is true, and gave his testimony to the truth; for the reverence of his person, and his testimony, sealed as it were with the seal of his honour, impressed faith upon the minds of his hearers, and confirmed his story by the seal of reason. Moreover, the full truth of these things is testified by a certain noble knight, valiant in war, Richard d'Argenton, who devoutly visited the east in his own person as a pilgrim, together with many others, and died afterwards as a bishop.

Villard de Honnecourt was probably the architect of Notre Dame de Cambrai, the reconstruction of which was begun in 1230 and finished in 1250. The following extract is from fol. 46 of his sketch-book, which by a fortunate chance has survived to the present day, and was published in facsimile by Lassus in 1858. His notes show that he specially studied the cathedrals of Reims and Laon, where he records his high admiration of that tower with its sculptured oxen which still looks out over the plain. He was also on the Rhine, at Lausanne, and in Hungary, where he probably built one of the churches of this date which show strong French influence. Apart from strictly technical points, his sketch-book shows an interest in such miscellaneous matters as perpetual motion, mechanical toys, trigonometry, engines of war, elementary surgery, and zoology. Its introduction runs (fol. 2): "Villard de Honnecourt saluteth you, and beseecheth that all those who labour at the divers kinds of works contained in this book may pray for his soul and keep him in remembrance; for in this book you may find great help to instruct yourselves in the principles of masonry and woodwork. You will find also the method of portraiture and draughtsmanship, after the laws and principles of geometry."

24. LION TAMING

(Fol. 46.)

Now will I speak to you of the instruction of the lion. He who would teach the lion hath two dogs. When he would fain make the lion do anything, he commandeth him to do it, and if the lion murmur, then he beateth the dogs; whereof the lion misdoubteth him sore, when he seeth the dogs beaten; wherefore he refraineth his courage and doeth that which hath been commanded. And if the lion be wroth, thereof will I speak no whit, for then would he obey neither for good nor evil usage. And know well that this lion here was portrayed from the life.

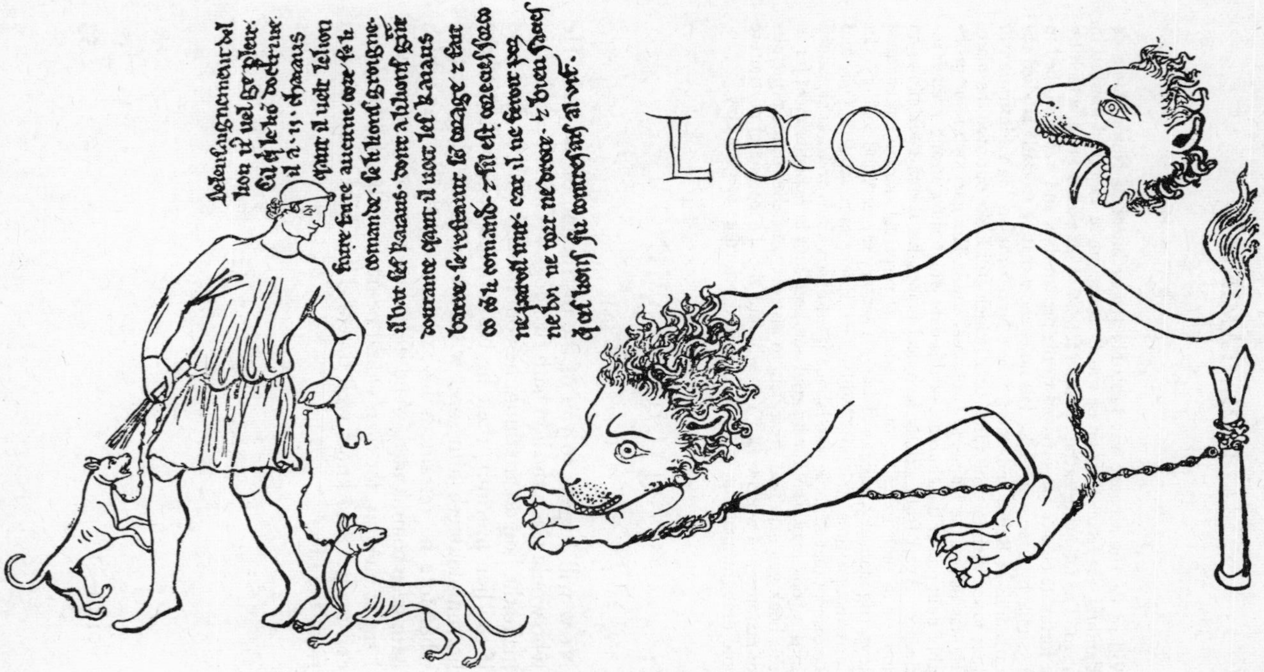

THE LION AND HIS TAMER

For a brilliant popular account of Roger Bacon see J. R. Green's *Short History*, chap. III, sect. iv; for a far more authoritative estimate of his work, Rashdall's *Universities of Europe in the Middle Ages*, vol. II, pp. 522 ff. Bacon, in Dr Rashdall's words, was "the most astonishing phenomenon of the medieval schools...unlike other medieval thinkers, orthodox or unorthodox, he saw that the study of Greek was the true key to the meaning of Aristotle, and a knowledge of the Bible in the original the true foundation for a fruitful study of theology. All the characteristic ideas of the sixteenth century are held in solution, as it were, in the writings of Roger Bacon, mixed up no doubt with much that is redolent of the age in which he lived; but, of all the anticipations of modern ways of thinking with which his works abound, the most remarkable is his plan of educational reform."

After twenty years of study and experiments, during which he expended on books and instruments the equivalent of nearly £40,000 modern money, Bacon joined the Franciscan Order, a step which he evidently lived to repent. His superiors forbade him to publish anything, and he would have died unknown but for the intervention of Clement IV, who had heard of him before his elevation to the papacy, and who in 1266 sent a letter bidding him write down his ideas "without delay, and with all possible secrecy, without regard to any contrary precept of your Superiors or any constitution of your Order." In less than two years Bacon wrote three works extending to some 600 folio pages of print—the *Opus Majus*, *Opus Minus*, and *Opus Tertium*. In 1271 he followed these up with the *Compendium Studii Philosophiae*, from which the following extracts are taken (ed. J. S. Brewer, R.S. 1859).

25. ROGER BACON'S DESPAIR
(p. 398.)

NEVERTHELESS, seeing that we consider not these hindrances from our youth upwards, but neglect them altogether therefore we are lost with infinite error, nor can we enjoy the profit of wisdom in the church and in the three other regions whereof I have spoken above.[1] For these hindrances bring it about that men believe themselves to stand in the highest glory of wisdom, so that there was never so great an appearance of wisdom nor so busy exercise of study in so many branches and in so many parts of the world, as in the last forty years.[2] For Doctors, and especially Doctors of

[1] *I.e.* the conduct of the State, the conversion of the heathen, and the repression of reprobate sinners (p. 397).

[2] *I.e.* since the rise of the Franciscan and Dominican Friars, the Student-Orders, as he calls them below, in contradistinction to the monks, who had already grown careless of learning. Cf. Richard de Bury's *Philobiblion*.

Divinity, are scattered abroad in every city and town and borough, especially by means of the two Student-Orders; and this hath been only for the last forty years, more or less. Yet the truth is that there hath never been so great ignorance and such deep error, as I will most clearly prove later on in this present treatise, and as is already manifestly shown by facts. For more sins reign in these days than in any past age; and sin is incompatible with wisdom. Let us look upon all conditions in the world, and consider them diligently; everywhere we shall find boundless corruption, and first of all in the Head. For the Court of Rome, which once was ruled by God's wisdom, and should always be so ruled, is now debased by the constitutions of lay Emperors, made for the governance of lay-folk and contained in the code of civil law. The Holy See is torn by the deceit and fraud of unjust men. Justice perisheth, all peace is broken, infinite scandals are aroused. This beareth its fruit in utterly perverse manners; pride reigneth, covetousness burneth, envy gnaweth upon all, the whole [Papal] Court is defamed of lechery, and gluttony is lord of all...if this be so in the Head, what then is done among the members? Let us see the prelates; how they run after money, neglect the cure of souls, promote their nephews, and other carnal friends, and crafty lawyers who ruin all by their counsels; for they despise students in philosophy and theology, and hinder the two Orders, who come forward to serve the Lord without hire, from living in freedom and working for the salvation of souls. Let us consider the religious Orders: I exclude none from what I say. See how far they are fallen, one and all, from their right state; and the new Orders [of Friars] are already horribly decayed from their first dignity. The whole clergy is intent upon pride, lechery, and avarice; and wheresoever clerks are gathered together, as at Paris and Oxford, they scandalize the whole laity with their wars and quarrels and other vices. Princes and barons and knights oppress and rob each other, and trouble their subjects with infinite wars and exactions, wherein each striveth to despoil the other even of duchies and kingdoms, as we see in these days. For it is notorious that the King of France hath most unjustly despoiled the King of England of that great territory; and Charles [of Anjou] hath even now crushed the heirs of Frederick [II] in mighty battles. Men care not what is done nor how, whether by right or wrong, if only each may have his own will; meanwhile they are slaves to gluttony and lechery and the wickedness of other sins. The people, harassed by their princes, hate them and keep no fealty save under compulsion; moreover, corrupted by the evil examples of their betters, they oppress and circumvent and defraud one another, as we see everywhere with our own eyes; and they are utterly given over to lechery and gluttony, and are more debased than tongue can tell. Of merchants and craftsmen there is no question, since fraud and deceit and guile reign beyond all measure in all their words and deeds.

There is another measure of the effect of this corruption. For the faith of Christ hath been revealed to the world, and certified already by saints without number. . . . And we have our Lord Jesus Christ in the sacrament of the altar; everywhere and daily we make it at our will, in accordance with that His precept, "Do this in remembrance of Me"; we eat and drink Him, and are turned into Him, to become Gods and Christs. . . . Certainly if men had faith, reverence, and devotion to this sacrament as they are in duty bound, then they would not corrupt themselves with so many errors and sins and wickednesses, but would know all wisdom and wholesome truth in this life: wherefore, seeing that they here play the ass [*hic asininant*], and many are infirm and weak and sleep (to use the Apostle's words) therefore they must needs become infirm and weak in all that region of wisdom, and sleep the sleep of death, and play the ass beyond common estimation; for this [sacrament] is at the end of the glory and goodness and comeliness of wisdom, and hath more certain proofs than any other kind. . . . Since therefore we know but little in so noble and so plain a matter, therefore all other profitable wisdom must needs be put farther away from us than tongue may tell.

The third consideration from effects is taken by comparing our state with that of the ancient Philosophers; who, though they were without that quickening grace which maketh man worthy of eternal life, and whereinto we enter at baptism, yet lived beyond all comparison better than we, both in all decency and in contempt of the world, with all its delights and riches and honours; as all men may read in the works of Aristotle, Seneca, Tully, Avicenna, Alfarabius, Plato, Socrates, and others; and so it was that they attained to the secrets of wisdom and found out all knowledge. But we Christians have discovered nothing worthy of those philosophers, nor can we even understand their wisdom; which ignorance of ours springs from this cause, that our morals are worse than theirs. For it is impossible that wisdom should coexist with sin, but she requireth perfect virtue, as I will show later on. But certain it is that, if there were so much wisdom in the world as men think, these evils would not be committed...and therefore, when we see everywhere (and especially among the clergy) such corruption of life, then their studies must needs be corrupt. Many wise men—considering this, and pondering on God's wisdom and the learning of the saints and the truth of histories, and not only the prophecies of Holy Scripture but also such salutary predictions as those of the Sibyls and Merlin and Aquila and Festo and many other wise men—have reckoned that the times of Antichrist are at hand in these days of ours.[1] Wherefore wickedness must needs be uprooted, and the Elect of God must appear; or else one most blessed Pope will first come, who shall remove all corruptions from University and Church and elsewhere, that the world may be renewed, and the fulness of the Gentiles may enter in, and the remnants of Israel be converted to the faith....God indeed, in His infinite goodness and long-suffering of wisdom, doth not at once punish mankind, but delayeth His vengeance until the iniquity be fulfilled, so that it may not and should not be longer endured....But now, seeing that the measure of man's wickedness is full, it must needs be that some most virtuous Pope and most virtuous Emperor shall arise to purge the Church with the double sword of the spirit and the flesh; or else that such purgation shall take place through Antichrist; or, thirdly, through some other tribulation, as the discord of Christian princes, or the

---

[1] The next greatest English friar of this age, Adam de Marisco, is even more emphatic on this subject, and more pessimistic generally, than Bacon.

Tartars and Saracens and other kings of the East, as divers scriptures and manifold prophecies tell us. For there is no doubt whatever among wise men, but that the Church *must* be purged: yet whether in the first fashion, or the second, or the third, they are not agreed, nor is there any certain definition on this head.

(P. 425.) The second principal cause of error in the present pursuit of wisdom is this: that for forty years past certain men have arisen in the universities who have created themselves masters and doctors in theology and philosophy, though they themselves have never learned anything of any account; nor will they or can they learn by reason of their position, as I will take care to show by argument, in all its length and breadth, within the compass of the following pages. And, albeit I grieve and pity these as much as I can, yet truth prevaileth over all, and therefore I will here expound at least some of those things which are done publicly and are known to all men, though few turn their hearts to regard either this or other profitable considerations, by reason of those causes of error which I here set forth, and whereby almost all men are basely blinded. These are boys who are inexperienced in the knowledge of themselves and of the world and of the learned languages, Greek and Hebrew, which (as I will prove later on) are necessary to study; they are ignorant also of all parts and sciences of the world's philosophy and of wisdom, when they so presumptuously enter upon the study of theology, which requireth all human wisdom, as the saints teach and as all wise men know. For, if truth be anywhere, here is she found: here, if anywhere, is falsehood condemned, as Augustine saith in his book *Of Christian Doctrine.* These are boys of the two Student-Orders, as Albert and Thomas[1] and others, who in many cases enter those Orders at or below the age of twenty years. This is the common course, from the English sea to the furthest confines of Christendom, and more

---

[1] *I.e.* Albertus afterwards called Magnus, and St Thomas Aquinas. Bacon (though no doubt he goes too far here in his disparagement) anticipates the main lines of modern criticism on scholastic philosophy—that it neglected almost altogether those physical and mathematical sciences on which all true philosophy must be based, and that even its principal sources—the Bible and Aristotle—were studied only in faulty translations, and often fatally misunderstood.

especially beyond the realm of France; so that in Aquitaine, Provence, Spain, Italy, Germany, Hungary, Denmark, and everywhere, boys are promiscuously received into the Orders from their tenth to their twentieth year; boys too young to be able to know anything worth knowing, even though they were not already possessed with the aforesaid causes of human error; wherefore, at their entrance into the Orders, they know nought that profiteth to theology. Many thousands become friars who cannot read their Psalter or their Donat;[1] yet, immediately after their admission, they are set to study theology. Wherefore they must of necessity fail to reap any great profit, especially seeing that they have not taken lessons from others in philosophy since their entrance; and, most of all, because they have presumed in those Orders to enquire into philosophy by themselves and without teachers, so that they are become Masters in Theology and in Philosophy before being disciples. Wherefore infinite error reigneth among them, although for certain reasons this is not apparent, by the Devil's instigation and by God's permission. One cause of this appearance is that the Orders have the outward show of great holiness; wherefore it is probable to the world that men in so holy a state would not presume on such things as they could not perform. Yet we see that all states are corrupted in this age, as I have discoursed in detail above. . . .

Bacon then goes on to set forth, under a series of numbered heads, the almost universal ignorance of Greek and Hebrew among Western philosophers and theologians, the small quantity and detestable quality of the accredited translations of Aristotle, and the consequent rottenness of contemporary science at its very foundation.

Wherefore all who know anything at all neglect the false translation of Aristotle, and seek such remedy as they may. This is a truth which men lost in learning will not consider; but they seek consolation for their ignorance like brute beasts. If I had power over the books of Aristotle [as at present translated], I would burn them all; for to study therein is but lost time, and a source of error and a multiplication of ignorance beyond all human power to describe. And, seeing that the labours of Aristotle are the foundation

[1] Latin Grammar; Donatus was the favourite grammarian of the Middle Ages.

of all wisdom, therefore no man may tell how much the Latins waste now because they have accepted evil translations of the Philosopher: wherefore there is no full remedy anywhere. Whosoever will glory in Aristotle's science, he must needs learn it in its own native tongue, since false translations are everywhere, in theology as well as in philosophy. For all the translators [of the Bible] before St Jerome erred cruelly, as he himself saith over and over again.... We have few profitable books of philosophy in Latin, for Aristotle wrote a hundred volumes, as we read in his life, whereof we possess only three of any importance: his Logic, his Natural History, and his Metaphysics.... But the vulgar herd of students, with their leaders, have nothing to rouse them to any worthy effort: wherefore they feebly dote over these false translations, losing everywhere their time, their labour, and their money. For outward appearance alone possesseth them; nor care they what they know, but only what they may seem to know in the eyes of the senseless multitude.

So likewise numberless matters of God's wisdom are still wanting. For many books of Holy Writ are not translated; both two books of the Maccabees which I know to exist in the Greek, and many other books of many prophets, which are cited in the Books of Kings and Chronicles. Moreover, Josephus in his *Antiquities* is utterly false as to the course of time, without which nothing can be known of the history of the Sacred Text; wherefore he is worthless until he be reformed by a new translation, and sacred history perisheth. Moreover, the Latins lack innumerable books of the Hebrew and Greek expositors, as Origen, Basil, Gregory Nazianzene, Damascenus, Dionysius, Chrysostom, and other most noble doctors, in Hebrew as well as in Greek. Therefore the Church slumbereth; for in this matter she doeth naught, nor hath done for these seventy years past, except that the lord Robert [Grosseteste] of holy memory, Bishop of Lincoln, translated into Latin from the books of St Dionysius, and Damascenus, and a few other consecrated teachers. We must marvel at the negligence of the Church; for there hath been no supreme Pontiff since the days of Pope Damasus [A.D. 384], nor any inferior pontiff who hath been solicitous for the profit of the

Church through translations, save only the above-mentioned glorious Bishop.

The thirteenth cause why Latin students need the knowledge of languages is the corruption which besetteth our studies through the ignorance of learned languages in these days. This cause is complementary of the Latins' error and ignorance. For such books of divine and human wisdom as have been well translated and truly expounded, are now become utterly faulty by reason of the disuse of the aforesaid learned languages in Latin countries. For thus, by the examples already cited, we may set forth clearly enough by way of compendious introduction, and see in general terms, how the Bible hath been corrupted. But he who would go into details would not find a single sentence wherein there is no falsehood, or at least no great uncertainty, on account of the disagreement of correctors: and this doubt falleth upon every wise man, even as we name that "fear" which falleth even upon a constant man. Yet there is falsehood wellnigh everywhere, even though doubts be interspersed. And would not these false or dubious passages be cleared away, to the quantity of half the Bible, if we introduced some certain method of proof, as the reasonable manner of correction demandeth? Wherefore all theologians nowadays, whether reading or preaching, use false texts, and cannot profit, and can consequently neither understand nor teach anything of any account.[1]

---

[1] In these last two sentences I have ventured on two emendations which seem required by the sense; viz. *nonne* for *non* and *proficere* for *proferre*. Bacon's complaint of the corruption of the medieval Vulgate text, exaggerated as it may seem, is borne out by proved facts. The late Sub-librarian of the Vatican, Father Denifle, wrote an article on this subject, in which he said: "It offers a melancholy spectacle, which would be still more darkened by a comparison of other manuscripts of the 13th century.... Roger Bacon was indeed right when he exclaimed with regard to the accredited Paris text, (which followed Correctorium E, and therefore contained the interpolations and belonged to the same family of MSS. as that above quoted), 'The text is for the most part horribly corrupt in the Vulgate, that is the Parisian, Exemplar.'" *Archiv f. Litt. und Kirchengeschichte* u.s.w., Band IV, S. 567.

Berthold von Regensburg, or of Ratisbon, was born about 1220 of a well-to-do citizen family. He joined the Franciscans while still a youth, and became the favourite pupil of David of Augsburg, whose writings were often attributed in the Middle Ages to St Bonaventura. He was already famous as a preacher in 1250; until his death in 1272 he tramped from village to village, like a Whitefield or a Wesley, through Bavaria, Rhineland, Switzerland, Swabia, Austria, Moravia, Bohemia, Silesia, Thuringia and Franconia. His fame spread all over Europe; he is enthusiastically extolled in the chronicles of Salimbene and the XXIV Generals; and Roger Bacon, speaking of contemporary preaching in words which do not err on the side of compliment, expressly excepts Berthold as one who "alone maketh more excellent profit in preaching than almost all the other Friars of either Order" (*Opp. Inedd.* R.S. p. 310). A thick volume of Berthold's sermons, translated into modern German, is in its third edition as a book of living theology (Regensburg, Manz, 1873). The text here used is that of Franz Pfeiffer (2 vols. Vienna, 1862). The abrupt changes from *thou* to *ye* are in the original.

26. A LESSON IN ANATOMY

(Band i, S. 431.)

In old days women were exceeding temperate, eating and drinking but little, yet now is gluttony become an ingrained custom with them. By the time the goodman hath drunk away his sword, the goodwife hath drunk away her ring and the veil from her head; and both have lost their honour for their gluttony's sake, and ruined soul and body, and health, and hope of long life.—"How, Brother Berthold, I had ever thought that, the better a man ate and drank, the stronger and stouter he would be, and live the longer for it."—That is false, and I will tell thee why. The stomach is in thy body; right in the midst of the body lieth a man's stomach, that receiveth first of all whatsoever thou eatest or drinkest; and this same stomach is shaped even like a cauldron on the fire, wherein we boil our food. Ye see well how, if the cauldron on the fire be filled too full, then must one of two evil things come to pass: either the cauldron will boil over and the food remain uncooked, or the food must burn in the cauldron, and so again stay uncooked; but if a man fill the cauldron in all temperance, then the food may be well sodden and find room to simmer quietly through and through....Now see and mark this, all and several. Even so is it with a man's stomach, that standeth in the midst of the body like a cauldron, and the liver lieth hard by the stomach like a fire, for the liver hath by nature the greatest heat of the whole body, and bringeth heat to the stomach wherewith all is seethed that a man may eat and drink.... If the stomach be too full, however hot the liver be, yet must the food stay uncooked; and if it boil over, then the superfluity rises either to the head, that a man's ears are dulled and he becomes deaf; or to the face, that his eyes grow weak or blind—heavy eyes, glassy eyes, or gravel-blind. ...And mark me this one thing! rich folk's children grow far more seldom to old age, or even to manhood, than poor folk's children; that cometh from the over-feeding that men practise on rich folk's children, for none can ever fill them so full that another will believe it is enough. That ariseth from the tenderness wherewith they are cherished, and also for that there is ever enough and to spare in the house. So the child's sister makes him a pap and coaxes it into him; now mark! his little cauldron, his little belly, is soon filled, and the pap begins to bubble out again, but she coaxes it in and in. Then cometh his aunt and doth likewise. Then cometh his nurse and crieth: "Alas! my child hath eaten nought this livelong day!" and she will straightway coax the pap in again as before, for all that the child may cry and toss his little limbs. Thus do all vie one with another in feeding rich men's children, so that few indeed grow to a good old age.

THE PROUD PROFESSOR

Thomas Cantimpratanus (of Chantimpré in Brabant) was the son of a noble who had fought under our Richard I in the Holy Land. A hermit near Antioch, to whom the father had confessed his sins, warned him that some of them would keep him long in purgatory unless he bred up one of his sons to the priesthood. The child Thomas was therefore sent to school at Liège, where (as he tells us in no. 69 in vol. I) he spent eleven years. At the age of fifteen he was much impressed by Jacques de Vitry's preaching. In early manhood he became a Canon Regular at Chantimpré, but passed over to the stricter Dominicans about 1231. He became a very distinguished preacher, a suffragan bishop, and a fairly voluminous writer. By far the most valuable of his works is the *Bonum Universale de Apibus*, a treatise on virtues and vices by analogy with the life of the bee, illustrated by personal and historical anecdotes. This was written somewhere about 1260; my extract is from the Douai edition of 1597.

27. THE PROUD PROFESSOR
(Lib. II, c. 48, p. 361.)

MASTER SIMON DE TOURNAI was Master of Theology at Paris, and excelled all others in his time; yet, contrary to the decorum of such an office, he was beyond measure incontinent and proud. Having a greater audience than all other Masters in that city, while he was publicly determining in the schools a question concerning the humility of the most lofty Christian doctrine, then at length, at the very end, he was given over to a reprobate mind and burst forth into execrable blasphemies against Christ, saying: "There are three who have ensnared the world with their sects and dogmas: to wit, Moses, Jesus, and Mahomet. Moses first infatuated the Jewish people; then Jesus Christ the Christians, called after His own name; thirdly, Mahomet the heathen folk." Then his eyes turned forthwith in his head, and his human voice changed into a bellow; and, falling straightway upon the ground in an epilepsy, he received on the third day the full punishment of that sickness. Wherefore the Almighty smote him with an incurable wound, depriving him of all his learning even to the first rudiments of letters; and the plague fell even more grievously upon his soul, for he remained as it were dumb until his dying day, and was compared unto the beasts that perish.

Don Ramon Muntaner (1265–1330?) was, like Joinville and Villehardouin, a soldier by profession and an author only in his old age: his chronicle, like theirs, gains by this combination. It is the best of Spanish medieval histories, and will bear comparison with those of any other nation. The author is best introduced by his own Prologue. The extracts are from the edition published by the Litterarischer Verein of Stuttgart.

28. AN AUTHOR'S FOREWORD

In the name of our Lord and true God Jesus Christ, and of His blessed Mother our Lady St Mary, and of all His blessed saints, both now and ever. Amen!

It behoveth every man to praise and thank God and His blessed Mother for the grace and mercy which have been vouchsafed to him; which blessings a man should not conceal but rather publish abroad, that every man may take thereby a good example, striving to do and speak well. For this is sure and certain truth, that whosoever doeth and speaketh and thinketh good, to him shall God give good for his reward; but to him that doeth evil, evil, unless it be that he amend his ways. Wherefore let every man strive, so far as in him lieth, to turn evil into good; for nothing can remain hidden from God. It is a good word that men commonly use in Sicily, when one man liveth at variance with another: "nay, let him go, and trust that God knoweth thine own way." Wherefore let every man strive to live in the faith that God seeth him; for to God all things are open. Even so, among other men in this world, must I also, Ramon Muntaner, born at Perelada and free of the liberties of Valencia, give manifold thanks to our Lord and true God and His blessed Mother, the holy Virgin Mary, and to all the Court Celestial, for the grace and mercy which they have vouchsafed to me, and for my rescue from many dangers wherein I have fallen; as for the two-and-thirty battles wherein I have fought by sea and land; in which wars I have oftentimes fallen into captivity and torment, and suffered many persecutions both in my prosperity and in mine adversity, as ye may presently hear among the deeds that were done in my time. I would indeed gladly forbear from the task of this story; yet it is my bounden duty to tell it, and for this cause more especially, that all men may

learn how we had no help in so great danger but through the
succour and grace of God and His blessed Mother, the holy
Virgin Mary. Know therefore that, when I went forth from
my home at Perelada, I was not yet eleven years old;[1] and
when I began by God's gracious help to write this book I stood
in my sixtieth year; which book I began on the fifteenth day of
May in the year of the glorious birth of our Lord and Saviour
Jesus Christ, one thousand three hundred and twenty five.

Chaps. 124–6. In the year 1283 Pope Martin IV proclaimed a crusade
against Peter of Aragon, who had thwarted his policy in Sicily and that
of his protégé Charles of Anjou. Philip the Bold of France caught at
this excuse to wage a holy war in Spain; he and his crusaders came and
besieged Muntaner's native town, but were beaten in several sorties.

29. THE SIEGE OF PERELADA

THERE was a lady at Perelada whom I knew and saw: men
called her Marcadera for that she sold merchandise [*mer-
caderia*]; she was a very doughty woman, stout and big of
bones. One day while the French host lay encamped before
Perelada, she went forth to fetch herbs from the garden without the walls: she put on a man's quilted doublet and armed
herself with sword and shield and lance, and thus went forth
into her garden. And as she stooped in the garden she heard
a sound of bells, whereupon she marvelled and left to pick
her colewort, and went to see what this might be: when lo!
in the way betwixt her garden and her neighbour's, she saw
a French knight fully harnessed on his horse, that was all
hung with little bells at his breastband; he rode hither and
thither to find issue from that path. When she was aware of
him, she strode forward a step and dealt him so shrewd a
thrust with her lance through the cuisses that she drove
through thigh and saddle, and even wounded the horse also.
When the beast felt the hurt, he reared and kicked again, and
would surely have thrown his rider but that he was bound
with a chain to the saddle. What more shall I say? She drew
her sword and ran round by a little gate and smote the beast

[1] He was probably sent out, according to the usual medieval custom, as page
in some knight's house.

so sore on the head that he staggered. What more? She seized the rein and cried to the Knight, "Yield thee, or thou art a dead man!" and he, that thought himself but dead, cast away his sword and yielded himself prisoner. She therefore took up the sword, drew the lance from his side, and led him to Perelada. The King and the Infante made merry over this story, and would oftentimes bid the lady tell them how she had taken him. In brief, the Knight and his armour were hers; he ransomed himself for two hundred gold pieces, which fell to her share. Thereby may ye know God's anger against the French.

[Meanwhile the King of Aragon thought the town strong enough to be left to the protection of a moderate garrison, assisted by 1000 Almugavars, or mercenary foot-soldiers.]

What think ye then? The King had with him some five thousand Almugavars, whereof he bade one thousand tarry behind at Perelada. These men, therefore, were sore grieved to be thus left, and they were cut to the heart to consider how they must now lose that spoil which the rest should win in skirmishes against the French; wherefore they purposed to get themselves some other satisfaction: hear ye therefore the iniquity which they devised in their hearts! About midnight, when the King and Infante were gone forth from Perelada, and already perchance at Vilabertran or Figueres, they went and set fire to a full hundred places of the town, and cried: "Forth, forth!" What more? When the good folk heard this tumult from their beds, and saw the whole town in flames, then each hastened to save his son or daughter, and the men thought only of their wives and children; and the Almugavars for their part set their minds to steal and pillage. In brief, the whole city was in flames, so that within a little while there stood not ten houses whole, save for the stone walls: the which was a sore pity, for Perelada was an exceeding ancient city, wherein no Saracens had been since the days of Charles the Great and Roland. . . . While, therefore, this fire raged throughout the town, all the folk hastened forth even to the last man, save only a lady whose name was Doña Palonavera, and who went to the altar of the Blessed Virgin, in whom she had great trust, saying that she would die there.

And therein she did well, seeing that it was all from love of the Virgin Mary.

So that night the King of France and his host were aware of this mighty fire; whereat they were amazed and sat harnessed, the whole night through, upon their horses. When the day dawned, and they saw the whole town burning, then they knew that it was altogether deserted; wherefore they entered in and did all that in them lay to quench the flames; for the good men were sorry that so fair and noble a city should burn to the ground; yet were they not all of one mind; for, even as the good extinguished the fire, so the evil fed the flames. Then they entered into the church and found that pious lady with the statue of the holy Virgin in her arms: then came the accursed Picards, who were the evillest folk of the host, and forthwith they hewed the good woman in pieces before the altar, and then they bound their beasts to the altars and wrought much outrage, whereof they had their full reward from God, as ye shall hereafter hear.

When therefore the King and the Infante and their host heard how miserably this town was destroyed, they were cut to the heart; yet nought could be done as matters then stood. Wherefore all Kings of Aragon, whosoever they be, are much bounden to show kindness to this little town of Perelada in general, and especially to all citizens thereof; for the Lord of Perelada, as ye may well think, lost in the king's service all that he had. Moreover I and other men, who then lost wellnigh all our worldly goods, have never seen our houses again; but have gone about the whole world, and sought our sustenance with the sweat of our brow, and suffered many perils; whereof the greater part are now dead in the wars of the King of Aragon.

30. A BRIEF ROMANCE
(Chap. 263, A.D. 1314.)

WHEN the son of the Count of Aria had married, he took possession of the barony of Matagrifo; and, if any lord ever showed himself a man of worth, this was he; for he was very wise and doughty in all things; and his wife bare him a daughter named the lady Isabel. Soon after her birth he died, to the sore distress of all his barons and vassals in Morea. (Now this count of Aria was of the lineage of Tous, which is the most ancient and most honoured house in all Provence, and near akin to the house of Anjou.) When therefore the lady of Aria had lost her husband, she was in sore distress and would take no other spouse; and when her sister the princess [of Morea] died, she herself desired the Principality; yet they who had it in possession gave her but a short answer. Hearing then that the Infante Don Fernando, son to the King of Majorca, was in Sicily, and that he had neither wife nor land, she thought no man in the world fitter for her daughter than he, because such a man would make good all his rights to the Principality, whether by favour or by force. Wherefore she sent ambassadors to the King of Sicily and the Infante Don Fernando; and at last they were accorded that the lady and her daughter should come to Messina, and then, if the damsel were such as they said, the marriage would please them for their part. So the lady came to Messina with her daughter, and ten dames and ten damsels, and twenty knights and twenty sons of knights, and other company to boot; and their hosts did them much honour. So when the King was come to Messina, and the Infante had seen the damsel, then he would not have changed her against another, even though a man had given him the whole world to boot; nay, he had so great pleasure in the sight of her that the day seemed a year to him until the whole matter was assured; and he declared outright to the lord King that he would have this damsel to be his wife, and none other that lived in the world. And it was no marvel that he loved her so hotly: for this was the fairest creature of fourteen years that ever man might see, the whitest and the rosiest and the best; and the wisest, for the years that she had, of any damsel that ever was in the world. What shall I say more? The lady of Matagrifo invested her daughter, both in her own lifetime and after her death, with all the barony of Matagrifo and all the right which she had to the Principality, to have and to hold at her own will, without further limitation whatsoever. So when this was done, and the spousal deeds were drawn, then by God's grace, with great feast and solemnity made by the King and Queen, and all the barons of Sicily and Catalonia, and Aragonese and Latin knights, and all other folk of Messina, the lord Infante took this lady Isabel to wife; and the Archbishop of Messina sang the mass, and the feast endured for fifteen days, so that all men marvelled at the joy and gladness that were there. And when the feast was past, the lord Infante led her with him to Catania, with her mother and all the company that had come with her; and he gave her Catalan dames and damsels, wives and daughters of knights. And when they were at Catania, the lord Infante gave great gifts to all her meinie; and thus they dwelt some four months at Catania. And then the lady mother-in-law of the lord Infante turned again to Morea with her following, glad and jocund of heart—glad also and jocund of heart was the lord Infante, who stayed with my lady Infanta.

And it pleased God that she became big with child, whereof was great rejoicing when it was noised abroad. When therefore the lady was thus with child, the lord Infante made ready to go with five hundred men-at-arms and a great multitude of footmen to Morea. While he thus made ready, I had news thereof at Gerba; then must I needs go with him whithersoever it might please him to go; the whole world should not have kept me back. Wherefore I sent word to the King, praying that it might please him to send me to Sicily. The King was pleased to grant his assent; so I took a galley and a smaller boat and came with the elders of that island to Sicily, leaving the castle and island of Gerba under good watch and ward. The first land which I touched in Sicily was at Catania, where I found the Infante safe and joyful, and his lady great with child (for eight days afterwards she bore a fair son, whereof they made great rejoicing). When therefore I had come down from my galley, I brought to land two bales of Tripoli carpets, and many other Moorish rarities and other jewels; all of which I bade my servants spread out before the lady Infanta and her lord, and offered them as gifts, whereof the lord Infante was much pleased. Then I departed thence and went to Messina; for the lord Infante said that he would come thither within a fortnight and speak at length with me. Yet before I had been a fortnight there, it was reported that the lady Infanta had brought forth a son, who was born on the first Saturday in April of this year 1315. God grant to every man such joy as I then felt! Ask me not whether the lord Infante was glad, with all that dwelt at Catania! more than eight days they feasted there; and the boy was baptized in the Cathedral of the blessed lady Saint Agatha, and they gave him the name of Jacme. If ever a child was born of good grace, it was this boy Don Jacme. What more shall I say? When the child was baptized, and his mother out of danger, the lord Infante came to Messina, where I proffered myself to him, both body and goods, to follow him whithersoever he would. He gave me hearty thanks, and said: "Go hence to the lord King, whom ye shall find at Plasa, and render into his hands the castle and the islands of Gerba and Querquens; then return to us, and I will teach you what ye shall do." Then I departed from him; and in the meantime word came that he must ride in all haste to Catania, for his lady was sick of fever and anguish of her reins. So he rode and came that night to Catania; and the lady was better for sight of him; yet she had already made her testament before the sickness came sorer upon her, and then she confirmed it; in which testament she had left to her son Don Jacme the barony of Matagrifo and her claim to the Principality: and in case of his death all should fall to her husband Don Fernando. In truth it was already two months since her mother was dead of mortal sickness at Matagrifo; but she knew nought thereof, nor would the lord Infante that any man should tell her aught while she was with child, or when she was brought to bed, or before she should have been churched. And, though the Infante was ready for his voyage, yet he hoped not to set out until the Infanta should be delivered and churched; then should she come to ship with him, for all were ready to set sail. In brief, the Infanta, by God's will, passed from this life two and thirty days after the birth of her child; and she breathed her last in the arms of her lord. If ever man saw grief, it was in this Infante Don Fernando and the whole city. With great solemnity (as for one who was purified and confessed and aneled and anointed), she was laid in a fair monument hard by the body of the blessed virgin my lady Saint Agatha, in her blessed church at Catania.

The next few chapters describe how Ramon was chosen to escort the little motherless Jacme to his grandmother, the Queen of Majorca: how he safely avoided all the enemies that lay in wait for them, and brought the child safe to Catalonia.

The following inquests are chosen as typical cases from the few surviving Oxford Coroners' Rolls which are printed on pp. 150 ff. of Prof. J. E. T. Rogers' *Oxford City Documents*. Of the twenty-nine inquests there recorded, thirteen disclose murders committed by students. This is partly attributable to the fact that the student, being a cleric, could not be hanged for his first murder. Robert of Bridlington, one of the heroes of no. (iv) here below, was apparently not even expelled from Oxford, but perished in a later affray between Town and Gown.

31. OXFORD MANNERS

(i) 1297.

It befel on the Monday next following the Purification of the Blessed Virgin Mary, in the 25th year of King Edward, that John Metescharp of Oxford died in the house of Ralph the surgeon in the parish of St Aldate's, and that same day he was viewed by John de Oseney coroner to the Lord King; and he had a wound in his left side from a certain small arrow of the breadth of half an inch, and the depth of five inches; and that same day an inquest was held before the aforesaid coroner by the oath of Thomas de Morton, Thomas le Parmenter, John de Stamford, Richard de Bampton, Thomas de Lewes, Geoffrey le Smith and Thomas le Turner, jurymen of the parish of St Aldate; Nicholas de Lincoln, Nicholas de Weston, Richard Sutton, John de Themele, William King and John le Furnur, jurymen of the parish of St Ebbe; Adam de Tilhurst, William de Godstow, Richard de Eynsham, Alexander de Bloxham, Robert de Quenynton and Robert de Fulbroke, jurymen of the parish of St Peter in the Bailey; Thomas de Weston, Thomas de Boleworth, Walter de Eynsham and Gilbert de Cowley, jurymen of the parish of St Martin; and all the aforesaid jurymen say on their oath that on the Saturday, on the feast of the Purification of the aforesaid year, a certain Michael, manciple to the clerks who dwell in Bull Hall in the parish of St Aldate, and a certain clerk named John de Skurf and one Madoc, a clerk of Wales, went through the streets with swords and bows and arrows shortly before the hour of curfew and assaulted all who passed by, wherefore the hue and cry was raised, and the aforesaid John Metescharp with others hearing the hue came forth from their houses to keep the Lord King's peace; and, when the aforesaid John came into the street, forthwith the aforesaid Michael shot him and inflicted the aforesaid wound, whence he died; but he had all his church rights;[1] and immediately after the aforesaid deed the said Michael and all the rest fled, so that they could not be attached; nor could anything of their chattels be found.

(ii) 1301.

It befel on Thursday, the morrow of St Nicholas' Day in the thirtieth year of King Edward, that John de Neushom, clerk and schoolmaster, was found dead by Cherwell bank hard by Petty-pont. Isabella his wife found him dead and raised the hue and cry: and he was seen that same day by John de Oseney, Coroner, and he had no wound nor any apparent hurt; whereof an inquest was held that same day, by the oath of John Pylle, William le Shoesmith, Henry le Slater, John le Cooper, John le Miller, Thomas le Taylor and Adam de Tew, jurymen of the parish of St Peter's in the east; and Ralph Baker, John le Lecche, Nicholas de Hanred, Henry le Cobbler, William de Clobber and Henry le Tailor, jurymen of the parish of St John; William de Milton, Thomas Bygod, Roger le Fletcher, Andrew de Cowley, and John de Cokesgrave, jurymen of the parish of St Mary the Virgin; Philip le Glover, Robert de Ocle, John le Smith and Ralph de Chilton, jurymen of the parish of All Saints. And all the aforesaid jurymen say upon their oath that, on the Monday late past, the said John de Neushom went after dinner to seek rods for the chastisement of the boys whom he taught, and

---

[1] *I.e.* absolution and extreme unction. The "clerks" were, of course, university students.

climbed upon a certain willow to cut such rods, hard by the mill-pond called *Temple Mill*, where by misadventure he fell into the water and was drowned. And the aforesaid jurymen say upon their oath that no man is guilty of his death. The pledges of the said wife who found him, that she would be etc.,[1] are John de Faringdon and Adam de Tew.

(iii) 1306.

It befel upon the Sunday next after the feast of the Assumption of the Blessed Virgin, in the 34th year of King Edward, that Gilbert de Foxlee, clerk, died at his lodging in the parish of St Peter in the East about the hour of noon, and on the Monday following he was viewed by Thomas Lisewys, Coroner of the Lord King for the City of Oxford; and he had a wound in his left leg, hard by the knee, of the breadth of four inches all around, and of the depth of an inch and a half. Whereof an inquest was held before the said Coroner by the oath of [etc., etc.]. . . . And [the jury] say on their oath that, on Thursday the Eve of St John last past, the tailors of Oxford and other townsfolk with them held a wake in their shops the whole night through, singing and making their solace with citherns, fiddles, and divers other instruments, as the use and custom is to do there and elsewhere on account of the solemnity of that Feast. And after midnight, finding that no man was wandering there in the streets, they went forth from their shops, and others with them, and held their dances[2] in the High Street in face of the Cloth Hall; and, as they thus played, there came the aforesaid Gilbert de Foxlee, with a certain naked and drawn sword in his hand, and began forthwith to contend with them, purposing by all means to break up that dance: but certain of them who were of his acquaintance, seeing this, came to him and would have led him away, and besought him to harm no man; yet for all that the aforesaid Gilbert would not promise, but forthwith broke away from

---

[1] *I.e.* that she would attend again if required for further inquiries or formalities: cf. Gross's *Select Coroners' Rolls*, p. 94 (Eynsham).

[2] Cf. Chaucer, *Miller's Tale*:

> In twenty manners he could skip and dance,
> (After the school of Oxenfordë though,)
> And with his leggës casten to and fro.

75

them and came back and assaulted one William de Claydon, whose hand he would have cut off with his sword as he went round in the dance, unless he had drawn suddenly back; whereupon Henry de Beaumont, Cruisor, fell upon Gilbert, together with Thomas de Bloxham, William de Leye servant to John de Leye, and the aforesaid William de Claydon; and the aforesaid Henry wounded him with a sword in the right arm, and the aforesaid Thomas with a misericorde[1] in the back, and the aforesaid William upon the head, so that he fell. Then William de Leye, with a certain axe called spar-axe, struck him forthwith upon the left leg and inflicted the aforesaid wound whereof he died on the Sunday aforesaid: yet he lived eight weeks and two days and a half, and had all his church rights.

(iv) 1314.

It befel, etc.... and [the Jury] say upon their oath that, on the Saturday aforesaid, after the hour of noon, the Northern clerks on the one part, and the Southern and Western clerks on the other, came to St John's Street and Grope Lane with swords, bucklers, bows, arrows and other arms, and there they fought together; and in that conflict Robert de Bridlington, Adam de Alderbeck, Richard de Louthby and Richard de Holwell stood together in a certain Soler[2] in Gutter Hall, situate in St John's Street, shooting down through a window into Grope Lane: and there the said Robert de Bridlington, with a small arrow, smote the aforesaid Henry of Holy Isle and wounded him hard by the throat, on the left side in front; and the wound was of the breadth of one inch, and in depth even unto the heart; and thus he slew him. Moreover the aforesaid jury say that [the others above-named] incited the said Robert to shoot the same Henry dead, and to slay him, and they were consenting unto his death.... And in the same conflict John de Benton came with a falchion into Grope Lane and gave David de Kirkby a blow on the back of the head, six inches in length and in depth even unto the brain. At which same time came William de la Hyde and

[1] Dagger.
[2] *Solar*, or *soller*: a private room, generally in an upper storey.

smote the aforesaid David with a sword across his right knee and leg: and at the same time came William de Astley and smote the said David under the left arm with a misericorde, and thus they slew him. Moreover, concerning the goods of the aforesaid evildoers, or those who have received them, the jury say that they know nothing.

Side by side with the coroner's view of these wounds it may be interesting to read the doctor's. The following extracts are from the recipes collected by Prof. Henslow (*Medical Works of the Fourteenth Century*, Chapman and Hall, 1899).

32. THE PERFECT LEECH

(p. 25. *Title in Latin.*) *Here we treat of wounds, if thou wilt know whether the wounded man may recover or no.*

TAKE pimpernole [salad burnet] and stampe hit and tempere hit with water and gif hym to drinke, and zif hit go out at ye wonde he schal live.

Another:

Zif hym to drynke letuse with water and zyf he spewe he schal be dyd.

Another:

Zif hym to drynke cristal [ice], and if he spewe hit he schal be dyde.

Another:

Zyf hym to drynke mensore[1] with ale and zef he holde hit tille that other day that same tyme he schal leve. . . .

For rankelyng of a wonde—take rede nettel and salt and stamp to-gedir, and drynke the Jus fastyng.

Another:

Good tret [ointment?] y-provyd wel, helyng everich wonde; (and if thou wilt prove it, take a cock and smite him in the brain and hold thee from [him] till he be almost dead, and then carve of this trete and lay it to his head and soon after he shall stand up and crow loudly; hit befallit so other-whyle; but how-so hit be, this he shall have;) take a good

---

[1] Prof. Henslow cannot identify this word.

handful of verveyne and another of pimpernole and another of bitayne [betony?] and grind them well together in a mortar, and seethe them well in a gallon of white wine till the half-deal be sodden away; then wring through a cloth and cast away the herbs and do the liquor into a pot for to seethe, and cast thereto a pound of resin or of clean coperose [copperas]; lue [dilute?] it a little of the small liquor cast thereto and do it boil together, then take 4 lb. of virgin wax and resolve it in a woman's milk that beareth a knave child[1] and do thereto afterward an oz. of mastic and an oz. of frankincense, and let them boil well together till it be well y-mellyd;[2] and then do it off the fire and in the doing a down look thou have y-broke half a pound of tormentille well y-powdered all ready, and cast therein, and stir all-a-way without boiling till it be cold and then take up that floateth above and smere thine hand with oil or with fresh butter and bear it again to the fire as thou wilt bear wax, till it be well y-mellid, and do therewith as thou wilt.

The *Limburg Chronicle*, which contains more details about costume and popular songs than any other of the Middle Ages, was written by Tilman von Wolfhagen, a married clerk and notary, settled at Limburg on the Lahn (see Frontispiece). From the year 1347 onwards, as he tells us, he himself remembers the events he chronicles. The record ends with the year 1398, and Tilman died in 1402. He was no historian; but his lively interest in the small events within his purview lends to his chronicle a very special value. The edition here used is that of A. Wyss in *Mon. Germ. Hist., Deutsche Chroniken*, tom. I.

33. A SMALL-BEER CHRONICLE

MOREOVER at this time (A.D. 1336) the town and folk of Limburg stood in very great honour and prosperity in population and in wealth; for all the lanes and corners were full of folk and goods; and, when they took the field, the citizens were counted at more than two thousand folk well armed with breastplates and harness and all appurtenances; and those who took God's Body at Easter were counted more than eight

---

[1] This same ingredient occurs again on p. 51, for wounds in the head.
[2] Mixed.

thousand folk.[1] Now thou must know that when so many folk are under government of one authority, whether of church or of state, he must needs have good sense and honesty, as Aristotle saith in the first book of his *Politics*: *Habentes rationem et intellectum utentes, naturaliter aliorum domini fiunt et rectores;* which is being interpreted, "Whoso seeketh honesty, and practise it who can, To bear the rule o'er other folk he is the proper man." Moreover the foundation of our good lord St George in that city stood then in great honour

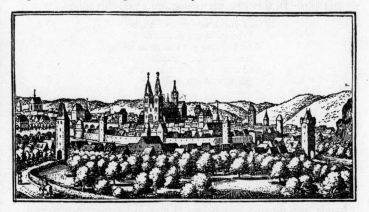

LIMBURG FROM THE SOUTH-WEST

From a view by Merian, about 1650.

and glory, so that it had a clear income of settled rents and moneys of no less than one hundred and twenty florins: and the foundation aforesaid was also governed by canons who were all men of this country and knights' sons.

In the year that men counted 1342, on St Boniface's day, well nigh half the city was burnt down....

(1347) King John's son of Bohemia, whom men called

---

[1] This would include all of both sexes above the age of fourteen years; in English medieval parlance they were called *housling-folk*. The Chantry certificates enrolled in the reigns of our Henry VIII and Edward VI always reckon populations in these terms: *e.g.* Sheffield is presented as having 2000 housling-folk, Beverley 5000 and Halifax even 8500.

Charles IV, and who was already King of Rome, became now full Emperor. This same Charles was wise and well-learned, so that he sought the disputations of the Masters at [the university of] Prague, and could bear himself well therein. And he had once a master who led him to school; to whom he smote an eye out, for that the master chastised him. This he well amended, creating him Archbishop of Prague and afterwards Cardinal. This Charles ruled and governed as a lion for more than thirty years....

(1359) In this year men sang and piped this song:

> God give him a year of blight
> Who made me to a nun,
> Who bade me put this tunic white
> And coal-black mantle on!
> And must I be a nun in truth,
> All against my will?...[1]

(1367) At the time of oat-harvest in this year, on the eve of St Peter ad Vincula, and in the Castle of Dern, a Freiherr von Dern stabbed Junker Johann, son of the Count of Dietz, so that he died on the spot. And he was a young man of less than thirty years and of goodly length, and had a long face with a lofty nose and smooth hair plaited in a long tail, as was the fashion of that time. And the said Johann would have been Count of Dietz if he had lived; but it came into other hands, as is written here below. The said Freiherr was named Friedrich, a stout knight of fifty years, and was a right Freiherr born of all his four ancestors. And he was cast into prison in the castle of Dern and brought to Dietz; and Count Gerhart, Junker Johann's brother, held a Land-Court at Reckenforst; and the aforesaid Freiherr was beheaded and buried forthwith among the Barefoot Friars of Limburg. Wherefore bethink thee when thou strikest; for Solomon saith: *Fremens ira nulli parcit*,[2] which is being interpreted: "Grim anger leaveth no man free, Thus Solomon doth

---

[1] Got gebe ime ein vurdrehen jar, Der mich machte zu einer nunnen, Und mir den swarzen mantel gap, Den wiszen rock darunden. Sal ich ein nunn gewerden Sunder minen willen, So wel ich eime knaben jung Sinen komer stillen. Und stillet he mir den minen nit, Daran mach he vurlisen.

[2] The nearest Biblical passage to this is Prov. xxvii, 4, *Ira non habet misericordiam*.

ALBERT III, DUKE OF AUSTRIA, AND FOUNDER OF THE ORDER OF TAILED KNIGHTS (1377)

From a window in the church of St Erhard, Styria, showing the case in which the tail was worn over his armour (A. Schultz, *Deutsches Leben*, fig. 246).

counsel thee." Now shalt thou know the form and countenance of this Freiherr. He was a square-built man with short crisp hair, and had a broad face with a flat nose....

(1374) Moreover at this time, some five or six years before, there was on the Main a Barefooted Friar who was driven out from among the people, for he was unclean [with leprosy]. He made the best songs and carols in the world, both words and melodies, wherein there lived not his like in Rhineland or in these parts. And, whatsoever he sang, all men sang it gladly after him; all masters, pipers, and other minstrels followed his songs and words. It was he who made that song:

> Far from the village am I bann'd,
> All doors are closed to wretched me!
> Unfaith, unfaith is all I see
> On every hand.

And that other:

> May, May! thy merry day
> Quickeneth me to joyous life.
> Tell me, what hath this to say?

And this again:

> Unfaith hath made her sport with me![1]....

(1384) In this year it came to pass that lords, knights, and squires wore short hair and crowns cut over the ears like laybrethren; and so also did burghers in general and the common folk and peasants after the fashion of the rest....

(1386) In these days was a Brother Minor, a Barefoot Friar of Brabant, Jacob by name. He bare himself as though he were a Bishop Suffragan, and had forged letters thereof; yet was he no bishop. This man went far and wide throughout the bishoprics of Mainz and Trier, and had consecrated and ordained more than three thousand acolites, subdeacons, deacons, and priests, who must needs now let themselves all be ordained afresh; and men called them all Jacobites, after the name of this aforesaid rascal Jacob. This same Jacob I

---

[1] (i) Des dipans bin ich uszgezalt, Man wiset mich armen vur di dure Untruwe ich nu spure Zu allen ziden.

(ii) Mei mei mei, dine wonnecliche zit Menliche freude git, An mir; waz meinet daz?

(iii) Der untruwe ist mit mir gespelet.

esteem more wicked than Judas who betrayed and sold Christ the Son of God; for the treason of Judas was made a balm and a salvation for the seed of men; but this other treason was a ruin and destruction to Christendom; for he caused mere layfolk to sing and read masses, whom men deemed to be priests, and yet were they none. For, whensoever men weened that they held up the Body of our Lord, then they held up a *simulacrum*, so that men called upon and adored an idol,[1] and many foul matters thus befel, which I cannot here write. Wherefore thou shalt know the man's form and his face; for I have oftentimes seen him. He was a slender man of even length, dark under the eyes, with a long face and a long sharp pointed nose; and his cheeks were somewhat ruddy, and he writhed with his body and bowed up and down in great courtesy. And he came to an evil end when he was caught in this matter; and that was no more than justice.... [2]

(1394) Moreover at this time a child was born at Nieder-brechen in the bishopric of Trier, that had lower limbs of a man and shapen in the upper parts somewhat like a toad. And this was a punishment from God; for, when men asked the woman whether she bare a child, she answered thereunto that she bare a toad; and such was her answer at every time....

(1394) (From the hand of a continuator, p. 107.) It was said that the lord of Arnburg was at ill accord with his wife, who was untrue to him; and his bitter wrath drove him into

---

[1] This is in strict accordance with scholastic theology: cf. Aquinas, *Summa*, pars III, quaest. lxxx, art. 6. Sir John Maundeville (chap. xviii) draws a slight distinction between a *simulacre*, and an *idol*; the former is an object of worship imitated from some natural object, while the latter is "an image made of the lewd will of man, that man may not find among kindly things, as an image that hath four heads."

[2] The *Magnum Chronicon Belgicum* (an. 1392) gives us further details. "Many of the priests and clergy in Holy Orders, finding that their ordination was false, married and lived as lay folk; but many were of a better mind, and let themselves be re-ordained by another true Catholic Bishop.... The Bishop of Utrecht, having summoned seven other Bishops to that city, brought this aforesaid forger of Papal letters in bonds before the people, clad in full pontificals, whereof he was despoiled again one by one: first of his crozier, then his mitre, then his chasuble, and so on even to his amice. Then the hair of his head was shaven away, and the skins of his finger-tips, wherewith he had been wont to handle the Lord's Body, were cut away down to the bone with a shard of glass." He was condemned to be boiled alive, but was finally beheaded instead, out of respect for his priesthood and the Franciscan Order.

a frenzy, so that he wandered abroad to beg his bread, and passed the seas and dwelt long in heathen lands, and bare always a naked coat of mail upon his naked flesh. And all his friends deemed him dead. And this endured so long until his wife was dead, and his children begat children of their own, and his sons died, and his grand-children begat him great-grand-children; and in the days of his grand-children he came again to his own land. And the time was so long that few folk knew him, and they were far advanced in age. And the lord of Arnburg also was old and grisly, so that the old folk knew him not well: yet by certain marks that he bare in his body, thereby they knew him better. Moreover he spake many true signs, whereof they knew part already, and the rest they found to be true. Wherefore the lords of Arnburg accepted him for their ancestor, and set him apart his own lodging in the castle of Arnburg, and did him great reverence. And he was sore bowed with age and crabbed of mood, and might not endure the lodging; and then they gave him a village to his own, and a fair house therein. This also he might not endure, and went out again to beg his bread in misery, and came to Cologne, and died within a brief space.

The beautiful manuscript commonly known as *Queen Mary's Psalter* contains a series of illustrations of Old Testament subjects, mainly drawn from the Bible but sometimes based on apocryphal legends; to each picture is appended a few lines of explanatory text. The book dates from about 1320, and shows "the high cultivation and great originality of the English School at this time." The page here given, from plate X of H. N. J. West-lake's edition, represents one of the many legends which grew round the history of Noah. Mr Westlake translates *cleyes* as *nails* (*clous*); but the picture itself, as well as the context, seems to point plainly to the far more natural rendering of *wattle-work* (*claies*).

34. THE ROMANCE OF NOAH

(Text to the three upper scenes reproduced on opposite page.)

How the Devil came in man's shape to Noah's wife and asked where her goodman was. And she said that she knew not where. "He is gone to betray thee and the whole world;

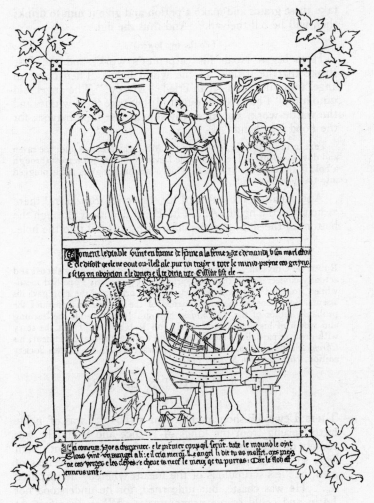

Cel moment le diable vint en forme de ferpent a la ferme ʒoe e demandeʒ b ſon mari eſtoit
E ele diſoit qeele ne eout ou il eſt ale pur tn traꝑ ꞇ tote le mūdo preyne ceſ grꝑnꝰ
e ſe teʒ vn aboꝺꝛion e le ꝺynetʒ e ſre diꝛia ꝩte Euſſint fiſt ele —

La comenſe Ʞoe a chargenter. e le ꝑmier coup qil ſeruit. tute le mounde oynt
Eſtoꝰ ꝩint vn euꝛugel a li: e il cꝛia merci. Ll angel li diſt tu aſ malfet. ceſ meꝛꝑ
ne ceſ ꝩꝛgeſ e leſ clepeſ ꞇ chꝛeue ta neef le meux qe tu purraſ: Car le ſtoꝺ eſt
enuꝰ uint ⸝

NOAH AND HIS ARK

From *Queen Mary's Psalter*, about A.D. 1320.

take these grains and make a potion and give it him to drink; then will he tell thee all." And thus she did.

(To the two lower.)

Here began Noah his carpenter's work; and the first stroke that he struck, all the world heard. Then came an angel unto him: and Noah cried, "Mercy!" The angel said unto him, "Thou hast wrought ill; but take these withies and the wattle-work, and finish thy ship as best thou mayest; for the flood is at hand."

Text to the next folio but one in the MS., which comes after the raven and dove incident, and represents the Devil falling head-foremost through a hole in the bottom of the boat, while a writhing snake's tail is plugged into the hole thus made.

And Noah at the entry of his ship cried *Benedicite!* there as he sat at the helm. And The Devil fled away through the bottom of the ship; and the dove thrust his tail into the hole.

Robert de Graystanes, Subprior of Durham, was canonically elected and actually consecrated to that bishopric in 1333; but the Pope had meanwhile "provided" Richard de Bury with the prize, and the king gave his assent. Bury, one of the most learned of the English bishops and the probable author of the *Philobiblon*, honourably commends the learning and worth of his unsuccessful rival; and Robert himself tells the story with great impartiality. He did not long outlive his disappointment; his *Chronicle* ends in 1336. The following extract is from the Surtees Society edition, *Hist. Dunelm. Scriptt. Tres.*

35. A BISHOP'S LATIN

(p. 118.)

THIS Lewis [Bishop of Durham 1316–33] was of noble birth, sprung from the kings of France and Sicily; he was comely of face but feeble in his feet, for he halted with both legs; so liberal that many called him prodigal; covetous of gain, but less scrupulous of the means whereby he procured it.... He was chaste, but unlearned, for he understood not Latin and could scarce pronounce it. When therefore, at his consecration, he should have made his formal profession, he could not read it, though he had been instructed therein for many days beforehand; and having at last arrived, with many promptings from others, at the word *Metropolitan*, which after many gasps he yet could not pronounce, at length he said in the French tongue "let that be taken as read!" All the bystanders were amazed, mourning that such a man should be consecrated bishop. Another time, when he was conferring Holy Orders, and could not pronounce that phrase *in aenigmate* [1 Cor. xiii, 12], he said in French to those that stood by, "By St Louis, the man was a clown that wrote this word!" Throughout almost all the days of his bishopric, he studied how he might extort money from the Prior and monks. He had a papal bull empowering him to promote to the dignity of prior whomsoever of the monks he would, and another giving him a fourth part of the priory revenues so long as the Scottish war should last; but, because these bulls had been obtained by suppression of the truth and suggestion of falsehood, therefore his council would not use them. He made no account of the palfreys and gifts which the Prior oftentimes gave him; for whensoever the prior made any request, he would answer, "'Sdeath, ye do naught for me, nor will I do aught for you; pray ye for my death, for so long as I live ye shall have nothing." Yet at the end of his life he had obtained a bull for appropriating the church of Ellewyk, in his own diocese and patronage, to the prior and convent; but death overtook him before he could complete this.

The University of Rome was founded by Boniface VIII in 1303. The removal of Boniface's successors to Avignon, and the long-standing lawlessness of the city, no doubt reacted unfavourably on the discipline of the Roman scholars. The following petition from the Senators to the absentee Pontiff is printed by F. Novati in *Giorn. Storico d. Lett. Italiana*, vol. II, p. 138, from a fourteenth-century manuscript; it belongs almost certainly to the first quarter of that century.

36. MANNERS AT THE UNIVERSITY OF ROME

To the most holy Father, etc.

The detestable infamy of crimes which are continually committed by certain sons of iniquity, who claim only in word the distinction of the clerical character, being themselves utter strangers to all honesty of morals and knowledge of letters, hath moved us to write to the feet of your Holiness. Know indeed, most Holy Father, that many in the city, furnished only with the shield and privilege conferred by the first tonsure, strive not in honesty of manners, but rather are ordinarily guided by the rule of horrible misdeeds; wandering armed from tavern to tavern and other unhonest places; sometimes going on to quarrel or fight in arms with laymen; committing manslaughter, thefts, robberies and very many other things that are far from honesty. For which things no safeguard or remedy is applied by the ecclesiastical judges holding the place of your most Holy See; but rather, when [these evildoers] are accused of the aforesaid misdeeds in our courts, they compel us to release them from our examination, saying that they themselves will see to the infliction of a fine upon them; and thus, under the cloke of such assertions, these so nefarious and most criminal men, hateful both to God and to man, pass unpunished; which is known to redound no little to the dishonour of the Holy See and to the damage of the Romans. Moreover, this is imputed to our official negligence, when misdeeds so enormous are not quelled by the rigour of our justice; and a most horrible and detestable belief haunts the minds of the Romans, who will say at times, in our presence or elsewhere: "Alas! these miscreants who call themselves clerics and yet comport themselves as layfolk, wherefore are they not punished out of their evil courses? In this the Senators do ill; for in the past, when our lord Boniface of blessed memory sat on the papal chair, the Senate made complaint to him concerning like matters, and he not only commanded their punishment but was as it were troubled in mind against them, for those who had gone scot-free; so likewise, if our present Lord learned the truth, he also would be displeased at their impunity." Wherefore we most piously beseech your Holiness, with all humility and devotion, that if it should so befall that our rigour should go so far as to punish them in virtue of our office as judges, then you would vouchsafe (if it so please you) to permit this unto us and to support us in future with the authority of your Holiness. For let not your clemency believe that we are on this account minded to go so far as to touch clerics in possession of church benefices, whom we are purposed and ready to treat with all due reverence, since we are unwilling to do anything derogatory to ecclesiastical liberties. For, most Holy Father, we fear lest, if the aforesaid impious fellows are not controlled to some extent by the secular arm, then the people of Rome will grow to such horror of these their misdeeds as to rise up in wrath and fury not only against these, but even against the aforesaid clerics who are zealous for the orthodox faith. Meanwhile we are ready from the bottom of our heart to carry out cheerfully whatsoever may conduce to the honour of the Papal See.

Sir Thomas Gray of Heton, son to the distinguished soldier mentioned in this first extract, and himself equally distinguished in due time, was taken prisoner by the Scots in 1355, and spent his leisure in writing the *Scalacronica*, a history beginning with the Creation, as usual, but possessing very great value for military and other matters during the reigns of Edward I, II and III. Joseph Stevenson edited the chronicle for the Maitland Club from the Norman Conquest onwards; the years 1274–1362 have been translated into English by Sir Herbert Maxwell, Bart. (1907).

37. A KNIGHT-ERRANT

(Ed. Stevenson, p. 145.)

TRUE it is that, after the town of Berwick was taken from the English (1318) the Scots had so gotten the upper hand, and were so presumptuous, that they made scarce any account of the English, who busied themselves no longer with the war but let it perish. In these days, at a great feast of lords and ladies in the county of Lincoln, a comely page brought to Sir William Marmion, Knight, a warrior's helm with a golden crest, and a letter from his lady withal, wherein she commanded him to go to the most perilous place in Great Britain and there make this helm known. It was there determined by the knights that he should go to Norham, as the most perilous and adventurous place in the country. Then the said Sir William went to Norham; where, within the fourth day of his coming, my lord Alexander de Mowbray, brother of the lord Philip de Mowbray who was then Warden of Berwick, came before Norham castle with the doughtiest chivalry of the Marches of Scotland, and arrayed more than eight score men-at-arms before the castle at the hour of noon. The hue and cry was raised in the castle, as they sat at meat; whereupon the Castellan, Sir Thomas de Gray, went forth with his garrison without the barriers,[1] where he saw the enemy arrayed for battle hard by. Then he looked round and saw the said Sir William Marmion coming on foot, all resplendent with gold and silver, marvellously arrayed, and bearing that helm on his head. Sir Thomas Gray had well heard of the manner of his coming, wherefore he cried aloud to him: "Sir Knight, ye are come here as a knight-errant to make known this helm of yours; wherefore it is better and more fitting that your knighthood be shown on horseback than on foot; mount therefore your horse; behold there your enemies; strike spurs into your steed, and go break into their midst; for I here deny my God if I rescue not your body alive or dead, but if I die myself!" Then that knight mounted a stout charger, and struck spurs into his sides, and brake into the midst of his enemies, who smote upon him and wounded him in the face and drew him from his saddle to the earth. Then came the said Sir Thomas with all his garrison, lance in rest, and smote the horses in the bowels so that they overthrew their masters. Thus they drave back their mounted enemies, raised up the fallen knight, mounted him again on his horse, and chased after their enemies; at which first encounter seven were slain, and fifty horses of price taken. The women of the castle brought the horses to their men, who mounted and made chase and smote down all whom they might overtake. Thomas de Gray slew in the Yair Ford one Cryn, a Fleming, an admiral of the sea and a robber, who was a great master with Robert de Bruce. The rest who escaped were chased even to the nunnery of Berwick.

---

[1] For the barriers outside a fortification see the illustration to vol. III, no. 48.

When Chaucer was called as a witness in the Scrope case, he deposed that, before his own capture, he had seen Sir Thomas Scrope bearing certain arms "before the town of Retters." It has been debated whether this was Retiers in Brittany or Réthel in the Ardennes; the question is decided by the following passage from the *Scalacronica*; for Château-Porcein is close by Réthel. The passage shows incidentally that Chaucer was with the Black Prince's division, which alone passed this way. It started, like the other divisions, from Calais in October, 1359. (Ed. Stevenson, p. 188.)

38. CHAUCER'S MARCH

THE prince, son to the king aforesaid, took the way by Montreuil and Hesdin, through Ponthieu and Picardy, crossing the Somme and passing by Neuilly and Ham into Vermandois; near which place Sir Baudouin Daukin, knight, Master of the Crossbowmen of France, with other French knights, was taken in fight by the men of the Prince's train, as he would have overrun by night the quarters of the earl of Stafford, who defended himself well.... So the Prince held his way aforesaid by St Quentin and Retieris, where the enemy themselves burned their town to hinder the passage; but the Prince's men passed [the river] by main force at Château-Porcein, and then passed through Champagne and joined his father's host before Reims.

I had occasion to point out, on p. 199 of *Chaucer and his England,* how much trade was done by the knightly and clerical classes, and how thoroughly medieval is the surviving Florentine custom by which you may buy a bottle of wine at the door of a princely palace. After many attempts on the part of church councils to forbid trade, and especially the liquor trade, to the clergy, this Council of Cologne set itself in 1333, probably with more success, to regulate rather than suppress it. See Hartzheim, *Concilia Germaniae*, vol. IV, p. 430.

39. CLERICAL INNKEEPERS

SEEING that our predecessor Henry, of pious memory, ordained by statute that no clerics, secular or monastic, should ply the trade of taverners—yet he would not that this statute should altogether prohibit the selling of such wine as a cleric

RÉTHEL IN THE ARDENNES

From a seventeenth-century view in Zeiller's *Topographia*.

may derive from his own benefice or from any other source than trade, provided always that this be done without deceit or fraudulent evasion of the aforesaid statute, and in such manners as have hitherto been used, and decent—yet some men call in question what may be the accustomed and decent manners of sale, to be kept by the clergy in this matter of wine-dealing. We therefore by this present statute have thought good to declare the following as customary and decent fashions of selling wine: to wit, that such sales should be conducted without vociferation or clamour of taverners and (so far as in the sellers lieth) without fraud; without tarrying or stay of men drinking such wines either within or at the door of the house, or within the privileged premises wherein such wines are sold; nor, when men would fain drink such wines, may any occasion be given of tarrying or staying at that same place, by the lending of cups or jugs, as is commonly done in taverns of laymen, nor may such be supplied in any way; and these manners aforesaid of selling wine are, in virtue of this present statute, to be used henceforth by clerics.

Henry Knighton was a Canon of Leicester Abbey; his *Chronicle* is extremely valuable from the middle of Edward III's reign to that of Henry IV. His evidence as to the Wycliffite movement and the Black Death has so often been quoted that I prefer to insert here two shorter extracts typical of the time.

40. TOURNEY AND MASQUERADE

(Vol. II, p. 57, A.D. 1348.)

IN those days there arose a great clamour and outcry among the people, seeing that in almost every place where tourneys were held they were attended by a band of ladies who formed part, as it were, of the spectacle. These came in divers and marvellous men's garments, to the number sometimes of forty, sometimes of fifty ladies, of the fairest and comeliest in the whole realm, yet not of the most virtuous. They were clad in motley tunics, half of one colour and half of another, with short hoods and liripipes[1] wound like cords round their heads, and richly-studded girdles of silver or gold, nay, even across their bodies they wore pouches containing those knives that are commonly called *daggers*; and thus they rode forth to the place of tourney on choice chargers or richly-decked palfreys, thus wasting their own goods and debasing their bodies with folly and scurrilous wantonness, as it was commonly reported. Thus they neither feared God nor blushed for the modest outcries of the people, but made nought of their marriage-vows. Nor did those in whose train they followed consider how great favour and how splendid a victory had been vouchsafed to the English arms by God the giver of all good things, in despite of all the enemies that beset us. But herein, as in all other matters, God brought a wondrous remedy by scattering their dissolute concourse; for He showered upon the places and times that had been appointed for such vain sports, rain and thunder and flashes of lightning, with all discomforts of wind and tempests.

41. THE FRENCH POPE

(*Ib.* p. 93, A.D. 1356, after the battle of Poitiers.)

IN those days, discord arose between the clergy and the Friars Minor concerning certain opinions, and both parties appealed to the Roman court: wherefore Master Richard [Fitzralph], Bishop of Armagh, crossed the sea with many other clerics to go to the Court in defence of the clergy. And this same Richard had a subsidy from the clergy, and the abbot of St Albans was his proctor. Moreover, seeing that the Pope ever favoured the French, and supported them so far as in him lay against the English, and that God had vouchsafed such a miracle to us in granting victory to so few men against so great a multitude of the French, therefore it was written in many places at Vienne [where the Pope lodged] and in many other towns, "Now is the Pope become French and

---

[1] Tails or streamers to a hood.

Jesus become English; now shall we see who will do most, the Pope or Jesus."[1] And this was written in derision.

Extracts 42 and 43 are two of the most picturesque passages omitted from the Globe edition of Froissart—an edition with which no fault can be found except its necessary incompleteness. No. 42 is wanting altogether in the text from which Lord Berners translated: it may be found in Buchon's edition, vol. i, p. 284; the other is on p. 62 of vol. iii.

42. THE SPANIARDS ON THE SEA

IN those days there was great rancour between the King of England and the Spaniards by reason of certain misdeeds and pillages which the said Spaniards had done upon the English by sea. Wherefore it befel in this year [1350] that the Spaniards who had come to Flanders for their merchandise had warning that they could not return to their own country but that they would first be met by the English. Wherefore they took counsel, and resolved not to take no too great account thereof; and they provided themselves at Sluys well and plenteously, both their ships and their boats, with all armour and good artillery; and they hired all sorts of people, soldiers and archers and crossbowmen, who would take their wages; and they waited one for the other, and made their bargains and their purchases even as their business demanded.

When the King of England, who hated them sore, heard how plenteously they provided themselves, then he said aloud, "We have long known the manner of these Spaniards, and they have done us much despite, and they come even yet to no amendment, but rather fortify themselves against us; wherefore we must needs sweep them up as they pass." To this speech his men gave ready assent, for they were glad to fight with the Spaniards. Therefore the King made a great and special levy of all his gentlemen who were then in England, and set forth from London and came to the county of

---

[1] Ore est le Pape devenu Franceys
E Jesu devenu Engleys.
Ore serra veou qe fra plus
Ly Pape ou Jesus.

Sussex, which sat upon the seaboard betwixt Hampton and Dover, facing the country of Ponthieu and Dieppe; thither he came and kept house in an abbey by the sea.... [1]

When the Spaniards had made their purchases and had laden their ships with cloth of wool and of linen and all that they thought good and profitable to bring home to their country, (and they knew well that the English would meet them, but thereof made they no account,) then came they to

A SHIP OF WAR

From a MS. of 1352 in Viollet-le-Duc, *Dict. du Mobilier*, t. v, p. 182.

the town of Sluys and came aboard their ships, wherein they had made so plenteous provision of artillery as it is marvel to think of; and withal they had great bars of iron ready forged and fashioned for casting and for sinking of ships, with launching of stones and pebbles beyond all number. When they saw that they had a fair wind, they weighed anchor; and they were forty great ships all of one fashion, so stout and fair that it was pleasant to see; and in the mast-trees they had built

[1] Probably Battle. The castle mentioned later would no doubt be the queen's castle of Pevensey.

crows'-nests well stored with stones and pebbles, and skir-mishers to guard them. Moreover their masts were hung with standards emblazoned with their bearings, which bellied and flew and fluttered in the wind; it was a full fair sight to see and imagine. And meseemeth that, if the English had great desire to find them, they themselves desired it yet more, as it appeared now and as I will hereafter tell you. These Spaniards were full a ten to one, what with the soldiers whom they had taken to wages in Flanders. Wherefore they felt themselves strong enough to fight by sea against the King of England and his power; with which intent they came sailing and scudding before the wind, for they had it at their stern, past the town of Calais. The King of England, who was at sea with his navy, had there ordered all his needs, and com-manded how he would have his men fight and bear themselves; and he had made my lord Robert of Namur master of a ship that they called King's Hall, wherein was all his household.

So the King stood at his ship's prow, clad in a jacket of black velvet, and on his head a hat of black beaver that became him right well; and he was then (as I was told by such as were with him that day) as merry as ever he was seen. He made his minstrels sound before him on their trumpets a German dance that had been brought in of late by my lord John Chandos, who was there present; and then for pastime he made the said knight sing with his minstrels, and took great pleasure therein; and at times he would look upwards, for he had set a watch in the top-castle of his ship to give tidings of the Spaniards' coming. While the King thus took his pleasure, and all his knights were glad of heart to see how merry he was, then the watch was aware of the Spaniards' fleet, and cried: "Ho! I see a ship coming, and methinks it is a ship of Spain!" Then the minstrels held their peace, and it was asked of him again whether he saw aught else; then within a brief space he an-swered and said: "Yes, I see two—and then three—and then four." Then, when he was aware of the great fleet, he cried, "I see so many, God help me! that I may not tell them." Then the King and his men knew well that these were the Spanish ships. Then the King let sound his trumpets, and all their ships came together to be in better array, and to lie more surely; for well they knew that the battle was at hand, since the Spaniards came in so great a fleet. By this time the day was far spent, for it was about the hour of vespers. So the King sent for wine and drank thereof, he and all his knights; then he laced on his helm, and the rest did likewise.

Meanwhile the Spaniards drew nigh; and they might well have departed without battle, if they had desired it; for, being well equipped and in great ships, and having the wind in their favour, they had no need to speak with the English but if it had been their will. Nevertheless through pride and presumption they deigned not to pass by without hail; wherefore they sailed straight on in full array to begin the battle. When the King of England saw how they came on, then he addressed his ship straight to a Spanish ship which came in the vanguard, crying to his steersman, "Lay your helm right upon that ship which cometh hither, for I would fain joust against him." The mariner, who would never have dared to gainsay the King's will, steered straight for that Spanish ship, which bore down boisterously before the wind. The King's ship was stout and well bound, else had it surely been burst; for it met with that Spanish ship, which was big and bulky, with such a crash that it seemed like the bursting of a storm; and, with the shock of their meeting, the top-castle of the King's ship smote so sore against the Spaniard that the force of that mast brake it from above the mast whereon it sat, and spilt it into the sea; so that all were drowned and lost who sat therein. With which shock the King's ship was so aghast that it cracked and drew water, whereof his knights were soon aware, yet said naught thereof to the King, but bestirred themselves to bale and empty her. Then said the King who saw before his face this ship against which he had jousted: "Grapple my ship with this here, for I would fain take her." Then answered his knights: "Sire, leave this alone; ye shall have a better." So that ship sailed on, and another great vessel came up, whereunto the knights grappled with chains and hooks of steel. Then began a battle both hard and sharp and strong; for the archers shot their shafts, and the Spaniards fought and defended themselves with a right good will; and this not in one place only, but in ten or twelve. When therefore they found themselves well matched against the stoutest of their enemies, then they grappled with them and did marvellous feats of arms. Yet the English had no whit of advantage. For the Spaniards were in those great ships of theirs, far higher and bigger than the English ships; whereof they had great advantage in shooting, in hurling, and in casting great bars of iron wherewith they gave the English much to suffer. The knights of the King of England who were in his ship, seeing that it drew water and was in peril of foundering, made hot haste to conquer that ship whereunto they were grappled; and there were many doughty deeds of arms done. At length the King and his men bare themselves so well that this ship was won, and all her crew cast overboard.[1] Then they told the King in what peril he was, and how his ship made water, and that he must needs come on board that which he had won. So he inclined to this advice and came on board with his knights and all the mariners, and left the other empty; and then they pressed forwards again to make assault upon their enemies, who fought right valiantly, and had crossbowmen who shot quarrels from strong crossbows, and gave much travail to the English.

This battle of the Spaniards and English was hard and strong and well fought; but it began late in the day, wherefore the English had much ado to achieve their task and to discomfit their enemies. Moreover the Spaniards, who are men trained to the sea and who had great and stout vessels, acquitted themselves loyally as best they might. On the other part fought the young Prince of Wales and those under his charge; their ship was grappled and fixed to a great Spanish vessel, and there the Prince and his men had much to suffer, for their ship was pierced and broken in several places, wherefore the water rushed in with great vehemence; and, for all that they might do to cast it forth, the ship waxed still the heavier. Wherefore all the Prince's men were in great anguish of fear, and fought most fiercely to win that Spanish ship; but in vain, for she was stoutly guarded and defended.

[1] Cf. the Shipman of Chaucer's *Prologue*:

> If that he foughte, and hadde the heigher hand,
> By water he sent hem hoom to every land.

Upon this peril and danger wherein the Prince and his men stood, then came the Duke of Lancaster sailing hard by the Prince's vessel, and learned how they could win no whit of advantage and how their ship was in sore straits; for men cast the water forth on every side. Therefore he went round and stayed at the Spanish ship, and cried, "A Derby to the rescue!" Then were these Spaniards assaulted and foughten most fiercely withal, that they lasted not long after. Thus was their ship won, and all were cast overboard without taking any mercy; and the Prince of Wales with his men entered into their ship. Scarce were they come in, when their own ship sank to the bottom; and then they considered more fully the great peril wherein they had stood.

On the other side fought the English barons and knights, each as he was ordered and established; and sore need had they to bear themselves stoutly and busily, for they found a sharp welcome. So it came to pass, late in the evening, that the ship of the King's Hall, whereof my lord Robert of Namur was chief, was grappled in fierce and tough fight with a great Spanish ship; and the said Spaniards, desiring to master their enemies better at their ease and to take the vessel with all that were therein, set all their intent upon carrying her away with them. Wherefore they hoisted sail, and took all advantage of the wind, and sailed away for all that my lord Robert and his men might do; for the Spanish ship was greater and bigger than theirs, and thus they had good advantage for the mastery. While they thus sailed, they passed by the King's ship: wherefore they cried aloud, "Rescue now the King's Hall!" But no man heard them, for the hour was late; and, even had they been heard, none could have rescued them. And methinks these Spaniards would have led them away at their ease, when a servant of my lord Robert, whose name was Hankin, did there a doughty deed of arms; for he made his spring, with a naked sword in his hand, and leapt into the Spanish ship; there he came to the mast and cut the rope that bare the sail, which fell without force to the deck—for, with great valiance of body, this Hankin cut four master-ropes that governed the mast and the sail—wherefore the said sail fell to the deck, so that the ship stayed still and might go no further. Then my

A SEA-FIGHT

From the C.C.C., Cambridge, miniatures to Matthew Paris, *Horda Angel Cynaan* (J. Strutt, pls. xxxi, xxxii).

lord Robert of Namur and his men, seeing their advantage, came forward and leapt into the Spanish ship with a right good will, having their drawn swords in their hands; and they made fierce assault upon all such as they found therein, until all were slain and cast into the sea; and the ship was won.

I cannot say of all these men, "This one did well, and that one better." But there was fought, the while it endured, a most fierce and bitter battle; and the Spaniards gave much ado to the King of England and his men. Yet at the last the victory remained with the English, and the Spaniards lost fourteen ships; the remnant sailed on and escaped. When they were all gone, and the King with his men knew no longer with whom to fight, then they sounded their trumpets for retreat and made head for England, and landed at Rye and Winchelsea soon after nightfall. Then forthwith the King and his sons, the Prince and the Earl of Richmond, the Duke of Lancaster and certain barons who were there, disembarked from their ships and took horse in the town and rode towards the Queen's manor which was two English leagues distant from thence. Then was the Queen glad at heart when she beheld her lord and her sons, seeing that she had suffered great anguish of heart that day for fear of the Spaniards; for men had seen the fight well enough from the hills on that part of the English coasts, for the air was full fine and clear. Wherefore the Queen, who had required to know the truth, had heard how the Spaniards had more than forty great ships; how great then was now her comfort to see her spouse and his sons! Then the lords and ladies passed all that night in great revel, devising of arms and of love. Next day the greater part of the barons and lords who had fought in that battle came to the King, who thanked them heartily for their deeds and their service; and then they took their leave and departed each to his own home.[1]

---

[1] The later text of Froissart printed by Siméon Luce describes how the queen had spent all day praying in an abbey; how the victors rejoined her only at two o'clock in the morning, and how the minstrels were arrayed next day in the fine cloth of Valenciennes taken from the Spaniards.

43. A PICTURESQUE BANDIT

AYMERIGOT MARCEL was sore displeased with himself in that he had sold and delivered the strong castle of Aloïse by St Flour: for he saw his own authority thereby greatly abated, and perceived well how he was the less feared: for all the season that he kept it, he was redoubted and feared, and honoured with all men of war of his party, and had kept a great estate always in the castle of Aloïse: the blackmail of countries that he held under subjection was well worth yearly twenty thousand florins. When he remembered all this he was sorrowful; his treasure he thought he would not minish; he was wont daily to search for new pillages, whereby he increased his profit, and then he saw that all was closed from him. Then he said and imagined, that he had too soon repented of well-doing, and that to kill and to rob even as he had done before, (all things considered), was a good life. On a time he said to his old companions, who had helped him with this device of war: "Sirs, there is no pastime nor sport, nor glory in this world but that of men of war, to use such life as we have done in time past. What a joy it was to us when we rode forth at adventure, and sometime found by the way a rich abbot or prior or merchant, or a route of mules of Montpellier, of Narbonne, of Limoges, of Fougaron, of Béziers, of Toulouse, or of Carcassone, laden with cloth of Brussels, or musterdevillers or peltryware, coming from the fairs or laden with spicery from Bruges, from Damascus, or from Alexandria; whatsoever we met all was ours, or else ransomed at our pleasures; daily we gat new money, and the villeins of Auvergne, and of Limousin, daily provided and brought to our castle wheat, meal, bread ready baken, oats for our horses, and litter, good wines, beeves, and fat muttons, pullets, and wild fowl; we were ever furnished as though we had been kings: when we rode forth all the country trembled for fear, all was ours going or coming. How took we Carlat, I and the Bourg[1] of Compiègne, and I and Pierrot of Béarn took Chalucet? How did we scale without other aid the strong

---

[1] Bastard.

castle of Marquay, pertaining to the Earl Dauphin! I kept
it not past five days but I received for it on a fair table five
thousand francs, and forgave one thousand for the love of the
Earl Dauphin's children! By my faith, this was a fair and a
good life, wherefore I repute myself sore deceived in that I
have rendered up the fortress of Aloïse: for it would have
been kept from all the world; and the day that I gave it up,
it was furnished with victuals to have been kept seven year
without any revictualling: this earl of Armagnac hath deceived me; Olivier Barbe, and Pierrot of Béarn, shewed me
how I should repent myself: certainly I sore repent me of that
I have done." And, when such of his companions as were
poor and had served him long heard him speak these words,
they perceived well how he spake them with all his heart
unfeigned; then they said to him: "Aymerigot, we are all
ready yet to serve you: let us renew again our war, and let
us get some stronghold in Auvergne, or in Limousin, and let
us fortify it; and then, sir, we shall soon recover our damages;
we shall make a goodly flight in Auvergne, and in Limousin;
for, as now, the Earl Dauphin and Hugh his brother are out
of the country, and divers other knights and squires in their
company into the voyage of Barbary, and specially the lord
of Coucy, who hath the sovereign regard under the king of
all those marches; therefore we shall not need to fear him,
nor the duke of Berry, for he is disporting himself at Paris,
so thus we shall have now a good season." "Well," quoth
Aymerigot, "I have good will thus to do, saving I am by
name expressed in the charter of the truce." "What for that,
sir," quoth his company; "ye need not care therefore if ye
list; ye are not subject to the French king, ye owe him
neither faith nor obeisance: ye are the King of England's man,
for your heritage (which is all destroyed and lost) lieth in
Limousin; and, sir, we must live; and though we make war
to live, the Englishmen will not be miscontent with us, and
such as be in our case will draw to us: and sir, we have now
good title to make war, for we in Auvergne, having all been
paid the blackmail which men owe us there, let us send to the
villeins of the villages when we be once in a stronghold, and
command them to pay us a tribute, or else to make them sore

war." "Well, so be it!" quoth Aymerigot, "first let us provide for a strong place to abide in, and to draw unto when we need." Some of them said, "Sir, we know where there is a dismantled stronghold, abandoned of all, pertaining to the heritage of the lord de la Tour: no man keepeth it: let us draw thither and fortify it, then when we have garnished it may we at our ease run into Auvergne and Limousin." "Where lieth this place?" quoth Aymerigot. "Sir," quoth they, "within a league of la Tour, and it is called la Roche de Vendais." "By my faith," quoth Aymerigot, "I know it well: it is a meet place for us; let us go thither and fortify it." Thus on this purpose they concluded, and on a day assembled together and went to la Roche de Vendais. Then Aymerigot aviewed the place to see if it were worth the fortifying thereof; and when he had well aviewed the situation thereof, and the defences that might be made there, it pleased him right well. Thus they took it and fortified it little and little, or ever they raided and began to do any displeasure in the country; and when they saw the place strong sufficiently to resist against siege or assault, and that they were well horsed, and well provided of all things necessary for their defence, then they began to ride abroad in the country, and took prisoners and ransomed them, and provided their hold with flesh, meal, wax, wine, salt, iron, and steel, and of all other necessaries; there came nothing amiss to them without it had been too heavy or too hot. The country all about, and the people, weening to have been in rest and peace by reason of the truce made between the two kings and their realms, they began then to be sore abashed; for these robbers and pillers took them in their houses, and wheresoever they found them, in the fields labouring; and they called themselves Adventurers.

The *Gesta Abbatum S. Albani* is a chronicle of the abbots of that great house compiled about 1350 by Thomas Walsingham, precentor of the abbey and last of the great English chroniclers. The writer had access to the wide collection of documents in his abbey; the *Gesta* extends from 793 to 1349, and Walsingham's own *Historia Anglicana* goes down to 1422. The edition of the *Gesta* here used is that published in the Rolls Series; it is brilliantly summarized by Froude in one of his *Short Studies* ("Annals of an English Abbey").

44. THE CONQUERED ENGLISH

(Vol. 1, p. 41.)

IN the days of this abbot [Frederic, 1064–1067] England was taken and subdued by the Normans, and evils began to multiply on the earth, according to the exposition of a vision of the sainted King Edward, who saw the Seven Sleepers turning from their right sides to their left. Which was an omen to mortals, and more especially to the English; robbery and envy, pride and nightlong dicing, swilling and divers forms of lechery, uncleanness and perjury, began their unhappy career, even as the little fire of charity began to wax cold. The country was full of wandering housebreakers and robbers. The nightlong dice, with horrible oaths contrary to English wont, stirred up strife and manslaughter; and the Age of Silver—nay, rather, of Clay—succeeded to the now fading Golden Age. The lords of England, who since Brutus' days had never known the yoke of slavery, were now scorned, derided, and trodden under foot: they were compelled to shave their beards and clip their flowing locks in the Norman fashion: casting aside their horns and wonted drinking-vessels, their feasts and carousals, they were compelled to submit to new laws. Wherefore many of the English nobles refused the yoke of slavery and fled with all their households to live by plunder in the woods, so that scarce any man could go safely abroad in his own neighbourhood; the houses of all peaceful folk were armed like a besieged city with bows and arrows, bills and axes, clubs and daggers and iron forks; the doors were barred with locks and bolts. The master of the house would say prayers as if on a tempest-tost bark; as doors or windows were closed, men said *Benedicite*, and *Dominus* echoed reverently in response; a custom which lasted even into our own days [probably about A.D. 1150].

The *Chronicon de Melsa* was compiled by Thomas de Burton, who was elected in 1396 to the abbacy of the Cistercian house of Meaux in Yorkshire. It throws much light not only on the business life of a monastery, but also on ecclesiastical politics as understood by an average churchman of the day. The following extract is from the Rolls edition, vol. III, p. 38.

45. A GOOD POPE

IN the year of our Lord 1342 died Pope Benedict XII, on the day of St Gregory the Pope and in the seventh year of his pontificate; of whom it is said that there was none more righteous than he since St Gregory. On his deathbed, the cardinals prayed him to commit his powers to one of them, who might thus give him plenary absolution for all that he had committed; but he refused, saying: "I will not give my glory to another; but I submit myself to God's mercy." Again, when they prayed him to think of his kinsfolk and friends, and to distribute of his goods among them, he made answer: "I am a monk, and possess nought of mine own; whereof then could I make a testament or a distribution? Think not that I shall take away the goods of the church to give them to my kinsfolk." They prayed him therefore to fix the place where he should be buried; but he answered: "I may not choose mine own sepulchre, seeing that I am a monk." For he had so loved his monastic state that, even as a Pope, he ever wore a cowl for his outer garment in his lower closet; and daily he sang mass in his monk's cowl within his private chapel. When therefore he must needs leave his closet and go in the sight of the people and put on his pontificals according to custom, then he would kiss his cowl as he laid it down, saying, "Farewell, monk!" and taking his pontificals he would say, "Welcome, lord Pope!" On his return, as he laid aside his pontificals and resumed his cowl, then would he say, "Farewell, Pope! and thou, monk, come hither!" For he was most humble and affable and ready to jest with all men; wherefore it is said that, while he drew almost his last breath, he was asked by those that stood by whether he could eat aught; to which he made answer: "No indeed, nor yet drink, whereof we have a more evil report."[1] So he held the papal see for six years and four months and twelve days, and died, and was buried in the cathedral church of Avignon.

Neville's Cross (1346) is one of the most glorious victories in our annals, because it was fought entirely in self-defence, and proved so triumphantly the value of the citizen-levies at a time when the more regular army was engaged abroad. The author of the following poem, probably a monk of Durham, lays even more stress than most other contemporaries upon the services of the clergy, from the Archbishop of York downwards. The whole Latin poem may be found on pp. 63 ff. of *Illustrations of Scottish History* (Maitland Club, 1834).

46. A NATION IN ARMS

THE English came on in three battles, the Northumbrians in the van, a good 20,000 fighting-men under Percy, whom we know well. "If we might bear down his standard, and Neville's that floats by its side, then within a brief space we would take the English and their Archbishop, like an orphan." Then again (as men say) spake King David to his barons: "In England are no men of war, but mere clerks, holy-water-sprinklers; we will turn these Confessors into Martyrs! This folk here gathered is but as chaff; the good corn is in France, hard bested; if fortune will, we shall take all these Englishmen as the fowler taketh the fowls with his birdlime. Philip of France, our special friend, hath written us by letter that there is no man or woman left in England who can defend his own head from evil."

Then ran the Scots to arms; the hills gleamed with golden shields; the strong men flocked to their king's side, and skipped

---

[1] Unfriendly contemporaries accused him of excess, and of having given rise to the proverbial saying: "Bibamus papaliter," "Let us drink like a Pope" (Baluze, *Vit. Pap. Aven.* vol. 1, pp. 240 ff.).

A MÊLÉE

From MS. Nero D. i, fol. 3 b; miniatures by a thirteenth-century monk of St Albans (Strutt, *l.c.* pl. xxxvii).

for the greatness of their rejoicing. At that moment a simple monk came to them, sent by the Prior [of Durham] to treat of peace; whom David in his fury commanded to be slain, yet the word of his mouth was not fulfilled. Forth from the wood came the Scots in close array, well furnished with swords and staves; yet, though they were so well equipped, they were but excommunicate. When the Scots arrayed their battles in order, then our own men came too in good array, advancing slowly with bray of trumpet, ready to meet with cut and thrust. Then ran our archers forth to meet the Scots, and sent angels to persecute them;[1] so shrewdly did we pick the Scotsmen's teeth that all may rue it still who outlived that day! English and Scots rushed together like furious lions greedy of the prey; but because the Scots had confessed their sins to no priest, therefore were they shriven now with cut and thrust.... Percy stood and fought stoutly with the Scots while many great lords tarried far off; seeing which, the Earl of Angus hastened to Percy with all his forces, and two hundred sworn companions. Neither the earl nor Percy turned his face until every foeman was overcome; scarce one stood his ground, rich or poor, whereby so much foul blood was spilt. Then came the Archbishop, Zouch by name, in a rough mood to shave and bless their crowns;[2] whosoever was thus ordained failed not to feel his blows; all such were henceforth his blessed brethren! He had a deacon, too, the polished Mowbray, and a subdeacon, the grey-headed Robert Okyll, who was so reckless in this ordination that he may never be chaplain henceforth.[3] For these clergy, these Confessors, whom David called holy-water-sprinklers, gave short shrift with oaken staves to their mockers, who lie thus dead for their sins.... Let no man take the glory of this deed of arms, for all that was done on that field was a miracle. God be praised Who keepeth His covenant, and who avenged the unjust violence done to St Cuthbert. Let us all refuse the deceitful praise [of men] and pour out prayers to the throne of

---

[1] Ps. xxxv, 6: "Let their way be dark and slippery, and let the angel of the Lord persecute them."

[2] Literally, "to confer Orders."

[3] To say mass after shedding man's blood needed a Papal dispensation.

grace that we may so pass through things temporal as finally to lose not the things eternal!

This should be compared with the account of the battle on pp. 348 ff. of the *Lanercost Chronicle*, evidently imitated in great part from a similar ballad. The author adds further particulars reminding us forcibly of Frère Jean des Entommeures.

"There was also [besides the Archbishop of York] another Bishop of the Order of Friars Minor; who bade the English fight like men to earn his blessing, adding threats of extreme penance if any should spare the Scots. And when he met the enemy he absolved them not *a poena et a culpa*, but with a certain staff of his he gave them an indulgence of days, not without grievous penance and effectual absolution; such power had he at that time that, without preliminaries of confession, he absolved the Scots with his aforesaid staff from every legal act [in this life]."

Not only did the clergy do their duty manfully in these wars, but we also find criminals sometimes pardoned on condition of joining the king's army. Of the Halidon Hill campaign Father Stevenson writes in his notes to the *Lanercost Chronicle* (p. 430, A.D. 1333): "It appears by the Rotuli Scotiæ that Edward, in his anxiety to obtain troops, had granted a free pardon of all crimes to all who joined the army. See 1, 254, dated 24 July. A letter from the king to his chancellor, written upon 4 November next following, shows that this officer had been beset by applicants who wished to avail themselves of this proclamation without having fought at Halidon. The king was consulted as to whether his proclamation should be interpreted in a literal manner, and his answer was that it should."

J. Thorpe, *Registrum Roffense*, p. 127, A.D. 1346. This document should be read in conjunction with the fact that, as early as 1246, the great Dominican Minister-General Humbert de Romans had urged upon the Pope in Council that some official manual should be drawn up for the guidance of the clergy in their preaching and other duties. Archbishop Peckham and Bishop Quivil compiled brief treatises of the kind during the thirteenth century; fuller but unofficial manuals began to be drawn up in the fourteenth century; yet in 1411 the University of Paris was still vainly urging upon the Council of Constance the necessity for some authoritative book for the whole Church.

47. A CLERICAL REFERENCE LIBRARY

To all sons of Holy Church to whose notice these letters present may come, Brother Hamo, by God's permission Bishop of Rochester, wisheth eternal salvation in the Lord. Know ye all how we have learned by frequent experience (as we sadly remember) that some churchmen of our diocese, bearing not only the cure of souls but even the office of penitentiaries,[1] although commendable both for their life and for their learning, yet have committed grievous and absurd errors [*non modicum delirasse*] for lack of books profitable to such cure or such office, especially in the matter of consultations and salutary advice to their flocks, of enjoining penances, and of granting absolution to penitents. We therefore, desiring greatly to bring such remedy as we can to the aforesaid evils, have thought fit to assign the following books, under the manners and conditions hereafter to be set down, for ministering some manner of [*aliqualem*] information in future times to the aforesaid priests with cures of souls or who hold the office of Penitentiary, and for advancing the salvation of souls. We give therefore hereby as a gift between living persons, and with all prerogatives and favour of our last will we bequeath and assign to the Prior and Chapter and Cathedral of Rochester, our glossed books of Decrees and Decretals, the sixth book of the Decretals with two glosses in one volume, the seventh book (or Clementine Constitutions) unglossed, bound up with divers Provincial Constitutions, the book of Pope Innocent on the Decretals, a volume of Matthew and Mark with glosses, the Historia Scholastica of the Bible; also a volume of the Summa of Raymond [de Pennaforte] and one of Avicenna on the counsel of medicine, and one little book of the Vices and Virtues, and two stitched books whereof one beginneth *Qui bene presunt* and the other treateth of the articles of faith, the beatitudes, and the petitions; and lastly the book of Papias the Elder on Grammar; willing, commanding and ordaining that all these books be laid up and kept within our Cathedral, in a chest under two locks, there to be preserved under safe custody for ever, or as long as they may last.... Provided that none of the aforesaid books be carried out of the said Cathedral, and that each, when it has been inspected [by the reader] for a reasonable time, be forthwith returned to the custodians; Excepting only, during our own lifetime, the use of the said books be at our good pleasure, whether within or without the aforesaid Cathedral.

---

[1] Select priests deputed by a Pope or bishop to hear and absolve reserved cases in confession.

John de Grandisson was one of the most notable English bishops of the fourteenth century. He was born in 1292, the second son of an English baron who was descended from the lords of Granson near Neuchâtel, and therefore nearly connected with some of the greatest families on the continent. One of his cousins was the Sir Otho de Granson, "flower of them that make in France," to whom Chaucer did the honour of translating three of his *balades*. In later life, the bishop himself inherited the barony (1358). His second sister was the famous Countess of Salisbury of the *honi soit qui mal y pense* legend. At seventeen he was a Prebendary of York; he studied in Paris under the future Pope Benedict XII, and became chaplain to Pope John XXII, who "provided" him in 1327 to the see of Exeter. Grandisson ruled this diocese with great vigour until his death in 1369.

48. EDUCATIONAL REFORM

(13 Feb. 1356-7. *Register*, p. 1192. A mandate directed by Grandisson to all the archdeacons of his diocese.)

WE ourselves have learned and learn daily, not without frequent wonder and inward compassion of mind, that among masters or teachers of boys and illiterate folk in our diocese, who instruct them in Grammar, there prevails a preposterous and unprofitable method and order of teaching, nay, a superstitious fashion, rather heathen than christian; for these masters,—after their scholars have learned to read or repeat, even imperfectly, the Lord's Prayer, the Ave Maria, the Creed, and the Mattins and Hours of the Blessed Virgin, and other such things pertaining to faith and their soul's health, without knowing or understanding how to construe anything of the aforesaid, or decline the words or parse them—then, I say, these masters make them pass on prematurely to learn other advanced [*magistrales*] books of poetry or metre. Whence it cometh to pass that, grown to man's estate, they understand not the things which they daily read or say: moreover (what is more damnable) through lack of understanding they discern not the Catholic Faith. We, therefore, willing to eradicate so horrible and foolish an abuse, already too deep-rooted in our diocese, by all means and methods in our power, do now commit and depute to each of you the duty of warning and enjoining all masters and instructors whatsoever that preside over Grammar Schools within the limits of his archdeaconry, (as, by these letters present, we ourselves strictly command, enjoin, and warn them), that they should not, as hitherto, teach the boys whom they receive as Grammar pupils only to read or learn by heart;[1] but rather that, postponing all else, they should make them construe and understand the Lord's Prayer, the Ave Maria, the Creed, the Mattins and Hours of the Blessed Virgin, and decline and parse the words therein, before permitting them to pass on to other books. Moreover we proclaim that we purpose to confer clerical orders henceforth on no boys but upon such as may be found to have learnt after this method. . . .

Geoffrey de la Tour-Landry fought in the Hundred Years' War at least as early as 1346 and as late as 1383. He wrote in 1371, for the instruction of his daughters, a book which became the most popular educational treatise of the Middle Ages. This "Book of the Knight of the Tower" was translated into German, and at least twice into English; it had passed through seven editions in the three languages before 1550. After Caxton's edition of 1483 there was none in English until it was reprinted in 1868 by T. Wright for the Early English Text Society, from a MS. of Henry VI's reign. It is from this edition that the following extract is taken.

49. A ROMANCE OF RUTH

(p. 119.)

ANOTHER example I shall tell you of a good lady named Ruth, of whom descended the king David. Holy Scripture praiseth much the same lady, for she loved God truly and she honoured Him. And she honoured and obeyed unto her husband as a good woman at all times, and for the love of her husband she honoured and loved all his friends, and bare them more favour and privity than unto her own friends; whereupon it befel that after, when her husband was dead, his sons that were of another wife, they would have left her nothing, nor lands, heritage, nor meuble;[2] and she was of a strange country,

---

[1] Literally, "learn in Latin," *discere literaliter. Literae, literalis, literatura*, etc., are frequently applied to Latin exclusively; cf. *Reg. Epp. Peckham*, R.S. vol. III, pp. 813, 816.

[2] Furniture.

and far from her friends. And the woman fell into a great heaviness by the occasion hereof, but the friends of her husband, that loved her for the great goodness and cherishing that they had found in her the time before in her husband's life, they withstood against the sons of her husband. And they were with her in her helping, insomuch that she had all that she ought to have by right and of custom. And in this wise the good woman saved and won her own, for the friendship and good company that she had y-done unto the kin of her husband, and unto his friends, while he was living. And therefore here is a good example how every good woman oweth to worship and to love kin and friends of her husband, for aye the more semblance of love that she showeth unto them, the more wealth she shall have among them.

From MS. Lansdowne, No. 762, written in the reign of Henry V.

50. THE MASTER OF OXFORD'S CATECHISM

(*Reliquiae Antiquae*, vol. i, p. 230.)
Questions between the Master of Oxenford and his Scholar.

THE *Clerk's question.* Say me where was God when he made heaven and earth? *The Master's answer.* I say, in the further end of the wind. *C.* Tell me what word God first spake? *M.* Be thou made light, and light was made. *C.* What is God? *M.* He is God, that all things made, and all things hath in His power. *C.* In how many days made God all things? *M.* In six days.... *C.* Whereof was Adam made? *M.* of viij things: the first of earth, the second of fire, the iijde of wind, the iiijth of clouds, the vth of air wherethrough he speaketh and thinketh, the vjth of dew whereby he sweateth, the vijth of flowers, whereof Adam hath his eyen, the viijth is salt whereof Adam hath salt tears. *C.* Whereof was found the name of Adam? *M.* Of four stars, this be the names, Arcax, Dux, Arostolym, and Momfumbres. *C.* Of what state was Adam when he was made? *M.* A man of xxx winter of age. *C.* And of what length was Adam? *M.* Of iiij. score and vj.

inches. *C.* How long lived Adam in this world? *M.* ix. c. and xxxty winter, and afterward in hell till the passion of our Lord God. *C.* Of what age was Adam when he begat his first child? *M.* An c. and xxx. winter, and had a son that hight Seth. . . . *C.* What was he that never was born, and was buried in his mother's womb, and since was christened and saved? *M.* That was our father Adam. *C.* How long was Adam in Paradise? *M.* vij. years, and at vij. years' end he trespassed against God for the apple that he ate on a Friday, and an angel drove him out. *C.* How many winters was Adam when our Lord was done on the cross? *M.* That was v. ml. cc. and xxxij. years. *C.* What hight Noes wife? *M.* Dalida; and the wife of Sem, Cateslinna; and the wife of Cam, Laterecta; and the wife of Japheth, Aurca. And other iij. names, Ollia, Olina, and Olybana. *C.* Whereof was made Noes ship? *M.* Of a tree that was cleped[1] Chy. *C.* And what length was Noes ship? *M.* Fifty fathom of breadth, and cc. fathom of length, and xxx. fathom of height. *C.* How many winter was Noes ship in making? *M.* iiij. score years. *C.* How long dured Noes flood? *M.* xl. days and xl. nights. *C.* How many children had Adam and Eve? *M.* xxx. men children and xxx. women children. *C.* What city is there where the sun goeth to rest? *M.* A city that is called Sarica. *C.* What be the best herbs that God loved? *M.* The rose and the lily. *C.* What fowl loved God best? *M.* The dove, for God sent His Spirit from heaven in likeness of a dove. *C.* Which is the best water that ever was? *M.* River Jordan, for God was baptised therein. *C.* Where be the angels that God put out of heaven and became devils? *M.* Some into hell, and some reigned in the sky, and some in the earth, and some in waters and in woods. *C.* How many waters be there? *M.* ij. salt waters, and ij. fresh waters. *C.* Who made first ploughs? *M.* Cam, that was Noes son. *C.* Why beareth not stones fruit as trees? *M.* For Cayme slew his brother Abell with the bone of an ass's cheek. *C.* What is the best thing and the worst among men? *M.* Word is best and worst. *C.* Of what thing be men most afraid? *M.* Men be most afraid of death. *C.* What are the iiij things that men may not live without?

---

[1] Called.

[*M*.] Wind, fire, water, and earth. *C*. Where resteth a man's soul, when he shall sleep? *M*. In the brain, or in the blood, or in the heart. *C*. Where lieth Moises' body? *M*. Beside the house that hight Enfegor. *C*. Why is the earth cursed, and the sea blessed? *M*. For Noe and Abraham, and for christening that God commanded. *C*. Who set first vines? *M*. Noe set the first vines. *C*. Who cleped first God? *M*. The devil. *C*. Which is the heaviest thing bearing? *M*. Sin is the heaviest. *C*. Which thing is it that some loveth, and some hateth? *M*. That is judgment. *C*. Which be the iiij things that never was full nor never shall be? *M*. The first is earth, the second is fire, the third is hell, the fourth is a covetous man. *C*. How many manner of birds be there, and how many of fishes? *M*. liiij. of fowls, and xxvj. of fishes. *C*. Which was the first clerk that ever was? *M*. Elias was the first. *C*. What hight the iiij. waters that runneth through paradise? *M*. The one hight Fyson, the other Egeon, the iijde hight Tygrys, and the iiijth Effraton. These be milk, honey, oil, and wine. *C*. Wherefore is the sun red at even? *M*. For he goeth toward hell. *C*. Who made first cities? *M*. Marcurius the giant. *C*. How many languages be there? *M*. lxij, and so many disciples had God without his apostles.

From MS. Lambeth, No. 306, p. 177 ro, b, of the reign of Edward IV.

51. VARIOUS HEIGHTS OF MEN

(*Ib.* p. 200.)

The longitude of men folowyng.

MOYSES xiij. fote and viij. ynches and half.
    Cryste vj. fote and iij. ynches.
    Our Lady vj. fote and viij. ynches.
    Crystoferus xvij. fote and viij. ynches.
    Kyng Alysaunder iiij. fote and v. ynches.
    Colbronde xvij. fote and ij. ynches and half.
    Syr Ey. x. fote iij. ynches and half.
    Seynt Thomas of Caunturbery, vij. fote save a ynche.
    Long Mores, a man of Yrelonde borne, and servaunt to Kyng Edward the iiijth, vj. fote and x. ynches and half.

52. INSCRIPTIONS IN BOOKS

(The first from MS. Bodleian 132 (thirteenth century); the rest from different MSS. of the fifteenth century, printed in *Reliquiae Antiquae*, vol. II, p. 163.)

THIS book belongs to St Mary of Robertsbridge; whosoever shall steal it, or sell it, or in any way alienate it from this House, or mutilate it, let him be anathema-maranatha. Amen.

Underneath, in the hand of Bishop Grandisson of Exeter (1327–1369).

I John, Bishop of Exeter, know not where the aforesaid House is, nor did I steal this book, but acquired it in a lawful way.

* * * *

"This book is one,
   And God's curse is another;
   They that take the one
   God give them the other."

* * * *

"He that steals this book
   Shall be hanged on a hook.
   He that this book stealë would
   Soon be his heartë cold.
   That it may so be
   Say *Amen* for charity!"

* * * *

"Whosoever this book find
   I pray him have this in his mind.
   For His love that died on tree
   Save this book and bring it to me,
   William Barbor of New Buckenham."

* * * *

"An I it lose and you it find
   I pray you heartily to be so kind
   That you will take a little pain
   To see my book brought home again."

* * * *

(From a MS. temp. Hen. VII (*Rel. Ant.* vol. i, p. 290).)

If this book of mine be defiled with dirt, the master will smite me in dire wrath upon the hinder parts....

* * * *

This abbey falleth in ruins, Christ mark this well! it raineth within and without: this is a fearful place!

* * * *

Three fingers write, and the whole body is in travail; yet they who know not to write deem it no labour!

53. STUDENT BANDITS IN 1422

(*Rot. Parl.* vol. iv, p. 190 (1 Hen. VI).)

MOREOVER the said Commons pray in this present parliament that, whereas divers manslaughters, murders, rapes, felonies, robberies, riots, conventicles, and other misdeeds have been committed afresh during these late days in the counties of Oxenford, Berks, Wilts, and Bucks, more frequently than of aforetime, and with impunity, as well by divers persons repairing to the city of Oxenford as by others dwelling in the city itself under the jurisdiction of the University there; some of whom are liege subjects of our lord the King born in Ireland, and the others are no lieges of his but enemies to our lord the King and to his realm, called *Wylde Irisshmen*; and whereas their malices, misdeeds, and robberies continue from day to day, to the great scandal of the said University, which is fountain and mother of our Christian faith, and to the greater damage and destruction of the whole country round; which malefactors and robbers, with their receivers and maintainers, openly threaten the officers and ministers of our said lord King in those parts, so that they dare not make or exercise execution of the law upon them according to their deserts; and they threaten likewise to slay the Bailiffs of the said city, for that they have lately arrested certain of the aforesaid robbers, and have them in prison with their leader, and by reason of the great menaces made on this occasion to the said Bailiffs, they dare not dwell in their own houses for fear of death, but hold themselves at large for the safety of their lives, seeing that the said Bailiffs are not [*blank*] to come to the said city for gathering and levying the fee-farm thereof in the King's service, nor doing or performing their said offices as they were wont and ought by right to do.... May it please you therefore, by assent of the Lords Spiritual and Temporal in this present Parliament, for peace and quiet's sake in the realm of England and for the settlement of the land of Ireland, that all Irish should be voided from this kingdom between the feast of Christmas now coming and the feast of Candlemas next ensuing, under pain of losing their goods and being imprisoned at the King's will; save only graduates in the schools, and men holding benefices of Holy Church in England, and such as have their heritage in England, or an English father or mother, and professed Religious, merchants, Burgesses, and other well-reputed inhabitants of cities and boroughs who can find surety for their good behaviour, and women married to Englishmen and Irishmen with English wives, so that they be of good report; and that all such Irishmen as have benefices or offices in the land of Ireland should remain there in their benefices or offices, under pain of losing and forfeiting the profits of the said benefices or offices for the defence of the aforesaid land of Ireland, according to the ordinance made in the first year of King Henry V, father of our King that now is. And that the said Graduates and holders of benefices should find surety for their good behaviour, nor should take upon themselves the principalship of any Hall or Hostel, but dwell among other English scholars under the principalship of others....

Answer. Be it as is desired by the petition.

See *Statutes of the Realm* under this year and also under the 8th Henry VI, where a statute was passed upon complaint of the Commons (*Rot. Parl.* vol. IV, p. 349) to deal with gangs of malefactors who terrorized and blackmailed the town and county of Cambridge, Essex, and elsewhere. There is however in this latter case no specific mention of students.

Mathieu de Coussy, the continuator of Monstrelet's *Chronicle*, was born about 1425 and died about 1480. He is a particularly conscientious writer, and rises here and there to vivid description. The following extract is from chap. LXXI of the edition published by J. A. C. Buchon, first as a supplement to Monstrelet and then independently in 1838.

54. TALBOT'S DEATH

WHEN therefore the men of Bordeaux were assembled in the presence of this Talbot, they showed him how King Charles and his army were already far entered, and had overrun the countries of Guienne and Bordeaux with great puissance of men-at-arms: then they reminded him how that they had given over the said town and city of Bordeaux on condition that he should fight against the King of France and his puissance if he came into the aforesaid country, and they submitted to him how he had said more than once, while they were making the aforesaid treaty of surrender, that he needed but ten thousand fighting men to make head against the French armies. "Wherefore," said they, "If you will keep your promise given when this city made obeisance and subjection to you, now is the hour and time for the accomplishment thereof. We pray you go and raise the siege which the French have laid to the town of Châtillon in Périgord." Talbot, hearing these words, and recognising that they had reason, showed no change of countenance at this complaint, but answered them coolly enough, for he was full of natural good sense and valiant in battle as any knight that bore arms in those days; thus then he said to them: "We may let them come nearer still; yet be sure that, God willing, I will keep my promise when I see due time and opportunity." Upon which answer those of the town of Bordeaux showed a face of discontent, misdoubting that this Talbot had no great intention and will to do what he said; nay, they even began to murmur sore one with the other, which was told to my lord Talbot; whereof he was inwardly troubled, and resolved forthwith to send for all who were dispersed in the garrisons of towns and fortresses that obeyed the English around Bordeaux, and for the garrison of the town of Bordeaux itself. He made such haste that within a few days he had from eight to ten thousand fighting men gathered together. Then on St Mary Magdalene's Day, which fell on a Monday that year (1453), he set out from the good city of Bordeaux with his company, and lay that same night at a place called Libourne, five leagues distant from Bordeaux and three leagues from the aforesaid town of Châtillon. But to know and better discover the bearing of the French his enemies, who were lodged before this town of Châtillon, he sent his spies secretly around their quarters; moreover he sent word to those who were within the said town that they should take courage, for he came with might and puissance, intending to succour them; and he bade them prepare themselves on the morrow when they should see him approach, that each man might be under arms and ready to sally forth without their walls and fall upon the enemy, for he was purposed, as he told them, never to turn back until he had driven away the beleaguering army or were slain himself in the fight. At which news those of Châtillon were filled with joy, and took good heart again, for it seemed to them that the lord Talbot had great will to succour them, forasmuch as he came so hastily and that the French had as yet only lain two days about the town; wherefore they sent back word that he should come when it pleased him, but they thought it fitting that he should first of all drive out those who were lodged in the abbey hard by their town, and that they, for their part, would come and help him with all their might, in this assault. Which news being thus brought back to him, he started without long delay from his lodging in Libourne and marched all night long until he came to a wood hard by the aforesaid abbey, wherein were lodged the free-archers of the duchies of Anjou and Périgord, who had with them Pierre de Bauval lieutenant to Charles of Anjou, count of Maine, who commanded this guard with the aforesaid Joachim Rohault. Since, therefore, this Talbot had purposed to carry out his enterprise, and the French that lay in the aforesaid abbey had no tidings of his coming, then the Tuesday following at daybreak he drew with all his company towards this abbey, raising a terrible shout, at the sound whereof the French, who were within, fell into rout, and issued forth with the purpose of gaining the park, whereof we have already spoken and wherein those of their party were lodged; and in this disorder the aforesaid free-archers sallied forth, and Pierre de Bauval and Joachim Rohault stayed behind, bearing the burden of the fight for a long space, making head against the English and withdrawing step by step towards the park. Yet, albeit the French who were therein became aware of the great travail which their own folk must needs undergo that had fled forth from the abbey, nevertheless they advanced not, nor brought no help nor succour to their comrades, by reason whereof in the very first onset five or six nobles were killed on the French part. Moreover the said Joachim, through his own valour, was more than once stricken to the ground; but by the help of the free-archers, who loved him well, he was raised up and remounted on his horse; whereon afterwards he did deeds of great prowess, for he had sworn to his free-archers that he would live and die with them; and, for all that the English might do, yet the French reached the park; but, before they had reached it, there were done great deeds and fair feats of arms on either side, and of the two parties some four-score or hundred men were left on that field. After which the lord Talbot, seeing that the French had gained the park, turned back to the abbey where he lodged, to take refreshment with his men; wherein he found much victual which the French had brought thither, with five or six pipes and barrels of wine, which were forthwith burst open and put at the mercy of all the soldiers, by reason whereof they lasted but a short while; and, seeing that the aforesaid skirmish had been begun and ended so early and that Talbot had as yet heard no mass, his chaplain made ready to sing one, and the altar with its ornaments was ready prepared. In the meanwhile he was of too light credence, for he gave faith to a man who brought him nought but lies, saying as it were in these words: "My lord, the French leave their park and flee away; now is the hour or never, if ye will accomplish your promise." Alas! here is a fair example for all princes, lords, and captains, who have people subjected to their governance, that they should not set too light faith in such tidings; for in so weighty a matter we must not build upon the tale of a jongleur, but of true and loyal officers-at-arms, as of a knight or gentleman, sure of his mouth. But my lord Talbot, for the great desire that he had to serve King Henry his sovereign lord, and also to keep his promise made to the aforesaid town and city of Bordeaux, did otherwise at this time; for, believing too lightly that these tidings were true, he left to hear the mass against his first purpose, and, issuing forthwith from this abbey, he was heard to say these words following: "Never shall I hear the mass until this day I shall have put to rout the company of the French whom I see before me in this park." Notwithstanding therefore that the French in the park were sore moved and troubled by the pursuit which my lord Talbot had made upon those who had fled from the abbey, yet they disposed their artillery straight in the vanguard on that side whereon they saw my lord Talbot come with his company, which advanced in excellent fair array with many trumpets and clarions sounding. Then these English uttered a horrible and terrible cry, shouting with all their voices: "Talbot, Talbot, St George!" but, as they drew near to the park, an ancient gentleman of England who had seen and experienced in his life many doughty deeds of war, perceived that the French within the park gave no ground, whereupon, seeing that they were posted in a strong and advantageous place and that the tidings of their pretended flight were false, he said to the lord Talbot: "My lord, my counsel would be that ye should return again, for ye may well see how the tidings brought unto you were untrue. Ye see their camp and their bearing; ye will gain nought at this time." At which words my lord Talbot was sore displeased, and made him a rough answer with exceeding injurious words: nay even, (if it be true that I have heard,) after this speech he struck him with the sword across the visage, of which stroke he died afterwards; but of this I have never learned the right truth. Certain it is, nevertheless, that my lord Talbot followed the counsel of his own great valiance and marched on towards the park, at the entry whereof he caused his standard to be planted upon one of the stakes wherewith the entrance-gate on that side was closed; and the standard-bearer, whose name I could never learn, clasped the stake with the lance of the

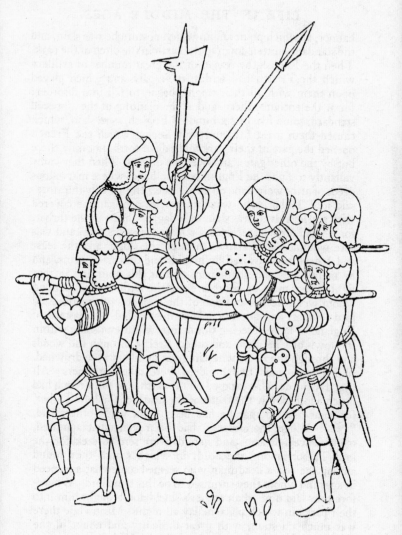

THE DYING WARRIOR

From MS. Reg. 13, c. IX (end of fourteenth century; reproduced in H. Shaw's
Dresses and Decorations).

banner, at which point and in which posture he was slain, and the standard smitten down to the earth in the ditch of the park. Then the English, by reason of the great number of artillery which the French had within their park and which played upon them with all their might, began to fall into disorder; for at the entrance there, and at the planting of the aforesaid standard, some five or six hundred English were slain, which caused them great fear and rout; seeing which the French opened the gate of their park and sallied forth, not only there but by the other gates, and over the ditches. Then they came valiantly to fight the English hand to hand, where marvellous deeds of arms were done on either side. In this sally the aforesaid lord Talbot, who was armed with a brigantine covered with scarlet velvet, was slain by a dagger-thrust in the throat, for he had already received a stroke across his face, and was sore wounded with arrows through the thighs and the legs; and I have been assured by heralds and officers-at-arms, and by many lords and gentlemen, that at this hour and in that fight 4000 men or more were slain with Talbot, among whom were the son and one of the nephews of the aforesaid lord Talbot, and another whom men called the Bastard of England. The rest, seeing this defeat, withdrew; some within the town of Châtillon, and others fleeing through the woods and through the river, wherein great numbers were drowned. Moreover a good two hundred were taken prisoners. All that day the dead lay exposed on the earth, and the French had much ado to know the truth of the death of the lord Talbot, for some assured that he had been slain, while others said, "No." When therefore all had been somewhat appeased, many officers-at-arms and heralds were sent to seek for the lord Talbot among the dead; in which search they found among the rest a dead man who seemed somewhat advanced in age, and whom they surmised to be this same lord. Wherefore they laid him on an archer's shield and brought him into their park; in which place he lay all night. Meanwhile there was much question, with great difficulty and doubt in the company of the lords and others, who said they had known and seen him in his lifetime, concerning the truth of his death; for, though such as affirmed themselves to have known and seen him well maintained that this was he, yet there were many others who said the contrary. But on the morrow there came upon the field many heralds and officers-at-arms of the English party, among whom was the herald of lord Talbot himself, who bare his coat-of-arms; which heralds besought grace to have leave and permission to seek for their master. Then men asked this herald of the lord Talbot whether he would know him well by sight, whereunto he answered joyously (deeming that he was yet alive and captive) that he would fain see him; whereupon he was brought to the place where Talbot lay dead upon the archer's shield, where the men said unto him: "Look and see if this be your master." Then forthwith his colour was changed; yet at first he withheld his judgment, not saying what he thought, for he saw his master much changed and disfigured by the stroke which he had in his face; moreover he had lain there since his death all that night through and all the morrow until that hour; wherefore he was much changed. Yet the herald kneeled down beside him, saying that he would presently know the truth. Then he thrust one of the fingers of his right hand into his lord's mouth, to seek on the left-hand side the place of a great tooth which he knew him certainly to have lost, which place he found, as his purpose was; and no sooner had he found it than, being on his knees as we have said, he kissed the dead man on the mouth, saying: "My lord and master, my lord and master, it is you! I pray to God that He pardon your misdeeds. I have been your officer-at-arms these forty years or more, and it is time that I render you all your loving-kindness!" making in the meanwhile piteous cries and lamentations, and raining piteously with salt tears from his eyes. Then he drew off his coat-of-arms and laid it on his master: by which recognition there was an end of the question and debate which had been made concerning the good lord's death.

Johann Busch was born at Zwolle in 1399. He showed brilliant scholarship as a boy; but as a youth he chose to join the same congregation of
Austin Canons to which his contemporary Thomas à Kempis belonged.
In 1440 he became Subprior of Wittenberg, and began his long and
arduous career as reformer of monasteries under a commission from the
Pope and the Council of Bâle. In this work he attained more success than
any of his contemporaries except the distinguished Cardinal Nicolaus
von Cusa. His chief writings were (i) a charming chronicle of the monastery of Windesheim, and (ii) the *Liber de Reformatione Monasteriorum*,
a minute and often very humorous record of his life's work. The edition
here used is that of K. Grube (Halle, 1887). A translation of it was begun,
but never completed, in the *British Magazine* for April, 1841, etc.; and
the reader may there find some strange things for which there is no place
here. Miss Eckenstein's account of these visitations in her *Woman under
Monasticism* is quite worthless; she takes it at second-hand from a not
always trustworthy monograph by Karl Grube. See Eileen Power,
Medieval English Nunneries, Cambridge, 1922, pp. 670 ff.

55. BOOK-KEEPING BY
DOUBLE ENTRY

Lib. Ref. Bk. IV, ch. 3, p. 730. The summary of this in Grube's monograph, p. 163
is very incorrect.)

A CERTAIN Lector[1] of the Dominicans had publicly
preached in the town of Zutphen, that layfolk should have
no books in the German tongue, and that no sermons should
be preached to the people save only in the church or churchyard. When therefore I heard this (for I was then a simple
Brother at Windesheim, and had been sent with Brother
Dietrich Willemzoon to conclude certain business of our
monastery in Zutphen) then, knowing that there were more
than a hundred congregations of Sisters and Béguines in the
diocese of Utrecht which possessed several books in the
mother tongue, which the Sisters read daily either by themselves or publicly in refectory, I stoutly gainsaid this friar,
seeing that they read and hear German books of this sort in
Zutphen, Deventer, Zwolle, Kampen, and everywhere in
the cities and country districts [of the Netherlands]. Wherefore I went to the Dominican convent and asked for the Prior,
to whom I said: "My lord Prior, I have heard that your

---

[1] "Reader," or Lecturer in a friary.

Lector hath publicly preached that layfolk ought not to have books in the German tongue. Herein he hath preached ill, and he must publicly revoke it: for the princes of the land, the common people, men and women throughout the whole world have many books written in the vulgar German tongue, wherein they read and study. Moreover ye and your Brethren preach oftentimes to the people in the vulgar tongue; would ye wish also that they might remember your sermons by heart?" "Yea," said he. Then I made answer, "If they had them in writing, then they would certainly keep them better in their memory; wherefore then should they not have books in German?" He answered, "The layfolk have many books in German, namely books of Sentences and suchlike, which a certain Doctor of our Order hath translated into German; and others have a missal, with the Canon of the Mass, in the vulgar tongue; therefore it is not good that they should have and read books in German." To whom I made answer, "I do not indeed approve that plain laymen and lay-women should have in German such lofty and divine books as that; nay, I myself burned a Canon of the Mass in German which was found in the possession of some nuns. Yet is it most profitable for all men, learned or unlearned, to possess and daily to read moral books treating of the vices and the virtues, of the Lord's incarnation, life, and passion, of the life and holy conversation and martyrdom of apostles, martyrs, confessors, and virgins, together with homilies and sermons of holy men provoking to amendment of life, moral discipline, fear of hell-fire, and love of the celestial country. If ye will not allow such books, then will I show you in writing the sayings of such Doctors of Holy Church as Austin, Gregory, Ambrose and Jerome, and other orthodox writers, to the effect that it is lawful and most profitable to have such books." Then said he, "If ye produce the written words of Doctors, we too will produce the contrary sayings of [other] Doctors." Then said I more plainly: "My lord Prior, your Lector must revoke publicly from the pulpit that which he hath publicly preached to the people against possessing books in the German tongue; otherwise I will so order things with the lord David bishop of Utrecht, and with his High Chapter, that neither you nor your Lector shall preach again in this diocese." Then said the Prior: "You seem to have a commission to this effect from the Bishop of Utrecht. Be at peace; I will see to it that our Lector shall revoke this." And when I would have gone of mine own authority to the Lector, who was lying on his bed, then said the Prior, "He is a most learned man." To whom I made answer, "I am all the more willing to speak with him since he is learned, for then he will the better understand his own error." Notwithstanding I desisted at the petition of the Prior and the Brother who was with me, and went not to the sick man; more especially because his Prior had promised me that he should revoke those words.

Another day as I journeyed by boat on the Yssel from Deventer to Zutphen, I questioned the men and women that voyaged with me, asking what the Preachers are wont to preach at Zutphen. Whereunto they made answer, "Our Lector formerly preached that layfolk should have no German books. This he hath revoked in brief, saying, 'Good folk, when I preach the gospel to you here, ye repeat it all awry to other men. I spake to you the other day in my sermon concerning German books, that the laity should not possess them, whereby I meant this: Certain women, or even men, sometimes lay certain writings in the German tongue under the altar-cloths, that a mass may be read over them; after which they take these same writings away and work therewith many incantations and divinations or auguries. Those were the writings that I forbade you to have and read; but ye may well and lawfully possess good and moral books in the German tongue, and read therein.'" And they who were in the boat added and said how they had marvelled greatly that he should so revoke his own words, not knowing who had compelled him thereunto. I for my part was well pleased to hear of this his revocation, for in that same town were two houses of Sisters that always read when they sat at meals by the table in the refectory.

On pp. 724, 729, 732, 733, the reader may find other instances of influential preachers who taught publicly similar falsehoods: *e.g.* "that all Béguines were in a state of damnation"; "that whensoever a mass is celebrated throughout the world, so often one soul is freed from the pains of purgatory"; "that is not usury to lend a man a meadow worth five florins a year by way of indemnity, until you have paid the hundred florins you owe him"; "that Caiaphas is in heaven." Busch first confuted these errors by quotation and logic, meeting No. 2 by the pertinent retort, "If that were true, then there could not be a soul left now in purgatory; seeing that more masses are daily sung in the whole world than the number of Christian men who die every day; wherefore it is in vain that masses are daily sung for the dead, since there is not a soul left there!" After which he roundly declared to the preachers, convinced or unconvinced, that they must publicly revoke forthwith or never preach again within his archdeaconry of Halle (for such authority he now had *ex officio* as Provost of Neuwerk); and he describes with much humour how three of them contrived to save their face under these trying circumstances. After which he gives the other side of the medal, p. 733.

Götz von Berlichingen "of the Iron Hand," born in 1480 of a knightly family in Württemberg, may be called the last of the robber-knights of the Middle Ages. For the first half of his life he played the part of a William of Deloraine with varying fortunes: from 1541 onwards he fought under Charles V in greater wars, first against the Turks (1541) and then against the French (1544). He died in his own castle of Hornberg (1562), leaving an autobiography on which Goethe founded his first play, and from which much of Sir Walter Scott's romantic spirit was indirectly derived. His descendants still flourish in two separate lines.

56. A PAGE'S QUARREL

(A.D. 1497, Götz aged 17.)

I was brought up as a page in the house of the Markgraf [of Ansbach]; on whom, in company with other pages, I must needs wait at table. Now it befel upon a time that I sat at meat beside a Pole, who had waxed his hair with eggs: and by chance I was wearing a long coat of outlandish fashion, which my lord Veit von Lentersheim had let make for me in Namur: so that, when I sprang up from my place beside the aforenamed Pole, I ruffled his fine hair with my skirt; and I was aware, even as I sprang up, that he thrust at me with a bread-knife, but missed me. Whereat I waxed wroth, and not without cause: so that, whereas I had both a long and a short blade by my side, yet I drew but the short one, and smote him therewith about the pate: notwithstanding I continued to wait on my wonted service, and stayed that night in the castle. In the morning betimes, the Markgraf went to hear mass at the parish church, as indeed he was a godfearing prince; after which, when we came back to the castle from the church, I found the gates shut behind me, and the Provost-Marshal came up and told me that I must yield myself prisoner. Then I bade him let me alone, for this might not be, and I must needs first get speech of the young Princes; and truly I gave him few gentle words for his pains. But the good man was wiser than I, and let me go; for, had he laid hands on me, I had surely defended myself; and fallen into an evil case. Then I went upstairs to the Princes, and told them of all that had befallen with the Provost-Marshal and this Pole: they were then about to go to table for their morning meal, wherefore they bade me stay where I was; and, if any came, that I should go into their chamber and hide myself in the inner room and lock the door from within. I did as they bade me, and waited till the Princes came back from table and reported how they had spoken on my behalf to the lord their father, and the royal lady their mother,[1] and besought them to save me from punishment in the matter of this Pole: but all their words had naught availed, and the old Markgraf might in no wise find peace with his lady, nor the Princes grace in the eyes of their mother, but she must first have assurance that her lord would cause me to be cast into the tower. Yet the two young Princes bade me in no wise resist, for they would not leave me there longer than one quarter of an hour. But I answered: "Wherefore should I to the tower, since the first offence was of the Pole's giving?" Yet they assured me over again that they would not suffer me to lie there but only for the space of a quarter of an hour: whereupon I let myself be persuaded, and was locked in of my own free will. Prince George would have given me a velvet cloak furred with marten and sable skins, to cover me withal: but I asked What should I with this? for in lying down with it, I might as well chance upon a foul spot as upon a clean; and seeing that my durance was like to be so short, I had no need of the cloak, but would go quietly without it to the tower. The Princes kept

[1] The Markgräfin was daughter to King Casimir IV of Poland.

their word, for I lay but a bare quarter of an hour in that tower; then came my brave captain, Herr Paul v. Absberg, and set me free again, bidding me tell him again the cause of the whole matter. Then this honest knight brought me before the Council, and spake in my behalf, and excused me: moreover, all the squires and noble pages who were at that time at the Markgraf's court, to the number of fifty or sixty, stood by me: and Herr Paul v. Absberg pleaded vehemently that the Pole also should be locked into the tower: yet here he might not prevail.

57. AN ANCIENT FEUD
(A.D. 1502.)

SHORTLY after the Nürnberg fight, (which was fought, as aforesaid, on the Sunday after St Vitus' day), about the time of Michaelmas, it chanced that I was riding down the Soden-berg with Neidhart von Thüngen, on whom I had waited in former times. We were aware, as we went, of two horse-men near a wood, close by the village of Obereschenbach. This was Endriss von Gemünd, Bailiff of Saaleck, with his squire, nicknamed the Ape.—Now you must know that before this, when first I came into Herr Neidhart's service, there had been a meeting at Hammelburg, whereat my cousin Count Wilhelm von Henneberg and Count Michael von Wertheim were present, and where the quarrel of the afore-said Michael von Wertheim with an enemy of his was judged and appeased. One day, then, when I would have joined Herr Neidhart and his troopers in their hostel, who indeed were mostly drunken, there among others I met this aforesaid Ape, and he was very heavy with drink and had much wind in his nose,[1] and spake strange words. "What brings this squireling hither?" quoth he; "is he also to be one of us?" and suchlike scornful words, wherewith he thought to provoke me to wrath. This angered me, and I answered him "What care I for thy scornful speeches and thy drunkenness? If we meet

---

[1] Cf. Chaucer, *Cant. Tales*, A 4151, and H 61.

one day in the field, then will we see who of us twain is squire, and who is trooper."—Now therefore, as we rode down the Sodenberg, I thought within myself, "That is the Ape with his master!" wherefore, galloping forthwith up a high hill, spanning my arblast as I went, I rode far across towards him. His master rode towards the village, to raise the peasants against me, as I supposed. The Ape also had a crossbow: but he fled like his master. Now, as I pressed hard after him, he must needs pass through a deep sunken way towards the village: and I had still far to go to the corner whereat this way led in [to the village]. So I let him ride into the sunken way, and shot after him as he fled. I would now have spanned my arblast again forthwith, since he too had a bolt ready in his own: but I thought that he would not abide me; wherefore I heeded not to span again, but spurred after him into the hollow way. When therefore he had marked how I had not spanned, he waited at the gate until I was hard upon him: then he let fly his bolt and struck me on the boss of my breast-plate, so that the shaft splintered and flew over my head. Suddenly I threw my arblast at his head, for I had no bolt in it; then I plucked forth my sword and ran him to the earth, so that his nag's nose lay on the ground. But he rose to his feet again; ever and again he cried unto the peasants, that they should come to his rescue. When therefore I rode into the village after him, I was aware of a peasant who had already laid a bolt in his bow; upon whom I sprang, and smote his bolt to the ground ere he could come to shoot. Then I reined up at his side, sheathed my sword, and gave him to know that I was Herr Neidhart von Thüngen's man, and that we were both good friends of the Abbot of Fulda. Meanwhile there came round me a whole rout of peasants, some with boar-spears, some with hand-axes or casting-axes or wood-axes, and some with stones. Here then was nought to be won save by hard blows and good adventure: for all this while the axes and stones buzzed so thick round my head, that methought my helmet was a-humming with bees. Then there ran up a peasant with a boarspear, at whom I spurred my horse: but, he, even as I drew my sword, thrust forward and dealt me so shrewd a blow on the arm, that methought he had smitten it in two. When again I would have thrust at him, he slid under my horse's belly, and I had not room to bend down after him. Then, however, I brake through the rout; and upon another peasant, who bore a wood-axe, upon him I dealt such a blow that he reeled sideways against the palisade. But now my horse would gallop no more, for I had overridden him: and I doubted sore how I should come forth from that gate again. Yet I made such haste as I might, for one fellow was on the point to close it: but I was beforehand with him and came safely through. Yet there stood that same Ape again, with four peasants by his side, and a bolt in his arblast, crying: "Upon him! upon him! upon him!" and shot after me, that I saw the bolt quiver in the earth. So I rode at him, and drove all five back into the village. Then the peasants raised their hue and cry after me; but I rode off with such speed as I might. As I came again to Herr Niedhart, who awaited me far away on the field, the peasants looked out after us, but none was so hardy as to come near us. Yet, even as I joined Herr Neidhart, there came a peasant running with his plough to the sound of the alarm-bell: him I took for my prisoner, and caused him to promise and swear that he would bring me out again my arblast, which I had thrown at the Ape when he shot at me: for I lacked time to pick it up again, but must needs leave it lying on the road.

58. THE IRON HAND
(A.D. 1504.)

I WILL now tell how I came by my wound. You must know that on Sunday, as I have related above, while we were skirmishing again under the walls of Landshut, the Nürnbergers turned their cannon upon friend and foe alike. The enemy had taken up a strong position on a dyke, and I would fain have broken a spear with one of them. But as I held myself still and watched for an occasion, suddenly the Nürnbergers turned their cannon upon us; and one of them, with a field-culverin, shot in two my swordhilt, so that the one

half entered right into my arm,
and three armplates there-
withal; the sword-hilt lay so
deep in the armplates that it
could not be seen. I marvel
even now that I was not
thrown from my horse; the
armplates were still whole;
only the corners, which had
been bent by the blow, stood
forth a little. The other half
of the sword-hilt and the blade
were bent, but not severed;
and these, I believe, tore off
my hand betwixt the gauntlet
and the arm-piece: my arm
was shattered behind and before. When I marked now
that my hand hung loose by
the skin, and that my spear
lay under my horse's feet, I
made as though nothing had
befallen me, turned my horse
softly round, and, in spite of
all, came back to my own folk
without let or hindrance from
the enemy. Just then there
came up an old spearman,
who would have ridden into
the thick of the fray: him I
called to me, and besought
that he would stay at my side,
since he must see how matters
stood with me. So he tarried
with me at my prayer, and
then he must needs fetch me
the leech. When I came to
Landshut, my old comrades
told me who had fought in

GÖTZ'S IRON HAND

From an engraving of the original still
preserved by his descendant, Freiherr v.
Berlichingen-Rossach.

the battle against me, and in what wise I had been shot, and that a nobleman, Fabian von Wallsdorf, a Voigtländer, had been struck and slain by the same shot, notwithstanding that it had struck me first; so that in this wise both friend and foe took harm alike. This nobleman was a fair and goodly gentleman, such that among many thousands you would scarce find any goodlier to behold. . . .

From that time forth, from the Sunday after St Vitus' day until Ash Wednesday, I lay in Landshut; and what pain at that time I suffered, each may well imagine for himself. It was my prayer to God that, if I stood indeed in His divine grace, then in His own name He might bear me away to Himself, since I was spoiled now for a fighting-man. Yet then I bethought me of a man at arms of whom I had heard my father and other old troopers tell, whose name was Köchli, and who also had but one hand, notwithstanding which he could do his devoir against his foe in the field as well as any other man. Then I prayed to God, and considered within myself that, had I even twelve hands, and His grace and help stood not by me, then were all in vain. Therefore, thought I, might I but get me some little help by means of an iron hand, then I would prove myself as doughty in the field, in spite of all, as any other maimed man. I have ridden since then with Köchli's sons, who were trusty horsemen and well renowned. And in all truth I can think and say nought else,—now that for wellnigh sixty years I have waged wars, feuds, and quarrels with but one fist,—but that God Almighty, Everlasting and Merciful, hath stood wondrously and most graciously by me and at my side in all my wars, feuds, and perils.

In 1536, the inhabitants of Bourges performed in their old Roman amphitheatre a "Mystery of the Holy Acts of the Apostles" which was perhaps the most elaborate ever recorded. It lasted forty days, and it was so admirably acted (as a contemporary historian assures us) "that the greater part of the spectators judged it to be real and not feigned." The performance began by a procession of the 494 performers from the Abbey of St Sulpice to the arena, in costumes which modern pageant-masters can only envy at a distance. "A demoniac, clad in green satin brocaded with golden apples, was led on a gilt chain by his father in yellow satin. A blind man and his varlet were in red and grey satin. A paralytic had a shirt of orange satin. The blind men, 'rascals,' and other beggars were clad in silk....After the Apostles came, 'in habit of humility, 62 [*sic*,? 72] disciples clad in robes of velvet, crimson satin, damask and taffeta, made in strange and divers fashions, some with embroidery and others with bands of ribbon or silk, all after the ancient fashion.'...'After all this devilry came a Hell fourteen feet long by eight feet broad in fashion of a rock crowned with a tower ever burning and belching flames, wherein Lucifer's head and body alone appeared...vomiting flames of fire unceasingly, and holding in his hands certain kinds of serpents or vipers which writhed and belched fire.'...'At the end of the procession came a Paradise eight feet broad by twelve feet long.'"

Baron de Girardot printed in t. XIII of Didron's *Annales Archéologiques*, pp. 16 ff., a manuscript which contained a list of the "properties" required for this performance. Everything was as realistic as possible: the flaying of St Bartholomew was made visible by a "nudity, or carnation" which he wore under his apparent skin; the beheading of Simon Magus was managed by the sudden substitution of a live sheep, which supplied the necessary blood; to out-devil the devil, "we must have a pair of spectacles for Satan." The following extract gives the properties required for the Virgin Mary's death, funeral, and assumption; see the whole description in the *Golden Legend* (Temple Classics, vol. IV, p. 234), or in Myrc's *Festial*. The accompanying illustration, representing the miraculous severance of Belzeray's hands, is from a series representing the same history, carved round the outside of Notre Dame de Paris from the north transept to the apse.

59. BEHIND THE SCENES AT A MIRACLE PLAY

W E must have a palm sent from Paradise for Gabriel to bring to Mary. There must be a thunder-clap in Paradise; and then we need a white cloud to come fetch and ravish St John preaching at Ephesus, and to bring him before the door of the Virgin Mary's abode. We must have another cloud to catch up all the Apostles from their divers countries and bring them all before the aforesaid house. We must have a white robe for the Virgin Mary to die in. We must have a little truckle-bed, and several torches of white wax which the virgins will hold at the said Lady's death. Jesus Christ must come down from Paradise to the death of the Virgin Mary, accompanied by a great multitude of angels, and take away her soul with Him.

A MIRACLE OF OUR LADY

At the moment when He cometh into the said Virgin's chamber, we must make great fragrance of divers odours. We must have the holy soul ready.[1] We must have a crown encircled with twelve stars to crown the aforesaid soul in Paradise. We must have a bier to bear the said Lady's body

---

[1] Probably in the shape of a little naked child issuing from the dying person's mouth, according to the usual medieval convention.

to the tomb. We must have a tomb. There must be sent down from Paradise to the tomb aforesaid a round cloud shaped like a crown, wherein are several holy angels with naked swords and javelins in their hands; and, if it may be, we must have these living, that they may sing. Belzeray, prince of the Jews, and others set off to go and prevent lest the body of the said Lady be laid in the tomb. The Jews strive to lay hands on the Virgin Mary's body to tear her from the Apostles; and forthwith their hands are withered and they are blinded with fire thrown by the angels. Belzeray laying hands on the litter whereon the Virgin Mary is borne, his hands remain fixed to the said litter, and much fire is cast down like unto thunderbolts, and the Jews must fall blinded to the earth. Belzeray's hands must be severed and joined again to his arms; then he is given a palm which he beareth to the rest, and whereby such as would believe were enlightened; then he brought back the said palm. We need a tomb wherein to lay the said Lady's body. Such as would not be converted are tormented by devils; some must be borne to hell. God purposeth to send to our Lady's tomb, to raise her and bring her up to Paradise, body and soul. St Michael should present the soul to Jesus Christ. This done, they come down accompanied by all the orders of angels in Paradise; and so soon as Jesus Christ is come to the tomb, a great light must be made, whereat the Apostles are amazed. Gabriel must raise the tombstone and the soul laid therein, so that it be no more seen. The soul is reunited to the body, and Mary riseth having her face clearer than the sun: then she must humble herself before Jesus Christ. Jesus, Mary, and all the angels must mount up; and in mounting they must stay awhile here and there, even as the Orders shall speak. Mary, for the doubt that St Thomas had, casteth him her girdle. A cloud must cover the Apostles: then let each depart underground and go unto his own region.

In the York miracle plays, the obnoxious Jew was named not Belzeray, but Fergus, probably in the same anti-Scottish spirit which prompted the contemporary author of the Wakefield plays to name the sheep-stealing shepherd Mac. The York Memorandum Book has a very interesting entry under the year 1420 (ed. Maud Sellers, Surtees Soc. vol. CXXV, p. 124). The goldsmiths of York complained that they were no longer able to meet the expense of acting two miracle plays yearly, while other crafts did only one each.

A representation of the Fergus scene, much damaged, is in Eton College Chapel, executed between 1479 and 1488, with a scroll referring to Vincent [of Beauvais], lib. VI, cap. 78.—Willis and Clark, *Archit. Hist. Univ. Camb.* I, pp. 412 and 599.

60. THE SAME

MEANWHILE, on the other hand, seeing that the masons of this city murmured among themselves concerning their pageant in the Corpus Christi play, wherein Fergus was scourged, for the reason that the matter of that pageant is not contained in Holy Scripture, and that it caused rather laughter and clamour than devotion, so that strife and contentions and fights sometimes arose thence on the people's part; seeing also that they could seldom or never produce and play the said pageant in full daylight, as the preceding pageants do, therefore the said masons desired with great desire to be exonerated from this their pageant, and to be assigned to some other pageant which may be in conformity with Holy Scripture, and which they will be able to produce and play by daylight.... The mayor, aldermen and council decided... that the masons should be exonerated and quit of the Fergus pageant, and that they should take for themselves and their craft the pageant of Herod, which the goldsmiths formerly had, to be produced and played at their own expense in the play of Corpus Christi, in the most honourable fashion that befits them, to the praise of the city, as often as the said play is played in the city aforesaid.

The documents quoted by Lucy Toulmin Smith (*York Mystery Plays*, Oxford, 1885, pp. xxviii ff.) show that in 1476 the linen-weavers were undertaking this play of Fergus; in 1485 it was again "laid apart"; in 1517, its revival was contemplated, if not carried out. The plot of the Fergus pageant is given in a single sentence in a Latin *Order of Pageants for the Play of Corpus Christi*, dated 1415: "Four apostles carrying Mary's bier, and Fergus hanging on the bier, with two other Jews [*in later hand*, and an angel]."

More's English Works (as Principal Lindsay writes on p. 17 of the third volume of the *Cambridge History of English Literature*) "deserve more consideration than they usually receive." Yet he vouchsafes them no further consideration; and later on Mr Routh mentions one of them only to disparage it (p. 80). Since they are practically inaccessible to the general reader (for the folio costs from £25 to £50 according to its condition) I give in these volumes some stories which show him at his best as a raconteur, and of which no. 61 in vol. IV is doubly interesting for the use that Shakespeare made of it. In the *Dialogue* More is arguing in his own person against a disputant of quasi-heretical leanings, generally alluded to as the *Messenger* or *your Friend*. The following extract, from *Dialogue* (bk III, chap. xvi), should be studied by all who have read those portions of *The Eve of the Reformation* in which Abbot Gasquet, after making free quotations from this chapter of More's, asserts: "This absolute denial of any attitude of hostility on the part of the Church to the translated Bible is reiterated in many parts of Sir Thomas More's English works.... It has been already pointed out how Sir Thomas More completely disposed of this assertion as to the hostility of the Clergy to the open Bible" (pp. 243, 246). The extract will, I cannot help thinking, bring fresh light even to readers of Dr Gairdner's *Lollardy and the Reformation*. It must be remembered that More's view (like Busch's already quoted in Extract 55) represents that of the most liberal and enlightened party among the orthodox.

61. THE HALF-CLOSED BIBLE

(p. 240.)

"Sir," quoth your Friend [the messenger], "yet for all this can I see no cause why the clergy should keep the Bible out of laymen's hands that can no more but their mother-tongue." "I had weened," quoth I, "that I had proved you plainly that they keep it not from them; for I have showed you that they keep none from them, but such translation as be either not yet approved for good or such as be already reproved for naught, as Wycliffe's was and Tyndale's; for as for other old ones that were before Wycliffe's days, [they] remain lawful, and be in some folk's hands had and read." "Ye say well," quoth he, "but yet, as women say, somewhat it was alway that the cat winked when her eye was out. Surely it is not for naught that the English Bible is in so few men's hands when so many would so fain have it." "That is very truth," quoth I, "for I think that, though the favourers of a sect of heretics be so fervent in the setting forth of their sect, that they let not to lay their money together and make a purse among them for the printing of an evil-made, or evil-translated book (which though it hap to be forbidden and burned, yet some be sold ere they be spied, and each of them lose but their part) yet I think there will no printer lightly be so hot to put any Bible in print at his own charge, whereof the loss should lie whole in his own neck, and then hang upon a doubtful trial, whether the first copy of his translation was made before Wycliffe's days or since. For, if it were made since, it must be approved before the printing. And surely how it hath happed that in all this while God hath either not suffered, or not provided, that any good virtuous man hath had the mind in faithful wise to translate it, and thereupon either the clergy, or at the leastwise some one bishop, to approve it, this can I nothing tell. . . ." "I am sure," quoth your Friend, "ye doubt not but that I am full and whole of your mind in this matter, that the Bible should be in our English tongue. But yet that the clergy is of the contrary, and would not have it so, that appeareth well, in that they suffer it not to be so. And, over that I hear, in every place almost where I find any learned man of them, their minds [are] all set thereon to keep the scripture from us; and they seek out for that part every rotten reason that they can find, and set them forth solemnly to the shew, though five of those reasons be not worth a fig. For they begin as far as our first father Adam, and shew us that his wife and he fell out of Paradise with desire of knowledge and cunning. Now if this would serve, it must from the knowledge and study of scripture drive every man, priest and other, lest it drive all out of Paradise. Then say they that God taught His disciples many things apart, because the people should not hear it, and therefore they would the people should not now be suffered to read all. Yet they say further that it is hard to translate the scripture out of one tongue into another, and specially, they say, into ours, which they call a tongue vulgar and barbarous. But of all things specially they say that scripture is the food of the soul, and that the common people be as infants that must be fed but with milk and pap; and if we have any stronger meat it must be champed afore by the nurse, and so put into the babe's mouth. But methinks, though they make us all infants, they shall find many a shrewd brain among us that can perceive chalk from cheese well enough, and if they would once take us our meat in our own hand we be not so evil toothed but that within a while they shall see us champ it ourselves as well as they. For let them call us young babes an they will, yet by God they shall, for all that, well find in some of us that an old knave is no child." "Surely," quoth I, "such things as ye speak is the thing that, as I somewhat said before, putteth good folk in fear to suffer the scripture in our English tongue; not for the reading and receiving, but for the busy champing thereof, and for much meddling with such parts thereof as least will agree with their capacities.... Finally methinketh that the Constitution Provincial,[1] of which we spake right now, hath determined this question already; for when the clergy therein agreed that the English Bibles should remain which were translated before Wycliffe's days, they consequently did agree that to have the Bible in English was none hurt. And in that they forbade any new translation to be read till it were approved by the bishops, it appeareth well thereby that their intent was that the bishop should approve it if he found it faultless, and also of reason amend it where it were faulty; but if [i.e. unless] the man were an heretic that made it, or the faults such and so many as it were more easy to make it all new than mend it, as it happed for both points in the translation of Tyndale. Now, if so be that it would haply be thought not a thing meetly to be adventured to set all on a flush at once, and dash rashly out Holy Scripture in every lewd fellow's teeth, yet thinketh me there might such a moderation be taken therein, as neither good virtuous lay folk should lack it, nor rude and rash brains abuse it. For it might be with diligence well and truly translated by some good catholic and well-learned man, or by divers dividing the labour among them, and after conferring their several parties together each with other. And after that might the work be allowed

---

[1] Abp Arundel's constitution of 1408, forbidding as heretical all unauthorized translations or portions of the Bible, but making no provision for any authorized translation.

and approved by the Ordinaries, and by their authorities so put into print, as all the copies should come whole unto the bishop's hand; which he may after his discretion and wisdom deliver to such as he perceiveth honest, sad, and virtuous, with a good monition and fatherly counsel to use it reverently with humble heart and lowly mind, rather seeking therein occasion of devotion than of despicion; and providing as much as may be, that the book be after the decease of the party brought again and reverently restored unto the Ordinary; so that, as near as may be devised, no man have it but of the Ordinary's hand, and by him thought and reputed for such as shall be likely to use it to God's honour and merit of his own soul. Among whom if any be proved after to have abused it, then the use thereof to be forbidden him, either for ever or till he be waxen wiser.... We find also among the Jews, though all their whole Bible was written in their vulgar tongue, and those books thereof wherein their laws were written were usual in every man's hands, as things that God would have commonly known, repeated, and kept in remembrance; yet were there again certain parts thereof which the common people of the Jews of old time, both of reverence and for the difficulty, did forbear to meddle with. But now, sith the veil of the temple is broken asunder that divided among the Jews the people from the sight of the secrets, and that God had sent His Holy Spirit to be assistant with His whole church to teach all necessary truth, though it may therefore be the better suffered that no part of Holy Scripture were kept out of honest laymen's hands, yet would I that no part thereof should come in theirs which to their own harm (and haply their neighbour's too) would handle it over-homely, and be too bold and busy therewith. And also though Holy Scripture be, as ye said whilere, a medicine for him that is sick and food for him that is whole, yet (sith there is many a body sore soul-sick that taketh himself for whole, and in Holy Scripture is an whole feast of so much divers viand, that, after the affection and state of sundry stomachs, one may take harm by the selfsame that shall do another good, and sick folk often have such a corrupt tallage in their taste that they most like the meat that is most unwholesome for them,) it were not therefore, as methinketh, unreasonable that the Ordinary, whom God hath in the diocese appointed for the chief physician, to discern between the whole and the sick and between disease and disease, should after his wisdom and discretion appoint everybody their part as he should perceive to be good and wholesome for them. And therefore, as he should not fail to find many a man to whom he might commit all the whole, so (to say the truth) I can see none harm therein, though he should commit unto some man the gospel of Matthew, Mark, or Luke, whom he should yet forbid the gospel of St John, and suffer some to read the Acts of the Apostles, whom he would not suffer to meddle with the Apocalypse. Many were there, I think, that should take much profit by St Paul's Epistle *ad Ephesios*, wherein he giveth good counsel to every kind of people, and yet should find little fruit for their understanding in his Epistle *ad Romanos*, containing such high difficulties as very few learned men can very well attain. And in like wise would it be in divers other parts of the Bible, as well in the Old Testament as the New; so that, as I say, though the bishop might unto some layman betake and commit with good advice and instruction the whole Bible to read, yet might he to some man well and with reason restrain the reading of some part, and from some busybody the meddling with any part at all, more than he shall hear in sermons set out and declared unto him, and in like wise to take the Bible away from such folk again, as be proved by their blind presumption to abuse the occasion of their profit unto their own hurt and harm. And thus may the bishop order the scripture in our hands, with as good reason as the father doth by his discretion appoint which of his children may for his sadness keep a knife to cut his meat, and which shall for his wantonness have his knife taken from him for cutting of his fingers. And thus am I bold, without prejudice of other men's judgment, to show you my mind in this matter, how the Scripture might without great peril and not without great profit be brought into our tongue and taken to laymen and women both, not yet meaning thereby but that the whole Bible might for my mind be suffered to be spread abroad in English; but, if that were so much doubted that perchance all might thereby be letted, then would I rather have used such moderation as I speak of, or some such other as wiser men can better devise. Howbeit, upon that I read late in the Epistle that the King's Highness translated into English of his own, which His Grace made in Latin, answering to the letter of Luther, my mind giveth me that His Majesty is of his blessed zeal so minded to move this matter unto the prelates of the clergy, among whom I have perceived some of the greatest and of the best of their own minds well inclinable thereto already, that we lay-people shall in this matter, ere long time pass, except the fault be found in ourselves, be well and fully satisfied and content." "In good faith," quoth he, "that will in my mind be very well done; and now am I for my mind in all this matter fully content and satisfied." "Well," quoth I, "then will we to dinner, and the remnant will we finish after dinner." And therewith we went to meat.

Jean de Bourdigné, whose *Chronicle of Anjou* ends in 1529, is well characterized by Quatrebarbes in his preface to the only modern edition (Angers, 1842, p. lxvii). "His double character of priest and nobleman comes out in every page. He has the same hatred for the enemies of the Faith and of France—the *monstre luthérique*, the Burgundians, and the English. Bourdigné is the last writer of the Middle Ages....His Chronicle, a faithful echo of ancient customs, has appeared to us the most precious historical document concerning our province." In reading these annals we see before our eyes the passing of the Middle Ages, and are ready to understand those wars of religion which devastated France in the next generation.

62. SHYLOCK IN PROVENCE

(T. ii, p. 237. Shortly after the death of Charles the Bold, A.D. 1477.)

THE good prince René of Anjou, King of Sicily, after having taken leave of his nephew King Louis in his town of Lyon, as you have already heard, returned to Provence. Now it befel that, while he was in the town of Aix, in his said County of Provence, there were then in that town several Jews his tributaries, men of great substance and fat merchants, one of whom at the Devil's instigation uttered several injurious words against the honour of the glorious Virgin Mary; which came to the ears of this devout and religious King of Sicily, who caused the blasphemer to be taken and clapped into prison. Then, a few days afterwards, he sent unto him several doctors of theology, men of great learning and good conscience, to preach to him and move him from his evil speech. Which doctors by lively and evident reasons proved unto him the error of all that he had said, and admonished him well to repent and unsay those false propositions which he had wished to maintain. But the poor wretch was so obstinate that he would never repent for all that could be said unto him. Moreover, what is worse, while continuing his evil speech he heaped error upon error, and uttered yet more villainies and insults than before. When therefore King René learned his obstinacy, he was sore displeased, and commanded his chancellor to try the Jew in form of law and do him good justice, saying that he would have no other man know of this matter but the chancellor, for fear lest (if any other took cognizance thereof) the other Jews, who were rich and wealthy, should suborn him by gifts and bribes.

The chancellor, after due form of trial, seeing the enormity of the case, condemned the obstinate merchant to be stripped stark naked upon a scaffold set up in front of his own house, and there to be flayed alive. Which sentence was forthwith published with sound of trumpet; and the crier proclaimed that this justice should be done after dinner on this same day. When therefore the other Jews of the city heard the horrible form of death whereby their companion was doomed to die, then were they in great doubt and trouble. Wherefore they held a council and set forth all means that could possibly be found to save him; nor could they find better than the counsel of one of the elders of the synagogue, who said unto them: "Sirs, the best means that I can see to save our brother from death is this; that the King of Sicily (as I have heard) hath at this time no great abundance of money; wherefore I counsel that we beseech him to pardon our fellow, and that for this request we present him twenty thousand florins, with a thousand or twelve hundred more to each of his three or four priviest and most familiar counsellors, that we may thus bend his purpose." Which counsel seemed most excellent to the Jews: wherefore they chose out some dozen of the most honourable from among them, and sent them on this business to the King of Sicily. These men, by gifts and promises, compassed their entry to the King and had leave to speak with him. When therefore they had done obeisance before him, they besought him to pardon their fellow and grant him his life; for which pardon they offered him 20,000 florins.

The good King, moved to indignation by this request of the Jews, left them without answer; and, entering into a closet where were five or six of his most familiar servants, he said to them with a smile: "What think ye, gallants? it lieth in my choice to have twenty thousand florins, which I have even now refused." Then he told them how the Jews had offered him so much to save their fellow's life; after which, he asked their counsel. And all the lords there present (who, perchance, were already corrupted with bribes) counselled that he should take the florins and let the miscreant go to the devil. "How?" quoth the good King: "ye would then that I should overlook the insults which by this traitor have been said concerning the mother of God, and that I should sell the punishment thereof! Certes, if this were so, I should then be an evil doer of justice, which shall never be. And albeit for the present I have certain most urgent business, to bring which to an end I have sore need of such a sum, yet would I rather have lost ten times as much than that my good Lady should not be avenged. God grant that no man say of me, nor no man write in chronicle, that under my governance so heinous a crime remained unpunished!"

When the virtuous King had thus spoken, then the rest knew well that they must hold their peace, for to speak would be but lost labour. But it chanced that one among them had a somewhat more lively wit than the rest, who said unto the King: "Sir, these Jews are evil miscreants, and have well deserved a great fine in that they have been so bold as to pray for the revocation of your just sentence, seeing especially that their fellow hath so well deserved death. Wherefore I pray you that it be your pleasure to command me to answer for you, and to avow whatsoever I shall say; and I hope, with

God's help, so to work that you shall be well pleased." "Yea in truth," said the King, "I grant it you, saving only that my doom already given shall be executed." "Sire," replied the gentleman, "that shall be done, trust me well." Then he sent an usher to tell the Jews (who were in the hall, awaiting the answer to their request) that the King was sending a gentleman of his chamber to declare unto them the finding of his Council. Within a brief space after this message, this gentleman came among them and began to look austerely upon them, saying thus: "Fair sirs, our lord the King and his noble Council cannot sufficiently marvel at the presumptuous temerity which hath moved you to petition him for the pardon of so execrable a crime as this of your fellow's, seeing that yourselves (by the conventions which stand between you and the Christian folk of this land) should have punished it; for it is laid down, in the law which suffereth you to dwell among Christian folk, that none of you should speak evil of our lord Jesus Christ nor of His glorious Mother. And, notwithstanding that ye have been duly advertised of the false and injurious words which yon fellow hath said of this matter, yet ye, though aiders and abettors in his crime, have had the hardihood to beseech a pardon for him, and have sought to corrupt the King's justice by bribes. Wherefore, in order that for all time to come no man among you may again be so presumptuous as to make or solicit such unlawful and importunate requests, therefore the King and his Council have judged irrevocably and sentenced that ye yourselves should flay this malefactor, the first royal sentence remaining still in full force and vigour. Wherefore I signify this doom unto you, according as it hath been commanded to me."

At this judgment the Jews were so amazed that they were ready to swoon with sorrow, and began to look most piteously one upon the other, as men who would rather have died than to do such hangman's work: which indeed they made shift to escape by working upon five or six favourites, to whom they gave great presents for their intercession with the King, that it might please him to absolve them from this execution whereunto his Council had doomed them; saying that they would give this sum of twenty thousand florins which they had before offered to save their fellow's life; whose death they left now to the sentence which the King had pronounced, confessing that he had spoken folly, and that they had been ill-advised in beseeching his deliverance. The King therefore, advised by his favourites of the device of his courtier who had condemned them, was well pleased and gave him good thanks, accepting the promised moneys to quit these Jews from the execution of the criminal. They held themselves fortunate to have thus escaped; and, that same day, after dinner, that sentence was carried out on the body of the unhappy Jew; for he was flayed alive by certain masked gentlemen who, to avenge the injurious words pronounced against the glorious Mother of God, willed of their own good zeal to execute the sentence. So miserably did this wretched Jew die, persisting to the last breath in his damned obstinacy.

63. THE END OF A WORLD
(T. II, p. 329. A.D. 1521.)

ALL the country parishes in Anjou were constrained to raise men-at-arms commonly called *francs-archers*, which was a grievous burden; for each parish furnished one man whom they had to fit out with cap, plumes, doublet, leather collar, hosen and shoes, with such harness and staff as the captain should command.[1] . . . Which innovation and raising of francs-archers was most grievous to the people of Anjou; for, albeit they were raised, fed, clothed and armed at so great a cost, yet were they unprofitable both to prince and to people; for they began to rise up against the common folk, desiring to live at ease without further labouring at their wonted trades, and to pillage in the fields as they would have done in an enemy's

[1] It is interesting to compare this with the far more businesslike militia system which worked so well in England from Edward I to James I, and which, instead of attempting to create by compulsion a small standing army, aimed at making each citizen responsible for his share of home defence, thus creating a whole population of roughly-trained men from which volunteer armies could be raised in times of emergency. The English militia was always looked upon as a steady constitutional force, and a valuable counterpoise to the danger of lawlessness which attends the formation of standing armies.

country; wherefore several of them were taken and given into the hands of the provost-marshals, ending their lives on the gibbet which they had so well deserved.

This year also the country of Anjou was infested by exceeding grievous rains, that did much harm to the fruit: moreover the earth quaked sore, wherefrom many had but evil forebodings. And certainly men heard daily reports of follies and barbarities committed by these francs-archers, to the great scandal of the Faith and detriment of the people. For about this season, after that the aforesaid miscreants had scoured and rifled the province of Maine, beating and grieving the people sore, then they feared not to do a most detestable deed; for, by instigation of the Devil, they took a calf and set it upon the holy font ordained for the giving of baptism to christian folk; and there one of them, taking the church ornaments and holy water, made a form and pretence of baptizing him and giving him such a name as one would give to a christian, all in scorn and disdain of the holy sacrament of baptism, which was a strange thing to christian folk.

Again, in the village called St-Côme de Ver, in the said country of Maine, as the francs-archers aforesaid had (according to their wont) done several insolences and derisions against the holy relics in that church, and against the sacraments and ceremonies of the Church, finally one of them came behind the said church of St-Côme, hard by the [great] glass window which giveth it light, where the said franc-archer found an apple-tree laden with fruit, which apples he plucked one by one, and threw them for his pleasure against the painted window of the church. And, having thrown several without being able to strike or break the glass, then it befel that, cursing and blaspheming, he cast one wherewith he smote the crown on a pictured St Cosmo that was in the window; which apple stuck there amidst the glass for a whole year's space, in the sight of all people, without decay or corruption; yet on the other hand all the other apples that hung on the tree fell to the ground from that day forward, and rotted in the twinkling of an eye, as though poisoned and infected by the touch of that wretch who had laid hands on the tree; who nevertheless escaped not our Lord's judgment and vengeance. For, in that night following, the arm wherewith he had cast the said apples was stricken with palsy, not without grievous pain and torment; whereof he was nevertheless afterwards cured to his own confusion; for, having done some deed that brought him into the hands of justice, he was hanged and strangled by the provost-marshal. Yet this shameful death of his amended not his fellows, but that they wrought many crimes and barbarities unwonted and unheard-of before this time; for they pillaged in their own country as in a foreign land, forced women and maidens, beat priests and men of all estates, and took horses or mares from the fields and meadows wheresoever they found them, to bear themselves and the raiment which they gathered by their robberies throughout the country; feeding their horses and mares on pure wheat which they took from the poor folk, and giving them wine to drink. And it befel in one place of Anjou that, after these miscreants had drunken outrageously of the best wine that was in the house wherein they lodged, then they began to cast the rest away; and as the master of that house, a man of holy church far advanced in age, gently reproved them, showing how it was a sin to waste the good things which God giveth for our sustenance, then these evil folk waxed wroth and constrained him to set a caldron on the fire, and fill it with wine, wherewith, when it was warmed he must needs wash their feet. And many other barbarities were wrought by the rabble, which would be tedious to tell of.... In the month of November of this year it rained in so great abundance that men thought the deluge had come (for some had foolishly foretold this the year before); whereof many men of light faith were sore afraid, both in Anjou and in Touraine. The river Loire swelled into so great a flood that it did much harm throughout the land; for in many places it brake the dikes and wrought piteous havoc in the lowlands; wherein some houses were overthrown by the violence of the waters, and much sown corn was lost, and many beasts drowned; so that the country folk were in sore poverty for many years after. And this same year, on the twelfth day of December, in the city of Freiburg in Germany, a cow brought forth a monstrous birth shaped like a man, yet hideous and deformed, bearing on his head a sort of tonsure, both broad and white, his body and tail shaped like a swine, and the whole colour as though he had been smoked. Moreover the skin round his neck was doubled and folded like a monk's cowl; and the shape thereof was soon afterwards brought into Anjou, wherefrom many drew manifold interpretations; and, among others, they attributed the form of this monster to the Lutheran doctrine, seeing that there was then in Germany a Friar, Martin Luther by name, who preached and dogmatized many articles and propositions which since by the Roman Church and the Sorbonne at Paris have been declared false and erroneous. Wherefore many folk named this misbegotten creature the Lutherick Monster, in mockery and derision of that same Luther and those of his damnable sect. . . .

Moreover in the month of March, the moon being in opposition, it was seen striped in many colours, to wit white and yellow and black and red, whereat folk marvelled sore. And soon afterwards came certain news of the enterprise which that unhappy enemy to the Christian Faith, Sultan Solyman called the Great Turk, had wrought upon the knights of Rhodes, whom we call Hospitallers, taking from them their most mighty and well-fortified city of Rhodes together with the whole island, and banishing them from those parts, to the great shame, confusion, and scandal of christian princes and prelates, and to the irrecoverable loss of all christendom. Whereof the knights of that same Order were much blamed; for the common rumour ran that (seeing how long warning they had received of that which the Turk meditated) they had very ill furnished their said town, both in victuals and in soldiers, artillery, powder, and other munitions of war; and thus they had done but little good for the great revenues which they gather wellnigh daily throughout all christian kingdoms, which revenues (as we may well believe) were given only to set the knights forward as the bulwark and defence of christendom, and especially of the said city of Rhodes.

INDEX TO PART I

References are to pages, unless otherwise stated

Abbot, abbots, bad, canonized, 16; dress of (fur caps), 32, (gold rings), 22; good, 22, 24; prince-, 22

Abelard, 15

Abraham, 131; *and see* Prateae

Acre, Bp of, 56

Adam, 40, 193, 208, 222; *and see* Eynsham, Vaux-Cernay

Agde, Council of, 35

Albert the Great, 132

Albigensians, 56, 67, 87

Alexander III, 125 n. 1

Alfrade, 132

Alice, *see* Stommeln, Christina

Almsgiving, 129, (neglected by clergy), 201

Alured, 173

Amici, *see* Midi

Amiens, Bp of, 21

Anastasius, Pope, 191

Ancona, Mark of, 228

Angers, 20; Bp **Guillaume Le Maire of, No. 113**, 205

Animals, 6, 10, 17, 34, 60, 68, 92, 160 ff., 172, 178, 197, 210, 219 ff., 239, 240; and plague, 33; ant-hills, 92; bees, 118, 120, and Host, 71; butterfly, 53; cats, 116 ff.; caterpillars and Host, 72; cows, 61, belled, 89 n.; cuckoo, 66; fish, 8, 238; horses, 60, 172, 197, wooden, 89, horse-litter, 183; goats, 118, accursed, 129; greyhound, 92 ff.; nightingale and anchorite, 174; wolves, 36, 94, 239 n. 1; *and see* Church, Clergy trading, Demons, Houses, Hunting, Reims

Anjou, 39, 80 n. 2

Anselm, *see* Bec

Antichrist, 1, 7, 40

Antioch, 118

Apostates, apostasy, 106, 236

Apostles, 202; by lot, 69

Aquila, church of St Francis at, 237

Arber, Prof., 42

Arc, Joan of, 210

Archbishops, and bribery, 121

Arles, 29 n.

Arnold and Addis, 20 n.

Arnold (heretic), 66; *and see* Cîteaux

Arras, Bp of, 21; Cathedral of, 126-7

Ars notoria, *see* Heresy

Art, artists, carving, 174, (from life), 175; "miracles of God painted," 192, 196

Arthur, King, vision of, 52

Arundel, Earl of, 233 n. 1

Assaults, 185

Assisi, 56

Auberville, 83

Augsburg, David of, 113

Augustinian, Augustinians, nuns, 72 n. 1

Augustinian Canons, 161 n. 1, 230

Augustinian Friars, *see* Mendicants

Aulayge, priest of, 79

Auleige, Peter de, 95

Aumale, deanery of, 80

Austin, *see* Augustinian

Austria, 113

Avignon, 164, 166

Azotus, 89

Babylon, 89, 184; prince of, 4

Bacon, Roger, 152; and Berthold of Regensburg, 113; on own times, 56

Bagdad, brocades of, 174

Bagnorea, 104; illustration of, 105

Bailiff, 228

Bailleul, 84

Bailly, 83

Bakon, William, 187

Bâle, Councils of, 210, 213, 214, 230; Dominicans at, 210; Geiler at, 239

Baluze, 166; -Mansi, 235

Barbarossa, Frederick, 22

Barcelona, John de Polomar, Archdeacon of, 214

Bartolomeo, Benedetto di Maestro, 216

Bath, Wife of, 223 n. 1

Bavaria, 112, 113

Bayeux, Odo, Bp of, 21

Bazinval .80

Beatific Vision, **No. 97**, 167

Beaubec, 83

Beaume, Jean de, No. 93; notes on, 156

Beauvais, 15, 16, 31 n.; **Vincent of** (*Speculum Historiale*), **No. 25**

Bec, Anselm, Abbot of, 16

Beds, bedding, 134; naked in, 60

Béguines, 144; age of entering, 132

Beleth, John, 209

Belleville, 84

Benedict IX, 7

Benedict XII, 177

Benediktbeuern, monastery of, 112

Bensington, Thomas, 55 n. 1

Bercy, Master Michel de, 95

Berg, Hilla von, 136

Berg, Lord of, 148

Berkeley, Lord, 39

Bernard, Brother, 60

Berneval, 83

Berthold, *see* Ratisbon

Bethlehem, 52, 110, 184

Beverley Chapter Act Book, 95; St John of, 176

Béziers, 67, 68 n. 1

Bible, the, 157; clerical ignorance of, 200; Douai version of, 131 n. 1, 194 n. 1; and heretics, 67, their knowledge of, 30 n.; history and legend in, 109; parodies on, 112; study of, 41; translations and free-thought, 229 n.

Biblinensis, Bp Hugh, 54

Bishops, Diocesan, 185 n. 1, 186, and refusal to consecrate, 187; election of, 119; excommunicate, 107; expense of entertaining, 56–7; friars as, 184; good, 23; hunting, 53; *in partibus infidelium*, 184 ff.

Bland, Mr C. C. S., 15

Bocheux, *see* St Omer

Bodmin, 182

Boethius, 18

Bogo, *see* Clare

Bohemia, Bohemian, 113; heretics in, 212; rebellion, 214

Bollandi, *Acta Sanctorum*, **Nos. 4, 13**

Bologna, 229 n. 1

Books in Middle Ages, 85, 138, 157; burnt, 121, 163; cost of, 163; for clergy, 232; *and see* Church

Bordeaux, Chapter General at, 148

Bordez, Master John, 96

Bouafles, 80

Bourbon, Etienne de, Nos. 10, 45–55; notes on, 84

Bourges, 24

Bouville, 83

Boy-archdeacons, 56, **No. 55**

Boy-bishop, 243

Bozon, *see* Smith

Brabant, 118, 125; dukes of, 126, 148; miracle of Psalter in, 123

Bracquemont, 84

Bradley, Henry, 8

Bran, 225

Braunweiler, Prior of, 142

Bribery, of clergy, 62

Brice, 32

Bricks, 222
Brie, Château en, 150
Britain, 8, 53
British Magazine, 230
British Museum MSS., Nos. 109, 110
Brittany, Godfrey, Earl of, 40; popular canonization in, 16, 17; St Fiacre in, 190
Brussels, 125
Buieval, 83
Burchard, *see* Worms
Bures, 79
Burgundy, Duke of, 212
Burials, burial-places, 115, 209; consecration of, 186–7; of criminals, 241; of Jews, 67; and money, 84, 243; service, 95; wakes forbidden at, 83 and note; and witchcraft, 34
Burne-Jones, 75
Busch, Johann, Nos. 119, 120; cited, 80 n. 1; notes on, 230
Butterfly, Bishop of the, 53
Buvyle, Richard, 180–2

Cadingdon, 172
Caesar, 197, 198
Caesarius, *see* Heisterbach
Cain, 193 n. 3
Calais, Greater and Lesser, 96
Calbe, 231
Cambrai, Bp of, 87
Cambridge, 186; *History of English Literature*, 42, 196, 245
Campneuseville, 82
Canaan, "seed of," 32 n.
Cannibalism, 3, 7
Canonization, *see* Saints
Canon Law, 180–1, 212, 214, 243–4
Canon *Si quis suadente Diabolo*, 185–6
Canons Regular, of Chantimpré, 118; of Lilleshall, 205; note on, 161 n. 1; of St Victor at Paris, 124

Canterbury, Archbishops of, 12 13, 16, 186; *Tales, see* Chaucer
Cantor, Petrus, 32 n., **No. 17**
Canus, Melchior, 20 n.
Carlisle, 52
Carlyle, T., 199
Carmelites, *see* Mendicants
Carmina Burana, No. 64; cited, 82 n. 1; notes on, 112
Carole, 188 n. 1
Carthage, 129
Carthusians, 135
Cassiodorus, 236
Cathari, 116 n. 1
Cathedral, finances, 95
Caudatus Anglicus, see Neilson
Caulibus, Joannes de, No. 63
Caxton, 189, 204; **Golden Legend, No. 124**
Celestine V, 12
Cesena, Michael of, 235 n. 1
Chalaronne, 94
Châlons, Bishop-Elect of, 126
Chantimpré, Thomas of, Nos. 62, 66–77; notes on, 118
Charles Martel, 209
Charles the Great, 26
Charles VII, 211–12
Château-Landon, 160–1
Chaucer, 39, 177, 188; his Archdeacon, 191; *Canon's Yeoman's Tale*, 161 n. 1; *Canterbury Tales*, 223 n. 1; his Doctor of Physic, 41; his good Parson, 205; his Host, 118 n. 1; his Prioress, 144 n. 1; *Prologue*, 223 n. 1; his Shipman, 186 n. 1
Chawsey, Walter de, 55 n. 1
Cherry, Mrs, 228 n. 1
Chester, 39
Chevreuse, 157
Children, 118; child-bearing (Bernardino of Siena on), 224–5; ill-treatment of, 33, 93; in church, 52, 102
Chiuso, *see* Fabriano
Christina, the Blessed, 170 ff.
Chudleigh, Manor of, 178–9

INDEX TO PART I

Church (medieval), finances (cathedral), 102; reform, 199

Churches (medieval), animals in, 103, 205, 207, 216, 242; business done in, 201, 242; children in, 52, in choir, 102; "Confession," 2 n. 1; dancing in, 91, 204–5; dedication of, 207; drunkenness in, 244; elections in, 69; empty, 201; feasting in, 201; gild commemorations in, 244; neglected, 55, 101; precedence in, 223; re-building of, 3; seats in, 223; talking in, 189, 208, 242; too numerous, 38; unpaved, 71 and note; wakes in, 83 and note; "white garment of," 3; women in, 95, 244–5; wooden beams of, 2

Church Ales, 244 n. 1

Church bells, 103, 177, (in illness), 41

Church Councils, 6, 160 n. 1; Ecumenical, 199, 200

Church doors, 37, 64

Church furniture and ornaments, altar-chests, 69; books (lack of), 204, (missals), 230; candles, 96, 101; crucifix, 75, 175, 188; fonts to be locked, 160 n. 1; images, 183, 188–9; irreverence in, 205, 242, 245; lamps, 43; organ, 242; paintings, 188; tiles (bronze), 2; vestments, 204; wax tapers, 183

Church Houses, see Church Ales

Church-porch, buying and selling in, 242; gambling in, 150

Church services, 243–4; absolution by laymen, 205; books for, 100–1; compline, 51; confirmation, 14; consecration, 14; dress at, 244; interruptions by clergy, 95, 204, 243; irreverence at, 37, 39, 95, 242–3; laymen and, 240; "Lord's Hours" and "Penny Hours," 37; and money, 36 and note, 83; necessity of shortening,

200; neglected, 79, 84, 201, 203; number of clerics at, 200; parodies of, 82 n.; talking at, 204–5; vestments at, 36; *and see* Clergy, Confession, Virgin Mary

Churchyards, bribery for burial in, 62; crosses in, 174; dancing in, 89, 204, and songs, 205; medieval beliefs about, 209, reasons for, 209

Church, Dean, *St Anselm*, 12

Cirencester, Abbot of, 233 n. 1

Cirrhus, 183

Cistercian, Cistercians, 36, 160; *Bibliotheca Patrum Cisterciensium*, 58; lay-brethren, 66; **Exord. Cisterc., Nos. 8, 9**

Cîteaux, Order of, 161, 175; Arnold, Abbot of, 67–8; lay-brethren, 157

Clairvaux, 22

Clare, Bogo de, 54, 55 n. 1

Clement V, 200, 205

Clergy (medieval), absentee (from parishes), 80 ff., 106, 122, 203, (from choir during services), 97; and almsgiving, 129, 201; armed, 80; at assizes, 83; books for, 202, (sermons), 207; and compurgation, 82 n. 3; discipline of, 91, 126; dress of, 101 ff., 184, 186, (ill-kept), 205, (improper), 79 ff., (lost by dicing), 82, 120, (neglected), 91, (no cassock), 80, 83; drunken, 79 ff., 95; education of, 118; evil, 55, 243; examination of, 38; excommunicate, 107; fined, 203; and Franciscans, 104; and gallows-rights, 55 n.; gambling, 36, 80 ff., 119; gluttonous, 202; good, 126, 129; Gower on, 190 ff.; on horseback, 14, 29, 57 n., 122; hospitality neglected by, 201; hunting, 83, (dogs and hawks), 205; ignorant, 97, 200, 202, 227; illegitimate, 107; immoral, 32 n., 47, 57, 70, 79 ff.,

95, 108, 127, 191, 199, 229, (and bribery), 62, 83, 200; incomes of, 55, 122 and note; and indulgences (feigned), 200; irreverent, 95 ff., 204–5; married, 15; and miracles, 18, (in miracle-plays), 193–4; and oaths, 193; pastimes of, 29, 83, 205; pluralism of, 54, 107, 122, 203, 239; promotion of, 7; punishments of, 98; quarrelling, 82; and sacrilege, 185 n. 1; and secular arm, 32 n., 66; sons of, 155 n. 1; in taverns, 79 ff., 119, 120; and taxes, 242; and tonsure, 79 n.; trading by, 79 ff., 95, 96; wandering, 82; and women, 125, 191; *and see* Church services, Parish priests

Clonfert, diocese of, 155
Clonmel, 33 n.
Clotworthy chapel, 185 n. 1
Clovelly, 183
Cloyne, 155 and note
Cluny, 1
Coblenz, 142
Cochem, Hartdyfa of, 72
Coggeshall, Chronicle of Ralph, Abbot of, No. 12
Coke, Arnulph and Thomasia, 182
Colgan, John, Nos. 2, 3; notes on, 8
Cologne, 58, 132, 133, 136, 138, 140, 143–6, 243; Abp Reinhold of, 66; Béguines at, 132, 142; Bro. Henry of, 121; Dominican Friary of, 132; eggs in, 141; heretics at, 66–7; Jews at, 67; inquisitors in, 211; lottery of Apostles at, 69; Bishop Siegfried of, 148; University of, 140, 210
Communion, and condemned criminals, 241
Compurgation, 82 and note
Confession, 66, 87; dangers of, 106; and Franciscans, 104; in Lent, 240; invalid, 108 n.; neg-
lect of, 203, (by clergy), 79, 122; twice a year, 44

Connaught, 155
Conrad, *see* Corvey
Constantine, 196, 198
Constantinople, 20
Conteville, 83
Conversion, by miracle-plays, 192 ff.
Corbeil, 21
Corinthians, 244
Cornwall, Archdeaconry of, 180–1
Corvey, monastery of, 22
Coucy, Nogent-sous-, 15
Court, Consistory, 175
Crane, Prof., 35, 56
Crediton, 99, 100 n. 1
Criel, Prior of, 83
Crime, criminals, 7; condemned, 241
Criticism of own times, 56
Croches, 157
Crusades, crusaders, 56, 79, 84; against Albigensians, 56, 67; and bishops *in partibus*, 184; dress of, 61; and money, 38; reasons for going on, 46, 60; vows broken, 46
Cursing, for tithes, 205–6
Cusa, Cardinal Nicolaus von, 230
Cushion, Ellen, 33 n.

Dacheux, L., *Jean Geiler*, 239
Damascus, 184 n. 1; Abp of, 187; Bp of, 185
Dancing, 89 and note, 90, **No. 75**, 188, 211; *and see* Churches, Churchyards, Holy-days
Daniel, 239; Book of, 32 n., 234
Dante, 42, 167, 191, 229 n. 1; cited, 52 n. 1, 63 n. 1; *From St Francis to*, 79, 82 n. 3; on St Bonaventura, 104
Dartmouth, 186 and note; Austin Friars at, 184 ff.; Mayor of, 187
David, quoted, 228
Debeler, Sir Gerard, 230

INDEX TO PART I

Demons, devils, 10, 45, 60, 63, 88, 90, 93, 129, 131, 145 n., 157, 176; and dancing, 90; on Etna, 54 n. 1; exorcism of, 231–2; and hallowing of churches, 207; names of, 162; and plague, 155; as owls, 45; as spiders, 144

Denifle, H., 166

Derchigny, 83

Derembourg, Ed., 37 n.

Deschamps, Eustace, No. 107; notes on, 188

Despair of own times, 199

Diana, 33

Didron, *Annales Archéologiques*, 190

Dijon, 86; St-Bénigne at, 1

Dilapidations, of church property, 83

Dillon, Philip, 33 n.

Discipline, difficulty of, 95 ff.

Documents, medieval use of early, 8

Dominicans, *see* Mendicants

Dormi Secure, **No. 121;** notes on, 232

Dorsetshire, 238

Douai, 210

Douvrend, 84

Dowry, *see* Marriage

Dress (medieval), 184, 231; cape, 10; of crusaders, 61; of lay folk on Sundays, 240; men's, 211 and note; perches for, 10–11 and note; ring (Pope's), 187; of Roman women, 218; of St Thomas of Canterbury, 169; *and see* Clergy

Drink, *see* Food

Drunkenness, at wakes, 180

Du Cange, cited, 63 n. 1

Dunstable, 170

Durand, *see* Mende

Eadmer, Nos. 5, 6; notes on, 12

Earth, goddess, 41

Eccleston, Thomas of, 54 n. 1

Eckenstein, Miss, 230

Ecouis, 80

Edmund, monk of Eynsham, 42

Education (medieval), of girls, 188; *and see* Schools

Edward III, and Villani, 167

Egypt, 141

Eifel, the, 141

Elder-trees, 92

Elne, diocese of, 89

Elphin, Bishopric of, 155 n. 1

England, English, 126, 164 n., 233 n.; bishops in, 184; Early Eng. Text Society, 189, 207; kings of, and pilgrimages, 174; Publicans in, 30; St Anselm in, 12; tailed, 238 and note; tongue (in cathedral service), 97, (ecclesiastical), 101; translations into, 189; wakes in, 83 n.; *and see* Masterman

Envermeu, deanery of, 83; St Mary at, 84

Erasmus, 141 n. 1

Esaias, cited, 109, 201, 203

Esdras, cited, 89

Eskilsoe, 32

Essigny, 83

Etampes, 162

Ethiopian, devil as, 90

Etna, 54 n. 1

Etrun, 84

Eu, deanery of, 83

Eucharius, 209

Europe, 113, 184; pilgrims in, 167; *Universities of, see* Rashdall

Eve, 62

Everard, Richard, 55 n. 1

Evesham, *see* Eynsham

Evreux, 243

Excommunicate, excommunication, 15, 22, 80 and notes, 167, 185–6; of animals, 22 ff.; greater, 178, 180; and miracles, 163; for witchcraft, 211

Exeter, alleged miracles at, 177 ff.; cathedral, ceremonies in, 185 n. 1; cathedral visitations, 96–100; leper-house at, 185 n. 1; **Poenitentiale of Bishop Bartholo-**

INDEX TO PART I

mew Iscanus of, **No. 14;** *and see* Grandisson

Exfestucatio, 63

Exodus, 229

Exorcism, *see* Demons

Eynsham, Revelation to a Monk of, Nos. 21-24; notes on, 42

Ezekiel, 229; quoted, 120

Fabriano, 238

Fairs and markets, 201

Famine, 3, 6

Fegatelli, 221 n. 1

Fidanza, Giovanni, *see* St Bonaventura

Fiddlers, 154

Flanders, Flemish, Count Philip of, 30; peasants and food, 142 n. 1

Fleury, 166

Floreffe, 62

Florence, Florentines, 167

Folquin, Brother, 144, 146, 148

Food and drink in M.A., abundance of, 6; ale (hot) and butter, 232; biscuits, 245 n.; cabbage-soup, 219; cheeses, 142; cherries, 142 n., 228; chick-peas, 228; corn (taxes on), 242; cracknels, 245; eggs, 141-2, 219, (value of), 224; fish, 148; ginger, 148; honey, 33; at inns, 219; meats (salt), 225; melons, 226; milk, 33; oil, 225; pig's liver, 221 and note; rye-bread, 3 n.; salad, 226; vinegar (wine turned to), 226; *wig, wigges,* 245 n.; wine, 226, in monasteries, 26, (taxes on), 242; *and see* Famine

Fosse, 82

Foucarmont, deanery of, 80

France, French, 1, 16, 35, 40, 127, 177; condemned criminals in, 241; heresies in, 3, 29; *Histoire Littéraire de la,* 156; holy-days in, 201; inquisitors in, 210, 213; Joan of Arc in, 211-2; kings of, 3, 29, 121, 165, 167, 168, 209, 211-12; queen of, 55; Société des Anciens Textes F., 188 Société de l'Hist. de, 84; Talmud in, 121

Franciscans, *see* Mendicants

Franconia, 113

Franks, 15; Pippin, King of the, 26

Fraticelli, 235, 238

Frederick II, 54 n. 1

Freethought in M.A., *see* Religion

Freiburg, 239

Friars, *see* Mendicants

Friars Minor, *see* Mendicants (Franciscans)

Friars Preachers, *see* Mendicants (Dominicans)

Froissart, 168

Froude, J. A., 42, 170

Fucci, Vanni, 63 n. 1

Gabriel, Angel, relics of, 168-9

Gairdner, Dr, *Lollardy and the Reformation,* 199

Galen, 230, note to 229

Gallican Church, and condemned criminals, 241

Gallows, 55 n

Gambling, 36, 80 ff., 150; illustration of, 81

Games, 80 ff., 84 n., 192

Gascoigne, 114 n. 1

Gasquet, Abbot, quoted, 114 n. 1

Gaul, 2, 4; rebuilding of churches in, 3

Gehazi, 37

Geiler, Johann, No. 125; and condemned criminals, 241; notes on, 239; *and see* Dacheux

Gelert, 94 n. 2

Generals, the XXIV, and Berthold of Regensburg, 113

Genesis, cited, 220, 229

Gerard the Advocate, 146

Germans, Germany, 89; children in, 52; inquisitors in, 210; Joan of Arc in, 211; superstitions in, 36; tongue, 135; translations into, 189; women in, 136

INDEX TO PART I

Gerson, 188

Gibbon, 40 n.; *Decline and Fall*, 167

Gild, gilds, and clergy, 201; commemorations, 244

Gilead, 144

Gilemerville, 80

Glaber, Ralph, No. 1; notes on, 1

Glasney, 99, 100 n. 1

Gluttony, 202, 221

Godchildren, 189

Godescal, *see* Cadingdon

Golden Legend, see Caxton

Good Friday, *see* Holy-days

Gottschalk, 60

Gournay, 15

Gower, John, No. 111; *Mirour de l'Omme*, 196; notes on, 196; on Jews and prostitutes in Rome, 198

Granaries, 225

Grandcourt, 82

Grandisson, Bp John de, Nos. 57–59, 104–6; character of, 95; on Friar-Bishops, 184; notes on, 177

Granson, 177; Sir Otho de, 177

Gratian, 178, 185 n. 1

Graystock, Baron of, 176

Great Toriton, 182

Greeks, Greek, 26 n., 237; Church, 6

Gregory VIII, Pope, 38

Gregory IX, Pope, 56

Gregory X, Pope, 79, 199

Greifen, Brother Gerard von, 142

Grenoble, Bp of, 91

Grey Friars, *see* Mendicants (Franciscans)

Grosseteste, *Epistolae*, cited, 83 n. 1

Guibert, *see* Nogent

Gyffard, Joan, 182

Halle, 230–1

Hamies, 80

Hartdyfa, *see* Cochem

Hartland, 182

Hartlepool, 54

Haucourt, 83

Hawks, .n church, 205

Haye, Père de la, 216 n. 1, 229

Healing, miracles of, 6

Heaven and hell, 109, 130, 193 and note 3, 195, 206, 208, 229, 230, 234, 240

Heidelberg, University of, 241

Heisterbach, Caesarius of, Nos. 33–5, 37–42; on abuse of sacraments, 72 n. 3; cited, 66, 68 n. 1, 82 n. 1; on medieval folk and prophecy, 72 n. 2; notes on, 58

Heisterbach, monastery of, 58; Hermann, Cantor of, 71

Hemmenrode, 65

Hemp, sold by priests, 84

Hennygan, Roger, 182

Henry II, 233 n. 1; ancestry of, 39–40; and heretics, 30

Henry III, 55 n. 1, 75

Henry V, Emperor, 126

Henry VI, 189, 212

Heraldry, and sorcery, 162 and note

Heresy, heretics, 29, 66, 84, 87, 113, 167, 191, 235; *ars notoria*, 162; banishment of, 30; and Bible, 67; Bible knowledge of, 30 and note; branding of, 30; burning of, 31, 32 and note, 67, 238; and communion, 67; growth of, in Italy, 6; and marriage, 30 and note; and miracles, 237; More and, 245; number of sects of, 237; and oaths, 118 and note; and sacraments, 57 n., 58

Herman, *Book of Miracles*, 17 n.

Hermann, *see* Heisterbach

Hermits, hermitages, 10, 40, 118, 124, 170

Herodias, 33

Higden, Ralph, *Polychronicon of,* **Nos. 18, 19**

Hildebrand, Pope, 57 n. 2

Hildesheim, 230

Hills, for burial, 209

Hingeston-Randolph, 96

Holland (Lincs.), 151

Holy-days, 199–205; dancing on, 129, 199, 204; and disorder, 89, 204, 242–5; fairs and markets on, 201, 243; hunting on Good Friday, 245; ploughing on, 129; processions on, 245; recreation on, 196

Holy Land, 15, 46–7, 118

Honi soit qui mal y pense, 177

Honnecourt, Villard de, cited, 188 n. 1; illustration by, 81; sketch-book of, 82 n. 1

Horst, 61

Hosea, 39

Hospitals, 218

Host, maltreated, **No. 89**; miracles concerning, 70–2, 151; and witchcraft, 160

Houses (medieval), animals in, 224; cleanliness of, 226; falling down, 144; floors of, 226; and incendiarism, 74; ovens in, 33; furniture of, beds and bedding, 169, 182, 226; chests, 151; oil-jars, etc., 225–6; pipkins and drinking-vessels, 224, 226; table-knives, 33; trenchers and wine-casks, 226

Houssaye, *see* Conteville

Hügel, Baroness von, 216

Hugh, Brother, 184

Hugh of St Victor, 124

Hundred Years' War, 189

Hunting, 178; by clergy, 53; dogs, 83, 88, 205; on Good Friday, 245

Huntingdon, 170

Huysmans, 132

Iceland, 54

Iconoclasm, 86

Imola, Benvenuto da, 229 n. 1

Indulgences and pardons, 113 ff., 168; feigned, 200; length of, 185 and note; price of, 114 and note

Innocent II, Pope, 125 n. 1; and sacrilege, 185 n. 1

Innocent III, Pope, 60; Register of, 68 n. 1

Innocents, Holy, 52; Feast of, 99, 143, 243

Inns, 219; *and see* Taverns

Inquisition, inquisitor, 161, 210, 211, 213, 235

Ireland, Irish, 10 n., 88–9; **Acta Sanct. Hib., Nos. 2–3;** devils in, 155; friaries, 152; plague in, 155; robbing in, 246; *and see* Colgan

Irreverence, 57, 67; in church, 37, 39, 242, 243; *and see* Clergy

Iscanus, *see* Exeter

Israel, 38

Israelites, 9

Italie, see Michelet

Italy, 2, 4; cities of, 110; heresy in, 3, 6; nicknames in, 228 n. 1; rebuilding of churches in, 3

Janssen, on freethought, 230, note to 229

Jehoshaphat (vale of), 169

Jerusalem, 38, 54, 110, 146, 171; church of Holy Sepulchre at, 4, 7; Jacques de Vitry, Patriarch of, 56; pilgrimages to, 7

Jesuits, 142 n. 1

Jews, 19, 25, 54, 80, 89, 115–6, 141–2, 179, 191, 193, 198; converted, 40; Eastern, 122; persecution of, 4; and medieval Popes, 198 n. 1; in Rome, 198; and Talmud, 121; *and see* Cologne

Joan of Arc, 210–12

Job, Book of, quoted, 240

Jocelin, 10 n.

John (schoolmaster), *see* Stommeln

John XIX, Pope, 7

John XXII, Pope, 177, 237; and Beatific Vision, 164 ff.; and heresy, 235–6

Joinville 80 n. 2

Jongleurs, **No. 93**

Jonquières, 83
Judas, 38, 69, 152, 206
Juries, 181
Justice in M.A., 156, 214, 242; and money, 197

Kaisersberg, 239
Kaltyseren, Heinrich, 211
Kenodoxia, 26 n. 1
Kent, 238
Ketzer, 116 and note
Koran, the, 232

Labbe-Mansi, 199
Labour, peasants', 200; *and see* Holy-days
Lambeth, 187
Lanercost Chronicle, Nos. 26, 27, 28; notes on, 52
Lanfranc, *see* Canterbury
Laon, Cathedral of, 17 n.
Lateran Council, 125 n. 1
Latin, medieval, 157; Greek words in, 26 n.
Launcells, 181
Lea, H. C., cited, 57 n. 2
Lecoy de la Marche, 84, 89 n. 1
Le Maire, *see* Angers
Leoteric, 4
Lepers, leprosy, leper-houses, 58; at Exeter, 185 n. 1; and clerical dress, 79 n.
Leviathan, 134
Liber Exemplorum, **Nos. 90-2**
Lichfield, 79
Liège, 68, 118; Albert, Bp of, 126; diocese of, 62; pluralism in, 122
Lilleshall, abbey of, 210; Canons Regular of, 205
Limburg Chronicle, 184
Lindsay, Principal, 245
Linen, wearing of, 218; making of, 225
Lippe, Dom Bernard of, 73
Lismore, *see* St Gerald, 8
Little, A. G., 75, 152, 154 n. 2, 155 n. 1
Livonia, 73

Llandaff, 79
Loksmyth, John, 102
Lollards, Lollardy, 118 n. 1; *and the Reformation*, 199
London, 54; British Museum, MSS. in, **No. 20;** Gower in, 196; St Martin's-in-the-Fields, 191
"Lord's Hours," 37
Lorraine, 84
Lortiey, 79
Lose, Count of, 68
Lots, lottery, 69
Louis VII, 29
Louvain, 8, 148; Duke of, 68
Louvechamp, 83
Lucy, 83
Ludlou, William, 181
Luxemburg, 148
Lynn News, 34 n.
Lyon, Lyons, 85; diocese of, 92; Ecumenical Council of, 79, 104; Pope's Court at, 89

Macaulay, G. C., on Gower, 196
Maccabees, Book of, 68
Madness and prophecy, 72 and note
Magic, *see* Witchcraft
Magus, Simon, 31, 37
Maire, Le, *see* Angers
Maitland Club, 52, 54 n. 2
Malachi, 70 n. 2
Malacopula, 83
Manichaeans, 30 n.
Manners (medieval), 226; at inns, 221; washing, 222; at weddings, 156; sleeping, 233; of peasant women, 18
Marchia, Beatus Jacobus de, Nos. 122, 123, 166; notes on, 235
Mark, the, 228
Markets, on holy-days, 243
Markyate, 170; nunnery at, 173
Marriage, married, 129, 220-1; confession and communion before, 227; and dowry, 65, 218; necessity of equality in, 152, 221; St Bernardino on, 216; spiritual, 146

INDEX TO PART I

Martene, Dom, 2 n.

Martin-Eglise, 84

Mass, masses, 2 n. 1, 189, 242; and condemned criminals, 241; doubts about, 70; early, 10; elevation of Host at, 177; and excommunicate clergy, 80; funeral, 78; incomplete, 204; and miracles, 70; and money, **No. 17**, 57, 80, 84; of monks, 240; and purgatory, 135; talking at, 189, 190, 222, 242; St Gregory at, 208; St Martin's (illustration), 190; of unworthy priests, 57–8, 108 n.; on week-days, 144; words of consecration at, 227

Mass books, without clasps, 101

Masterman, Mr C. F. G., *Condition of England*, 199

Maurice, Brother, 140

Maximilian, Emperor, 239

Maxwell, Sir Herbert, 52

Measures (medieval), ell-yard, 221

Meaux, Abbey of, 175; Abbot Hugh of, 175; Cathedral statutes of, 95 n. 1; *and see* Melsa

Medicine, and common-sense, 232; and magic, 34, 41–2

Melsa, Chronicon de, **No. 102**

Mencken, J. B., cited, 70 n. 1

Mende, Guillaume Durand of, Nos. 114, 205

Mendicants, 84, 88, 191; bad, 229; and Beatific Vision, 164 ff.; as Bishops, 184; preaching of, 113; and marriage, 220; wandering, 74; (Augustinian friars), 167; in Dartmouth, 184, 186, (Carmelite friars), 167; (Dominicans), 88, 118, 121, 132, 135, 139, 156, 164 n. 1, 199, 210, 214; at Evreux, 243; on Immaculate Conception, 232; in Paris, 84, 140; (Franciscans), 36, 52, 79, 104, 106, 108, 109, 113, 164 n. 1, 232; British Society of F.

studies, 152; English, 97 n. 1; friary in Paris, 152; and Immaculate Conception, 234 n. 1; Jacques de Vitry and, 56; Ministers-General of, 235 n. 1; observants, 237; Odo Rigaldi and, 79; at Paris, 152, 167; Strict, persecuted, 235; and women, 106

Mesnières, 79

Mesnil-David, 82

Mesnil-Mauger, 82

Metz, 211

Meulers, 80

Michaelists, 235 ff.

Michelet, on fasting, 191

Middleton (?), Richard of, 238

Midi, Nicolas, 212 n. 1, 213

Migne, *Pat. Lat.* **Nos. 8, 9**, 32 n., 36

Milan, Archbishopric of, 235

Mill, mills, 60 ff., 91; illustration of, 59

Millennium, belief in, 1

Minstrels, 62

Miracle plays, by clergy, 193; sermon against, 191

Miracles, 123, 173–4, 212; by children, 163; false, 6, 17 and note; and heresy, 237; popular, 177 ff.; of Virgin Mary, 233–4 *and see* Ordeal, Relics

Mirk, *see* Myrc

Mohammedans, 193 n. 1; and Immaculate Conception, 232

Molières, town of, 159

Monasteries, books in, 77, 127; manuscripts in, 112; cellarers in, 26; granges belonging to, 157, 159; lay-brethren in, 65–6, 157, 160, 175, (choir of), 175, (serving priests), 205; novices in, 58; pets in, 23; quarrels in, 1; relics in, 29; sacrilege in, 115, 185 n. 1; scandals in, 1; schools in, 1, 28; servants in, 23, 26; simony in, 115; thefts from, 160; wine in, 26; women in, 175

Monasteriorum, Liber de Reformatione, 230–1

Monasticism, decay of, 1, 2; *Women under*, 230

Money and absolution, 191; value of, 241–2

Monk, monks, and absolution of excommunicates, 185, 186; and almsgiving, 239; apostate, 161–2, 229 n. 1; armed, 159; bad, 229; beds and bedding, 24; and books, 163, *and see* Monasteries; changeling, 26; and confessions, 44, 184–5; conversion, 58; difficulties of strict, 239; and discipline, **No. 73**; dress of, 77, 126, 239, patched, 24; fasting by, 44, 240; feasting by, 240; good, 36, 43 ff., 155, 239–40; and habit, 184, 186; harvester, 58; and heirs, 241; and heresy, 18; on horseback, 157; and Jews, 25; and labour, 24; and money, 18, 241, 244; and personal property, 25, 115; and punishments, 127, (corporal), 124; and relics, 18, *and see* Monasteries; and services, 240; in taverns, 185–6; temperate, 240; and tonsure, 239; and women, 239; writing by, 15, 58, 132, 157, 163; *and see* Abbots, Clergy, Mendicants, Monasteries, Nuns

Monod, Bernard, 15

Monod, G., 1

Montenaeken, 68

Montpezat, illustration from tapestry of, 190

Morals, in M.A., 7

Moravia, 113

More, Sir Thomas, No. 128; notes on, 1, 245

Morigny, abbey of, 162

Morinie, la, 168

Morinie, Mém. Hist. de la Soc. des Ant. de la, 168

Mortagne, collegiate church of, 95 n. 1

Mortemer, 82 and note 1

Morville, 80

Moselle, 72 n. 1

Moses, 122, 169; rod of, 4; horned statue of, 190; times of, 6

Munistero, *see* Siena

Murray, T. Douglas, 212 n. 1

Myrc, John, Nos. 115, 116; *Festial* of, 130 n., 207; *Instructions for Parish Priests*, 205

Naphtali, 184 n. 1

Narbonne, Arnold, Abp of, 67

Nassyngtone, William de, 98

Nature, medieval ideas on, 54

Neckam, Master Alexander, 233 and note

Neilson, Dr George, *Caudatus Anglicus*, 238 n. 1

Nemours, Lord Walter of, 80 n. 2

Neuchâtel, 177

Neufchâtel, deanery of, 82

Neuilly, 80, 82

Neuwerk, monastery of, 231

Neville's Cross, Battle of, 54 n. 2

New Forest, 75

Newport, R.C. Bishop of, 115

Nicholas V, Pope, 238

Nicknames, 228 n. 1

Nider, Johann, Nos. 116 A, 116 B; notes on, 210

Niniveh, 184 n. 1

Nogent, 83

Nogent, Guibert de, No. 7; 17 n., 21; notes on, 15

Nogent-sous-Coucy, 15

Normandy, 75; parish priests of, 79

Northam, 182

Northawe, 174

Norway, 54

Nunneries, 72

Nuns, 92; age of, 132; bad, 229; dress of, 144 n.; personal property of, 25; *and see* Eckenstein, Power

Nuremberg, Dominicans at, 210

INDEX TO PART I

Oaths, 33, 193

Odo, *see* Bayeux, Rigaldi

Offa II, King, 5

Oignies, Blessed Mary of, 56, 109

Oil-jars, care of, 225

Olivet, Mt, 54

Olmütz, Bp of, 199

O'Quinn, Brother Thomas, 155 and note

Ordeal, by hot iron, 32 n., 73, 156; and miracle, **No. 42**

Orkneys, the, William, Bp of, 54

Ottery St Mary, 99, 100 n. 1

Otto IV, 29 n.

Ousâma, 37 n.

Oxford, 42, 114 n. 1; and Bogo de Clare, 55 n. 1; Holywell, 55 n. 1; Publicans at, 30

Pagham, 55 n. 1

Palestine, 154 n. 1

Panliu, 83

Papal commissioners, 184

Papal Nuncio, 241

Papal Registers, 166

Paradise, 42, 47; in east, 208; Vision of, 47 ff.

Pardoners, *see* Indulgences

Paris, 141, 161, 163–7, 213; Canons Regular at, 124; Cathedral School at, 36; Dominicans at, 140; Etienne de Bourbon at, 84–5; Franciscans at, 152, 167; Grandisson at, 177; Jacques de Vitry at, 56; Odo Rigaldi at, 79; St Bonaventura at, 104, 234; Ste Geneviève, 32; Talmud in, 121; University, 140, 152, 164, 177, 212, (eggs), 141 and note; *and see* Sweden, Peter of

Paris, Matthew, No. 43; death of, 77; illustration from, 19; notes on, 75; *Vita offae Secundi,* 5

Paris, Paulin, 157

Parishes (medieval), 200; appropriated, 204

Parish priests (medieval), 104 ff., 141 n., 144–5, 200 ff.; good, 134; hospitality of, 133; *Instructions for,* 205; in Normandy, 79; *and see* Clergy, Mass

Parma, John of, 104

Parody of Gospels, 112

Pear-trees, 219

Peasants, scarcity of work for, 200

Peckham, Abp, 14 n.

"Penny Hours," 37

Pepin, Guillaume, No. 127; notes on, 243

Percy Society, 149

Persant, Jean, 161–2

Pessimism of Middle Ages, 199

Peter the Precentor, *see* Cantor

Petit, Jehan, 232

Petra, 80

Philip Augustus, King of France, 29

Philip VI, King of France, 165–8

Philip, Brother, *see* Reims

Philip the Bold, 157

Pierrepont, 82

Piers Plowman, 184

Pilate, 72

Pilgrims, pilgrimages, 89, 167, 177 ff., 180; disorder at, 245; offerings and quarrels at, 174–5; women on, 7

Pinchbeck, 151

Pippin, *see* Franks

Plague, and demons, 155; great, 167; priests and, 35; *and see* St Antony

Plantagenet, Geoffrey, 39

Ploughing, 231

Pluralism, pluralists, *see* Clergy

Plympton, 183

Poaching, 75

Polomar, *see* Barcelona

Pomerevalle, 79

Pomponne, 163

Popes, bad, 7 n. 1; and Beatific Vision, 164 ff.; and heresy, 235; infallibility of, 164, 168; and monastic reform, 230; and sacrilege, 185 n. 1; youthful, 7

INDEX TO PART I

Power, Dr Eileen, *Medieval English Nunneries*, 230

Poys, Robert de, 80

Praemonstratensians, 62, 161 n. 1, 184

Prateae, Abraham, Abbot of, 24

Preachers, preaching, 84, 91, 94, 113, 118, 130 n. 1, 155, 185 n. 1, 235; good, 230, 239, 243; Franciscans, 104; manuals for, 84, 149, 152, 232; penny-, 114; *and see* Sermons

Prévost, Jean, 160 ff.

Prices, cost, of book-making, writing, 163; of corn, 151; of indulgences, 114 and note; legal, 175; of money, 241–2; of relics, 21

Priests, children of, 155; and oaths, 193; and trade, 79 ff.; unlucky to meet, 34–6; *and see* Clergy, Parish

Priscian, 229 n. 1

Prophets, the, 122

Proverbs, 6, 223, 240

Prüm, monastery of SS. Peter and Paul at, 26

Psalms, Psalmist, Psalter, 122–3, 128, 192, 234; as charms, 41; gabbled, 95, 149–50; quoted, 89, 109; size of, 40

"Publicans," 29, 30

Puff, William, 174

Punishments (medieval), for deer-stealing, 75; for incendiarism, 74; for witchcraft, 94, 162; *and see* Clergy

Purgatory, 42, 232; priests in, **No. 23**, 47

Puritans, puritanism, 29, 244 n. 1

Pyk, *see* Redbourn

Pynson, 207

Quaracchi, Friars of, 106 n. 2

Quicherat, J., *Mélanges d'Archéologie*, cited, 188 n. 1

Quoits, *see* Games

Rabulas, 17

Raguel, 194

Ralph, *see* Coggeshall

Rashdall, Dean, cited, 82 n. 3, 166

Ratisbon, 132; *and see* Regensburg

Raynaldus, 199

Realcamp, 82 and note 2

Redbourn, 172–4

Red Sea, 9

Reformation, 101, 199, 244 n. 1; and wakes, 83 n. 1; *and see* Gairdner

Regensburg, 213–15

Regensburg, Berthold of, No. 65, 36; and freethought, 193 n. 3; notes on, 113

Regnaud, Abp, 85

Reims, 126; Abp William of, 29 ff.; diocese of, 87; Dominican convent at, 91; Jackdaw of, 22; Rotard, Archdeacon of, 126

Reinhold, *see* Cologne

Relics, 3, 21, 32, 145, 168, 242; and alms, 17; cost of, 21; false, 17 ff.; method of keeping, 169; and miracles, 4, 33; in monasteries, 29

Religion of M.A., 1, 200, 202, 229; Beatific Vision, 164 ff.; confirmation (of children), 185, (rare), 14 and note; contemporary criticism of, 18; few saved, 230; freethought, 229 and note; future life, 131; prayers to dead, 178; salvation through saints, 168; *and see* Church Services, Confession, Heaven and Hell, Indulgences, Mass, Miracles, Relics

Reliquiae Antiquae, No. 110

Renan, on Christina von Stommeln, 132

Renier, *see* Jonquières

Rents, 55 n.

Rheindorf, 70

Rheineck, Elias von, 61

Rhine, the, 52

Rhineland, 113

Rhys, *Celtic Folklore*, 154 n. 2

Riccardus, 238

Rich and poor, in Middle Ages, 12, 32 n., 153; burial of, 84, 209, 226

Richard [? of Middleton], 238

Richard I, 40, 75 ff., 118, 233 n.

Richard II, cited, 162 n. 1

Rigaldi, Odo, Nos. 44, 56; notes on, 79, 95; and St Bonaventura, 104

Rigaud, Eudes, *see* Rigaldi

Riley, 170 n. 1

Rimita, forest of, 93

Riom, 12

Ripon Chapter Acts, 95

Robbery, 246

Robert, King of France, 3

Roches, des, *see* Winchester

Roche-Scise, 85

Roger the Hermit, 170 ff.; burial-place of, 173–4

Roland (jongleur), 156

Roman Church, and miracles, 180; reform necessary to, 201

Roman Empire, 121, 202; and Jews, 4

Romanorum, In Gestis, 209

Romans, Epistle to, quoted, 104

Romans (France), 94 n. 2

Romans, Humbert de, No. 112; notes on, 199

Rome, Romans, 112, 125, 128, 173; the Capitol, 167; dress of women in, 218; fire in, 2; and friars, 184; pilgrims to, 167; St Peter's, 2

Rome, Court of, 185, 206, 236; clergy detained at, 203; Gower on, 196; prostitutes in, 198; simoniacal, 197

Rotard, *see* Reims

Rotherfield, 55 n. 1

Rouen, Cathedral visitation at, 95; Council of, 79 n. 1; synods of, 79 n. 1; *and see* Rigaldi

Rourkes, Anastatia, 33 n.

Routh, Mr, 245

Roy, Jules, 1

Runkel, Siegfried of, 70

Ruskin, J., 199

Russia, 235

Rusticus, Bishop, 10

Sabatier, his *St François d'Assise*, 56

Sabbatarian, 243

Sacraments, 70; and animals, 71; despised, 229; and money, 38, 84, 87; of unworthy priests, 57; and witchcraft, 38, 70 ff.

Sacrilege, 67, 71, 125 and note, 185 and n. 1

Saints, canonization of, 12–13, popular, 15 ff.; and evil petitions to, 246; patron, 18, 20

St Abban, 10 n.

St Agnes, 146

St Aicaire, 12

St Aignan, 83

St Albans, 5, 77, 186, 233 n. 1; Abbot Geoffrey of, 170, 173; discovery of bones of (illustration), 5; *Gesta Abbatum*, 170 ff.; Matthew Paris and, 75; pilgrimages to, 174; St Peter's at, 174; shrine of, 19; tombs at, 174

St Amable of Riom, 12

St Andrew, 69, 130 n. 1

St Anselm, 12–14

St Anthony (fire of), 3 n.

St Asaph, 79

St Augustine of Canterbury, 208, 238

St Augustine of Hippo, 124; on Beatific Vision, 166; on Church, 237; on dancing, 128–9

St Barry, 8

St Bartholomew, 129, 130

St Benedict, black monks of, 158

Saint-Benoit, Miracles de, 1

St Bernard, 15, 16 n., 40; on Beatific Vision, 166; and Immaculate Conception, 233–4 and note

INDEX TO PART I

St Bernardino of Siena, Nos. 117, 118, 229 n. 1, 237; on child-bearing, 224–5; on lottery of Apostles, 70 n. 1; notes on, 216

St Bonaventura, 79, 80 n. 3, **No. 61,** 106 n. 1; 109; confounded with David of Augsburg, 113; on Immaculate Conception, 233–4; notes on, 104

St Boniface, 169

St Brandan, 8 n.

St Brice, 189

St Catherine of Siena, 132, 239 n. 1

St Clement, 203

St Crisipinian, 148

St Crispin, 148

St David, 8 n.

St Denis, Grandes Chroniques de, Nos. 94–7; monastery of, 21, 157; notes on, 157

St Elizabeth of Hungary, 70 n. 1

St Elphege, 13

St Eninu, 10 n.

St Exuperius, 21, 22

St Fiacre, 190

St Firmin, 21

St Francis, church of, at Aquila, 237; *Fioretti,* 104; *St F. to Dante,* 79

Ste-Geneviève, *see* Paris

St Gerald of Lismore, 8–9

St Germer, abbey-church of, 15

St Goar, Life of, 10, 12

St Gregory, 207, 208, 237; *Moralizations upon Job,* 240

St Greyhound, 92

St Guinefort, 92, 94 n. 2

St Hilary, 236

St Hugh of Lincoln, 42; *Metrical Life of,* 188 n. 1

St James (Apostle), 69, 169

St James of the Mark, *see* Marchia

St Jerome, 17, 202

St John, 69, 70 n. 1, 234; and Beatific Vision, 165; Feast of, 99

St John Baptist, 13, 20–1; Feast of, 182–3

St John Gualbert, 75

St Joseph, 109 ff.

St Jude, 69

St Laurence, 67

St Laurent-le-Petit, 84

St-Lô, Master John de, 95

St Louis, 80 n. 2, 84, 121, 157; and Odo Rigaldi, 79; and Talmud, 121

St Lydwine of Schiedam, 132

St Margaret, 169

St Martin du Bois, 82

St Martin-en-Campagne, 84

St Martin of Tours, 18, 189

St Matthew, 69; cited, 220

St Michael, 206

St Modestus, 142

St Nicholas, 43 ff., 162, 206; Feast of, 243

St Nicolas Insel, 72

St Omer, 14; relics at, 168–9

St Patrick, Acts of, 10 n.

St Paul, 22, 38, 111–12, 140, 178; and Beatific Vision, 168; Corinthians, 220, 244; Ephesians, 221–2; and preaching, 120; Romans, 229; Thessalonians, 229

St Peter, 2, 9, 31 n., 70, 121, 169, 206, 235 ff.; and Beatific Vision, 168; Feast of, called *Ad Vincula,* 183

St Pyro, 16

St Remy, 18, 80

St Samson, 16

St Scothinus, 8

St Stephen, 206, 239; Feast of, 36–7, 99

St Sulpice, 83

St Thomas Aquinas, 132; on unworthy priests, 57 n. 2

St Thomas à Kempis, 230

St Thomas-du-Paraclet, 32

St Thomas of Canterbury, 40, 169, 179

St Valery, 80

INDEX TO PART I

St Victor, Hugh of, 25–6, 124

St Vitus, 142

St William, Life of, No. 13; notes on, 32

Salemonville, Master William de, 95

Salicosa Mara, 83

Salimbene, and Berthold of Regensburg, 113

Salisbury, Countess of, 177

Sanctuary, at wayside cross, 76

Sara, 194

Saracens, 56, 58

Saragia, Madonna, 228

Sardinia, 169

Sarquenciaux [Serquigny?], 161

Satan, 60, 63, 90, 112, 114, 152, 178, 213, 215

Sathanas, 44

Sauchay-by-the-Sea, 83

Sauchay-in-the-Forest, 83

Saxo, Brother, 32

Scandinavia, 235

Schaffhausen, 239

Schiedam, see St Lydwine

Schools, scholars, schoolmasters, 136, 141 n., 145, 202; wandering, 29 n. 1; and see Monasteries

Schott, Peter, No. 126, 205; notes on, 241

Schultz, A. (illustrations from), 129, 223

Scipio Nasica, 128

Scothin, see St Scothinus

Scottish history, Illustrations of, 54 n. 2

Scottish Historical Review, 52

Scotus, Duns, 238

Scriptures (medieval), 128 n.; meaning of, 231 and note; quoted, 223

Seez, 40

Selfe, Miss Rose, 167

Sens, 3; Abp of, 161

Sermons, 207, 216, 228, 230; and see Preachers

Servants, 226

Sexes, difference between, 222; equality of, 221; miracles of change of, 9 and note; worth of, 224

Shakespeare, 245

Shaw, Mr Bernard, 210

Shaw, H., *Dresses and Decorations,* 27

Sicily, condemned criminals in, 241; King Robert of, 168

Siebengebirge, 58

Siegfried, see Cologne *and* Runkel

Siena, 216, 228; convent of Munistero at, 228; *and see* St Bernardino

Sigar, 174

Sigismund, Emperor, 213

Silesia, 113

Simonburn, 55

Simony, 15, 37, 107, 197, 200

Singing, in churches and cemeteries, 205

Skenninge, 142

Skynner, John le, 179

Slavery, slaves, 9

Slow and Mrs Worry, Mrs, 223 n. 1

Smale, William, 186

Smith, Toulmin, *Contes de Nicole Bozon,* cited, 52, 97 n. 1

Soissons, 91

Solomon, 7, Song of, 233; quoted, 7, 113, 225

Sommery, 82

Songs, 82 n. 1

Southwell, Visitations of, 95

Spain, 40; King of, 67

Speaker, The, 199

Speyer, 52

Spirituals, 104

Sports in M.A., greased pig, 37; *and see* Games

Stevenson, Father, 52

Stoke, Master Roger de, 174

Stolloke, Lavinia, 183

Stommeln, 132, 141; Béguines of, 144, 146

Stommeln, Christina von, Nos. 80, 83, 132 ff.; *and see* Sweden, Peter of
Strange, Joseph, 58
Strasbourg, 239 ff.
Strood, 238
Strutt, J., 77; *Manners and Customs,* 19; *Sports and Pastimes,* 37 n.
Suicide, temptation to, 132
"Sunday's child," 171 n. 1
Superstitions, 33, 92
Sussex, *Victoria History of,* 55 n. 1
Sutton, Brother Hugh de, 154
Swabia, 113
Sweden, 32, 141-2, 145
Sweden, Peter of, Nos. 78, 79, 81, 84; death of, 149; notes on, 132 ff., 142, 148; in Paris, 137; on student's life in Paris, 139
Switzerland, 113

Tails, of English, 238 and note
Tallies, 55 n.
Talmoud, 116, 121
Taverns, 60, 79, 80, 221; clergy in, 79 ff., 119, 120; and holy-days, 199, 201; monks in, 185-6
Taxes, 242
Theban Legion, 145
Thessalonians, Epistles to, cited, 239
Thoresby, *see* York
Thorpe Bassett, 176
Thureau-Dangin, Paul, 216
Thuringia, 113
Thurstan, *see* York
Tiber, 104
Tilbury, Master Gervase of, 29 and note, 30
Times, evil, 199
Tissier, Father B., on Caesarius of Heisterbach, 58
Tithes, cursing for, 205-6
Tityvillus, 150
Tobias, Book of, 194 n. 1
Toledo, 40; Council of, 202
Tonsure, neglected by clergy, 79 n.

Torre, Praemonstratensians at, 184, 186
Torture, 161, 214
Tour-Landry, Geoffrey de la, No. 108; notes on, 189
Tournaments, 62; and hell, 68
Tournay, Bp of, 36
Tours, Abp of, 189
Towers (medieval), Italian, 110 n.
Townships, 9
Trades in M.A., barber, 217; blacksmith, 67; church-carving on Fridays only, 174-5; cobblers, 118; clockmaker as stone-carver, 174; dyeing, 34; fishers, 73; goldsmith, 43; shearman of cloth, 216; shipman (armed), 186; spinning, 225; spurrier, 118; woollen, 34
Trading, by clergy, 79 ff.
Transport, by chariot, 232; of letters, difficulties of, 141
Travel, travellers, 219; dangers of, 15, 153; by pack-mules, 220; tales of, 54
Trede, Th., 241
Trèves, 26, 211; Bp of, 10
Trevisa, John, 39
Tunstall, 184-5

Ulster, 8
University, universities, 210, 212, 241; scholars, 108 n.; *and see* Cologne, Paris, Rashdall
Unkel, Fr Karl, on Caesarius, 58
Usurers, usury, 58 ff., 86, 114
Utrecht, diocese of, 58, 73; synod of, 62

Vallombrosa, Order of, 75
Vaux-Cernay, 157
Venus, 129
Verden [Werden], John of, **No. 121;** notes on, 232
Vesuvius, Mt 2
Vienne, Ecumenical Council of, 200; University of, 210
Vieux-Rouen, 80

Vignes, Master Jean des, 91

Villani, Giovanni, No. 98;
notes on, 167

Villars, de, 92

Villeneuve [diocese of Lyons], 92

Vincennes, 121, 165

Vineyards, 29, 228

Vinquenel, *see* Bracquemont

Viollet-le-Duc (illustration by), 59

Virgil, parodied, 144; quoted, 140 and note

Virgin Mary, 25, 40, 52, 87, 110, 158, 206, 238; Assumption of, 20 and note, (Feast of) 183; and Beatific Vision, 168; blasphemed, 150; Caesarius and, 58; and Christ, **No. 34;** Feasts of, 182, 243; images of, 150, 152, 163, 188; Immaculate Conception of, 232; Mass of, 135, 177; Mattins of, 97, 135; miracles of, 150, 152, 233–4; Nativity of, 144; and Psalter-miracle, 123; relics of, 168

Virgins, Eleven Thousand, 145

Visitations, of cathedrals, churches, **Nos. 56–60;** and neglect of locking fonts, etc., 160 n. 1; of rural deaneries, 79

Vitry, Cardinal Jacques de, Nos. 15, 29–32; on dancing, 89 n. 1; his influence on Chantimpré, 118; and money for burials, 84; notes on, 56; on Petrus Cantor, 36

Vulcan's Caldron, 2

Wadding, 232

Wakes, 180

Wales, Welsh, 154 n. 2, 246

Wallis, Thomas, 164 n. 1

Walsingham, Thomas, Nos. 100, 101, 103; notes on, 170

Walter, Brother, 132

Ward, Mr H. L. D., 42

Warwickshire, 152

Weeping, 194–5; and prayer, 137

Weimar, illustration from Museum at, 129

Welsh, Alice le, 55 n. 1

Werden, *see* Verden

Wesley, 113

Whitefield, 113

Whitstone, 180, 182

Wicksteed, Mr P. H., 167

Widekind, 70

Wife-beating, 223, (illustration) 224

Wig, wigges, 245 and note

Wildenburg, 70

Wilkins, *Comilia,* cited, 83 n. 1

Winchester, Peter des Roches, Bp of, 52–3

Windesheim, monastery of, 230

Windsor, 233 n. 1

Wine, in monasteries, 26

Winkleigh, 181

Wisdom, Book of, quoted, 239

Wissant, 14

Wit, of Middle Ages, 79

Witches, witchcraft, 33 ff., 85, 92, 149, 160, 210; burning of, 31, 162, 213; and heraldry, 162 n. 1; punishment for, 35, 94

Wittenburg, 230

Wodward, Sir Thomas, 210

Wolsey, Cardinal, 55 n. 1

Women in Middle Ages, 29, 69, 93; -beating, 35; "of bone," 222; churching of, 83; and confession, 106; duties of wives, 225; employments of, 18, 85; at Jerusalem, 7; and letters, 141; and monks, 175, 239; names of, 222–3, 228; *and see* Nuns

Woodford, 183

Worcester, Chronicle of John of, No. 11; on Bogo de Clare, 55 n. 1

Woringen, 148–9

Worms, Burchard, Bp of, 41

Wright, T., 189; *Homes of Other Days,* 82 n. 1, (illustration from), 11; *Latin Stories,* 56, (quoted), **Nos. 15, 16, 36, 86–9**

INDEX TO PART I

Writing, in M.A., 15, 168; of letters, 140–1; manner of, 216

Württemberg, Count of, 211

Wycliffites, 57 n. 2

Wyke, St Mary, 181

Wykeham, William of, 55 n. 1

Xanten, John, Master of Schools at, 58

Yarn, 225

York, Abp Thoresby of, 83 n. 1; Abp Thurstan of, 172; *Fabric Rolls*, 101; Grandisson and, 177; Visitation Board of, 95

Yorkshire, 175, 185 n. 1

Zacharias, 70

Zwolle, 230

INDEX TO PART II

References are to pages, unless otherwise stated

Abbeys in war, 122; *and see* Froude

Abbots, 50, 94, 106–7, 134; good, 7, 8; wealth of, 103; writing, 7

Abelard, Peter, No. 9, 7, 14, 16; notes on, 11

Abell [Abel], 116

Abraham, 25, 117

Absberg, Paul von, 133

Absolution, 74 n.; plenary, 107; of reserved cases, 112 n.

Academe, The, 12

Acre, 38

Adam, 45, 115, 143

Adhémar, *see* Chabannes

Aeneas, 18

Ai, 25

Aimery, *see* Rochechouart

Aix, 147

Albert III, *see* Austria

Albertus Magnus, 59

Albigensians, 38

Albin, bishop, 39

Alexander, 6

Alexander IV, 46

Alexander the Great, 117

Alexandria, 103

Alfarabius, 58

Almsgiving and building, 26

Almugavars, 68

Aloïse, castle of, 103

Alpine climbing, **Nos. 3, 4, 5**

Amiens, Thierry, Bp of, 18

Ananias, 51

Anatomy, **No. 26**

Ancourt, 44

Angels, 116

Anglicana, Historia, see Walsingham

Angus, Earl of, 110

Animals, 38–9, 117; bears, 3,

(baiting of) 8; bees, 65, 134; birds in high air, 5; calf and baptism, 152; capercailzie, 38; cats, 142; chamois, 3; cows, 153; goats, 3; God's favourite, 116; horses, 134–5, (fed on wheat and wine) 153; lion-taming, **No. 24,** (illustration) 54; mules, 103; in mystery-play, 138; raven and dove, 86; serpent, 1; sheep, 4; snake, 86; stag, 2; toad, 83; wolves, 27; *and see* Monstrosities

Anjou, 70; Charles of, 5 n., 57, 67, 122; militia in, 151 ff.; René of, 147; *and see* Bourdigné

Ansbach, Markgraf of, 131

Antichrist, 58

Antioch, 50, 65

"Ape, The," 133 ff.

Apocalypse, 146

Apostles, Acts of the, 146; "Mystery of the Holy Acts of the," 138

Appropriations of parish churches, 87

Aquila, 58

Aquitaine, 60

Aragon, K. Pedro III of, 5 and note, 67 ff.

Arblast, *see* Crossbow

Arborfield, John of, 41

Arcax, 115

Archbishops, in war, 110; *and see* Canterbury

Archdeacons and education, 113

Archers (English) 98, 110, (French) 151, (free) *see* francs-archers

Architects, architecture, art, artists, **Nos. 8, 15,** 37, 84; masons, 10, lodges of, 99; on strike, 9

Ardennes, 91, 92

Ardres, Lambert of, No. 19; Count Arnold II of, 35; earthworks of (illustration), 36

Arduin, 4

Arduzon, R., 12

Areopagite, Dionysius the, 11

Argenton, Richard d', 52

Aria, Count of, 69

Aristotle, 1, 55, 58, 79; bad translations of, 59 ff.

Armagh, 94

Armagnac, Earl of, 104

Armenia, 29; Archbishop of, 50

Arms, armour, 131, 133 ff.; *and see* Weapons

Arnburg, 83

Arnold, *see* Ardres, Guisnes

Arostolym, 115

Arundel, Abp, 144 n.

Assisi, *see* Sabatier

Atlas, Mt, 29

Augsburg, David of, 63

Augustinian Canons, 128

Aumâle, 42, 44

Aurca, 116

Austin, *see* Augustinian

Austria, 63; Albert III, Duke of, 81

Auvergne, 103 ff.

Avicenna, 1, 2, 58, 112

Avignon, 87, 108

Aymerigot, *see* Marcel

Babel, 26

Bacon, Roger, 14, 38, **No. 25;** notes on, 55; on preaching, 63

Bailiffs, 119, 133

Baker, Ralph, 74

Baldwin, *see* Canterbury, Jerusalem

Bâle, Council of, 128

Baluze-Mansi, 8

Bampton, Richard de, 73

Bandits, **Nos. 43, 53**

Barabbas, 51

Barbary, 1c

Barbe, Olivier, 104

Barbor, *see* Buckenham

Bastard of England, 126

Battle, 96 n.

Bauval, Pierre de, 122–3

Bavaria, 63

Béarn, Pierrot of, 103, 104

Beauvais, 7; Vincent of, Nos. 1, 4, 31 n. 2; notes on, 1

Beds and bedding, 139

Béguines, 128, 130

Belgicum, Magnum Chronicon, 83 n. 2

Belzeray, *see* Jews

Benedict, *see* York, Jews in

Benedict VIII, 24

Benedict XII, 107, 113

Benedictine, Benedictines, 1; *and see* Mabillon

Berkeley, Lord, 2

Berkshire, 119

Berlichingen, Götz von, Nos. 56–58; notes on, 131

Berlichingen-Rossach, Freiherr von, 136

Bernetot, 42

Berry, Duke of, 104

Berwick (nunnery) 90, (town) 89

Bethel, 25

Beverley, 79 n.

Béziers, 103; Council of, 39; Raymund Trenchaval, Viscount of, 23

Bible, 58, 59, 84; Bacon on, 55; Bibliolatry, 3 n. 1; in cathedral library, 112; Genesis, 45–6; ignorance of, 13; illustrations of, 84–5; Job, 44; as material for miracle-plays, 141; Old Testament, 12; "Open Bible," 142 ff.; Proverbs, 80 n. 2; restriction of, 146; translations of, 61–2, (Church's attitude to) 142, (and Bishops) 144; *and see* Clergy

Bishop, bishops, 34; avaricious, 87; and clerical examinations, 43; election of, 25, 86; false, 82; few, 17 n.; good, 62, 113; ignorant,

86; incomes of, 49; and Jews, 24; Latin of, **No. 35**; learned, 34, 48; as monk, 25, 86; and translations of Bible, 14 n.; in war, 111; worldly, 48

Black Death, the, 93

Black Prince, the, 91

Bleneau, 42, 44

Bloxham, Alexander de, 73

Bodleian MS., 118

Bohemia, 63, 79

Boleworth, Thomas de, 73

Bondeville, 44

Boniface VIII, 87

Bonnin, 44 n.

Book-keeping, **No. 55**

Books, 2, 55; burnt, 143; and clergy, 111–2; denied to layfolk, 128; educational, 114; encyclopaedias, 1; in Germany, 128–9; inscriptions in, **No. 52**; locked up, 112; missals, 129; stitched, 112; superstitions about, 130; in wills, 112; *and see* Bible, Monasteries

Bordeaux, 121, 124

Boulogne, Count of, 35

Bouquet, Dom, 23

Bourdigné, Jean de, *Chronicle of Anjou,* **No. 63**

Bourg, *see* Compiègne

Bourges, 138

Brabant, 65; Barefoot Friars of, 82

Bridlington, Robert of, 73

British Magazine, 128

Bruce, Robert de, 90

bruer, 38

Bruges, 103

Brussels, cloth of, 103

Brutus, 106

Buckenham, New, 118

Buckinghamshire, 119

Building, buildings, (medieval) 26–7; and almsgiving, 26; implements, 37; materials for, 19, 37; methods, 53; *and see* Church

Bullock, Richard, 41

Burgundians, 147

Burgundy, 3; Duke Philip the Good of, 48

Burial, of Jews, 34; of monks, 107; of rich men, 49

Burton, Thomas de, 107

Bury, Richard de, 55 n. 2, 86

Busch, Johann, No. 55, 142

Bygod, Thomas, 74

Caiaphas, 131

Calais, 91, 97

Cam, *see* Ham

Cambrai, 42, 53

Cambridge, 120; *C. Hist. Eng. Lit.,* 2, 142

Canigou [Canigosus], Mont, 5

Canons, Augustinian, 128; Regular, 65; youth of, 34

Canterbury, Abp Baldwin of, 31, 34

Cantimpratanus, *see* Chantimpré

Cantor, Petrus, No. 15; notes on, 25

Carcassone, 103

Carlat, 103

Carloman, 24

Cartaphilus, *see* Jew, The Wandering

Casimir, *see* Poland

Catalonia, 71, 73

Catania, 71 ff.

Catchpolls, 37

Cateslinna, 116

Cathedral, cathedrals, 112; almoner of, 15; reconstruction of, 28 n.

Caucasus, 29

Caxton, 114

Cayme, 116

Cerauneys, 29

Chabannes, Adhémar de, *Chronicle of,* **No. 14**

Chalucet, 103

chamium, 38

Champagne, 91

Chandos, John, 97

Changelings, 38

Chantimpré, Thomas of, No. 27; notes on, 65

Chantry certificates, 79 n.
Charlemagne, 68; and Jews, 24
Charles IV, 80
Charles V, 131
Charles VII [of France], 121
Charles the Bold, 147
Chartes, Bibliothèque de l'École des, 18
Chartres, 18 ff.
Chartreuse, the, 10
Château-Porcein, 91
Châtillon [Castillon], siege of, 121 ff.
Chaucer, 2; *Canterbury Tales*, 133 n.; *C. and his England*, 91; his march, 91; *Miller's Tale* (quoted), 75 n.; and Otho de Granson, 113; his *Prologue* (quoted), 99 n.
Cherwell, 74
Chester, 2, 40
Chevet, 28 n.
Chichester, 41
Children, 83; and church-building, 18 ff.; feeding of, 143–4; at meals, 146; over-feeding of, 64; as pages, 67; and wet-nurses, 38
Chilton, Ralph de, 74
Chronicles, 63; Belgian, 83 n.; English, 50, 106; monastic, 23, 128; Monstrelet's, 121; **Novaliciense, No. 3**; Spanish, 66; *and see* Limburg
Church (medieval), its attitude to Jews, 23 ff.; its attitude to translated Bible, 142; and manuals for preachers, 111; needed reform of, 58, 59
Churches, appropriations of, 87; east end of, 28 n.; horses in, 69; images in, 24; irreverence in, 152; jealousy between, 14; singing in, 39, 40; stained glass in, 152
Church bells, 22
Church building, 8 ff., **No. 11**; associations for, 18; sinfulness of, 28

Church furniture (altar-cloths), 130
Church ornaments, 15, 152; (waxen tapers) 21
Church rights, 74, 76
Church services, absolution, 74; baptism, 39, 57, 117, (mock) 152; churching, 72; communion, 57, (age of) 79 n.; extreme unction, 74; *and see* Mass
Church vestments, 15
Churchyards, apple tree in, 152; preaching in, 128
Cistercian, Cistercians, 107; Rule, 8
Cîteaux, Order of, 8
Citizen-levies, *see* Militia
Clairvaux, 16
Clédat, Prof. Léon, 45 n. 2
Clement, Count, 4
Clement IV, 55
Clementine Constitutions, 112
Clergy, and books, 111; examinations of, **Nos. 21, 22**; good, 40; ignorance of, **No. 22 A**, 39 ff., 59, 113, 142; incomes of, 49; as innkeepers, **No. 39**; and Jews, 23; living as lay-folk, 83 n. 2; married, 78, 83 n. 2; medieval criticism of, 56; morality of, 43; multiplicity of, 49; as notaries, 78; and open Bible, 142 ff.; ordination of, 39 ff.; quarrelling, 56; as soldiers, 108; and trade, 91; in war, 111; youth of, 60, 114
Clobber, William de, 74
Cloth, trade in, 96
Cluny, 11
Cobbler, Henry le, 74
Cokesgrave, John de, 74
Colbronde, 117
Colewort, 67
Cologne, 84; cathedral, 28 n.; **Council of, No. 39**
Comestor, Petrus, 5, 30
Compiègne, 103
Condé, Master Nicholas of, 46

Confession, 16; of reserved cases, 112 n.

Confirmation, rare, 17 n.

Constance, Council of 111

Constantine, Emperor, 8

Constitution Provincial, 144 and note

Cooper, John le, 74

Co-operation (medieval), in Bible translation, 144–5

Coroners' Rolls, No. 31

Corpus Christi, Order of Pageants for the Play of, 141

Coucy, Lord of, 104

Councils, of Bâle, 128; of Constance, 111; English Church, 39; Lateran, 39; of Lyons, 43 n. 1

Courcelles, Robert of, 46

Courtrai, 44

Coussy, Mathieu de, No. 54

Cowley, Andrew de, 74

Cowley, Gilbert de, 73

Crane, Prof., 38

Crime, criminals, 73, 106, 119; in war, 111

Cross, adoration of, 24

Crossbowmen, crossbows, 91, 95, 99, 134

Cruisor [*sic* in Rogers' text, but probably a misreading for *Cissor, i.e.* tailor], 76

Crusades, contemporary criticism of, 154; failures of, 38; in Spain, 67

Cryn, 90

Culverin, 135

Curfew, 74

Cusa, Cardinal Nicolaus von, 128

Dalida, 116

Damascenus, Johannes, 30

Damascenus, St John, 61

Damascus, 103

Damasus, Pope, 61

Dances, dancing, German, 97; on holy-days, 75; at Oxford, 75 n.

Dante, on Charles of Anjou, 5 n.; *Purgatorio* (cited), 5 n.

Daukin, Sir Baudouin, 91

Dauphin, the, 104

David, 114

David II, K. of Scotland, 108 ff.

Decretals, books of, 112

Deloraine, William of, 131

Demons, devils, 20, 116; Noah and, 86

Denifle, Father, 62

Denmark, 60

Derby, House of, 100

Dern, Castle of, 80

Deventer, 128, 130

Déville, 42, 44

Didron, *Annales Archéologiques*, 138

Dieppe, 42, 95

dies Egipciacus, 31

Dietz, Count of, 80

Diogenes, 12

Dionysius the Areopagite, 11, 61

Dives, Haimon of, No. 11; notes on, 18

Dives, St Pierre-sur-, 18

Donat, *see* Donatus

Donatus, 47 n. 1, 60 n.

Dorset, 41

Douai, 1

Dover, 96

Dress (medieval), 78; of bishops, 83 n. 1; of French militia, 151; kings', 97–8; of knights, 81, 89, 90, 132; minstrels', 102 n.; in mystery-plays, 138; pages', 131; warriors', 125–6; women's, 63 (in men's), 93; *and see* Hairdressing, Monks and habit, Nuns

Drunkenness, 133

Duchesne, 23

Durham, monks of, 108; Prior of, 110; **Robert de Graystanes**, Sub-prior of, **No. 35**

Dux, 115

Earth, medieval beliefs about, 29, 30

INDEX TO PART II

Earthquakes, 24

Eckenstein, Miss, 128

Eden, 30

Education (medieval), Bacon on, 55; of princes, 1; reform of, **No. 48**; *and see* Schools

Edward the Confessor, 106

Edward I, 73 ff., 89, 151 n.

Edward II, 89

Edward III, 89, 93, 95, 97, 111

Edward IV, 117

Edward VI, 79 n.

Effraton, 117

Egeon, 117

Egipciacus, dies, 31

Egypt, Egyptians, 2, 29, 30

Elias, 30, 117

Elisha, 12, 26

Ellewyk, 87

Emperor, ideal, 58

Enfegor, 117

England, English, bandits in, 119 ff.; in battle (illustration), 109; Bible translation in, 142 ff.; chroniclers, 18; The Conquered E., **No. 44**; dissolution of monasteries in, 48; E.E.T.S., 114; kings of, 56, 104; Mendicants, 58 n.; militia in, 108, 151; relics in, 50; taxation by Pope of, 34; *and see* Walsingham

Ennius, 2

Enoch, 30

Entommeures, Frère Jean des, 111

Ephesus, 138

Epilepsy, 65

Erasmus, No. 22 A; on number of priests, 49

Esaias (quoted), 26

Essex, 120

Ethiopia, 29

Eu, 42, 44

Euphrates, 29

Europe, chroniclers in, 50; learning in, 25; preaching in, 63; *Universities of,* 55

Eve, 116

Excommunication, 33

Exeter, 14; *and see* Grandisson

Ey, Sir, 117

Eynsham, Richard de, 73; Walter de, 73

Fairs, 103

Famine, 35

Faringdon, John de, 75

Fécamp, Abbot of, 46

Fergus, *see* Jews

Fernando, Infante Don, 70

Festo, 58

Figueres, 68

Fitzralph, *see* Armagh

Flanders, Flemings, 90, 95, 97; *Corpus Chronicorum Flandriae,* 14, 32

Flax, 37

Fletcher, Roger le, 74

Florence, wine-selling in, 91

Flowers, *see* Plants

Fontbois, 43

Fontevraud, 31

Food and drink in M. A., 63, 117; of bandits, 103; black poppy as, 1–2; eggs (used for hairdressing) 131; pigs' flesh, 9; storing of food, 104; waste of, 153; wine, 98, 117, 123; *and see* Monks

Forgery, 82

Fougaron, 103

Foxlee, Gilbert de, 75

France, French, 68, 113, 131, 147; chronicles, 18; clergy (youth of) in, 60; crossbowmen of, 91; *Hist. Litt. de la,* 14; kings of, 16, 56, 67, 69, 86, 104, 108; language, 44–5, 87; militia in, 151; Pope's favour towards, 94; religious wars in, 147

Franconia, 63

francs-archers, 123, 151

Franks, 7

Frederick II, 57

Freiburg, 153

Froissart, Nos. 42, 43, 102 n.

Froude, J. A., *Annals of an English Abbey,* 106

Fulbroke, Robert de, 73
Fulda, Abbot of, 134
Furnur, John le, 73
Fyson, 117

Gabriel, 138, 140
Gairdner, Dr, *Lollardy and the Reformation*, 3 n. 1, 142
Gallic War, 17
Gambling, 106
Gardens, 37
Gasquet, Abbot, *Eve of the Reformation*, 142
Gemünd, *see* Saaleck
Generals, xxiv, 63
Genesis, book of, 30
Gentiles, 58; buildings of, 27
Geoffrey, Prior, *Chronicle of,* **No. 12**
Geometry (medieval), 53
Gerard (priest), 15
Gerba, 71–2
Gerhart, Count, 80
Germany, Germans, 60, 114, 153; books in, 128; *Mon. Germ. Hist., Deutsche Chroniken,* 78; *Mon. Germ. Hist. Script.,* 4; *and see* Hartzheim
Girardot, Baron de, 138
Glanville, *see* Rochester
Glover, Philip le, 74
Gluttony, 63
Godstow, William de, 73
Goethe, 131
Golden Legend, The, 138
Gospels, clerical ignorance of, 39
Gournay, 7
Grammar, clerical ignorance of, 42 ff.
Grandisson, Bp John de, No. 48, 118
Granges, 37; castellated, 28
Granson, 113; Sir Otho de, 113
Gray, Sir Thomas de, 90; *and see* Heton
Graystanes, *see* Durham
Greece, Greek, 61; language, 55, 59, (ignorance of) 60

Green, J. R., 55
Green, Mrs, *Town Life in Fifteenth Century,* 14
Gregory IX, 38, 50
Gross, 75 n.
Grosseteste, 34, 61
Grube, Karl, 128
Guienne, 121
Guisnes, 35; Count Arnold II of, 35

Haimon, Abbot, 18
Hainault, Philippa of, 102
Hairdressing, 80, 82; of English under Normans, 106; of Poles, 131
Halidon Hill, 111
Halifax, 79 n.
Halle, 131
Ham 91, [Cam] 116
Hammelburg, 133
Hamo, *see* Hythe, Rochester
Hampton [Southampton], 96
Hankin, 100
Hanred, Nicholas de, 74
Haqueville, 42
Harcourt, *see* St Richard
Hartzheim, *Concilia Germaniae,* 91
Health (in M. A.), and over-eating, 64
Heathen, conversion of, 55 n.
Heaven and hell, 115, 116; books on, 129; in mystery-play, 138
Hebrews, ancient, 20; language, 30, 59, (ignorance of) 60
Hegesippus, 3 n. 1
Héloïse, 11
Henneberg, Count Wilhelm von, 133
Henry II, 31
Henry III, 50
Henry IV, 93
Henry V, 114, 120
Henry VI, 114, 119, 120, 124
Henry VIII, 79 n., 147
Henslow, Prof., 77 n.
Heralds, 126–7
Heretics, and Bible, 143 ff.
Heriman, 14

Hermits, hermitages, 11, 12, 27, 65

Herod, 141

Hesdin, 91

Heton, Sir Thomas Gray of, Nos. 37, 38

Higden, Ralph, *Polychronicon,* **Nos. 2, 16, 17, 18,** 3n., 33 n.; notes on, 2

History, natural, **No. 20**; writing of in M.A., 14, 50, (military) 89

Holy-days, 37; and disorder, 75, 141

Holy Land, 7, 65

Honi soit qui mal y pense, 113

Honnecourt, Villard de, No. 24; notes on, 53

Hornberg, castle of, 131

Horses, war- (harness of), 67

Hospitallers, *see* Rhodes

Host, consecration of, 41 n.

Households, knightly, 132–3

Houses, floors of, 132; fortified, 106; furniture of, bread-knife, 131; pages in, 131

Housling-folk, 79 n.

Hoveden, Roger of, 33 n.

Hue and cry, 90, 135

Hugh, chaplain, 25

Hungary, 53, 60

Hurst, John of, 40

Hythe, Bp Hamo of, No. 47

Impostors, The Three, 65

India, 30

Indulgences and money, 27

Infante, 68–9

Innocent II, 17 n.

Innocent IV, 34, 111, 112

Innocent VI, 94

Inns, innkeepers, clerical, **No. 39**

Inquests, **No. 31**

Ireland, Irish, 119; bishops, 39, 41, 94; "wild," 119 ff.

Iron Hand, 131, 135–7

Isidorus, 1, 2, 29, 30

Israel, 2; conversion of, 58

Italy, 60

Jacme, Don, 72

Jacobites, 82

James I, 151 n.

Japheth, 116

Jerusalem, 14, 23; Baldwin, K. of, 7; Patriarch of, 38

Jew, Jews, 14, 27, 51; *auto-da-fé* of (illustration), 32–3; baptism of, 33; Belzeray, Prince of, 140–1; and Bible, 145; and Church, 23 ff.; and crucifix, 24; Fergus, Prince of, 141; massacres of, 31 ff.; Moses and, 65; persecution of, 23 ff.; in Provence, 147; Richard I and, 31; synagogues of, 24–5; the Wandering, **No. 23**

John XXII, 86, 113

Joinville, 66

Jongleurs, 123

Jordan, R., 12, 20, 116

Joseph, *see* Jew, wandering

Josephus, 3 n. 1, 29, 61

Jovinian, 11

Judas, 52, 83

Judgment, Last, *see* World

Julius Caesar, 17

Juries, jurymen, 73–4

Justice (medieval), difficulty of, 119; and money, 148

Kampen, 128

King's Hall, 97 ff.

Knighton, Henry, *Chronicle of,* **Nos. 40, 41**

Knights (medieval), 89; dress of, 89; and trade, 91

Köchli, 137

Lahn, R., 78

Lambert, *see* Ardres

Lambeth MS., 117

Lancaster, Duke of, 100, 102

Land-courts, 80

Landshut, 135–6

Lanercost Chronicle, 111

Langton, Abp Stephen, 39

Laon, cathedral of, 53

Laterecta, 116

Latin, a Bishop's, 86; grammar, 60 n.; need of, 62; philosophical books in, 61; in schools, 114

Latins, 61

Lausanne, 53

Lecche, John le, 74

Lectors, 128 and note

Leicester, Abbey, 93

Lentersheim, Veit von, 131

Leprosy, 82

Letters dimissory, 47 n.

Lewes, Thomas de, 73

Libourne, 122

Liège, 65

Limburg, Barefoot Friars of, 80; **Chronicle, No. 33**; illustration, 79; notes on, 78

Limoges, 8, 103

Limousin, 103 ff.

Lincoln, 33, 89; bishop of, 39; Nicholas de, 73; *and see* Grosseteste

Lindsay, Principal, 142

Linen, trade in, 96

Liripipes, 94

Lisewys, Thomas, 75

Loire, R., 153

Lollardy, *see* Gairdner

London, 40, 95; Jews in, 34

Lorey, Stephen of, 42

Lot, 25

Louis VII, 16

Louis XI, 147

Luce, Siméon, 102 n.

Lucifer, 138

Luther, 147, 154

Lynn, 33

Lyon, 147

Lyons, Council of, 43 n.

Mabillon, *Annales Benedictini*, 18

Mac, 141

Maccabees, Books of, 61

Madoc, 74

Magic and Mass, 130

Magus, Simon, 138

Mahomet, 65

Main, R., 82

Maine, 152; *and see* Anjou, **Charles of**

Mainz, 82

Majorca, King of, 70; Queen of, 73

Manciple, 74

Manners, waiting at table, 131

Marcadera, 67

Marcel, Aymerigot, 103

Marcurius, 117

Marisco, Adam de, 58 n.

Marmion, Sir William, 89

Marquay, castle of, 104

Marriage, married, 83; age of, 70

Martin IV, 67

Mary, Queen, *Psalter of,* **No. 34**; illustration of, 85

Masons, *see* Architecture

Masquerades, 93

Mass, masses, 16, 17, 71, 123, 132; canon of, 39, 40 and note, (burnt) 129; daily, 107, 131; by lay-folk, 83; and magic, 130; and manslaughter, 110 n.; and parish priests, 39; and purgatory, 130; Roger Bacon on, 57

Matagrifo, 69, 72

Mathematics (medieval), 53

Maundeville, Sir John, 83 n. 1

Maxwell, Sir Herbert, 89

Meaux, 107; *and see* Melsa

Medicine (medieval), 1, 7, 77; books on, 112; *and see* Health, Surgery

Megara, 27

Melsa, Chronicon de, No. 45

Mendicants, 39, 56, 58; ignorant, 60; as preachers, 63, 154; (Dominicans) 1, 55 n. 2, 65, 111, 128; (Franciscans) 38, 42, 43, 82, 83 n. 2, 111; Berthold von Regensburg as, 63; Roger Bacon as, 55; quarrels with clergy, 94

Mercenaries, 95, 97

Merian (illustration by), 79

Merlin, 58

Mesopotamia, 29

Messiah, 23

Messina, 70, 72

Metescharp, 73–4

Militia, 108, 151 and note

Miller, John le, 74

Milton, William de, 74

Minières, Bro. Walter de, 43

Minstrels, 82, 102 n.; in war, 97

Miracle-plays, **Nos. 59, 60**; expense and length of, 141

Miracles, 18, 25, 35, 152

Misericorde, 76

Momfumbres, 115

Monasteries, books in, 17; business life of, 107; cells dependent on, 18; chronicles of, 23; Dissolution of, 48; in Germany, 128; jealousy between, 14; patron saints of, 11; reform of, 128; sick in, 8; wealth of, 28

Monasteriorum, Liber de Reformatione, 128

Monasticism, 8; *Women under, see* Eckenstein

Monks, and almsgiving, 28; building by, 10; buildings of, 27, 28; burial of, 107; criticised by contemporaries, 56; food of, 12; good, 25; and habit, 107; Irish, 120; and Jews, 23; labour of, 10; lay-brethren, 82; learned, 2, 7; learning neglected by, 55 n. 2; and private property, 107; and schools, 13; and usury, 28; in war, 110; writing by, 3, 108; youth of, 59, 60; *and see* Abbots

Monod, Bernard, on Guibert of Nogent, 7

Monstrelet, *Chronicle* of, 121

Monstrosities, 83, 153–4

Mont Cenis, 3

Montpellier, 103

Montreuil, 91

Monumenta Germaniae, 4, 78

Moors, 71

Moravia, 63

More, Sir Thomas, No. 61

Morea, 70, 71

Mores, Long, 117

Morton, Thomas de, 73

Moses, 65; height of, 117

Mountains, 3–6; medieval fear of, 6

Mowbray, 110

Mowbray, Alexander de, 90

Muisis, Abbot Gilles li, 32

Muntaner, Don Ramon, Nos. 28, 29, 30; notes on, 66

Murky, Mount, 5

Musical instruments, 75

Musterdevilliers [cloth from Montevilliers in Normandy], 103

Myrc, *Festial*, 138

Mystery-plays, *see* Miracle-plays

Namur, 131; Robert of, 97, 100, 102

Narbonne, 103; Théodard, Bp of, 23

Natural History, **No. 20**

Nebuchadnezzar, 18

Nervii, the, 17

Netherlands, 128

Neuchâtel, 113

Neuilly, 91

Neushom, John de, 74

Neuwerk, Provost of, 131

Neville's Cross, 108

Niederbrechen, 83

Nile, R., 29

Noah, 25, 52, 84, 116

Nogent, Guibert de, No. 6, 27 n.; notes on, 7, 14

Nogent-sous-Coucy, 7

Nogent-sur-Seine, 11

Norham, 89

Norman Conquest, 89

Normandy, 18

Normans, 106

Northampton, 33, 34

Northumbrians, 108

Novalese, monastery of, 3

Novaliciense, Chronicon, No. 3

Noyon, Simon, Bp of, 17 n.

Nuns, nunneries, 90; books in, 128, 130; Canon of Mass in,

129; dress of, 80; *Medieval English*, *see* Power; widows in, 7

Nürnberg, 133, 135

Oaths, 87, 106
Obazine, *see* St Stephen
Oberschenbach, 133
Ocle, Robert de, 74
Oignies, 38
Okyll, Robert, 110
Olina, 116
Ollia, 116
Olybana, 116
Olympus, Mt, 5
Ordination, false, 83 n. 2; repeated, 82, 83 n. 2
Origen, 61
Oseney, John de, 73, 74
Osmund, Brother, 43
Ovid (quoted), 27
Oxford, 39; Catechism of Master of, **No. 50**; clergy in, 56; Coroners' Rolls, 73; County of, 119; Manners, **No. 31**; St Aldate's, 73; St Ebbe, 73; *and see* Rogers

Pageant, *see* Miracle-plays
Pages, 67 n., 131
Palonavera, Doña, 68
Papal letters, forged, 83 n. 2
Papias the Elder, 112
Paraclete, 13
Paradise, 138; Adam and Eve in, 143; earthly, 28 ff., 31 n. 2
Pardoners, *see* Indulgences
Paris, 38, 45, 65, 104; Cathedral School at, 25; clergy in, 56; Grandisson at, 113; Notre Dame de, 25, 26 n., 138; St Denis, 11; Sorbonne, 154; University of, 111
Paris, Matthew, No. 23; miniatures to (illustration) 101; notes on, 50
Parish churches, 132; appropriations of, 87

Parish priests, 35; examinations of, 39 ff.; households of, 41; influence of Mendicants on, 39
Parliament, Pleas to, No. 53
Parmenter, Thomas le, 73
Paul (hermit), 27
Pavilly, 44
Peasants and squires, 134
Peckham, Abp, 111, 114 n.
Peltryware [skins], 103
Penitentiaries, office of, 112 and note
Pennaforte, Raymond de, 112
Percy, 108, 110
Perelade, 66–7
Périgord, 121
per saltum, 49 and note
Peter the Venerable, 11
Petiville, 43
Pevensey, 96 n.
Pfeiffer, Franz, 63
Philip the Bold, 67
Philip VI, K. of France, 108
Philippa, *see* Hainault
Philobiblon, 86
Picards, Picardy, 69, 91
Pilate, 51
Pilgrims, pilgrimages, 50, 52
Plants, flax, 37; God's favourite, 116; medicinal, 77; poppy (black), 1
Plasa, 72
Plassay, 42
Plato, 12, 58
Ploughing, 135
Poitiers, 94
Poland, King Casimir IV of, 132 n.
Poles, 131–3
Ponthieu, 91, 95
Pope, popes, 34 ff., 46, 47; and absolution, 107; "bibamus papaliter," 108 n.; French favoured by, 94; good, 107; ideal, 58; intelligent, 55; and Jews, 23; kinsfolk of, 107; and mass, 107; and monastic reform, 128; negligent of learning, 61; and taxation of England, 34

Population (medieval), of English towns, 79 n.; of German towns, 79

Power, Dr Eileen, 128

Prag, University of, 80

Preachers, preaching, 23, 38, 65, 128; and falsehoods, 130; few, 49; manuals for, 111; in vulgar tongue, 129

Prices, cost, of ransom, 68; for castle, 104

Priors, 110, 128; wealth of 103

Prisons, 31

Processions, religious, 138

Provence, 5, 60, 70, 147

Proverbs, 28, 66, 142, 144; Book of, 80

Psalms, psalmist, psalter, 60; and church-building, 21; clerical ignorance of, 40; *Queen Mary's*, 84; quoted, 51, 110 n.

Punishments, 148; corporal, 74, 80; hanging, 73; and strangling, 153

Pythagoreans, 12

Quatrebarbes, 147

Quenynton, Robert de, 73

Querquens, 72

Quesnel, Nicholas, 46

Quintilian, 12

Quivil, Bp, 111

Rabbi, 33

Ransom, 68, 104

Rashdall, Dean, 55

Ratisbon, *see* Regensburg

Raymund, *see* Béziers

Reading, 41

Reckenforst, 80

Red Sea, 29

Reformation, the, 39; *and see* Gairdner, Gasquet

Regensburg, Berthold of, No. 26; notes on, 63

Reims, 26, 91; cathedral of, 53; Samson, Abp of, 16

Relics, 14, 50, 152; and church-building, 21; false, 33; *and see* Nogent

Religion of M. A., 50, 137; fervour in church-building, 18 ff.; in miracle-plays, 138 ff.; revivals, 21; *and see* Education

Reliquiae Antiquae, **Nos. 50, 51**

Rents, 79

Réthel, 91; illustration of, 92

Retieris, *see* Retters

Retiers, *see* Retters

Retters, 91

Rhasus, 2

Rhine, the, 53

Rhineland, 63; minstrelsy in, 82

Rhodes, knights of, 154

Rich and poor in M. A., 18, 27, 49, 153; feeding of, 64

Richard I, 65; and the Jews, **No. 17**

Richmond, Earl of, 102

Rigaldi, Odo, 46 n. 1; notes on, 42; his relations with Pope, 47; *Visitation-Register* of, **No. 22**

Robber-knights, 131

Robbers, robbery, 119

Robertsbridge, St Mary of, 118

Rochechouart, Aimery, Viscount of, 25

Rochester, Bp Gilbert de Glanville of, 41; Bp Hamo of, 111; Cathedral, 112

Roffense, Registrum, No. 47

Roger, Bro., 43

Rogers, Prof. J. E. T., *Oxford City Documents*, 73

Rohault, Joachim, 122–3

Roland, 68

Romans, Humbert de, 111

Rome, Roman, amphitheatre, 138; buildings in, 27; building of, 2; Court, 56, 94; earthquake at, 24; Jews in, 24; king of, 80; University of, 87

Romuleo, Monte, 3, 4

Romulus, 3, 4

Ross [? *Rosam*], 40

Rothoirs, 45

Rot. Parl. 119, 120

Rouen, 42; Hugh, Abp of, 18; *and see* Rigaldi

Routh, Mr, 142

Ruscombe, 41

Rusticus (monk), 12

Ruth, Romance of, **No. 49**

Rye, 102

Saaleck, Bailiff of, 133

Sabatier, *St François d'Assise*, 38

Sacrilege, 69

Saints, and Jews, 23; patron, 11

St Achaire, 15

St Albans, 50; abbot of, 94; monks of, 101, 169; **Gesta Abbatum S. Albani, No. 44**

St Aldate's, *see* Oxford

St Ambrose, 129

St Anthony, 27

St Augustine of Hippo, 59, 129; *De Civitate Dei* (quoted), 2

St Bartholomew, in mystery-play, 138

St Basil, 29, 61

St Bernard, 16, 23; and Cistercian buildings, 27; Guibert de Nogent and, 7; and See of Tournai, 17 n.

St Bonaventura, 43 n., 63

St Boniface, 79

St Cecilia, 42

St Christopher, 117

St Chrysostom, 61

Ste-Côme de Ver, 152

St Cuthbert, 110

St Eleutherius, 15 ff.

St Eloy, 15

St Erhard, church of, 81

St Flour, 103

St Francis, *see* Sabatier

St George, 79, 124

St-Germain, 42

St Germer, abbey of, 7

St Gregory the Great, 107, 129

St Gregory Nazianzene, 61

St Jerome, 48, 61, 129; quoted, 2, 3, 11, 12, 27

St John, 138; Gospel of, 146

St John Damascenus, 61

St Lawrence, Feast of, 17

St Louis, 1, 47, 87

St Luke, Gospel of, 146

St Marie du Port, 20

St Mark, Gospel of, 146

St Martin, Feast of, 39

St Mary of Oignies, 38

St Matthew, Gospel of, 146

St Michael, 140

St Omer, 35

St Osmund, Register of, *see* Sarum

St Paul, 48, 52; baptism of, 51; 1st Epistle to Corinthians, 87; Epistle to Ephesians, 146; Epistle to Romans, 146

St Peter, 52

St Peter ad Vincula, 80

St Pietre-sur-Dives, 18

St Quentin, 91

St Richard de Harcourt, 43

St Stephen of Obazine, Life of, Nos. 7, 8

St Théodard, Life of, No. 13

St Thomas, 140

St Thomas Aquinas, 59; on idolatry, 83 n.

St Thomas à Becket, 117

St Thomas à Kempis, 128

St Vitus, 133, 136

Salimbene, Brother, No. 5, 63; notes on, 4

Salisbury, Bp Herbert of, 41; Countess of, 113; William, Dean of, 39; *and see* Sarum

Salomonville, William of, 42

Salustius, 29

Samson, *see* Reims

Sandhurst, 41

Saracens, 7, 24, 38, 59, 68

Sarica, 116

Sarum Registers, No. 21

Satan, 138

Scalacronica, 89, 91

INDEX TO PART II

Schools, schoolmasters, 13, 65, 74, 80; grammar-, 113; *and see* Monks

Scotiae, Rotuli, 111

Scotland, Scots, Scottish, 108 ff., 141; *Illustrations of S. History*, 108; Marches of, 90; war, 87, 89

Scott, Sir Walter, 131

Scrope, Sir Thomas, 91

Sellers, Maud, *see* York

Sem [Shem], 116

Seneca, 1, 58

Sens, 16

Sermons, *see* Preachers

Seth, 116

Seven Sleepers, 106

Shakespeare and More, 142

Shatton, 41

Sheffield, 79 n.

Shepherds, huts of, 27

Sherborne, John of, 41

Shillingford Letters, 14

Shipman, Chaucer's, 99 n.

Ships, shipping, illustration of, 96

Shoesmith, William le, 74

Shylock, 147

Sibyls, the, 58

Sicily, 66 ff.; kings of, 86, 147

Silesia, 63

Simon (chaplain), 39

Simon the Dyker, 37

Simulacre, simulacrum, 83

Singing, clerical ignorance of, 43, 47

Skurf, John de, 74

Slater, Henry le, 74

Sluys, 95, 96

Smith, Geoffrey le, 73

Smith, John le, 74

Smith, Lucy Toulmin, *see* York

Socrates, 58

Sodenberg, 133-4

Sodom, 28

Solar, soller, 76 n.

Solomon (quoted), 80

Solyman, Sultan, 154

Somme, R., 91

Songs, 80, 82

Sonning, 39, 41

Souls, medieval conception of, 139 and note

Southampton [Hampton], 96

Spain, Spaniards, 5, 60, 66; on the sea, **No. 42**

Spices, 103

Spigurnel, Henry, 50

Sponges, 5

Squires, 133

Stafford, Earl of, 91

Staffordshire, 18

Stamford, 33; John de, 73

Statutes of the Realm, 120

Stevenson, Father, 111

Strike, of masons, 9

Stuttgart, 66

Styria, 81

Surgeons, surgery, 7, 53, 73

Sussex, 96

Swabia, 63

Switzerland, 63

Tailed Knights, Order of, 81

Tailor, Henry le, 74

Talbot, 121 ff.

Tarquinius Priscus, 18

Tartars, 59

Taxation, papal, 34

Taylor, Thomas le, 74

Tears, religious, 20 ff.

Tew, Adam de, 74-5

Themele, John de, 73

Théodard, *see* Narbonne

Thierry, *see* Amiens

Thorpe, J., 111

Thüngen, Neidhart von, 133-4

Thuringia, 63

Tigris, 29

Tilhurst, Adam de, 73

Titus, 14

Tonsure, first, 88; and learning, 39

Toulouse, 24, 25, 103

Tour-Landry, Geoffrey de la, No. 49

Tour, Lord de la, 105

Touraine, militia in, 153

Tournai, *see* Tournay

Tournaments, 93

Tournay, 25; **Chronicle of, No. 10**; Cathedral of, 17 and note; foundation of town of, 18; Master Simon de, 65

Tourney, *see* Tournaments

Tous, 70

"Tower, Knight of the," *see* Tour-Landry

Towns (medieval), burned, 68, 79, 91; fortified, 35, 90, 105; population of, 17 n.; prosperous, 78; rivalry between, 14; walls, 18

Trade, trading, by clergy and knights, 91; and miracle-plays, 141

Trades (medieval), 73-4; goldsmiths, 141; leathermongers, 49; linen-weavers, 141; tailors, 75-6; *and see* Architects

Transport (medieval), dangers of, 95; difficult, 134

Trenchaval, *see* Béziers

Trevisa, John, 2, 28, 30, 33 n.

Trier, 82-3

Tripoli carpets, 71

Troyes, 11

Tully, 58

Turk, Turks, 131; the Great, *see* Solyman

Turner, Thomas le, 73

Turnus, 18

Tutbury, 18

Tygry, 117

Tyndale, 142 ff.

University, 58; of Prague, 80; students armed, 74 ff.; students and crime, 73 ff., 119; *and see* Paris, Rashdall, Rome

Usury, 28, 131

Utrecht, bishops of, 48, 83 n. 2, 129; monasticism in, 128

Valencia, 66

Valenciennes, cloth of, 102 n.

Valerian, 45

Valmont, 46 n. 1

Vatican, 62

Vendais, la Roche de, 105

Vermandois, 91

Vespasian, 14

Vexin, 42

Vienne, 94

Vilabertran, 68

Villehardouin, 66

Vines, 117

Viollet-le-Duc, 96

Virgil, 2

Virgin Mary, 10, 18 ff., 44, 66-8; girdle of, 140; height of, 117; Jews and, 23, 148; miracles of (illustration), 139; in mystery-plays, 138 ff.; services of, 113

Visitations, (archidiaconal) 39, (monastic) 128

Vitalis (priest), 39, 41

Vitry, Jacques de, Exempla, No. 20; notes on, 38; on Petrus Cantor, 25; preaching of, 65

Vivisection, **No. 6**

Voigtländer, 137

Vulgate, *see* Bible

Wakefield, miracle-plays of, 141

Wakes, 75

Wales, 74; Prince of, 99

Wallsdorf, Fabian von, 137

Walsingham, Thomas, *Hist. Anglicana* of, **No. 44**

War, wars, 56, 67 ff., 108 ff.; and criminals, 111; engines of, 53; English and French, 121 ff.; Hundred Years', 114; Scottish, 87, 89; by sea (methods of), 96; Spanish, 66

Wattle-work, 84

Weapons (medieval), 76, 134 ff.

Weights and measures, heights of men, 117

Wells, Hugh of, 39

Wertheim, Count Michael von, 133

Wesley, 63

Westlake, Mr, 84

Weston, Nicholas de, 73

INDEX TO PART II

Weston, Thomas de, 73

Whitefield, 63

Willemzoon, Bro. Dietrich, 128

William the Dean, 15

Wills, books in, 112

Wiltshire, 119

Winchelsea, 102

Winchester, 40, 41

Windesheim, 128

Windsor, 41

Wine, medieval trading in, 91; by clergy and knights, 93

Wittenberg, 128

Wokingham, 40

Wolfhagen, Tilman von, *see* Limburg

Women, 63, 67, 83; in battle, 90; in church, 49; dress of, 63, (men's) 93; education of, 114; on horseback, 94; at tournaments, 93; *and see* Eckenstein, Nuns

Worcester, Florence of, 3 n. 1

World, end of, 26–7, **No. 63**

Wright, T., *Latin Stories*, 38

Writing, labour of, 119; *and see* Monks

Württemberg, 131

Wyclif, Wycliffites, 93, 142 ff.

Wynemerville, 46, 47

Yair Ford, 90

York, Archbishops of, 108, 110–11; Grandisson and, 113; Jews in, 33–4; *Memorandum Book*, 141; *Mystery-Plays*, 141; St Mary's Abbey at, 33

Yorkshire, 107

Yssel, R., 130

Zeiller, *Topografia*, 36, 92

Zoology (medieval), 53

Zouch, *see* York

Zutphen, 128, 130

Zwolle, 128